THE GREAT DEPRESSION IN EASTERN EUROPE

THE GREAT DEPRESSION IN EASTERN EUROPE

Edited by
Klaus Richter,
Jasmin Nithammer, and Anca Mândru

CEU PRESS
Central European University Press
Budapest – Vienna – New York

Published in 2025 by
Central European University Press

Nádor utca 9, H-1051 Budapest, Hungary
Tel: +36-1-327-3138 or 327-3000
E-mail: ceupress@press.ceu.edu
Website: www.ceupress.com

ISBN 978-963-386-894-2 (hardcover)
ISBN 978-963-386-895-9 (ebook)

A catalogue record for this book is available from the Library of Congress.

Contents

List of Tables and Figures

Tables

Figures

Chapter 1

INTRODUCTION

Klaus Richter, Jasmin Nithammer, and Anca Mândru

The year 2029 will mark the centenary of the beginning of the greatest economic crisis known to the modern world—the Great Depression. Strikingly, while we know much about its impact on the United States and parts of Europe, its effect on the much larger rest of the world is almost unknown. "The Great Depression dealt a harsh blow to the leading powers of the world," Iván T. Berend wrote in his landmark study *Decades of Crisis: Central and Eastern Europe Before World War II*: "Small wonder that the relatively poor countries at the periphery of the European and world economy suffered even more."[1] Our book puts the focus on this periphery: Eastern Europe. Although Eastern Europe was more heavily affected by the economic crisis of the 1930s than most other parts of the continent, the history of the Great Depression has remained largely unwritten for this region. Neither regional nor transnational or comparative studies exist that reconstruct the crisis and assess its impact on politics, societies, and economies.[2] We intend this book to fill this gap and, in addition, make a significant contribution to the broader scholarship on the economic turmoil that shattered the interwar order and paved the path toward World War II. We would like to thank the Gerda-Henkel Foundation for making the editing of this volume possible as part of their generous funding commitment to

1 Iván T. Berend, *Decades of Crisis: Central and Eastern Europe before World War II* (Berkeley, CA: University of California Press, 1998), 253.

2 The pathbreaking comparative volume *Wirtschaftskrisen als strukturelle Umbrüche* is paradigmatic: It investigates the transformative impact of economic crises on Eastern Europe and beyond across ten centuries, but does not mention the Great Depression, except for a chapter on Cyprus. Dariusz Adamczyk and Stephan Lehnstaedt, eds., *Wirtschaftskrisen als Wendepunkte: Ursachen, Folgen und historische Einordnungen vom Mittelalter bis zur Gegenwart* (Osnabrück: Fibre, 2015).

the project *The Liminality of Failing Democracy: East Central Europe during the Interwar Slump.*

The majority of scholarship on the Great Depression focuses on its origins on Wall Street and subsequent proliferation across the world, structured around the principal questions of its root causes, the causes for its global spread, and the causes for the world's collective failure to contain it.[3] The perennial question around the roots of the slump revolves around a US-centered answer (a disrupted monetary system resulting in the Wall Street Crash of 1929) and a Europe-centered one (the consequences of World War I: reparation payments, the loss of British financial hegemony, erosion of the Gold Standard, and—most importantly—a dramatic overproduction resulting from the entry of the nonbelligerent countries into the global market).[4] Inquiries into the depression's impact on Europe concern themselves with the failure to find a coordinated international response to reverse the downturn and with its significance in causing a breakdown of international relations that paved the way to World War II.[5] Yet readings of the Great Depression in Europe—let alone Eastern Europe—remain strangely segregated into international histories and economic histories. We lack knowledge on the Great Depression as a much broader historical force—a force that shaped politics, societies, cultural practices, and subjectivities.

Laying the groundwork for this analysis, this volume provides, in the first instance, a reconstruction of the depression's impact on the individual countries of Eastern Europe and of responses to mitigate

3 For example, Charles P. Kindleberger, *The World in Depression, 1929–1939* (Berkeley, CA: University of California Press, 1973); Barry J. Eichengreen, *Golden Fetters: The Gold Standard and the Great Depression, 1919–1939*, NBER Series on Long-Term Factors in Economic Development (New York: Oxford University Press, 1992); Douglas A. Irwin, *Trade Policy Disaster: Lessons from the 1930s*, The Ohlin Lectures (Cambridge, Mass: MIT Press, 2012).

4 Clarence L. Barber, "On the Origins of the Great Depression," *Southern Economic Journal* 44, no. 3 (1978): 432–56.

5 Patricia Clavin, *The Great Depression in Europe, 1929–1939* (New York: St. Martin's Press, 2000); Nikolaus Wolf, "Europe's Great Depression: Coordination Failure after the First World War," *Oxford Review of Economic Policy* 26, no. 3 (2010): 339–69; Roger Middleton, "The Great Depression in Europe," in *The Oxford Handbook of European History, 1914–1945*, ed. Nicholas Doumanis (Oxford: Oxford University Press, 2016), 179–206.

the impact. This volume covers Eastern Europe as the cluster of states located in between Germany and the Soviet Union—a region whose conflictual and postimperial character is often stressed by labels such as "Shatterzone of Empires," "European Rimlands," or "East European borderlands."[6] This approach excludes the Soviet Union itself, which experienced the Great Depression in a fundamentally different way, but allows the investigation of the large part of the European continent stretching from Estonia to Greece and from Romania to Austria as a coherent region structured by the shared challenges that arose from the fundamental consequences of the European reordering that followed World War I. Here, national sovereignty was particularly contested.[7] Countries such as Czechoslovakia and Austria were similarly hit by the depression as the industrialized countries of Central and Western Europe, yet it was particularly the drop in agricultural prices that brought the states of Europe's East to the verge of collapse. At the same time, most states in this region suffered from external challenges to their existence as independent states and to their territorial integrity, which made protectionist and isolationist policies seem without alternative.

Traditional economic histories of Eastern Europe, which structure their historical inquiry along the lines of economic mechanisms and sectors, have paid surprisingly little attention to the broader impact of the Great Depression on the region. While they acknowledge the implications that overbearing protectionism had on international politics, we learn much less from them about how the slump shaped domestic policies and social change.[8] Berend is

6 Omer Bartov and Eric D. Weitz, eds., *Shatterzone of Empires: Coexistence and Violence in the German, Habsburg, Russian, and Ottoman Borderlands* (Bloomington, IN: Indiana University Press, 2013); Mark Levene, *Devastation. The European Rimlands, 1912–1938* (Oxford: Oxford University Press, 2013); Alexander Victor Prusin, *The Lands Between. Conflict in the East European Borderlands, 1870–1992* (Oxford: Oxford University Press, 2010).

7 John Connelly, *From Peoples into Nations: A History of Eastern Europe* (Princeton, NJ: Princeton University Press, 2020).

8 Michael Charles Kaser and E. A. Radice, eds., *The Economic History of Eastern Europe, 1919–1975* (Oxford and New York: Clarendon Press; Oxford University Press, 1985); David Turnock, *The Economy of East Central Europe, 1815–1989: Stages of Transformation in a Peripheral Region* (London and New York: Routledge, 2014).

the only historian who has viewed Central and Eastern Europe's latter half of the interwar period entirely through the lens of the Great Depression. The depression led to trauma among peasants, thus destabilizing societies. Because of their traditional social structures, the states of the region failed to adapt to the dramatically changed market conditions. Soaring debts and lack of credit further constrained their economic and political agency to the extent that state sovereignty was increasingly limited. While responses to the depression—including the lowering of commercial exchange rates, promotion of exports, and raising of prices for imports—successfully revitalized the economy, they isolated the states from the world economic system and drew them into the sphere of influence of Nazi Germany's quest for economic control over Eastern Europe. They also constituted a "gaming of the system" rather than a genuine reform. Berend concludes:

> The Great Depression in Central and Eastern Europe was thus not only deeper and more devastating because of the agrarian character and indebtedness of the region's countries, but, most significantly, was not accompanied by technological-structural renewal, a fact that determined the long-term destiny of the area by conserving its peripheral status in Europe.[9]

The Great Depression thus struck Eastern Europe primarily—but not exclusively—in the form of an agricultural crisis. Although Eastern Europe suffered to a particularly high degree from the global collapse of agricultural prices, scholarly studies tend to stress the severity of the agricultural crisis and its societal consequences in the United States and mention Eastern Europe only at the margins.[10] Even Charles P. Kindleberger makes only minimal references to Eastern Europe in his landmark study *The World in Depression*. Nonetheless, Kindleberger was the first to decisively shift the focus

9 Berend, *Decades of Crisis*, 265.

10 Gérard Béaur and Francesco Chiapparino, "Introduction," in *Agriculture and the Great Depression: The Rural Crisis of the 1930s in Europe and the Americas*, eds. Gérard Béaur and Francesco Chiapparino (London and New York: Routledge, 2023), 1–18.

from monetary explanations to the disruptions caused by World War I, especially the issue of rising stocks and falling prices of primary products.[11] These were indeed the factors that had the largest impact on Eastern Europe as a predominantly agricultural region. Here, the decline in agricultural prices, the inaccessibility of foreign loans, and the escalation of protective tariffs had disastrous consequences.

Kindleberger has also pointed out that Eastern Europe's economic crisis started earlier than in autumn 1929, as the world's agricultural countries were losing gold earlier than others. Hungary, Europe's largest grain producer, lost a fifth of its gold reserves before autumn 1929. Already before the Wall Street Crash, agricultural prices were falling and stocks were rising. Kindleberger stresses a process of "structural deflation" for 1925–29, as the supply of agricultural produce vastly exceeded demand. By stocking surpluses, some producers only deferred the problem. By exporting surpluses at dumping prices, other producers contributed to the downward spiral of global prices. By autumn 1929, global agricultural prices had dropped to 70 percent of the 1925 prices. In the same period, stocks of agricultural surplus increased by 75 percent. By late 1932, prices dropped further to below 25 percent of the 1925 prices, while stocks were at 260 percent of their 1925 value. This was aggravated by the Soviet Union's entry into the global wheat market: As prices collapsed, the Soviet Union ramped up production to make up for the losses, flooding the world market with cheap agricultural goods while laying the ground for the disastrous Soviet famines of the early 1930s.[12]

Interwar economic experts—many associated with the League of Nations—were acutely aware of the specific manifestations and severity of the depression in Central and Eastern Europe. Twenty international conferences were convened to address the issue of agricultural prices following 1929. Seven of these dealt exclusively with Eastern Europe.[13] League experts stressed that prices no longer covered the cost of production. Taxes and debts remained unpaid,

11 Kindleberger, *The World in Depression.*

12 Kindleberger, *The World in Depression*, 100, 110–11, 121, 125–27.

13 Kindleberger, *The World in Depression*, 109.

and farmhands were laid off. This was accompanied by a dramatic scissors effect as manufacturing prices remained far more stable than agricultural prices, making machinery unaffordable (whereas 1929 agricultural prices were at only 87 percent of their 1927 level, industrial prices had not only remained stable but even increased slightly by 3 percent).[14] The League experts also noted a catastrophic rise in debt burdens, as American loans to Europe seized up—a situation that was further aggravated by the Central European banking crisis of 1931, with the collapse of the Austrian *Credit-Anstalt* (May 1931), of the *Rheinische Landesbank*, and of the *Danat Bank* (July 1931). As long-term loans became unavailable, farmers were forced to resort to high-interest short-term loans, leading in Hungary, for instance, to more than a doubling of interest rates. In some parts of Eastern Europe, the League observers noticed interest rates of 18 to 50 percent.[15] Hungary's debt burden increased from 1.17 billion Pengő in 1928–29 to 2.18 billion in 1932–33, with the repayment burden rising from 9 percent of income to 25 percent. This triggered a deep crisis in government and an escalation of both interventionist and far-right policies.[16] In Poland, the income of farms halved from 1929 to 1932 and fell further to below 40 percent of prewar income by 1934. Whereas market consumption in Polish cities had dropped to 87 percent of its predepression levels by 1933, it had dropped to 47 percent in villages and would drop further to 43 percent a year later.[17]

As a response, the countries of Eastern Europe resorted to protectionist measures in an effort to prevent the collapse of their shattered agriculture and fledgling industries. György Ránki and Jerzy Tomaszewski have argued that the Great Depression represented

14 Economic Committee (League of Nations), *The Agricultural Crisis*. Vol. 1 (15.06.1931), LON, 0000765460_D0001, 7–8, 11.

15 Economic Committee, *Agricultural Crisis*, Vol. 1, 14.

16 Zsuzsanna Varga, "The 1929 Crisis in Hungary's Dual Agriculture," in *Agriculture and the Great Depression: The Rural Crisis of the 1930s in Europe and the Americas*, eds. Gérard Béaur and Francesco Chiapparino (London and New York: Routledge, 2023), 145–48.

17 Tadeusz Janicki, "Impact of the Crisis on the Polish Agriculture (1929–35)," in *Agriculture and the Great Depression: The Rural Crisis of the 1930s in Europe and the Americas*, eds. Gérard Béaur and Francesco Chiapparino (London and New York: Routledge, 2023), 158, 165.

a watershed, separating the 1920s, which were largely guided by prewar logics, from the protectionism-charged 1930s. They have stressed the disastrous economic consequences suffered by those that had lost the war (Bulgaria, Hungary), but also by those who faced hostile revisionism (Poland, Romania, Yugoslavia). Moreover, all states were in the process of either state-building, reconfiguring their territories, or both, which required a high degree of state intervention. As Europe entered the slump, this political rationale for state intervention turned into an economic necessity. Not least, the depression thus eroded liberal norms that had rested on the favorable contingencies of rising agricultural prices, credit boom, and growing foreign investment. As these ceased, so did the attractiveness of liberalism more broadly.[18] As Hans Raupach stressed, Eastern European post-1929 protectionism "came close to autarky, not because they had an ideological preference for this system, but because the self-isolation of the world powers – the USSR, the British Empire (the sterling bloc set up at Ottawa in 1932), and the United States (retreat at the World Economic Conference of 1933) – left them no other way out."[19]

In fact, using the "potential tariff levels" calculated by Heinrich Liepmann in 1938 to reconstruct tariff changes during the depression, we see that two Eastern European states—Bulgaria and Poland—did indeed impose the highest import tariffs on foodstuffs in 1931. Yet Romania, Czechoslovakia, and Yugoslavia were very much in line with Germany, whereas Hungary and Austria were even at the lower end of the spectrum. Moreover, if we look at the extent to which European states ramped up tariffs during the depression, we get a different picture altogether: As the industrialized countries (Germany, France, Italy, and Austria) increased their tariffs twofold to fourfold, the agricultural countries of Eastern

18 György Ránki and Jerzy Tomaszewski, "The Role of the State in Industry, Banking and Trade," in *The Economic History of Eastern Europe, 1919–1975. Vol. II: Interwar Policy, the War, and Reconstruction* (Oxford: Clarendon, 1986), 5–6, 21.

19 Hans Raupach, "The Impact of the Great Depression on Eastern Europe," *Journal of Contemporary History*, 4, no. 4 (1969): 81.

Table 1.1 Potential Tariff Levels on Foodstuffs in Europe

Country	*1927 (%)*	*1931 (%)*	*Increase (%)*
Bulgaria	79.0	133.0	68.0
Poland	72.0	110.0	53.0
Finland	57.5	102.0	77.0
Romania	45.6	87.5	92.0
Czechoslovakia	36.3	84.0	131.0
Germany	27.4	82.5	201.0
Spain	45.2	80.5	78.0
Yugoslavia	43.7	75.0	72.0
Italy	24.5	66.0	169.0
Hungary	31.5	60.0	90.0
Austria	16.5	59.5	261.0
France	19.1	53.0	177.0
Switzerland	21.5	42.2	96.0
Sweden	21.5	39.0	81.0
Belgium	11.8	23.7	101.0

Source: Heinrich Liepmann, *Tariff Levels*, 413.

Europe (Yugoslavia, Bulgaria, and Poland) did so only by factors 1.5–1.75[20] (Table 1.1).

1.1 The Depression's Transformative Impact

Yet how did this maelstrom of economic hardship and desperate state responses transform societies, cultures, and states in Eastern Europe? This volume assesses the depression's profound impact on the relationships between societies and states, between genders, social classes, and different nationalities. Existing studies of such changing relationships have hitherto been largely confined to the history of the depression in the United States.[21] However, with regard to Eastern Europe, the book can build on studies that

20 Heinrich Liepmann, *Tariff Levels and the Economic Unity of Europe* (London: Unwin & Allen, 1938), 413.

21 Lara H. Campbell, *Respectable Citizens: Gender, Family, and Unemployment in Ontario's Great Depression* (Toronto: University of Toronto Press, 2009); Laura Hapke, *Daughters of the Great Depression: Women, Work, and Fiction in the American 1930s* (Athens, GA: University of Georgia Press, 1995); Iwan Morgan and Philip John Davies, eds., *Hollywood and the Great Depression: American Film, Politics and Society in the 1930s* (Edinburgh: Edinburgh University Press, 2016).

examine aspects of welfare, labor, and gender relations more broadly. As Tomasz Inglot has shown, the depression prompted Eastern European states to increase state involvement in welfare, albeit in very different forms: Poland centralized welfare, Czechoslovakia reformed welfare but maintained its autonomous system, and Hungary introduced a new type of corporatist model of social policy.[22] Not least, the states of Eastern Europe expanded public welfare in an effort to not fall behind Nazi Germany's responses to the depression, which were increasingly seen as a successful model to emulate.[23] As pertains to other policies, welfare policies constituted an instrument of state-building across Eastern Europe, meaning their reforms had repercussions across a broad range of institutions, with specific implications for the relationship between state and society.[24] The responses to the Great Depression, which focused on public works and the modernization of infrastructure and industries, led to ambitious projects that radically reconfigured the region's national economies. One such case was Poland's Central Industrial District, which had dramatic implications for the cities located in the heart of Poland.[25]

The whole region covered in this volume was fundamentally multi-ethnic. As Rogers Brubaker has famously stressed, the states emerging here from the collapsed empires were conceived of as "nation-states," but they were far from ethnically homogeneous. Rather, they were "nationalizing states" that deployed mechanisms and policies designed to strengthen the mono-ethnic character and ownership of the state.[26] Did the Great Depression forestall

22 Tomasz Inglot, *Welfare States in East Central Europe, 1919–2004* (Cambridge and New York: Cambridge University Press, 2008).

23 Radka Šustrová, "A Dilemma of Change and Cooperation: Labour and Social Policy in Bohemia and Moravia in the 1930s and 1940s," in *Nazism Across Borders: The Social Policies of the Third Reich and their Global Appeal*, eds. Sandrine Kott and Kiran K. Patel (Oxford: Oxford University Press, 2018): 105–38.

24 Sergiu Delcea, "A Nation of Bureaucrats or a Nation of Workers? Welfare Benefits as Nation-Building Modernization Tools in Interwar Romania," *Journal of European Social Policy* 32, no. 1 (2022): 75–90.

25 Jerzy Gołębiowski, *Centralny Okręg Przemysłowy: COP*, Prace Monograficzne 284 (Cracow: Wydawnictwo Naukowe Akademii Pedagogicznej, 2000).

26 Rogers Brubaker, "National Minorities, Nationalizing States, and External National Homelands in the New Europe," *Daedalus* 124, no. 2 (1995): 107–32.

such efforts, or did it even facilitate them? How did the depression change the relationship between those nationalities viewed as the new bearers of statehood versus those now conceived of as national minorities at best or as agents of revisionist neighbors at worst? The depression did not only deepened divides between nationalities, but also between genders. Concerning the depression's impact on gender relations, Ruth Milkman has argued that the main impact of the depression in Romania was not the involvement of women in the labor market, but that the main arena of struggle was that of unpaid domestic labor.[27] This book sheds light on how these structures and relationships—domestically and internationally—changed and how actors from Eastern Europe responded to these changes.

1.2 Eastern European Perspectives on the Global Depression

Most studies of the Great Depression cast an external view on Eastern Europe, be it that of the League of Nations or that of revisionist Germany. Given the inherent weaknesses of the reconstituted post-1918 liberal order and the failures to recover prewar economic networks, several economic historians speak of a two-decade-long interwar slump rather than a depression confined to the early 1930s. More recently, scholars of international and political history have broadened this economic rationale to speak of a profound, sustained interwar crisis: With efforts stretching across the 1920s to recover prewar prosperity and establish viable international institutions failing, the Great Depression crushed fledgling, fragile, and unfinished political and economic projects. This had particularly disastrous consequences for Eastern Europe, where states and state institutions were in the process of construction and consolidation and often were not accepted as uncontested members of the international community yet.[28] At the same time, interna-

27 Ruth Milkman, "Women's Work and Economic Crisis: Some Lessons of the Great Depression," *Review of Radical Political Economics* 8, no. 1 (April 1, 1976): 71–97.

28 Robert W. D. Boyce, *The Great Interwar Crisis and the Collapse of Globalization* (Basingstoke: Palgrave Macmillan, 2012); Nathan Marcus, *Austrian Reconstruction and the Collapse of Global Finance, 1921–1931* (Cambridge, Mass.: Harvard University Press, 2018); Klaus Richter, *Fragmentation in East Central Europe: Poland and the*

tional involvement in the Eastern European economies was substantial, as the League of Nations dispatched delegations to Central and Eastern Europe to aid financial reconstruction. However, these delegations' missions were not of a purely economic nature. For the League's missions to Vienna and Budapest, nothing less than the viability of the former Habsburg Empire's centers of power, Austria and Hungary, as sovereign states seemed at stake. Additional missions aided in financial reconstruction to ensure the survival of new states such as Estonia and the Free City of Danzig in a dramatically changed international order.[29] Existing studies indicate a decisive shift in international mood from support for crisis-stricken Eastern Europe toward a framing of these new states as the culprits for Europe's failure to recover from the depression, thus laying the groundwork for the success of Nazi encroachment into the region.[30]

Yet how far was there a specifically Eastern European subjectivity of the interwar slump? Did the Great Depression constitute a liminal moment, that is, a period of time in which changes were perceived as so profound that they led societies and elites to question the validity of existing knowledge, orders, and norms? In what arenas did politicians, economists, intellectuals, and "common people" from Eastern Europe articulate their interpretations of the economic turmoil? It is safe to assume that mass unemployment, debt crises, political chaos, and social unrest had a decisive impact on subjective views of the world, and on expectations toward the future of communities and their countries. At the same time, the Great Depression in Eastern Europe has to be contextualized in the sustained instability that stretched across the interwar period, starting from the collapse of empires and the immediate threats arising to the newly formed states from both German revisionism and Soviet aggression.

Baltics, 1915–1929 (Oxford: Oxford University Press, 2020); Mark Mazower, *Greece and the Inter-War Economic Crisis* (Oxford: Oxford University Press, 1991).

29 Patricia Clavin, *Securing the World Economy: The Reinvention of the League of Nations, 1920–1946* (Oxford: Oxford University Press, 2015); Marcus, *Austrian Reconstruction.*

30 Klaus Richter, "The Catastrophe of the Present and That of the Future: Expectations for European States from the Great War to the Great Depression," *Contemporary European History* (2023), http://dx.doi.org/10.1017/S096077732200100X: 1–19.

We lack knowledge on how far the overly optimistic assessments of the course that the depression was about to take, which characterized the mainstream of American and Western European economists, dominated Eastern European expert discourse, too.[31] However, to assess the impact of the Great Depression on Eastern European politics and society, we need to understand how this relatively short period of sudden and compressed change reshaped dominant concepts of political order, of macroeconomic rationale, of the relationship between states and society, and of the relationship between Eastern Europe and the wider world. This approach goes far beyond the existing scholarship, which has reconstructed economic and political thinking during the 1930s using mainly approaches from intellectual history.[32] There is a broad consensus among scholars that economic nationalism played a crucial role in the history of social and national movements across the modern history of Eastern Europe, and that the Great Depression increased its dominance further. However, although scholars have highlighted the broader social and cultural contexts of economic nationalism, its depression-era manifestations feature in the literature almost exclusively in the form of economic doctrine: tariff policies and exchange controls.[33] The authors of this book, on the other hand, focus on economic nationalism as a social project and as an instrument of nationalism more broadly—a turn long demanded by scholars, but rarely empirically enacted.[34] The volume thus moves

31 Gabriel Mathy and Herman Stekler, "Expectations and Forecasting during the Great Depression: Real-Time Evidence from the Business Press," *Journal of Macroeconomics* 53 (September 2017): 1–15; Natalya Oliynyk and Iryna Shevchenko, "Conceptualisation of Economic Crisis in Discourse: From the Great Depression to the Great Recession," *Advanced Education* 6 (2016): 76–81.

32 Stefan Cristian Ionescu, "Theorists of Economic Nationalism in 1930s–1940s Romania," *Nationalities Papers* 47, no. 2 (2019): 264–79; Nikolay Nenovsky, "Theoretical Debates in Bulgaria during the Great Depression: Confronting Sombart, Marx and Keynes," *OEconomia* 2-1 (March 1, 2012): 67–101.

33 Helga Schultz and Eduard Kubů, *History and Culture of Economic Nationalism in East Central Europe* (Berlin: Berliner Wissenschafts-Verlag, 2006).

34 George Crane, "Economic Nationalism: Bringing the Nation Back In," *Millenium* 27, no. 1 (1998): 55–76; Eric Helleiner, "Economic Nationalism as a Challenge to Economic Liberalism? Lessons from the 19th Century," *International Studies Quarterly* 46 (2002): 307–29; Andreas Pickel, "Explaining, and Explaining with, Economic Nationalism," *Nations and Nationalism* 9, no. 1 (2003): 105–27; Thomas

the study of economic nationalism from economic history to the center of social and political history. We hope it will thus contribute to a much enhanced understanding of Eastern European nationalism in the 1930s.

In addition, the authors address a wide gap in the scholarship concerning the authoritarian states' continued engagement with the European order of states. There is no denying that responses to the interwar slump centered on national, protectionist solutions.[35] However, international cooperation and federative ideas continued or even gained traction—not least among right-wing groups.[36] The Depression-era "Agrarian Bloc" of East-Central European states contained elements of deep economic integration.[37] Yet studies of 1930s' international cooperation are limited to diplomatic efforts—even in the case of integrationist projects, such as a Danubian Federation, that explicitly aimed at overcoming postimperial economic fragmentation.[38]

Fetzer, "Beyond 'Economic Nationalism': Towards a New Research Agenda for the Study of Nationalism in Political Economy," *Journal of International Relations and Development* 25 (2021): 235–59; Stefan Berger and Thomas Fetzer, eds., *Nationalism and the Economy: Explorations into a Neglected Relationship* (Vienna: CEU Press, 2020).

35 Patricia Clavin, *The Great Depression in Europe, 1929–1939* (London: Macmillan, 2000); Kindleberger, *The World in Depression.*

36 Holly Case, "The Strange Politics of Federative Ideas in East-Central Europe," *Journal of Modern History* 85 (2013): 833–66.

37 Irena Stawowy-Kawka, "Blok Rolny a koncepcje integracji Europy Środkowej i Południowo-Wschodniej w latach 1930–1932," in *Międzymorze: Nadzieje i ograniczenia w polityce II Rzeczypospolitej,* ed. Elżbieta Znamierowska-Rakk (Warsaw: Uniwersytet Warszawski, 2016), 419–45.

38 Eero Medijainen, "The 1934 Treaty of the Baltic Entente: Perspectives for Understanding," *Ajalooline Ajakiri* 1/2 (2012): 183–200; Mustafa Türkeş, "The Balkan Pact and its Immediate Implications for the Balkan States, 1930–34," *Middle Eastern Studies* 30, no. 1 (1994): 123–44; Piotr Wandycz, "The Little Entente: Sixty Years Later," *Slavonic and East European Review* 59, no. 4 (1981): 548–64; Ignác Romsics and Béla K. Király, eds., *Geopolitics in the Danube Region: Hungarian Reconciliation Efforts, 1848–1998* (Budapest: Central European University, 1999).

1.3 The Great Depression and the Decline of Democracy

As Adam Tooze has argued, the immediate impact of the Great Depression was not to blow up the international order, but rather to "tighten the constraints of the existing order" as deflationary policies had become an entrenched norm. Yet later, it would erode an order based on ambitious visions of international cooperation and peace. Austerity responses to the Great Depression played into the hands of nationalists and of the enemies of democracy and international cooperation.[39] How did these dynamics play out in Eastern Europe? In what other ways did the depression facilitate the rise of authoritarian rule?

Although democracy survived the depression in some cases, parliamentary systems were eroded across much of the region. The authors assess how far the economic crisis changed the political landscape and eroded the legitimacy of parliamentary democracy and liberalism. Central and Eastern Europe saw the emergence of a series of democratically constituted new states as a result of the collapse of Russian, German, and Austro-Hungarian imperial rule at the end of World War I. The majority of these states—Poland, Yugoslavia, the Baltic States, and Romania—shifted to authoritarian rule in the late 1920s and 1930s. Comparative studies have argued that inexperience with political participation precluded the formation of resilient democracies.[40] Eastern Europeanists, on the other hand, have de-emphasized this shift, highlighting the ethno-centric, "nationalizing" thrust of these states instead, which transcended changes in the political system.[41] Only recently have scholars begun to seek the roots of democracy's failure in the specific character of interwar East-Central European statehood, stressing that the "double transformation" from empires to nation-states and from monarchies

39 Adam Tooze, *The Deluge: The Great War, America and the Remaking of the Global Order, 1916–1931* (London: Allen Lane, 2014), 487. For a brilliant case study of these dynamics, see also Tobias Straumann, *1931: Debt, Crisis, and the Rise of Hitler* (Oxford: Oxford University Press, 2020).

40 Dirk Berg-Schlosser and Jeremy Mitchell, eds., *Authoritarianism and Democracy in Europe, 1919–39: Comparative Analyses* (Basingstoke: Palgrave Macmillan, 2000).

41 Rogers Brubaker, *Nationalism Reframed: Nationhood and the National Question in the New Europe* (Cambridge: Cambridge University Press, 1996).

to democracies overstrained their governments, which prioritized national at the expense of democratic values.[42] Democratization never became a process of broadening political participation, but remained at the level of a continuous challenging of democratic concepts.[43] However, we still lack knowledge of how democracies were dismantled and authoritarian regimes installed in what were mostly bloodless coups. Sociological approaches that focus on decision-making during transitions from and to democracy in East-Central Europe have ignored crucial economic contexts.[44] Neither do regional studies exist that investigate the mutual dynamics of the relationship between regimes and societies. Popular support is mostly understood as something the authoritarian regimes aspired to by means of institutional and cultural nationalism, yet it remains unclear how far they were successful.[45]

Berend has claimed that the emergence of dictatorships in Eastern Europe was part of the "direct and immediate political repercussions" of the Great Depression.[46] However, neither economic nor political historians of interwar East-Central Europe have examined economic crises as preconditions for democratic failure, which has been so thoroughly studied with regard to Hitler's rise to

42 Heidi Hein-Kircher and Steffen Kailitz, "'Double Transformations': Nation Formation and Democratization in Interwar East Central Europe," *Nationalities Papers* 46, no. 5 (2018): 745–58.

43 Agnes Laba and Maria Wojtczak, "'Aufbruch zur Demokratie?' Aspekte einer Demokratiegeschichte Ostmitteleuropas (1918–1939)," *Zeitschrift für Ostmitteleuropa-Forschung* 62, no. 2 (2015): 159–71.

44 Juan J. Linz and Alfred Stepan, *The Breakdown of Democratic Regimes* (Baltimore, MD: Johns Hopkins University Press, 1978); Guillermo O'Donnell et al., eds., *Transitions from Authoritarian Rule: Comparative Perspectives* (Baltimore, MD: Johns Hopkins University Press, 1986); Giovanni Capoccia, *Defending Democracy: Reactions to Extremism in Interwar Europe* (Baltimore, MD: Johns Hopkins University Press, 2007); Michael Bernhard, *Institutions and the Fate of Democracy: Germany and Poland in the Twentieth Century* (Pittsburgh, PA: University of Pittsburgh Press, 2005).

45 Heidi Hein-Kircher, *Der Piłsudski-Kult und seine Bedeutung für den polnischen Staat, 1926–1939* (Marburg: Verlag Herder-Institut, 2002); Deniss Hanovs and Valdis Teraudkalns, "'Happy Birthday, Mr Ulmanis!' Reflections on the Construction of an Authoritarian Regime in Latvia," *Politics, Religion & Ideology* 15, no. 1 (2014): 64–81; Eva Plach, *The Clash of Moral Nations: Cultural Politics in Pilsudski's Poland, 1926–1935* (Athens, OH: Ohio University Press, 2006).

46 Berend, *Decades of Crisis*, 300.

power.[47] This is partially due to the fact that this authoritarian turn is more muddled than in the case of the Nazi's ascent, which happened exactly at the high point of the depression. Yet while Latvia and Estonia saw the introduction of dictatorship in 1934, Hungary's Miklós Horthy, Poland's Józef Piłsudski, and Lithuania's Antanas Smetona came to power years before the depression. It is only when we look at how their regimes were challenged that we see a significant lurch to the right, as Horthy appointed the extremist Gyula Gömbös as prime minister in 1932, the followers of the fascist Augustinas Voldemaras tried to oust Smetona from power in 1934, and Poland passed a new constitution in 1935, thereby formally ending parliamentary rule. The depression hit economies already fragile as a consequence of sweeping economic reforms, state-building processes, political conflicts, dependence on agricultural exports, and the disruption of trade networks through new borders.[48] This put existing authoritarian regimes under considerable pressure and caused remaining democracies to collapse.[49]

But how did these pressures translate into antidemocratic, antiliberal, and anti-integrationist policies and how did they enter the political mainstream? Scholars have emphasized the central role that Depression-era economists played in authoritarian regimes and the subjection of economic decision-making to political considerations.[50] Detailed studies exist on discrete antiliberal policies,

47 See the classic texts: Alice Teichová, *Kleinstaaten im Spannungsfeld der Großmächte: Wirtschaft und Politik in Mittel- und Südosteuropa in der Zwischenkriegszeit* (Vienna: Oldenbourg Wissenschaftsverlag, 1988); Joseph Rothschild, *East Central Europe between the two World Wars* (Washington, DC: University of Washington Press, 1977).

48 Derek H. Aldcroft, *Studies in the Interwar European Economy* (London: Routledge, 1997).

49 For example, Jan Tomicki, "Konflikty społeczne i polityczne w okresie wielkiego kryzysu gospodarczego. Problematyka robotnicza," *Dzieje Najnowsze* 7, no. 2 (1975): 49–68; Mindaugas Balkus, "1935–1936 m. Užnemunės ūkinkų streikas. Propagandos ir viešosios nuomonės apžvalga," *Lietuvos istorijos metraštis* 1 (2012): 103–18.

50 Nikolay Nenovsky, "Theoretical Debates in Bulgaria during the Great Depression"; Mario Pomini, "The Great Depression and the Corporatist Shift of Italian Economists," *The European Journal of the History of Economic Thought* 18, no. 5 (2011): 733–53; Nikolaus Wolf, "Should I Stay or Should I Go? Understanding Poland's Adherence to Gold, 1928–1936," *Historical Social Research / Historische Sozialforschung* 32, no. 4 (2007): 351–68.

such as the escalation of protective tariffs, the introduction of state monopolies, the establishment of state-operated enterprises that scooped up struggling private businesses and banks, the introduction of corporatist systems in all East-Central European states, the extreme state intervention in the agricultural sector, and the various economic measures aimed at weakening national minorities; yet we have almost no knowledge of the extent of popular support for these policies.[51] By gauging how the depression changed political structures, political cultures, and societal views on these changes, the authors of this book enhance our understanding of the nature of democratic collapse in Eastern Europe, building on recent studies that focus on the lack of political practice in Eastern Europeans and on the significance of external threats.[52]

1.4 Structure of the Book

The book opens with a chapter on the League of Nations' involvement in Eastern Europe before moving along the lines of national case studies, starting with Austria, Poland, and Czechoslovakia. With the Baltic states, the book then covers three countries that had emerged from the collapsed Russian Empire, before turning toward Southeast Europe, with chapters on Romania, Hungary, Bulgaria, and Greece. At the same time, these case studies are grouped into thematic sections that allow addressing the key questions laid out above from multiple perspectives, actors, and institutions: the relationship of states with the interwar international order, the response

51 Gertrude Enderle-Burcel, "Government and Industry in Austria in the 1930s," in *Business and Politics in Europe, 1900–1970*, ed. Terry Gourvish (Cambridge: Cambridge University Press, 2003), 269–88; Jutta Günther and Dagmara Jajeśniak-Quast, eds., *Willkommene Investoren oder nationaler Ausverkauf? Ausländische Direktinvestitionen in Ostmitteleuropa im 20. Jahrhundert* (Berlin: BWV Verlag, 2006); Antonio Costa Pinto, ed., *Corporatism and Fascism: The Corporatist Wave in Europe* (London: Routledge, 2017); Alice Teichová, Herbert Matis, and Jaroslav Pátek, eds., *Economic Change and the National Question in Twentieth-Century Europe* (Cambridge: Cambridge University Press, 2000).

52 Heidi Hein-Kircher, ed., *Verflochtene Herausforderungen politischer und gesellschaftlicher Demokratisierung. Ostmitteleuropas Demokratien zwischen den Kriegen* (Marburg: Verlag Herder-Institut, 2023); Kurt Weyland, *Assault on Democracy. Communism, Fascism, and Authoritarianism during the Interwar Years* (Cambridge: Cambridge University Press, 2021).

of business networks to the crisis, changing state-society relations, and the impact of the crisis on political and economic thought.

The first three case studies address the impact of the Great Depression in its international context. In their chapter "The League of Nations, Eastern Europe, and the Great Depression," Klaus Richter, Jasmin Nithammer, and Anca Mândru argue that the League of Nations was well aware of the challenges that the states of Eastern Europe faced during the Great Depression. Political and economic actors from the region consistently articulated their demands, with a specific focus on preferential treatment, which would have eased the impact of the agricultural depression. Yet the League, overwhelmed at its basis and structured by highly normative views toward Eastern Europe, failed to throw its weight behind these demands. Instead, the Great Powers would incorporate these into their own geopolitical agendas, resulting in the formation of trade blocs. The chapter covers agricultural conferences convened by the countries of Eastern Europe and the efforts of the Commission for Inquiry into European Union to aid (Eastern) Europe's economic recovery.

In his chapter on Austria ("The Toll of Economic Orthodoxy"), Nathan Marcus provides a comprehensive overview over the course of the depression and the dynamics between the economy on the one hand and domestic and international politics on the other. Austria was among the countries that were the hardest hit by the depression, especially since the 1931 collapse of the Viennese Credit-Anstalt. Moreover, Austria was under considerable external pressure—from Germany (especially since Hitler's rise to power), but also at the international level more broadly, as the Habsburg Empire's disintegration had resulted in a small Austrian state that most thought was too small to be economically viable. The chapter thus fundamentally enhances our understanding of the weaknesses of Austrian parliamentary democracy, but also of the Austrian *Ständestaat* in light of the failures to achieve economic recovery and international hostility.

In his chapter on "Foreign Capital and Economic Nationalism during the Great Depression," Jerzy Łazor examines the international entanglement of Poland's slump through the lens of Polish policy regarding foreign capital. Through a close study of four government takeovers of French- and German-owned companies between 1934 and 1936, the chapter provides a detailed reconstruction of how economic nationalism came to dominate Polish policy. The chapter argues that while the close timing of the takeovers suggests a wide-ranging turn toward nationalization and Polonization, a closer inspection undermines this interpretation: The four conflicts appeared in different contexts, and the underlying motivations had little in common. Rather than being guided by any theoretical or political design, they reflected the general Polish political climate, statist tendencies, and power struggles within the authoritarian regime in Warsaw.

The second section of the book includes two case studies that address the fundamental question of how economic actors made sense of the crisis and how they responded to it. In his chapter "'The Last Straw': Bat'a and Endicott-Johnson during and after the Great Depression," Zachary Doleshal shows how the Great Depression recast the business strategies of the Czechoslovak shoe manufacturer Bat'a and its US counterpart Endicott-Johnson as examples of welfare capitalism. Astonishingly, Bat'a and Endicott-Johnson not only survived the Depression, but maintained high employment rates even in its peak years. Their strategies, however, diverged profoundly and ultimately pitted both companies against each other. Strikingly, Bat'a embraced globalization in a time of surging economic nationalism, thus ensuring its survival not only beyond the Depression but also beyond World War II and the Cold War.

In her chapter "Between Economic Recovery and the Great Depression: Multi-ethnic Entrepreneurship, Fragmentation, Nationalization," Katja Wezel examines the dynamics between Latvia's state policies and the activities of businesses and entrepreneurs in the context of post-1918 economic recovery and post-1929 decline. The chapter provides a detailed study of the impact that Latvian financial policies, ranging from protectionism to currency devaluation, had on the country's industrial enterprises. Decision-making became less and less influenced by business strategies or economic considerations. Given the prominence of Baltic Germans and Jews in the industries, the chapter also demonstrates how the Great Depression interacted with political efforts to strengthen ethnic Latvians vis-à-vis the national minorities. Finally, the chapter shows how the authoritarian coup of Kārlis Ulmanis led to an increase in state takeovers of private companies through Latvia's state-run bank, resulting in the disenfranchisement of Latvia's formerly independent economic institutions.

The third section puts a focus on how the Great Depression changed the relationship between states and societies in Eastern Europe. As David Feest shows in his chapter, many Estonians asked themselves, "Is This the Estonia We wanted? How the Interwar Slump Reshaped Estonia's Society" as the country descended into depression. By studying how the economic crisis forced Estonian society to reconsider the nature, success, and future prospects of the young state, the chapter focuses on how the Great Depression fundamentally reshaped the understanding of national sovereignty in a region where it seemed under permanent threat from a hostile international order. The depression thus closely interacted with the fear that the project of building an Estonian nation-state was on the verge of failure. This fear did not only directly contribute to Konstantin Päts's 1934 authoritarian coup but also to an increased hostility toward national minorities, who were regarded as agents of foreign forces that posed an immediate threat to the existence of Estonia as such.

In his chapter "The Great Depression, Social Divisions and Economic Nationalism," Klaus Richter shows how the Great Depression fragmented Lithuanian society along both social and ethnic lines. Focusing on the impact of the depression on the countryside, the chapter reconstructs the experience of peasants across the peak years of the depression from 1931 to 1933, arguing that the existential crisis of the peasants caused profound divides between debtors and creditors, between small and large farmers, and between the towns and the countryside. The Lithuanian Nationalist Union of authoritarian ruler Antanas Smetona harnessed these divides to further an agenda of economic empowerment of ethnic Lithuanians, promoting the entry of struggling peasants into urban professions that were traditionally dominated by non-Lithuanians—especially Jews.

Alexandra Ghiț's chapter "Serving Fewer by Design: Austerity Welfare Politics during the Great Depression" argues that Romanian welfare policy was designed in a general context of austerity. At a time when most other countries enacted protectionist policies, the ruling National Peasant Party promoted foreign investments and enacted austerity policies in exchange for a stabilization loan mediated by the League of Nations. As the standard of living deteriorated rapidly in both urban and rural areas, the authorities stubbornly refused to acknowledge and address the existence of unemployment. The decline in welfare provisions, the chapter argues, was not brought about only by the unfolding economic crisis or Romania's obligations toward international organizations. Instead, it was the culmination of a longer trend toward limiting both the benefits and beneficiaries of the emerging welfare system. Austerity affected all categories of workers, but it had specific effects on women as workers and mothers, leaving them particularly vulnerable.

The book's final section examines how the Great Depression catalyzed changes in economic and political thought. In his chapter "Social and Political Consequences of the Great Depression," Béla Tomka examines how Hungary's depression marked a shift in popular opinion, with state intervention becoming increasingly welcome and judged capable of solving social and economic problems. The Hungarian state counteracted the crisis in agriculture with far-reaching measures, including financial support for farmers, centralization of exports, and the restructuring of rural debt. Although Hungary fared comparatively well during the depression, this increasing acceptance of state-centered economic policies directly contributed to the rise of the extreme right, first with the 1932 appointment of Gyula Gömbös as prime minister and subsequently with the 1935 dissolution of parliament after Gömbös's death in 1936. Depression-era policies, which represented an intensification of existing trends, paved the ground for the consolidation of authoritarian politics.

Apart from providing an overview of the course of the depression in Bulgaria, Nikolay Nenovsky and Tsvetelina Marinova reconstruct cultural and intellectual responses to the Great Depression in their chapter "Economic Thought and Structural Change during the Great Depression," thus addressing not only the question of how the Great Depression intensified the trend toward increasing state intervention in the economy, but also how it highlighted the inability of international organizations to provide support. Bulgaria was particularly vulnerable to external shocks given the nature of its economy, that of a poorly diversified agricultural country, and its status as a defeated country of the Balkan Wars and World War I. The responses of the state included protectionist measures and the promotion of industrial goods, nationalization of the banking system, and an increasing reliance on clearing agreements with Germany. As the authors show, this led to a fruitful proliferation of theories and debates on economic protectionism, autarky, corporatism, and planned economy. Not least, these legitimized authoritarian and corporatist solutions, first with the military coup of 1934 and then with the instatement of Tsar Boris's authoritarian regime in 1935.

In the chapter, "Institutional Strategies and Political Actors in a Period of Increasing Economic Protectionism," Catherine Brégianni examines the fiscal and economic impact of the Great Depression in Greece, as well as its repercussions on economic and political thinking, particularly the consolidation of protectionism and the rise of authoritarianism. Unlike other Balkan countries, Greece had already begun a process of modernizing its agriculture in the 1920s, establishing an agricultural credit bank, switching from cereals to tobacco, and increasing harvest yields. These policies resulted at least in part from the massive influx of refugees from Asia Minor after the Greco-Turkish War (1919–22), which required a redistribution of land and increased productivity. These early efforts likely contributed to the substantial recovery of Greek agriculture by 1934. Not least, the case of Greece showcases the decline in significance of the League of Nations as an international actor of economic recovery, as the Venizelos government eventually rejected the austerity measures and fiscal supervision stipulated by the League, subsequently defaulting on its debt in May 1932.

The conclusion, which brings the findings of the individual chapters into a single frame, posits the Great Depression as "The Watershed Moment of Eastern Europe's Interwar." It stresses the slump's transformative effects on political regimes, on social and economic policies, on the relationship of minorities and the state, on the relationship of Eastern Europe with the wider world, and on how individuals interpreted their lives more broadly. The conclusion argues that the impact of the depression on Eastern Europe has been concealed by the horror and destruction of World War II, but that the path to war—and to the region's Communist postwar period—can only be understood if we view them through the lens of the profound economic collapse of the interwar period.

PART ONE

Eastern Europe's Great Depression in Its International Context

Chapter 2

THE LEAGUE OF NATIONS, EASTERN EUROPE, AND THE GREAT DEPRESSION

Klaus Richter, Jasmin Nithammer, and Anca Mândru

Recent scholarship has vindicated the League of Nations (further: the League) by shifting the focus from causes for its failure to reconstructing its role in promoting innovative and surprisingly durable structures of international cooperation. Scholars of international history have traditionally stressed international efforts to stabilize hyperinflationist Germany in the wake of World War I to prevent it from becoming a breeding ground for Bolshevism. However, a new generation of historians argue that it was rather the broader region of "Central and Eastern Europe" (primarily meaning the successor states of the Habsburg Empire and of the western border regions of the Russian Empire) that was the focus of international efforts to stabilize Europe.[1] This had several reasons. Not least, as opposed to Germany, these countries were members of the League, which made direct support possible—be it voluntary or through assertive interventions. Moreover, at the international level, there were serious doubts concerning the viability of the newly established states. Many of these were involved in border disputes with neighboring countries and had ethnically mixed populations. This heterogeneity was increasingly seen as an impediment to long-term stability—and as something to be solved by internationally steered resettlement, population exchanges, and ethnic cleansing (as in the case of the 1923 Treaty of Lausanne, which stipulated the deportation of Greeks from Turkey and Muslims from Greece and was internationally

1 Patricia Clavin, *Securing the World Economy: The Reinvention of the League of Nations, 1920–1946* (Oxford: Oxford University Press, 2013); Natasha Wheatley, *The Life and Death of States: Central Europe and the Transformation of Modern Sovereignty* (Princeton, NJ: Princeton University Press, 2023).

regarded as a success).[2] In this chapter, we will examine how far the League's efforts to address the challenges of the Great Depression were guided by such normative views on the states of Central and Eastern Europe, and, in turn, what agency these states had in shaping the League's responses. We will focus specifically on two sets of institutions: a series of agricultural conferences, convened at the initiative of these states themselves, and the so-called Commission of Enquiry for European Union, set up by the League to aid Europe's economic recovery through rapprochements and the abolition of trade barriers.

Financial and economic reconstruction had not been among the core tasks of the League's founding vision, but it quickly moved to its center in the early 1920s as the short-lived postwar boom came to an end, the new states of Central and Eastern Europe failed to overcome their financial crises, and Austria, Hungary, Poland, and Germany descended into hyperinflation and mass unemployment (Czechoslovakia, which attained political stability earlier than its neighbors, and the Baltic states, which consolidated the multitude of different currencies in circulation after the Russian Revolution and German military occupation, avoided it).[3] The centrality of financial reconstruction in the League's portfolio is reflected in the International Financial Conference in Brussels, organized by the League in 1920 as a matter of priority. Without financial aid, Austria, Hungary, Poland, and Germany seemed on the verge of state failure. Although the conference did not solve these crises, it established the League as an organization for economic diplomacy, created an open forum for international economic expertise, and distanced international economic policy from the political rationale

2 Robert Gerwarth, *The Vanquished: Why the First World War Failed to End* (London: Allen Lane, 2016); Klaus Richter, *Fragmentation in East Central Europe: Poland and the Baltics, 1915–1929* (Oxford: Oxford University Press, 2020).

3 Jose A. Lopez and Kris James Mitchener, "Uncertainty and Hyperinflation: European Inflation Dynamics after World War I," National Bureau of Economic Research Working Paper Series, Working Paper 24624, Cambridge, Mass. (May 2018), 5, 13–15; Oldřich Krpec and Vít Hloušek, "Czechoslovak Tariffs in the 1920s: An Example of Historical Specificity in Economic Policy," *Slavic Review* 80, no. 3 (2021): 523–43; François R. Velde, "Hyperinflations of the Early Twentieth Century," in *Money in the Western Legal Tradition: Middle Ages to Bretton Woods*, eds. David Fox and Wolfgang Ernst (Oxford: Oxford University Press, 2016), 676–78.

of the Paris peace negotiations.[4] At a smaller follow-up conference in Porto Rosa (1921), states that had emerged from, or inherited parts of, the Habsburg Empire—Austria, Hungary, Italy, Poland, Romania, Czechoslovakia, and the Kingdom of Serbs, Croats, and Slovenes—agreed to undertake efforts to mitigate the fragmentation of Central European railway lines, which, however, were never fully implemented due to diverging political interests.[5]

From its creation, the League's relationship with the states that had emerged from the former European borderlands of the Habsburg, Russian, German, and Ottoman Empires was of a special nature. Conceived of as a "custodian of the principle of self-determination" (Patricia Clavin), the League acknowledged that it had a special responsibility for the consolidation and preservation of these "nation-states" that the Entente victory had liberated from centuries of imperial oppression.[6] Political actors of these states tended to be enthusiastic about the League, regarding it as the foundation for an equitable international order that would respect their sovereignty at eye level with that of the European "Great Powers." This enthusiasm abated when the Western Entente enshrined the protection of minorities in the League's covenant and compelled the governments of the "new" states to sign Minority Treaties. As the "old" states refused to sign similar treaties (claiming that no minorities lived on their territories), Eastern European politicians saw this as evidence that the sovereignty of their own states received less respect than that of others.[7]

In their relationship with the League, the countries of Eastern Europe are usually regarded as passive recipients. However, Eastern Europeans made considerable contributions to the League's work. With Momčilo Ninčić (1926–27), Nicolae Titulescu (1931–32), and Edvard Beneš (1935–36), three key politicians from this region

4 Clavin, *Securing the World Economy*, 11–46.

5 Irene Anastasiadou, *Constructing Iron Europe: Transnationalism and Railways in the Interbellum* (Amsterdam: Amsterdam University Press, 2011), 110–13.

6 Clavin, *Securing the World Economy*, 11–46.

7 Carole Fink, *Defending the Rights of Others: The Great Powers, the Jews, and International Minority Protection, 1878–1938* (Cambridge: Cambridge University Press, 2004); Mark Mazower, "Minorities and the League of Nations in Interwar Europe," *Daedalus* 126, no. 2 (1997): 47–63.

served as presidents of the General Assembly. Between 1920 and 1939, 71 citizens of Eastern European states (excluding Austria) served as assistants, clerks, and section members. According to nationality, the largest cohorts of these were Poles, Czechoslovaks, Yugoslavs, and Romanians. With the Health Section, Poland was also one of the few Eastern European countries to hold a senior League post, with the Polish physician and UNICEF founder Ludwik Witold Rajchman serving as director for the whole duration of the section's existence. In addition to Rajchman, the Greek diplomat Thanassis Aghnides served as director of the Disarmament Section (1930–39) and Branko Lukač (Yugoslavia) as Chief of the Communications and Transit Section (1939–46). The Health Section and the Economic and Financial Section employed the largest numbers of Eastern European citizens (15 each), followed by the Information Section (11). Strikingly, the number of Eastern European citizens employed with the League increased gradually across the 1920s and dropped significantly during the Great Depression. No Eastern European citizens were appointed to League posts in 1932 and only one in 1933[8] (Table 2.1, Figure 2.1).

The League's primary economic support for Eastern Europe took the form of loan mediation. The League acted as a de facto seal of quality for these loans, which were provided by a diverse range of banks. The first of these loans was acquired for Austria in 1923 as part of the League's extensive mission to reconstruct the failing state's finances.[9] Loans for Greece (1924) and Bulgaria (1926) were mediated specifically to aid with the resettlement of the hundreds of thousands of refugees displaced by the Greco-Turkish War. Both countries received two further League-endorsed loans in 1926 to stabilize their currencies. Hungary received a loan in 1924, Danzig in 1925 and 1927, and Estonia in 1927. As historians arguing for the failure of these schemes have stressed, all nine loans ended in defaults. However, others stress that the economic conditions brought about by the Great Depression were so fundamentally

8 All figures from the League of Nations Search Engine (LONSEA), http://www.lonsea.de/.

9 Nathan Marcus, *Austrian Reconstruction and the Collapse of Global Finance, 1921–1931* (Cambridge, MA: Harvard University Press, 2018).

Table 2.1 Employees in League of Nations Sections by Nationality

Country	*Employees*[a]
Poland	21
Czechoslovakia	14
Yugoslavia	9
Romania	8
Hungary	6
Lithuania	4
Greece	3
Latvia	2
Albania	1
Bulgaria	1
Danzig	1
Estonia	1

[a] Assistants, clerks, section members, and senior officials.

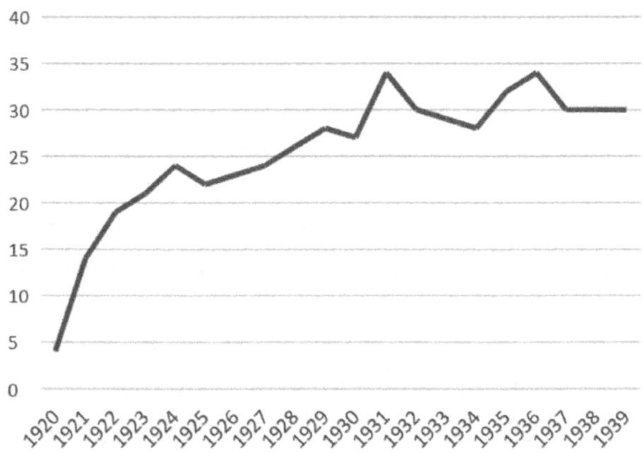

Figure 2.1 Citizens of Eastern European States Employed by the League of Nations

(*Source*: Compiled by the Authors on the Basis of the League of Nations Database LONSEA.)

different (and more challenging) than those under which the loans were established, and that anything else than default would have been a miracle. Greece, Hungary, and Bulgaria defaulted on their five loans in 1932–33 at the fulcrum of the depression; Austria, however, defaulted only after its incorporation into Germany in 1938, Danzig only 2 months before the Free City's occupation by the Nazis, and Estonia only in winter 1940–41, when it was already under Soviet occupation.[10]

Recent scholarship has stressed the nature of the League of Nation—especially in its initial phase in the absence of the United States, the Soviet Union, and Germany—as a "League of Empires," in which norms around development, sovereignty, and international relations were articulated through the lens of its two dominant European member states, Britain and France.[11] Patricia Clavin has emphasized that the relationship of the League's Economic and Financial Organization (EFO) with the states of Central and Eastern Europe was characterized by ideas of nineteenth-century humanitarian imperialism. This was illustrated by the rather patriarchal terms characterizing the efforts to promote those states benefiting from League-mediated loans and advice from the League's financial missions. Greece's League delegate Nicholas Politis praised John Campbell, a former vice-chairman of the Refugee Settlement Commission (RSC) in Greece, for his "practical knowledge thanks to his long colonial experience."[12] A Greek RSC colleague congratulated the RSC's chairman, Charles Howland, for his achievement in "hellenizing" Macedonia by organizing the resettlement of Greek refugees in localities previously inhabited by Slavs and Turks: "You can, certainly, boast that your great Colonization work has not only contributed to the 'Renaissance' of Greece, but also that it has helped

10 J. F. Zendejas, "Contesting the Preferred Creditor Status of the League of Nations, 1931–3," *Economic History Review* 74, no. 4 (2021): 1069; Yann Decorzant and Juan H. Flores, "Public Borrowing in Harsh Times: The League of Nations Loans Revisited," IFCS—Working Papers in Economic History, WH. (Universidad Carlos III de Madrid. Instituto Figuerola) 2012, https://ideas.repec.org/p/cte/whrepe/wp12-07.html.

11 Susan Pedersen, *The Guardians: The League of Nations and the Crisis of Empire* (Oxford: Oxford University Press, 2015).

12 Clavin, *Securing the World Economy*, 11–46.

settle most definitely the age-long and most difficult . . . diplomatic problem, that of the 'Macedonian Riddle', thus establishing Peace in the 'Volcanic' Balkans."[13]

However, not everyone shared such positive assessments of the quasi-colonial practices of the League's experts. The League's General Commissioner for the Economic Reconstruction of Austria, Alfred Rudolph Zimmerman, who was dispatched to oversee the stabilization of the Austrian currency, recommended economic cuts that resulted in a surge in unemployment. This culminated in the layoff of 100,000 state officials, hospital closures, and the collapse of industries in 1924, making him the target of press campaigns by socialists who portrayed him as the personification of foreign intervention, which colonized Austria on behalf of foreign (Jewish) capitalism.[14] In a striking parallel to the controversial financial interventions of the European Commission, the European Central Bank, and the International Monetary Fund in Greece following the 2009 European debt crisis, these reservations regarding the implications of the League's economic and financial assistance for national sovereignty obstructed a meaningful response of the League to the Great Depression in Eastern Europe. Arthur Salter, head of the EFO until 1930, and his successors, Pietro Stoppani and Alexander Loveday—who presided over the Economic Section and Financial Section respectively after the EFO's split in 1931—openly wondered whether the League's overseeing role "was a poisoned chalice" and whether it might be better "to give advice to members of the League without taking any responsibility in regard to the acceptance of such advice . . . to remove the fear felt by some states that a request for advice might involve League interference in financial policy."[15]

13 Papadakis to Howland, October 19, 1926, Yale University, Howland Papers, Box 7, Folder 141. Quoted in: Matthew Frank, *Making Minorities History: Population Transfer in Twentieth-Century Europe* (Oxford: Oxford University Press, 2017), 83.

14 Marcus, *Austrian Reconstruction*, 204; Klaus Richter, "The Catastrophe of the Present and that of the Future: Expectations Towards European States from the Great War to the Great Depression," *Contemporary European History* (2023), https://doi.org/10.1017/S096077732200100X: 13.

15 "Comment by Loveday, 'Minutes of Directors' Meeting,' February 12, 1930, 3–4, League of Nations Archive (hereafter: LON) R3565, 50/25831/767, Directors Meetings 1931; Comment by Salter, 'Minutes of Directors' Meeting,' October 8, 1930, LON

It was amid these tensions that the Great Depression reshaped the relationship between the League of Nations and the Eastern European states. National governments were worried about the League's interference in national sovereignty and its alleged nature as an agent of international, exploitative, and imperialist powers on the one hand. But on the other, there remained a genuine (if diminishing) enthusiasm about the League, as Eastern Europe depended on international loans and political support more than ever in the face of (primarily German and Soviet) revisionism.

During the slump, the region became synonymous with the "Agricultural Depression." With notable exceptions (most strikingly, Czechoslovakia), all countries in the region were primarily agricultural in character. Thus, they were all heavily affected by the fall in prices for agricultural products. "Agriculture plays such an important part in the economic life of Poland that the effects of its depression cannot but be generally felt," the president of Poland's Land Credit Society, Tomasz August Popławski, reported to the League.[16] Stressing the economic vulnerability of the "new" states of Eastern Europe as compared to the large agricultural producers overseas, the League's Economic Committee reported in 1931 that the agricultural depression "operates with unequal intensity according to the economic development of the countries, their capacity for resistance and the relative advantages which they enjoy as agricultural producers. They do not suffer to the same extent from the same evils."[17] Yet within the region itself, countries were also affected to various degrees, with some countries of Southeastern Europe hit particularly hard and the Baltic states, which had already begun a transition from grain exports to meat and dairy products, affected relatively less.

R3565, 50/16937/767, Directors Meetings 1930, 4. Quoted in: Clavin, *Securing the World Economy*, 72 [Ch. 2, note 101].

For all references to the League of Nations Archive, we have decided not to use the original call numbers but rather the reference codes assigned by the Total Digital Access to the League of Nations Project (LONTAD) for ease of access (https://archives.ungeneva.org/lontad).

16 Economic Committee (League of Nations), *The Agricultural Crisis*. Vol. 1 (15.06.1931), LON, 0000765460_D0001, 253.

17 Economic Committee, *The Agricultural Crisis*, 7.

Initially, this agricultural depression was not regarded as a rupture. Agriculture had taken a downturn already before the Wall Street Crash. The League's report on the World Economic Conference of 1927 stressed the widening gap between prices for manufactured products and slumping agricultural prices, which meant that agricultural producers "no longer receive sufficient return for their labour and their capital."[18] The conference recommended removing obstacles to industrial production and international trade to increase demand for agricultural products. In addition, delegates discussed the provision of agricultural credit, measures to increase productivity, and new social legislation.[19] However, in the aftermath of the conference, the conditions of European agriculture rapidly deteriorated further. In 1929, the League Assembly reviewed the implementation of these recommendations and had to admit that "no decisive movement had occurred in the reduction of trade barriers and no serious effort had been made to carry out the fundamental idea of the Conference – namely, the idea of closer co-operation between nations in their economic life and reduction of opportunities for international conflict."[20]

2.1 The Agricultural Conferences

In early 1931, Vojislav Marinković, Yugoslavia's Minister for Foreign Affairs, vented his frustration at this lack of action. Notably, he did so at a meeting of a new enquiry commission set up to facilitate European cooperation, reduce trade barriers, and secure peace: The Commission for Enquiry into the European Union (further: the Commission), established on May 17, 1930, based on a proposal by Aristide Briand. Initially, the commission's aim was a deep economic entanglement of European states to make their future disentanglement through wars untenable ("rapprochements"). It represented the first diplomatic effort to fulfill the old idea of

18 Cited in Economic Committee, *The Agricultural Crisis*, 11.

19 R. R. Enfield, "The International Situation in Agriculture and the World's Economic Conference, 1927," *International Affairs* 8, no. 1 (1929): 43–44.

20 Commission of Enquiry for European Union (=CEEU), "Minutes of the Second Session of the Commission. Held at Geneva from January 16–21, 1931," LON, C-144-M-45-1931-VII_EN, 13.

European unification.[21] However, when Marinković spoke, the economic depression had already achieved an intensity that made this plan seem utopian. Instead, the commission became the League's main incubator for debates on Europe's economic recovery.

Marinković stressed he did not think "that the economic experts have yet understood this truth, which is a very simple one [. . .]. The agricultural countries [. . .] came to Geneva with several resolutions, the adoption of which would, they thought, improve their position to a certain extent." He added: "I do not know whether they were right or wrong, but I do know that these schemes were discussed in a manner which absolutely precluded any satisfactory result." The key issue was that the Great Powers—and the League's economic experts for that matter—failed to understand the specific implications of national sovereignty in a region where state-building was an ongoing process, where economic structures were backward as a consequence of imperial neglect, where the countryside was overpopulated, and where both Bolsheviks and the vanquished of the war sought destabilization in order to revise the fragile political order. Instead, they erroneously lumped the agricultural states of Eastern Europe together with those of the Americas:

> We were told that we ought to lower Customs barriers and even abolish them. As far as the agricultural States of Europe are concerned, if they could keep the promises they made in 1927 . . . and could carry that policy right through, we might perhaps find ourselves able to hold our own against overseas competition in the matter of agricultural products. But, at the same time, we should have to sacrifice four-fifths of our population; we should have to create in Poland, Roumania and Yugoslavia the same conditions as exist in Canada and the Argentine, where vast territories are inhabited by a scanty population and where machinery and other devices are employed. Obviously, none of us could decide to adopt a system which would be very like Moscow's five-year

21 "Documents Relating to the Organisation of a System of European Federal Union," 15.09.1930, LON 0000676824_D0004, 5; Pauli Heikkilä, "Northern Replies to the Briand Memorandum 1930," *Scandinavian Journal of History* 32, no. 3 (2007): 215.

> plan. We would not sacrifice our people by shooting them, but they would nevertheless be killed off by famine – which would come to the same thing.[22]

As the agricultural crisis deepened, the Eastern European states began to make efforts to address the crisis themselves. Of the sixteen international conferences organized worldwide to address the agricultural depression, seven were held by representatives of Eastern European countries: three in Bucharest (July 21–23, 1930 and October 18–21, 1930; February 16–18, 1931), one in Sinaia (July 30, 1930–August 1, 1930), two in Warsaw (August 28–30, 1930 and November 10, 1930), and one in Belgrade (November 10–13, 1930).[23] The Romanian economist and League delegate Virgil Madgearu, who successively served as Minister of Industry and Trade, Minister of Finances, and Minister of Agriculture and Royal Domains when the Great Depression struck, stressed the international reluctance to implement the recommendations of 1927 and the failure of the League-sponsored Conference of Agricultural Experts (1930) to make practical recommendations as the main reason for the concerted activities: "The initiative for these conferences was due also, in part, to the atmosphere of deception produced by the lack of positive results from the economic activity of the League of Nations."[24] Not least, the agricultural conferences were a testimony to Madgearu's long-term advocacy for the creation of an "Agrarian Bloc" that would promote the interests of Eastern European agricultural exporting countries, especially in relation to their industrialized Western and Central European counterparts.[25]

Both contemporary and historical assessments of these conferences tend to be negative. Romanian corporatism theorist Mihail

22 CEEU, "Minutes of the Second Session of the Commission," 16.02.1931, LON, C-144-M-45-1931-VII_EN, 31.

23 Alonzo E. Taylor, "The International Wheat Conferences during 1930–31," *Wheat Studies of the Food Research Institute* 7, no. 9 (1931): 440.

24 Virgil Madgearu quoted in *L'Europe Nouvelle*, no. 657, September 13, 1930, 1320, translated into English in D. G. H., "The European Agrarian Bloc," *Bulletin of International News* 7, no. 10 (November 6, 1930): 3.

25 On Madgearu's ideas see: Keith Hitchins, *Rumania, 1866–1947* (Oxford: Clarendon Press, 1994), 320–25; D. G. H., "The European," 3–11.

Manoilescu, one of Madgearu's fiercest critics, deplored the conferences' "poverty of ideas" and "utopian solutions," which rendered them "sterile, empty and unproductive."[26] Historians have criticized the conferences' narrow focus on extracting concessions, lowering tariffs, and removing import restrictions, instead of more ambitious efforts to influence cereal prices by limiting exports.[27] Newspapers also tended to be critical of both the League and the Eastern European representatives, who did "very, very little" and "very, very slowly."[28] Still, these conferences remain significant both for their debates and the attempts to form, if not a truly agrarian, then at least a concerted regional bloc.

The Eastern European agricultural conferences were characterized both by a remarkable sense of unity and by profound divergences in interests. That Hungary joined the Little Entente (Romania, Czechoslovakia, Yugoslavia) at the first Bucharest conference (July 1930) to work on a unified response to the Leagues was a remarkable political feat. However, the participants were reluctant to include the missing Habsburg Empire's successor state, Czechoslovakia. At the Little Entente's annual conference, they stressed that Czechoslovakia was "too industrialized" to fully share the concerns of the other countries. Still, Czechoslovakia dispatched an observer to the Sinaia conference, where Romania and Yugoslavia discussed the prospect of forming a "Danubian" customs union.[29]

By far the most significant of these conferences, the Agricultural Conference in Warsaw (August 1930) included eight East-Central European countries: Romania, Yugoslavia, Hungary, Czechoslovakia, Poland, Bulgaria, Estonia, and Latvia. Lithuania declined the invitation due to its conflict with Poland, while Finland sent an observer. In Warsaw, delegates developed previously

26 Mihail Manoilescu, *Memorii* (Bucharest: Editura Enciclopedică, 1993), vol. 2, 231.

27 Bogdan Murgescu, *România și Europa: Acumularea decalajelor economice, 1500–2010* (Iași: Polirom, 2010), 237–38.

28 "Cuvântul d-lui Briand," *Adeverul*, September 18, 1931.

29 See M. Baumont's report, "La Conférence Internationale Agricole de Varsovie," in *Meeting of Eastern European Agricultural Correspondents in Warsaw, August 27–30, 1930*, LON, R2804-10D-21543-2016, 2–3. For a comprehensive discussion of the international debates on the numerous plans for a Danubian federation and customs' union see Wilfried Loth and Nicolae Păun, eds., *Disintegration and Integration in East-Central Europe, 1919 – post 1989* (Baden-Baden: Nomos, 2014).

theoretical and disjointed debates into a coherent agenda and a set of policy recommendations. Polish delegates proposed the creation of a closely integrated "Agrarian Bloc."[30] Representatives agreed to rationalize and coordinate agricultural products, especially cereals, organize networks of storage facilities, establish financial institutions that would advance payments to farmers, and unify statistical methods so that all countries could have easy access to accurate data about quantities and prices.[31] Given its own experiences and advances in the centralization of agricultural exports, it was agreed that Poland should take the lead.

The hierarchies, alliances, and divergences between the delegates are reflected in the report of the League's observer, the historian Maurice Baumont. According to Baumont, Polish representatives regarded Poland as the ideal mediator between the Balkan countries and the East-Central European states, both by virtue of its geographic position and its success in alleviating the effects of the agricultural crisis through the centralization of cereal and livestock exports via a national agency, the Union of Grain Exporters (*Związek Eksporterów Zboża Rzeczypospolitej Polskiej*, established in 1929). At the Belgrade conference of November 1930, the participating countries agreed to use the union's charter as a model to establish a network of national institutions to fix prices and terms of sale.[32] Poland aside, Romania, Yugoslavia, and Hungary were the only countries to play an active role at the Warsaw conference. The Baltic states were mere "spectators," while Czechoslovakia was in a "delicate situation" due to its industrialized economy.[33] When they opposed draft resolutions, they were largely ignored.[34] Still, the conference concluded with unanimous agreement on its requests and recommendations, which Virgil Madgearu afterward presented to the League as representative for all the eight countries present at the

30 Poland first approached Yugoslavia with a proposal for the creation of a broad European agricultural bloc with shared interests. See D. G. H., "The European," 5–6.

31 "Records of the Eleventh Ordinary Session of the Assembly. Annex 3: Text of the Resolution Adopted by the International Agricultural Conference at Warsaw (30.08.1930)," 1930, LON A-PLENARY-MINUTES-1930_EN, 489–90.

32 Economic Committee, *The Agricultural Crisis*, Vol. 1, 65.

33 Baumont, "La Conférence Internationale Agricole," 3.

34 Baumont, "La Conférence Internationale Agricole," 4.

conference. International observers stressed that the conference's significance transcended the agricultural crisis by framing Eastern Europe as a coherent economic region that was markedly different from North America: "The meeting brought into greater prominence than hitherto the concept of the central European region as a cereal belt opposed to the overseas cereal areas."[35]

2.2 From Preferential Treatment to Agricultural Credit

The most contentious resolution of the Warsaw conference was the request for preferential treatment, in the form of reduced tariffs for agricultural products originating from Eastern Europe, in a derogation of the most favored nation (MFN) clause. This reflected a broader global pushback against the MFN, for which 1930–31 was a watershed moment: Almost any bilateral treaty concluded before 1931 contained the MFN clause, whereas only 40 percent of post-1931 treaties did so.[36] Various other members of the League challenged the MFN across the 1920s and would ramp up these efforts throughout the 1930s. However, the request made by Virgil Madgearu on behalf of the Warsaw conference countries at the 1930 General Assembly represented the one occasion when Eastern European countries acted as a unified bloc and presented this demand in an assertive manner.[37] Madgearu pointed out that a precedent already existed in "the Baltic clause, the Scandinavian clause, the Iberian clause and the South American clause," wondering why, "since the right of exceptions to the most-favored-nation clause has already been admitted in the case of these economic units, . . . in reason and equity, should it be refused to other regions."[38]

35 Taylor, "The International Wheat Conferences," 443.

36 Richard Carlton Synder, *The Most-Favored-Nation Clause: An Analysis with Particular Reference to Recent Treaty Practice and Tariffs* (New York: King's Crown Press 1948), 132.

37 Records of the Eleventh Ordinary Session of the Assembly, Twentieth Plenary Meeting, 1.10.1930, LON, A-PLENARY-MINUTES-1930_EN, 178–84.

38 Records of the Eleventh Ordinary Session of the Assembly, Twentieth Plenary Meeting, 182.

However, as scholars have noted, these regional agreements had largely been "Platonic clauses" with little impact, as these neighboring states shared too many economic characteristics, thus making them rival exporters.[39] The largely ineffective Baltic -clause was rarely implemented, and Finland, the main driver behind its inception, regarded it not as an instrument for achieving economic union, but rather as a means of gaining advantages without further economic integration.[40] Madgearu's request went much further in terms of the scale and depth of integration. Moreover, the League's agreements regarding the MFN clause, drafted in 1927 and 1928, referred to these regional clauses as exceptions considered due to the "special ethnic, historical, geographical, or other ties" that united the respective countries.[41] Two years prior to the Ottawa Conference, when Britain would grant its colonies and dominions exactly this kind of preferential treatment, the British representative was quick to point out that the existence of past exceptions did not justify "the right of any group of countries to come to such arrangements in the future."[42] According to the British Press, the delegate supposedly dismissed "artificially created groupings."[43] Britain threw its weight behind those non-European countries that strongly opposed the Warsaw resolutions, including the British Dominions, Canada, Australia, and India, as well as Japan, which condemned the idea of preferential treatment as discrimination against non-European countries.[44]

In his aforementioned speech at the Commission, Vojislav Marinković stressed the unjustness of the hierarchies between

39 Jacob Viner, *The Customs Union Issue* (New York: Carnegie Endowment for International Peace), 22.

40 Antti-Jussi Nygård, "The Formation of the Baltic Clause: A Finnish Initiative?," *Acta Historica Tallinnensia* 18, no. 1 (2012): 73–96.

41 "Report by M.M. Brunet and di Nola on the Drafting of the [Most Favored Nation] Clause and the Extension of its Application," 27.12.1928, LON, R2728-10C-3278-578-Jacket2, 22.

42 "Work of the Economic and Financial Organisation," 11th Session of the Assembly, 23.09.1930, LON, R3349-15-22402-22311-Jacket2, 17.

43 D. G. H., "The European," 8.

44 "Work of the Economic and Financial Organisation," 11th Session of the Assembly, 20.09.1930, LON R3349-15-22402-22311-Jacket1, 27–29, 43–49.

"Great Powers" and the "small states" of Eastern Europe that structured these debates. Dropping tariffs would amount to the sacrifice of national sovereignty, Marinković claimed, and if the economic experts were to comprehend the bind that the Eastern European states were in, they would realize that the MFN, in its current sacrosanct form, could not be maintained:

> Last year, when I was in the Yugoslav mountains, I heard that the inhabitants of a small mountain village, having no maize or wheat on which to live, were simply cutting down a wood which belonged to them under a decision of the Council of State and were living on what they earned by selling the wood. Unfortunately, the forest grew smaller and smaller. I went to the village, collected together some of the leading inhabitants and endeavored to reason with them, just like the great industrial States reason with us. I said to them: "You possess plenty of common sense. You see that your forest is becoming smaller and smaller. What will you do when you cut down the last tree?" They replied to me: "Your Excellency, that is a point which worries us: but, on the other hand, what should we do now if we stopped cutting down our trees?" I can assure you that the agricultural countries of Europe are in exactly the same situation. You threaten them with future disasters; but they are already in the throes of disaster. The agricultural countries are unable to make both ends meet, and cannot buy from the industrial countries of Europe.[45]

As predicted, the failure to obtain preferential treatment for agricultural products led to divisions among the eight Warsaw countries, who now turned to discussing the imposition of quotas for imports of manufactured goods from industrial countries. This approach, however, went against the interests of so-called "semi-industrialized" Czechoslovakia, as well as noncereal exporting countries like Latvia, Estonia, and even Bulgaria, which refrained from taking a

45 CEEU, "Minutes of the Second Session of the Commission," 16.02.1931, LON, C-144-M-45-1931-VII_EN, 31–32.

stand. By October 1930, when the second Bucharest conference took place, the "Agrarian bloc" was again reduced to Poland, Romania, Yugoslavia, and Hungary.[46] Reconciling the interests of the entire region seemed increasingly impossible.

By that time, the matter of preferential treatment was already moving out of the focus of League discussions. When the League's Economic Committee met in late October, Yugoslavia's delegate, Milan Todorovič, declared preferential treatment as the "essential point for the agricultural states of Eastern Europe," with all other measures discussed at the Warsaw Conference secondary:

> So far as the importing countries were concerned, in view of the fact that the production of the countries of Eastern Europe would remain the same as would their consumption, imports would not change, and, consequently, the preferential treatment would simply mean a small reduction in fiscal revenues. For the overseas countries, who were the competitors of the agricultural countries in the east, the consequences would be nil, for their exports would remain the same.[47]

However, the majority of the Economic Committee's members broadly argued in support of maintaining the MFN clause.[48] At a further economic conference in Geneva, the "Danubian countries" made a last attempt to secure preferential treatment, where the issue was again postponed.[49]

For Eastern European politicians, international opposition against preferential treatment betrayed a gross injustice in the international order, where the "new," "small" states were constantly refused the right to "catch up" with the more established and more

46 "Protocol of the Conference of the Agricultural Experts of Central and South-Eastern Europe, Held at Bucarest, October 18–20, 1930," LON R2804-10D-23363-2016, 6–8.

47 Economic Committee, "Thirty-Third Session," 15.11.1930, LON, 0000765306_D0007, 20.

48 Economic Committee, "Thirty-Third Session," 18.

49 "Proceedings of the Second International Conference with a View to Concerted Economic Action (First Session), Held at Geneva from November 17–28, 1930," LON C-149-M-48-1931-II-B_EN, 101–15.

modern economies of the West. This is reflected in the argument between Hungarian delegate István Winchkler and the Canadian Advisory Officer to the League, Walter Alexander Riddell. At the 1931 League Assembly meeting, Winchkler attempted to dissuade Riddell's concerns that preferential treatment for Eastern Europe would put Canadian agricultural exporters at a disadvantage. All wheat-exporting countries could voice their views on bilateral treaties through diplomatic channels, Winchkler assured Riddell. Preferential treatment would not erode the MFN principle, which was "completely safeguarded." The demands of the Agrarian Bloc "had never been directed against the extra-European wheat-growers; on the contrary, they believed that their proposals would ultimately prove to be in the interest of the latter." In Winckler's view, the culprit for the catastrophic collapse in wheat prices was America. However, whereas America could mitigate overproduction and the fall of prices by rationalizing production, the peasants of Eastern Europe could not: "The resulting margin between the cost of production in America and in Europe was enormous; and all that the preference was intended to do was to compensate for that margin." It was America, in fact, that had increased its agricultural output by as much as 100 percent, whereas the "Danubian states" had remained at prewar levels. "Mr. Riddell had appealed to 'equal rights' and 'justice,'" Winchkler protested: "He might remember the maxim *Summum jus, summa injuria*."[50]

While the League's member states rejected the appeal for preferential tariffs, they proved willing to work on another important resolution of the Warsaw conference, the establishment of a credit institution for Eastern European farmers. With the League's blessing, all eight East-Central European countries reconvened in Warsaw in November 1930 to examine the issue. As the League's representative observed, the usual tensions resurfaced. Czechoslovakia and Hungary were indifferent, while Estonia and Latvia did "not desire their peasants to entangle themselves in foreign debts."[51]

50 "Work of the Economic Organisation," 12th Session of the Assembly, Minutes of the Second Committee, 19.09.1931, LON, A-C2-MINUTES-1931_EN, 41.

51 "Note on the Warsaw Conference for Agricultural Credit (November 10–13, 1930)," 10.11.1930, LON, R2851-10D-24025-9867, 5.

Nonetheless, like before, all countries present saw benefit in showing a common front and eventually produced a memorandum recommending medium-term loans (from 6 months to 5 years), less secure than long-term loans but more appropriate to the local farmers' needs.

The Warsaw countries' proposal was simultaneously considered by the Financial Committee, a smaller consultative body answering to the League's Council, and the Commission of Enquiry for European Union.[52] After lengthy discussions, the Financial Committee recommended the establishment of a Delegation for Agricultural Credits.[53] The only Eastern European representative of the delegation was Feliks Młynarski, a Polish economist and banker and member of the Financial Committee. The group drew up a draft convention for the establishment of the International Agricultural Mortgage Credit Company (IAMCC), which would gather capital by selling shares to Western banks and then provide loans to farmers in Eastern Europe through national agricultural credit banks.[54] Whereas only European banks were allowed to apply during the first 5 years, the scheme would then open to overseas countries as well. As Madeleine Dungy notes, based on agricultural debt estimates provided by Poland and Romania in Warsaw, the capital of the IAMCC, as designed, would have been enough to make a "significant impact" on the Eastern European rural economies plagued by exorbitant interest rates that at times reached 500 percent.[55]

The Commission's support for the establishment of the IAMCC has to be seen in the context of further initiatives that were based on a genuine desire to assist the states of Eastern Europe in overcoming the agricultural depression. As a short-term measure, the Commission organized a meeting in February 1931 to help dispose

52 "Extract from Minutes of the 7th Meeting of the 62nd Session of the Council," 23.01.1931, LON, R2852-10D-25549-9867, 4–5.

53 Financial Committee, "Report to the Council on the Work of the Fortieth Session of the Committee (Geneva, January 15–20, 1931)," 27.01.1931, LON, R2852-10D-25488-9867, 3–5.

54 "Convention for the Creation of an International Agricultural-Mortgage Credit Company, with Charter and Statutes, Geneva, May 21, 1931," *Official Journal*, 1931, 1428–44.

55 Madeleine Lynch Dungy, "The Global Agricultural Crisis and British Diplomacy in the League of Nations in 1931," *The Agricultural History Review* 65, no. 2 (2017): 308.

of the 1930 grain stocks and to inquire into the exportations of the surplus of future grain harvests. The Commission made crucial contributions to two Conferences of wheat-exporting and importing countries that took place in Rome (March 1931) and in London (May 1931).[56] France's League delegate André François-Poncet was jubilant about these achievements. "All this work has been accomplished," he claimed: "A practical plan, the creation of an international company for agricultural mortgage credits complete in every detail is ready for your consideration."[57] As we know, however, the Austrian Credit-Anstalt's collapse on 11 May—4 days before François-Poncet declared the Commission's work a success—rendered the IAMCC a pipe dream. In September 1930, Britain withdrew its backing following the turbulent political changes around the decision to abandon the Gold Standard.[58]

2.3 Assigning the Blame: Eastern Europe and the Failure of European Integration

Why did the League fail to throw its weight behind those measures that could have made a real difference in terms of Eastern Europe's economic recovery in those years? The League was certainly increasingly overwhelmed as its basis—the consensus that a recovery of the (highly idealized) prewar liberal international order was desirable and achievable—was eroded by the spiral of protectionist measures initiated in 1930. Moreover, the dislocations caused by the Great Depression even in the wealthiest and most powerful of the League's member states—France and Britain—challenged the very notion of international solidarity. Yet the causes can also be found in normative views on the nature of statehood in those parts of Europe—Eastern and Southeastern Europe—that had formerly been under (Ottoman, Habsburg, Russian, and German) imperial rule. While

56 "List of Questions Relating to International Trade," 28.10.1932, LON, 0000679921_D0001, 11; CEEU, "Minutes of the Third Session of the Commission," 25.06.1931, LON, C-144-M-45-1931-VII_EN, 9.

57 CEEU, "Minutes of the Third Session of the Commission," 25.06.1931, LON, C-144-M-45-1931-VII_EN, 20.

58 Dungy, "The Global Agricultural Crisis," 317; Clavin, *Securing the World Economy*, 119.

the broader approach of the League of Nations was grounded in the idea that the Great Depression was universal, the League recognized the special position and particular vulnerability of the states of Eastern Europe due to their economic structure. "In agricultural exporting countries," the Economic Committee stated in 1931, "the economic organization is more severely hit if the products of the soil are sold at a loss."[59] At the same time, the League's experts were well aware that there were huge internal differences in the economic structure—and their vulnerability to the crisis—among the states of Central and Eastern Europe. A Swiss expert, dividing the states of Europe into four different categories, assigned the "Danubian States" to the category of countries that could both grow corn to satisfy their own needs and have enough left to export.[60] The Delegation on Economic Depression, tasked in 1938 with identifying the causes for the slump and its long-term impact on states and societies across the world, came to the conclusion that "agricultural over-capacity" had been at the root of the Great Depression, as well as the failure of the three major groups of countries to cooperate: the industrial countries, which limited imports to maintain price levels, those agricultural countries with highly mechanized methods, which depended on agricultural exports and thus squeezed prices to keep their exports competitive, and the "peasant countries." The latter, including Eastern Europe, were characterized by "low agricultural efficiency," "acute capital underequipment," and "small size of individual holdings." They depended on exports but were in no position to compete with the price policy of the former.[61] Western European representatives in the League's Economic Committee regularly claimed that the depression was not a result of overproduction but of "bad organization" of the Eastern European economies, and that the League should not concern itself with improving

59 Economic Committee, *The Agricultural Crisis*, Vol. 1, 7.

60 "Notes on the Cereal Problem, Switzerland," 05.08.1930, LON, 0000679919_D0001, 1.

61 Delegation on Economic Depressions, "Agricultural Over-Capacity as a Cause of Depression," 06.06.1939, LON, D-D-E-51_EN, 1; "Economic Depressions—Circular Letter," 18.02.1938, LON, R4450/10A/32446/32446, no pagination.

their conditions, given that such improvements would have no significant impact on the production of cereals.[62]

These normative views were deeply embedded in the work of the Commission of Enquiry into the European Union. Initially, the Commission viewed Eastern Europe as a region that was struck particularly severely by the depression and was, as a consequence, particularly worthy of assistance. In a 1931 session, Briand referred specifically to the agricultural depression in Eastern Europe and requested that the Commission explore instruments to overcome the stagnation of the grain market and possibilities to provide agricultural credits.[63] This resulted in the establishment of an Economic Co-ordination Sub-Committee that investigated problems of agricultural production and trade, credits, preferential treatment, and "pacts of economic non-aggression."[64] The Commission recognized the need for a preferential agricultural regime to ensure better returns for Central and Eastern European grain exporters. However, they deemed these facilities temporary and subject to third-party interests, and explicitly ruled out preferential treatment.[65]

Yet, instead of facilitating agricultural exports and loans for Eastern Europe, the Committee increasingly demanded one-sided tariff reductions from the states of Eastern Europe, accusing them of petty particularism and excessive protectionism. "The causes of the crisis were to be found mainly in the desire of countries to be self-supporting and to endeavor to produce and manufacture everything they required without taking into account their consumption requirements and without any regard for the reciprocal nature of trade," France's Minister of Commerce, Louis Rollin, claimed at one of the Commission's meeting: "That was one of the reasons for the over-production and the economic disorder which had given

62 Economic Committee, "Thirty-Third Session," 15.11.1930, LON 0000765306_D0007, 21.

63 CEEU, "Minutes of the Third Session of the Commission," 25.06.1931, LON, C-144-M-45-1931-VII_EN, 9.

64 CEEU, "Resolutions on Economic Questions," 28.05.1931, LON, C-395-M-158-1931-VII-Extract_EN;

65 Economic Committee, *Agricultural Crisis*, Vol. 1, 55–56.

rise to the crisis with all its direful effects."[66] In the view of Eastern European Committee members, the charge that the states of Eastern Europe were obstructing recovery through protectionist measures was deeply unfair. The high tariffs introduced across the region in the 1920s were, in their view, existential measures for the protection of their "backward" industries, in line with the Listian ideas that had legitimized Germany's nineteenth-century policy to protect its "infant industries."[67]

Yet more broadly, the Commission's work suffered from an increasingly strained relationship with its Eastern European members. In January 1931, the Commission voted to pursue a thorough study aimed at overcoming the economic crisis, which they regarded as necessary to maintain "harmony" in Europe and fight the continent's "inorganic condition" (i.e., its descent into a downward spiral of protectionist measures). The study, the Commission stressed, should zoom in on regional causes and manifestations of the slump, indicating its continued interest in Central and Eastern Europe's role in causing and overcoming the depression.[68] When the Commission's Sub-Committee of Economic Experts presented the report in summer 1931, the delegates from Eastern Europe were outraged. The experts had concluded that Europe's failure to overcome the depression was "largely due to its division into a large number of units," indicating that the post-1918 emergence of independent nation-states was an obstacle that threatened to impoverish the continent as a whole. Although the report did not question these states' sovereignty, it did suggest that their nature as "small states" was "out of harmony with the growth in facilities for communication and intercourse . . . which need an enlargement in the scale of production."[69] The report's lack of clearly articulated recommenda-

66 "Work of the Economic Organisation," 12th Session of the Assembly, Minutes of the Second Committee, 19.09.1931, LON, A-C2-MINUTES-1931_EN, 28.

67 David Levi-Faur, "Friedrich List and the Political Economy of the Nation-State," *Review of International Political Economy*, 4, no. 1 (1997): 154–78.

68 CEEU, "Minutes of the Third Session of the Commission," 25.06.1931, LON, C-144-M-45-1931-VII_EN, 9.

69 CEEU, "Report of the Sub-Committee of Economic Experts," 29.08.1931, LON, C.510.M.215.1931.VII, 3–4; CEEU, "Minutes of the Fourth Session of the Commission," 30.10.1931, LON, C.681.M.287.1931.VII, 43–44.

tions opened a space for delegates from other countries to link territorial revisionism to a broader agenda of European recovery. A jubilant German delegate immediately framed the report as a clear case for Austria's *Anschluss* to Germany.[70] The Polish delegate was quick to claim that the "organic weakness of the economic situation of Europe" was rather grounded in the Great Powers' negative view of the "small states" of East-Central Europe and thus of "the failure to understand the part played in that economy by the states of Central and Eastern Europe, and in particular the vast territories situated between the Baltic Sea and the Black Sea, with their population of a hundred million inhabitants, or approximately a quarter of the total population of Europe."[71]

2.4 Stresa and Conclusion

The Stresa Conference of September 5–20, 1932, was mandated by the Lausanne Conference, which was held in 1932 to dissolve the payment of reparations by Germany to the former Allied and Associated Powers of World War I, with the aim to prepare proposals for the Commission of Enquiry for European Union to restore Central and Eastern Europe's economy. Attended by delegates from the region, plus the United Kingdom, Belgium, Netherlands, and Switzerland, it constituted the final attempt at coordinating international assistance for Eastern European agriculture. Stresa signaled a shift in the League's preoccupation with Eastern Europe, looking primarily into financial and monetary questions and only cursorily at agriculture, where it mostly reiterated earlier recommendations. The Stresa report recommended that all European countries should gradually return to a system of free trade. However, against the background of Britain's declaration of "Imperial Preference" at the recent Ottawa Conference, the Stresa Conference included stipulations to adjust tariffs through bilateral agreements. Essentially, this constituted the preferential treatment the Eastern Europeans had so arduously

70 Richter, "The Catastrophe," 17.

71 "Observations of Governments on the Report Submitted on August 29, 1931, by the Sub-Committee of Economic Experts to the Commission of Enquiry for European Union," 28.01.1932, LON, C.E.U.E.71–C.129.M.55.1932.VII, 3.

militated for. In a statement on the work of the Stresa conference, its chairman, Georges Bonnet, pointed out the main achievement of the conference: "Its object may be expressed in a few words. It will enable the nations of Central and Eastern Europe to sell the whole of their cereals, and to sell abroad above the world price, thus revalorising internal prices."[72] The conference even recommended that the IAMCC convention "be put into force as quickly as possible," although this seemed highly unlikely.[73] Ultimately, Stresa failed. As Patricia Clavin notes, the London World Economic Conference of 1933, which was convened to implement the recommendations made at Stresa, collapsed "in undignified recrimination among the major powers," marking "the end of attempts at international economic co-operation in the interwar period."[74]

From 1931, there was a notable decrease in speeches made by Eastern European representatives at the League, but they continued to seek international support for their crisis-ridden agricultures and continuously adapted their rhetoric to changing discourse within the League. In the mid-1930s, the League's concern with agriculture gave way to a broader interest in the quality of "rural life."[75] Therefore, the Eastern European delegates, too, connected the crisis in agriculture to questions of health, nutrition, and purchasing power.[76] However, even as they adapted to the evolving discourse and priorities of the League, they obtained little in economic terms. Prompted by the League, the focus of debates returned from agriculture to the stabilization loans, which the League helped several countries secure in the late 1920s and early 1930s. From 1932, the discussions thus moved from agriculture to finance and the activities

72 CEEU, "Minutes of the Sixth Session of the Commission (30.10.–01.11.1932)," 15.10.1932, LON, 0000767623_D0006, no pagination.

73 CEEU, "Report by the Stresa Committee for the Economic Restoration of Central and Eastern Europe," 24.09.1932, LON, R2923-10D-39020-38450-Jacket1, 76.

74 Patricia Clavin, "Explaining the Failure of the London World Economic Conference," in *The Interwar Depression in an International Context*, ed. Harold James (München: Oldenbourg Wissenschaftsverlag, 2002), 77.

75 Clavin, *Securing the World Economy*, 161.

76 "Work of the Economic and Financial Organisation," 15th Session of the Assembly, Minutes of the Second Committee, 20.09.1934, LON, A-C2-MINUTES-1934_EN, 36–41.

of the "money doctors," the financial missions sent by the League to Austria, Hungary, Estonia, Romania, Bulgaria, and Greece.[77]

Ironically, as the states of Eastern Europe were refused preferential treatment on their terms, the idea itself rapidly gained traction, albeit as a measure for "Great Powers" to extend their economic reach as their economies gradually recovered from the depression. Preferential treatment, in the form of bilateral trade agreements, was increasingly viewed as an instrument to forge large trade blocs in a world of disintegrating free trade, "Imperial Preference" being only one of these. Anticipating the Commission's concluding report that the states of Eastern Europe hindered European recovery, the eminent German economist Max Sering regarded preferential treatment as an economic instrument to further German revisionism. In a speech held at Cornell University in 1930, Sering framed Briand's Commission as a political scheme aimed at consolidating European fragmentation and Eastern Europe's "conglomeration of antagonistic national elements" with the aim of restricting Germany's economic potential: "We, on the other hand, desire to guarantee Europe's economic progress by clearing away the obstructions to sound recovery and thus also strengthen Europe's purchasing power for the benefit of the entire world. That is why the Briand plan is doomed to fail."[78] Political elites of the Weimar Republic had repeatedly attempted to abrogate adherence to the MFN principle in its trade with Eastern Europe, yet respective treaty negotiations held with Poland and Czechoslovakia in the 1920s and with Romania

77 "Work of the Economic and Financial Organisation," 13th Session of the Assembly, Minutes of the Second Committee, Annex 6: "Statement by the Rapporteur on Economic and Financial Questions," 1932, LON, A-C2-MINUTES-1932_EN, 49; "Work of the Economic and Financial Organisation," 14th Session of the Assembly, Minutes of the Second Committee, Annex 3: "Report of Economic and Financial Questions," 1933, LON, A-C2-MINUTES-1933_EN, 41–42; Dominique Torre and Elise Tossi, "Charles Rist and the French Missions in Romania 1929–1933. Why the 'Money Doctors' failed," in *Economic and Financial Stability in Southeast Europe in a Historical and Comparative Perspective (Conference Proceedings of the 4th Meeting of the South-Eastern European Monetary History Network)*, eds. Branko Hinić, Ljiljana Đurđević, and Milan Šojić (Belgrade: National Bank of Serbia, 2009), 91–106.

78 Max Sering, "Causes of the International Depression of Agriculture," in *Proceedings of the Second International Conference of Agricultural Economists Held at Cornell University*, Ithaca, NY, August 18–29, 1930 (Menasha, WI: George Banta, 1930), 34–35.

and Hungary in 1931 failed under domestic and international pressure. This changed with the rise of the Nazis. The Nazis signed the first bilateral trade agreement, based on preferential treatment, with Bulgaria in 1933. Treaties with Hungary, Romania, and Yugoslavia followed in 1934.[79] Yet, although contributing to economic recovery in Europe's East, these agreements were a harbinger to the end of sovereignty, as Nazi Germany established its "informal empire" across Southeastern Europe by means of commercial control.[80]

79 Kerry A. Chase, *Trading Blocs: States, Firms, and Regions in the World Economy* (Ann Arbor, MI: University of Michigan Press, 2009), 101–103.

80 Hans-Jürgen Schröder, "Südosteuropa als 'informal Empire' Deutschlands 1933–1939. Das Beispiel Jugoslawien," *Jahrbücher für Geschichte Osteuropas* 23, no. 1 (1975): 70–96; Alfred Kube, "Außenpolitik und 'Großraumwirtschaft'. Die deutsche Politik zur wirtschaftlichen Integration Südosteuropas 1933 bis 1939," *Geschichte und Gesellschaft*, 10 (1984): 185–211.

Chapter 3

AUSTRIA

THE TOLL OF ECONOMIC ORTHODOXY

Nathan Marcus

In the final months of 1931, a group of young sociologists descended on the small industrial town of Marienthal, 25 km south of Vienna. Since its only factory had shut down in 1930, its 1,200 workers were now unemployed and almost three-quarters of the population were dependent on government support. Covered by a series of articles in the socialist newspaper *Das Kleine Blatt*, Otto Bauer, leader of the Austrian Social Democratic Party, suggested investigating the town to settle an ongoing debate: whether prolonged unemployment led to apathetic inactivity, or instilled a revolutionary spirit among the unemployed. After months of study, the researchers concluded that resignation and idleness experienced by the out-of-work community led to reduced political interest, particularly among men. The long-term unemployed, so they concluded, were unlikely to furnish protagonists for a socialist revolution. The published study became a classic of sociological research and the unemployed of Marienthal exemplary for the material and psychological hardship of prolonged unemployment in Austria during the 1930s.[1]

The Austrian economy was among the hardest hit by the Great Depression. In terms of economic contraction, only Germany and the United States suffered more, though Austria's downturn lasted longer.[2] Like in Germany and the United States, Austria's particu-

1 Marie Jahoda, Paul Lazarsfeld, and Hans Zeisel, *Die Arbeitslosen von Marienthal: ein soziographischer Versuch über die Wirkungen langdauernder Arbeitslosigkeit; mit einem Anhang zur Geschichte der Soziographie* (Leipzig: Hirzel, 1933); Marie Jahoda, Paul Lazarsfeld, and Hans Zeisel, *Marienthal: The Sociography of an Unemployed Community* (New Brunswick, NJ: Transaction Publishers, 2002).

2 Karl Aiginger, "A Comparison of the Current Crisis with the Great Depression as Regards Their Depth and the Policy Responses: Lecture at the NERO-Meeting on "The

larly deep crisis stemmed from the fact that the Great Depression coincided with a home-grown financial crisis. In May 1931, Austria's largest bank, the Credit-Anstalt, admitted to enormous losses, provoking a run on the bank by concerned customers and creditors. Letting the big bank fail would have endangered its industrial conglomerates, which employed up to half of Austria's workers, but the exorbitant state bailout triggered continual currency flight, to which the Austrian National Bank reacted by suspending gold convertibility and introducing capital controls.[3] The financial crisis exacerbated Austria's economic depression because the bailout curtailed government expenditure, capital controls damaged international trade, and capital flight reduced available credit.

Austria's economy still grew 1.5 percent in 1929, though its industrial activity had already shrunk the year before. When it entered a recession in 1930, with a 10 percent fall in industrial output and a 26.5 percent rise in unemployment, most economists still predicted a quick recovery, but in fact, Austria would not return to its 1929 production levels throughout the 1930s.[4] In the wake of the crisis triggered by the Credit-Anstalt collapse, Austria's economy contracted severely. From 1929 to 1933, industrial production fell almost 40 percent and the annual turnover of 300 industrial corporations dropped 35 percent.[5] In 1932, more share companies were loss-making than profit-making and a year later, two-thirds

---

Causes and Consequences of the Financial Crisis," OECD, Paris, September 21, 2009 (Vienna: Österreichische Institut für Wirtschaftsforschung, 2009), 8; Felix Butschek, *Die österreichische Wirtschaft im 20. Jahrhundert* (Vienna: Österreichische Institut für Wirtschaftsforschung, 1985), 50; Fritz Weber, "Die Weltwirtschaft und das Ende der Demokratie in Österreich," in *Der 4. März 1933. Vom Verfassungsbruch zur Diktatur*, ed. Erich Frösch (Vienna: Verlag der Wiener Volksbuchhandlung, 1984), 40; Günther Chaloupek, *Die Risiken der Deflation und Wege zu ihrer Vermeidung* (Vienna: Kammer für Arbeiter und Angestellte für Wien, 1999), 42.

3 Roman Sandgruber, *Ökonomie und Politik. Österreichische Wirtschaftsgeschichte vom Mittelalter bis zur Gegenwart* (Vienna: Überreuter, 1995), 388–89.

4 Felix Butschek, "Die CA-Krise 1931," *Wirtschaft und Gesellschaft* 35, no. 1 (2009): 71; Gerhard Senft, "Der Börsenkrach 1929 und seine Folgen in Österreich," in *Wirtschafts- und Finanzkrisen im Kapitalismus. Historische und aktuelle Aspekte*, ed. Manfred Mugrauer (Vienna: Alfred Klahr Gesellschaft, 2010), 10.

5 Karl Haas, "Industrielle Interessenpolitik in Österreich zur Zeit der Weltwirtschaftskrise," *Jahrbuch für Zeitgeschichte* 1 (1978): 103.

of those publishing balance sheets paid no dividend.[6] The severity of contraction varied by sector, with exporters, the capital goods industry, specifically the iron and metal industry, and the construction sector and food and beverage sectors hit worst. In November 1931, for example, orders at the *Donawitz Hüttenwerk* stood at less than a tenth of normal times and the following year the ironworks closed its gates thrice, then fired all its workers and closed for good in December, before reopening in spring 1933, with orders at 16 percent of what they had been in 1929.[7] The number of insolvencies in 1932 was more than double the figure of 1929, with failures disproportionate among farmers and artisans.[8]

The external factors contributing to Austrian economic contraction can be gauged from trade statistics. Throughout the 1920s, Austria pursued a liberal trade policy and in per capita terms had one of Europe's highest rates of trade, making it more dependent on international exchange than other Central European states. Exporters were challenged by protectionist trade measures and new competitors in neighboring countries, but around a quarter of domestic production was sold abroad, of which almost half were industrial products.[9] Capital imports and invisible exports (services and tourism) covered the trade deficit, more than half of which was on account of food (cattle, wheat, fats) or coal imports, though the country also depended on importing chemicals, rubber, and raw materials to produce textiles (wool and cotton), iron and metal goods, or machines.[10] In 1929, in terms of imports per capita, Austria

6 Josef Nussbaumer, "Sozial- und wirtschaftsgeschichtliche Aspekte der Weltwirtschaftskrise in Österreich" (PhD diss., University of Innsbruck, Innsbruck, 1980), 54–55.

7 Gertrude Enderle-Burcel, "'Planwirtschaft' als Krisenbekämpfung. Aspekte österreichischen Staatsinterventionismus 1930 bis 1938," *Mitteilungen des Österreichischen Staatsarchivs* 46 (1998): 38; Siegfried Mattl, "Die Finanzdiktatur. Wirtschaftspolitik in Österreich 1933–1938," in *"Austrofaschismus" Beiträge über Politik, Ökonomie und Kultur 1934–1938*, eds. Emmerich Tálos and Wolfgang Neugebauer (Vienna: Verlag für Gesellschaftskritik, 1984), 135.

8 Haas, "Industrielle Interessenpolitik," 104; *Monatsberichte des österreichischen Institutes für Konjunkturforschung* 9, no. 2 (February 1935): 26.

9 Hans Kernbauer, "Österreichische Währungs-, Bank- und Budgetpolitik in der Zwischenkriegszeit," in *Handbuch des politischen Systems. Erste Republik 1918–1938*, ed. Emmerich Tálos (Vienna: Manz, 1994), 568.

10 Weber, "Die Weltwirtschaft," 47.

ranked second after Switzerland among a group of European countries, and in terms of exports, fourth (after Switzerland, Germany, and France).[11]

During the Great Depression, Austrian foreign trade, which had reached a record in 1929, fell by half in the wake of the massive surge of global tariffs following the passage of the Smoot-Hawley Tariff Act in 1930.[12] The Austrian tariff reform of July 1930 signaled the end of Austria's liberal trade policy, increasing customs and introducing import bans favoring Austrian farmers and producers.[13] In July 1931, existing trade agreements were replaced with quota and preference treaties, and in April 1932, twenty-three import bans were introduced to confine imports to countries buying Austrian exports.[14] Austrian exporters suffered particularly because Austria had not devalued its currency. From 1929 to 1934, imports were reduced by half and exports fell 60 percent, which was especially damaging for Austria's export-oriented economy.[15] The export decline was the highest among cars, machines, and motors, followed by other finished goods, such as electronic machines, semifinished goods, and raw materials.[16]

11 The group includes Bulgaria, Czechoslovakia, France, Germany, Hungary, Italy, Romania, Switzerland, and Yugoslavia. "Die Handelspolitik und der Aussenhandel Österreichs in den Jahren 1918 bis 1936," *Monatsberichte des österreichischen Institutes für Konjunkturforschung* 10, no. 12 (December, 1936): 270.

12 Felix Butschek, *Österreichische Wirtschaftsgeschichte* (Vienna: Böhlau, 2012), 225; Nussbaumer, "Sozial- und wirtschaftsgeschichtliche Aspekte," 47; Sandgruber, *Ökonomie und Politik*, 383.

13 Eduard März, "Die große Depression in Österreich 1930–1933," *Wirtschaft und Gesellschaft* 16, no. 3 (1990): 413–14.

14 Gertrude Enderle-Burcel, "Government and Industry in Austria in the 1930s," in *Business and Politics in Europe, 1900–1970*, ed. Terry Gourvish (Cambridge: Cambridge University Press, 2003), 271; Josef Villa, "Ökonomische und politische Krisenstrategien in Österreich, den Vereinigten Staaten von Amerika und Deutschland zwischen 1930 und 1938: Konvergenzen und Divergenzen" (PhD diss., University of Vienna, Vienna, 2016), 41.

15 Jürgen Nautz, "Between Political Disintegration and Economic Reintegration. Austrian Trade Relations with the Successor States after World War I," in *Economic Transformations in East and Central Europe. Legacies from the Past and Policies for the Future*, ed. David F. Good (London and New York: Routledge, 2004), 261–76.

16 Kernbauer, "Österreichische," 564; März, "Große Depression," 413; Senft, "Börsenkrach," 10; Weber, "Die Weltwirtschaft," 42–43.

The contraction of industry and trade increased unemployment and spread poverty so that the number of beggars in the streets of Vienna grew noticeably.[17] Unemployment had been high during the 1920s, reaching 18 percent in 1926–27, as producers cut costs by streamlining production, but in 1929, unemployment had fallen to a low of 8.8 percent.[18] From 1929 onward, unemployment spread strongly among Austria's population of 6.7 million, but only 56 percent of the almost 2 million employed were actually insured against unemployment, with tenured state workers, the self-employed, their family members, or agricultural hires being excluded.[19] The official number of unemployed in 1930 was 385,000; in 1931, 440,000; and in 1932, 557,000, of which less than two-thirds received official support.[20] Official statistics excluded recent graduates, women following maternal leave, or "Ausgesteuerte," who were excluded because of their age and given a small pension instead, so that only 40 percent of those without work received support in 1934.[21] In 1933, approximately 680,000 Austrians were actually without work; a year later 741,000 or almost 40 percent of salaried workers, but only 278,500 received unemployment support.[22] Over 40 percent of the unemployed in 1933 had worked in the iron or metal industry or in construction and in 1934, 44.5 percent of industrial workers were unemployed. Among those still employed in the metal industry in 1934, 28 percent worked part-time, a phenomenon that spread to

17 According to reported statistics, of more than 30,000 Viennese beggars in 1932, only half had been beggars in 1927. See Nussbaumer, "Sozial- und wirtschaftsgeschichtliche Aspekte," 225.

18 Dieter Stiefel, "Der Arbeitsmarkt in Österreich in der Zwischenkriegszeit," *Studia Germanica et Austriaca* 2 (2002): 4–5.

19 Jörg Tittes, "Weltwirtschaftskrise 1929–1933: Wirtschaftspolitik in Österreich und Deutschland in der Weltwirtschaftskrise und die wirtschaftspolitische Diskussion um aktive Arbeitsbeschaffung zur Überwindung der Krise" (MA diss., Wirtschaftsuniversität Wien, Vienna, 1984), 43; Weber, "Die Weltwirtschaft," 37.

20 Herbert Matis, "Österreichs Wirtschaft in der Zwischenkriegszeit: Desintegration, Neustrukturierung und Stagnation," in *Bank Austria Credit-Anstalt: 150 Jahre österreichische Bankengeschichte im Zentrum Europas*, eds. Oliver Rathkolb et al. (Vienna: P. Zsolnay, 2005), 142.

21 Gerhard Senft, "Wirtschaftspolitische Leitlinien in der Ära des Austrofaschismus," in "*Wir werden ganze Arbeit leisten . . ." Der austrofaschistische Staatsstreich 1934*, ed. Stephan Neuhäuser (Norderstedt: Books on Demand, 2004), 238–39.

22 März, "Die große Depression," 410.

leather and textile factories, where work could easily be stretched and employers wished to preserve employee know-how.[23] Women were possibly less affected than men, since employers paid them less, but the young suffered disproportionately.[24]

Those lucky enough to remain employed suffered a steep drop in income. In Vienna, average wages and salaries fell 44 percent from 1929 to 1934, and taxable income from salaries and enterprises dropped 25 percent. Over the same period, the number of individual tax cases dropped 26.4 percent, and the amount of taxes paid by self-employed 45 percent.[25] A study by the Chamber of Labor showed that before the crisis, the average members of a working-class household consumed 3,000 calories a day, but in 1933, that figure had dropped to 2,525 and in 1934 to 2,496 calories as unemployed households cut back on 33 out of 36 food categories.[26] The only three categories they spent more on were black bread, lard, and legumes.[27] In 1934, the average household expenditures were only 64 percent of what they had been 5 years earlier.[28] Reflecting the drop in living standards, from 1928 to 1933, beer production in Austria fell 58 percent (from 5.4 million to 2.3 million hl), Vienna's milk supply fell 10 percent (from 251,000 hl to 226,000 hl), while coffee consumption had dropped 45 percent since 1931.[29]

According to Austrian economists, the root of their country's economic problems lay in the fact that bad investments, oversized welfare programs, and high wages had reduced productivity and

23 Fritz Weber, "Sonderfall Österreich. Warum die österreichische Wirtschaftspolitik nach 1931 auf entschiedene Maßnahmen zur Bekämpfung der ökonomischen Krise verzichtete und warum dieser restriktive Kurs in eine Diktatur mündete," in *Wirtschafts- und Finanzkrisen im Kapitalismus*, ed. Manfred Mugrauer (Vienna: Alfred Klahr Gesellschaft, 2010), 24; Sandgruber, *Ökonomie und Politik*, 383–84; Stiefel, "Der Arbeitsmarkt," 5–9; Weber, "Die Weltwirtschaft," 38.

24 Sandgruber, *Ökonomie und Politik*, 383–84.

25 Nussbaumer, "Sozial- und wirtschaftsgeschichtliche Aspekte," 166–72; Senft, "Börsenkrach," 11–2; Weber, "Die Weltwirtschaft," 39.

26 Villa, "Ökonomische und politische Krisenstrategien," 42.

27 By 1933, the consumption ratio of dark to white bread, which from 1926 to 1930 was 3:1, reached 5:1, and in unemployed households, it was 11:1. See, Nussbaumer, "Sozial- und wirtschaftsgeschichtliche Aspekte," 185–91.

28 Nussbaumer, "Sozial- und wirtschaftsgeschichtliche Aspekte," 186.

29 Nussbaumer, "Sozial- und wirtschaftsgeschichtliche Aspekte," 180–84; Weber, "Die Weltwirtschaft," 39.

competitiveness.[30] During its initial years, the Austrian Republic had put into law progressive workers' rights such as the 8-hour workday, paid vacations, state-funded unemployment support, and the right to collective bargaining, all of which were opposed by bourgeois employers and industry.[31] Workers' wages rose compared to before the war, but at a quarter of US real wages, half of real wages in the United Kingdom and two-thirds of real wages in Germany, they were still comparatively low.[32] The economist Ludwig von Mises nevertheless criticized the demands of workers' unions, which ensured that wages kept rising despite unemployment, and he argued that a successful return to market equilibrium needed currency stability and balanced budgets.[33] His student, Friedrich Hayek, claimed that business cycles were unavoidable and that any state intervention would only exacerbate the crisis.[34] In 1930, a committee of experts appointed by the government and including von Mises attacked trade unions for distorting market mechanisms, recommended lowering production costs and government expenditures to enhance exports and investments, and advised against increasing government spending to stimulate the economy.[35]

Facing a fall in tax revenues and large expenditures from saving Credit-Anstalt, covering the loss-making federal railways, and rising unemployment, the Austrian government in 1931 faced a budget deficit of 215 million Schilling, or 16 percent of government

30 Weber, "Die Weltwirtschaft," 53.

31 Dieter Stiefel, "The Great Depression in a Small Country: Austria, the World Economic Crisis of the 1930s and its Significance for the Present Day," in *The Economic Development of Austria since 1870*, ed. Herbert Matis (Aldershot: Elgar, 1994), 467; Weber, "Die Weltwirtschaft," 54; Weber, "Sonderfall Österreich," 24.

32 "Das Lohn- und Preisproblem," *Neue Freie Presse*, January 1, 1931, 20.

33 Franz Baltzarek, "Ludwig von Mises und die österreichische Wirtschaftspolitik der Zwischenkriegszeit," *Wirtschaftspolitische Blätter* 28, no. 4 (1981): 135; Senft, "Börsenkrach," 12–13; Senft, "Wirtschaftspolitische Leitlinien," 235; Sandgruber, *Ökonomie und Politik*, 395.

34 Chaloupek, *Die Risiken*, 27.

35 Redaktionskomitee der Wirtschaftskommission, *Bericht über die Ursachen der wirtschaftlichen Schwierigkeiten Österreichs* (Vienna: Druck der österreichischen Staatsdruckerei, 1931), 28–33; Baltzarek, "Ludwig Mises," 136; Senft, "Wirtschaftspolitische Leitlinien," 237; Chaloupek, *Die Risiken*, 56–57.

revenues.[36] Large deficits stirred painful memories of hyperinflation, but Socialist opposition prevented a reduction of state contributions to unemployed welfare, and to raise a new loan Austria still needed the League of Nations' consent. To gain its approval, Austria's parliament in October 1931 almost unanimously committed to balancing the budget through radical cuts in expenditures on productive investments, wages, and pensions, as well as the introduction of new taxation on beer, sugar, petrol, cars, income, and wealth.[37] The Lausanne loan issued in 1933 produced 308.6 million Schilling, but incurred the presence of a League financial advisor, the Dutch Meinoud Rost van Tonningen, whose presence in Vienna from 1931 to 1936 was to ensure that Austria kept to a balanced budget.[38] Government expenditure indeed fell from 2.3 milliard Schilling in 1931 to 1.9 in 1932 and 1.5 in 1933, but revenues also dropped from 2 to 1.9 and 1.3 over the same period.[39] The cost of social insurance had risen from 4 million Schilling in 1928 to 90 million in 1931, but any changes to the system needed parliamentary approval.[40] Thus budget deficits remained, not least due to bailing out Credit-Anstalt and other banks, while productive investments, which had stood at 10.9 percent of expenditures in 1930, dropped to 0.6 in 1932, rising back to only 5 percent in 1934.[41]

36 März, "Große Depression," 418; Fritz Weber, "Staatliche Wirtschaftspolitik in der Zwischenkriegszeit," in *Handbuch des politischen Systems. Erste Republik 1918–1938*, ed. Emmerich Tálos (Vienna: Manz, 1994), 547.

37 Peter Berger, "The Austrian Economy, 1918–1938," in *Economic Development in the Habsburg Monarchy and in the Successor States*, ed. John Komlos (Boulder, NY: Columbia University Press, 1990), 280; Matis, "Österreichs Wirtschaft," 139; Emmerich Tálos, *Das austrofaschistische Herrschaftssystem: Österreich 1933–1938* (Vienna: Lit-Verlag, 2013), 324; Tittes, "Weltwirtschaftskrise 1929–1933," 65; Weber, "Sonderfall Österreich," 32.

38 Berger, "The Austrian Economy," 280; Butschek, *Österreichische Wirtschaftsgeschichte*, 222.

39 März, "Große Depression," 418.

40 *Public Finance, 1928–1935, III Austria* (Geneva: League of Nations, 1936), 7.

41 Matis, "Österreichs Wirtschaft," 141; März, "Große Depression," 418; Stiefel, "Der Arbeitsmarkt," 9; Dieter Stiefel, "Utopie und Realität: Die Wirtschaftspolitik des Ständestaates," in *Tirol und der Anschluss: Voraussetzungen, Entwicklungen, Rahmenbedingungen 1918–1938*, eds. Thomas Albrich et al. (Innsbruck: Haymon, 1988), 412.

The Austrian National Bank, which during 1931 had massively increased the money supply to salvage Credit-Anstalt and had lost most of its foreign reserves doing so, prioritized exchange rate and price stability, and therefore opted for capital controls instead of devaluation.[42] Officially upholding gold parity reduced the real value of Austria's foreign debt service, while devaluation would have increased the price of imports and the cost of living, making wage increases unavoidable.[43] A transfer-moratorium for most foreign debt was declared in 1932 before the proceeds of the Lausanne loan replenished the central bank's foreign reserves, upon which the gold value of the Schilling, which had fallen abroad and on the black market, was officially reduced by 22 percent in March 1933.[44] From 1929 to 1933–34, money supply (M2) fell slightly more than the economy contracted, while the number of banknotes in circulation dropped only by 10 percent, thus not really contributing to the contraction.[45] Together with the government, the national bank focused its policies on salvaging Austria's ailing banks and keeping the currency stable to avoid price inflation, while fighting unemployment and/or stimulating the economy were given only secondary importance.[46]

Government efforts at actively relieving unemployment were accordingly modest. Starting in December 1930, the *Aktion Jugend in Not* offered programs and meals to the 100,000 unemployed youth, while *Winterhilfe* provided similar relief to others during the cold winter months.[47] Since 1922, the *Produktive Arbeiterfürsorge* had provided funds from unemployment insurance to provinces that created employment, and in 1932 this initiative was extended to the private sector, but by 1934 it gave work to no more than 24,000.[48]

42 Hansjörg Klausinger, "'Misguided Monetary Messages': The Austrian Case, 1931–1934," *The European Journal of the History of Economic Thought* 12, no. 1 (2005): 27.

43 Kernbauer, "Österreichische," 568–69.

44 Heinz Handler, "Two Centuries of Currency Policy in Austria," *Monetary Policy & the Economy* 3 (2016): 67; Tittes, "Weltwirtschaftskrise 1929-1933," 61–62; Sandgruber, *Ökonomie und Politik*, 391; Chaloupek, *Die Risiken*, 37.

45 Handler, "Two Centuries," 67; Hans Kernbauer, *Währungspolitik in der Zwischenkriegszeit: Geschichte der Österreichischen Nationalbank: 1: Von 1923 bis 1938* (Vienna: Austrian National Bank, 1991), 401.

46 Sandgruber, *Ökonomie und Politik*, 390–91; Chaloupek, *Die Risiken*, 27.

47 Nussbaumer, "Sozial- und wirtschaftsgeschichtliche Aspekte," 217–23.

48 Matis, "Österreichs Wirtschaft," 141.

A new government program, *Freiwilliger Arbeitsdienst*, introduced in 1932, gave work to 20,000 unemployed people below the age of twenty-five, but in 1933, 13,000 recruits had to be turned away for lack of employment.[49] The beneficiaries, three-quarters of whom were male and were mostly housed in camps, received shoes, clothing, and pocket money in return for working 40 hours a week.[50]

There was a reigning consensus in almost all quarters that increasing government deficits would not bring about economic recovery and only lead to price inflation.[51] The government had therefore canceled its orders from Austrian industry in August 1931, and even Socialist leader Otto Bauer, himself schooled in classical economics, did not believe that running fiscal deficits could ultimately raise employment and induce growth.[52] Writing in the socialist *Arbeiter-Zeitung* in May 1931, Bauer stressed that economic recovery could only come from technological innovation and that expensive housing programs, railway electrification, or the expansion of hydroelectricity would need to wait until the state had paid for the expensive Credit-Anstalt bail-out.[53] His party would focus on protecting existing welfare programs and suggested alleviating unemployment by shortening the work week and work hours, clamping down on double earners, reducing management costs, and reforming preferential tariffs and state monopiles.[54] In 1932 the party became more proactive, launching a newspaper specifically targeting the out-of-work community (*Der Stempler, das Blatt der Arbeitslosen*), offering afternoon programs for the unemployed at party centers, and initiating the *Jugend am Werk* initiative in reaction to the government's

49 Stiefel, "Der Arbeitsmarkt," 12.

50 Nussbaumer, "Sozial- und wirtschaftsgeschichtliche Aspekte," 158–60.

51 Agrarian Deputy Chancellor Franz Winkler's appeals to fellow ministers for state intervention or the *Heimwehr's* proposed work program were exceptions. Sandgruber, *Ökonomie und Politik*, 392.

52 Weber, "Staatliche Wirtschaftspolitik," 547, 550.

53 Otto Bauer, "Wird die Weltwirtschaftskrise überwunden werden?," *Die Arbeiter Zeitung*, May 24, 1931.

54 Senft, "Wirtschaftspolitische Leitlinien," 237; Stiefel, "Great Depression," 470; Weber, "Sonderfall Österreich," 29–30; Weber, "Staatliche Wirtschaftspolitik," 63; Chaloupek, *Die Risiken*, 58–59.

Freiwilliger Arbeitsdienst.[55] During a parliamentary debate in 1932, influential Socialist MP Robert Danneberg still mobilized the fear of inflation to argue for balanced budgets.[56] The party also opposed a successful experiment in Wörgl am Inn in Tyrol, which reduced unemployment by issuing regional currency to expand infrastructure, before it was shut down for undermining the Austrian National Bank's note privilege.[57]

Adolf Hitler's rise to power in Germany in 1933 increased pressure on the Socialist party from its unions, resulting in a joint plan: *Arbeit für 200 000.* The plan, put forward by Bauer himself, suggested spending 300 million Schilling from the Lausanne loan and money from a future domestic loan to create work for 60,000 workers, plus another 60,000 jobs from an export boost through changes in trade and tariff policies, and finally 80 to 100,000 additional jobs by shortening the workweek from 48 to 40 hours.[58] A similar plan put forward in 1932 by the economic editor of the liberal *Neue Freie Presse,* also proposed issuing a loan to fight unemployment. An *Aufbauanleihe* of 400–500 million Schilling would be used to initially put 165,000 unemployed to work in state infrastructure projects running from railways, roads, and bridges to agriculture, electrification of the railways, and hydroelectricity, and use the windfall of savings from the reduction of unemployment and annual profits of 450 million to create another 375,000 jobs over 10 years.[59] Finally, an innovative plan by the Chamber of Labor from March 1933 proposed financing employment by saving over 206 million Schilling through budgetary modifications without requiring fresh funding, but it, too, was criticized as inflationary and ultimately detrimental to state credit and the principle of balanced budgets.[60]

55 Wolfgang Russ, "Zwischen Protest und Resignation. Arbeitslose und Arbeitslosenbewegung in der Zeit der Weltwirtschaftskrise," *Österreichische Zeitschrift für Geschichtswissenschaften* 1, no. 2 (1990): 33.

56 Stiefel, "Great Depression," 473–74; Weber, "Die Weltwirtschaft," 64.

57 Senft, "Börsenkrach," 15.

58 Sandgruber, *Ökonomie und Politik,* 393–94; Senft, "Börsenkrach," 15; Stiefel, "Great Depression," 474; Weber, "Die Weltwirtschaft," 63; Weber, "Staatliche Wirtschaftspolitik," 550; Chaloupek, *Die Risiken,* 65–66.

59 Sandgruber, *Ökonomie und Politik,* 392; Senft, "Börsenkrach," 15; Tálos, *Herrschaftssystem,* 323–24; Chaloupek, *Die Risiken,* 59–63.

60 Chaloupek, *Die Risiken,* 63–65.

Socialist and liberal proposals became obsolete, however, as political developments destroyed Austrian democracy. Austria's conservative and right-wing forces were disenchanted with parliamentarism, and already in 1929, upon pressure from the right-wing *Heimwehr*, a new constitution had empowered the Federal President to the detriment of parliament.[61] Following his resignation during the Credit-Anstalt crisis in June 1931, Chancellor Otto Ender had made his return dependent on handing parliamentary control of economic policies to a smaller committee, but in September, the opposition had foiled a proposal to enact economic policies by decree.[62] Since the Pan-Germans had left the government following the failed Austro-German customs union project, the right-wing coalition of Christian-Socials, agrarians, and the *Heimwehr* was left with a fragile single vote majority, while Bauer refused to join their coalition and serve as the savior of capitalism.[63] In June 1932, before parliament ratified the Lausanne loan with the smallest possible majority, Austria's finance minister had called on the President to dismiss it if no agreement was reached; and when on October 1, 1932, the Austrian government used a 1917 emergency decree to indict leading functionaries of Credit-Anstalt, it was side-stepping parliament in broad daylight and exceeding its own authority.[64] With Socialists and Trade Unions staunchly opposed to curtailing Austrian welfare and labor laws, conservative industrialists increasingly supported silencing parliament and, in early 1932, asked Chancellor Karl Buresch to install an authoritarian regime that would govern by decree.[65]

With the illegal National Socialist Party (NSDAP) gaining support from exasperated farmers, artisans, and industrialists or entrepreneurs, government ministers themselves started considering

61 März, "Große Depression," 411.

62 Weber, "Sonderfall Österreich," 34.

63 Butschek, *Österreichische Wirtschaftsgeschichte*, 232.

64 Berger believes that the socialists' "stubborn resistance" added to Dollfuss's determination to "do away with democracy." See Berger, "The Austrian Economy," 281.

65 Weber, "Sonderfall Österreich," 25, 28; Mattl, "Die Finanzdiktatur," 136; Haas, "Industrielle Interessenpolitik," 113.

ways to circumvent parliament and break the socialist opposition.[66] Engelbert Dollfuss, who took over as Chancellor on May 20, 1932, finally used a failed parliamentary session prompted by a railway workers' strike to cynically declare that the representative body had in fact dissolved itself.[67] On March 1933, upon a quarrel surrounding the disputed validity of a single vote, the Socialist Head of Parliament resigned, followed by his Christian Social and Pan-German deputies. Thereupon, the MPs had gone home, after which the Dollfuss government prevented a reconvention and forbade new elections. The Socialists appealed to the Constitutional Court, which was dissolved in May, after government appointed judges had stepped down. The government quickly outlawed the Communist and National-Socialist parties, though the Socialists remained in charge of Vienna, where they continued their municipal welfare programs. The party's armed organization, the *Schutzbund*, was declared illegal, however, and following Dollfuss' meeting with Mussolini in August and a speech on September 11, 1933, in which he announced a new corporatist and authoritarian Austria, the party's left wing attacked Bauer's defeatism, threatening a general strike should Dollfuss try to curtail their hold on Vienna or dare to dissolve the party and its unions.[68]

On January 24, 1934, a raid of the Socialist Party offices in Vienna, ordered by the *Heimwehr* Minister of the Interior, uncovered large firearms deposits, upon which the offices were occupied and the *Schutzbund* leadership arrested for allegedly planning a coup d'état. On 12 February, the armed *Schutzbund* repelled a similar raid in Linz and fighting spread the same day to Styria and Tyrol. In Vienna, Socialist leaders approved, by one vote, an immediate general strike, but railway workers did not walk out, so the strike

66 Stefan Eminger, "Gewerbepolitik und gewerbliche Organisationen in Österreich zur Zeit der Weltwirtschaftskrise" (MA diss., University of Vienna, Vienna, 1995), 73–74; Herbert Matis, "An Economic Background to Berchtesgaden: Business and Economic Policy in Austria in the 1930s," in *Business and Politics in Europe, 1900–1970*, ed. Terry Gourvish (Cambridge: Cambridge University Press, 2003), 57–58.

67 März, "Große Depression," 430; Weber, "Sonderfall Österreich," 34.

68 Wolfgang Maderthaner, "12 February 1934: Social Democracy and Civil War: Austria in the Twentieth Century," in *Austria in the Twentieth Century*, eds. Rolf Steininger et al. (New Brunswick, NJ: Transaction Publishers, 2002), 56.

collapsed by the evening. The government, meanwhile, dispatched army units and heavy artillery, occupied Vienna's First District and City Hall, outlawed the Socialist Party, and arrested Socialist dignitaries, including Vienna's Mayor Karl Seitz and Theodor Körner, Chair of the Federal Council. Fighting continued for 3 days, and the government-controlled radio broadcast amnesty offers to those who laid down their arms, an offer eventually not honored, though only a few summary death sentences were actually carried out.[69] A new constitution promulgated on May 1, 1934, and inspired by the recent encyclical Quatragesimo Anno and the authoritarian teachings of Othmar Spann, replaced Austria's democratic institutions with a one-party system in which Dollfuss' *Vaterländische Front* restructured the country into the corporativist *Ständestaat* and handed economic legislation and planning to a board of business leaders and trade representatives.[70] Taking advantage of the political unrest, Austrian national socialists attempted their own unsuccessful coup d'état on July 25, 1934. Donning SS uniforms, they occupied a central radio station and the Federal Chancellery, arrested present government ministers, and broadcast that Dollfuss, who had been shot trying to escape, had stepped down. But many government members remained free, Mussolini mobilized troops on Austria's southern border preventing Hitler from intervening, and the coup collapsed.[71] Dollfuss' Minister of Justice Kurt Schuschnigg took power and used the Nazi attack to curtail remaining freedoms of press and assembly.

In terms of economic policy and measures to fight the Great Depression, the dictatorial *Ständestaat* recognized earlier expert opinions that solving the crisis required reducing wages and social costs to increase productivity and exports. It therefore upheld the primacy of balanced budgets and largely continued existing economic policies and programs.[72] Strikes and walk-outs became illegal, and collective labor agreements between unions and employers

69 Maderthaner, "12 February," 64–71.

70 Karl Vocelka, *Österreichische Geschichte* (Munich: Beck, 2005), 105–6.

71 Vocelka, *Österreichische Geschichte*, 107–9.

72 Heimwehr Finance Minister Ludwig Draxler repeated in December 1935 that a stable currency and balanced budget were the prerequisites for a healthy economy. See, Weber, "Staatliche Wirtschaftspolitik," 548. Tálos, *Herrschaftssystem*, 315.

were replaced with new regulations that cut workers' pay, unemployment benefits, and compensation for overtime.[73] Already in 1930, the Alpine Montan had cut workers' pay, ignoring the collective agreement and infringing on workers' rights, and almost all industrial sectors, as well as Austria's civil service, had followed suit over the years.[74] Gradually, employers were also able to extend the workday beyond 8 hours and ignore the legal limit of 44 weekly work hours for women and youths.[75] In March 1935, a new social insurance law drastically reduced the eligibility and amount of unemployment benefits and sick pay, as well as accident insurance and pensions, but upon advice from leading civil servants, the government abstained from completely abolishing all social insurance benefits.[76]

Though disavowing direct economic intervention, the government did enact some measures in support of its voter base, which it identified among small shopkeepers and farmers.[77] To support artisans, it limited the number of new business licenses and shop hours, restricted the expansion of department stores and prohibited them from selling food, outlawed the sale of shoes via postal mail, and regulated the work of peddlers.[78] Farmers had been particularly hurt by the drop in the price of agricultural products, and the indebtedness of farms in Austria was rising alarmingly.[79] Following the example of Upper Austria, which in July 1931 had fixed the price of milk, minimal prices for milk and rye were set nationally in August 1933, and a production limit for milk and fixed prices for other agricultural products were set in 1934. Import tariffs on wheat and beef had already been increased by 200 and 250 percent,

73 Maderthaner, "12 February," 57.
74 Stiefel, "Great Depression," 471.
75 Tálos, *Herrschaftssystem*, 368
76 Butschek, *Österreichische Wirtschaftsgeschichte*, 244–45; Gabriele Singewald, "Sozialpolitik in der Weltwirtschaftskrise in Österreich: Die Jahre 1929 bis 1934 im Spiegel der Zeitung 'Arbeit und Wirtschaft'" (MA diss., Wirtschaftsuniversität Wien, Vienna, 1995), 97–99; Tálos, *Herrschaftssystem*, 373–74.
77 Tálos, Herrschaftssystem, 315.
78 Eminger, "Gewerbepolitik," 130–32.
79 Liabilities per square hectare of agricultural land rose from 136 million Schilling in 1920 to 247 million in 1935. See Villa, "Ökonomische und politische Krisenstrategien," 36.

respectively, in May 1931, and in 1932 and 1934 the amount of cattle allowed to be imported for slaughter was reduced.[80]

Rigorous restrictions on access to trade and commerce resulted in a dire lack of apprentices and a lack of competition that put a halt to productive rationalization or modernization.[81] And while higher prices helped farmers, they hurt consumers, who bought less, so that from 1929 to 1934, the number of farms that had to be auctioned off in Lower Austria rose more than threefold and in Tyrol by a factor of ten.[82] But thanks to protectionism, after 1933, exports rose twice as fast as imports and in 1937, the economy enjoyed a current account surplus.[83] Overvaluation had shifted imports from raw materials to consumption goods, however, and the level of Austrian trade as a share of gross national product, which from 1929 to 1932 had fallen from 18 to 8 percent, reached only 12 percent in 1937, far lower than 22 percent in 1924.[84]

By 1933, the average company share price had fallen to 58 percent of its nominal value, but stirred by hopes in the corporativist state, dividends and shares on the Vienna Stock Exchange rose in 1934 and 1935.[85] Indeed, business friendly policies altered the share of national income, so that from 1933 to 1937, labor's share dropped from 58.4 to 54.2 percent, whereas that of income from property, undertakings, and corporations rose from 41.6 to 45.8.[86] But the strong currency hurt exports, falling wages and higher taxation dampened consumption, while ending collective agreements, extending work hours, or restricting social welfare did little to help

80 Consequently, Vienna meat consumption dropped 25 percent from 1931 to 1936. See Villa, "Ökonomische und politische Krisenstrategien," 42.

81 Eminger, "Gewerbepolitik," 133–35.

82 In the province of Salzburg, almost 80 percent of farms were threatened by debt collection in 1931; see Villa, "Ökonomische und politische Krisenstrategien," 44–48; Maderthaner, "12 February," 49; Tálos, *Herrschaftssystem*, 317.

83 Clemens Jobst and Hans Kernbauer, *The Quest for Stable Money: Central Banking in Austria, 1816–2016* (Frankfurt am Main: Campus, 2016), 188; März, "Große Depression," 413–14.

84 Kernbauer, "Österreichische," 568.

85 Nussbaumer, "Sozial- und wirtschaftsgeschichtliche Aspekte," 54–55.

86 Anton Kausel, *Österreichs Wirtschaft 1918 bis 1968* (Vienna: Verlag für Geschichte und Politik, 1968), 20.

industry.[87] Industrialists, upset about the preferential treatment of agrarian producers, requested their own export subsidies, industrial embargoes, or forced cartelization and called for increased state procurements, but the government refused to subsidize industrial exports, there were almost no public orders, while tariffs and import bans often conflicted with industrial needs.[88] Government efforts to control the industrial economy through a state commissioner were met with resistance and got him removed by October 1935.[89] Like elsewhere in the world, industrial production in Austria did pick up in 1934, but at an average of 2.8 percent per annum, annual growth of domestic product between 1933 and 1937 was timid.[90] With wage levels frozen after dismantling the unions, there could be no stimulus from increased consumption, and the recovery was mainly led by growth in capital goods and raw material production that supplied the armaments boom.[91] In 1937, industrial production was still 20 percent below its level of 1929 and gross national product was 9 percent lower.[92]

In terms of unemployment relief, the *Ständestaat* continued its efforts along familiar lines. There were still a total of 700,000 unemployed in Austria in 1935, 692,000 in 1936, and 621,000 in 1937, but the number of unemployed receiving government support was only 261,000, 259,200, and 231,300, respectively.[93] By 1938, the total number of salaried employees reached 81 percent of its level in 1928, while the share of women among the workforce had dropped from 29.7% in 1934 to 26.8% in 1937.[94] The *Freiwilliger Arbeitsdienst* was continued and at its height engaged about 25 percent of young unemployed, but from 1935 onward got wound down, since it was more expensive than the *Produktive Arbeitslosenfürsorge*.[95] The latter program continued to engage unemployed in labor-intensive

87 Eminger, "Gewerbepolitik," 133–35; Tálos, *Herrschaftssystem*, 319.

88 Enderle-Burcel, "Government and Industry," 270–73; Enderle-Burcel, "Planwirtschaft," 35.

89 Enderle-Burcel, "Government and Industry," 279–81.

90 Mattl, "Die Finanzdiktatur," 136.

91 Mattl, "Die Finanzdiktatur," 142–44.

92 Jobst and Kernbauer, *The Quest*, 188; Sandgruber, *Ökonomie und Politik*, 384.

93 Weber, "Die Weltwirtschaft," 38.

94 Matis, "Österreichs Wirtschaft," 143; Weber, "Sonderfall Österreich," 30.

95 Stiefel, "Der Arbeitsmarkt," 12.

street and bridge constructions, but without successfully reducing overall unemployment.[96] The first large employment program initiated under the Dollfuss regime was financed through a new loan, the *Trefferanleihe* of 1933, over 265 million Schilling, of which 75 million were used to pay for the construction of roads and waterways, electrification of the Tauernbahn, or investments in agrotechnology and the Austrian post and telegraph administration. But the larger part was used to finance the merger between Credit-Anstalt and Wiener Bankverein.[97] The Schuschnigg regime issued a further loan, the *Arbeitsanleihe* of 1935 for 150 million Schilling, which financed the *Arbeitsschlacht*, which engaged 42,000 workers in 1934 and 52,000 workers in 1935 (10% of all unemployed) in mainly manual labor, but which got discontinued in 1936 to reduce the budget deficit.[98] Of the *Arbeitsanleihe* only 66 million were used to alleviate unemployment, whereas the rest financed the consolidation of Federal short-term debt.[99] Similarly, of the 125 million Schilling raised by the Investment loan of 1937, only 40 percent was used to pay for productive investments, while 54 percent went to reduce federal debt.[100]

The Austrian National Bank had gradually reduced its discount rate from 8 percent in 1932 to 3.5 percent in 1935, which was still higher than in other industrialized countries, but lower than in neighboring states.[101] Saving deposits increased over the same period, and although Austria's ailing banks reduced their liabilities toward the central bank, the money supply (M2) remained almost unchanged from 1933 to 1936, as did the amount of bank notes in

96 Singewald, "Sozialpolitik," 97–99.

97 Mattl, "Die Finanzdiktatur," 137; Tálos, *Herrschaftssystem*, 324; Weber, "Staatliche Wirtschaftspolitik," 547.

98 Weber called the *Arbeitsschlacht* "eine Karikatur von Arbeitsbeschaffung," see Fritz Weber, "Hauptprobleme der wirtschaftlichen und sozialen Entwicklung Österreichs in der Zwischenkriegszeit," in *Aufbruch und Untergang: österreichische Kultur zwischen 1918 und 1938*, ed. Franz Kadrnoska (Vienna, Munich, and Zurich: Europa-Verlag, 1981), 615; Weber, "Staatliche Wirtschaftspolitik," 548; Sandgruber, *Ökonomie und Politik*, 394.

99 Mattl, "Die Finanzdiktatur," 137.

100 Tálos, *Herrschaftssystem*, 324; Weber, "Staatliche Wirtschaftspolitik," 547–48.

101 Kernbauer, *Währungspolitik*, 396–97.

circulation.[102] Austria's central bank thus did not follow a policy of active deflation, but not joining the rounds of devaluations in other countries meant a practical appreciation of the Austrian currency, while commercial banks had long stopped borrowing from the ANB, offering industry only expensive short-term credit.[103] By 1935, foreign loan issues and currency repatriation had restored the central bank reserves sufficiently to end exchange controls and allow the resumption of foreign debt service, which appreciation and loan conversions had reduced significantly.[104] When in 1936, remaining gold-block countries opted for another currency devaluation, Austria's central bank chose not to join them, further damaging exports.[105] Some foreign observers and Austrian exporters were of the opinion that Austria should have participated in the devaluation, but it would have increased stable prices and incurred wage demands, given the low living standards of workers, which would have strengthened the influence of the now illegal socialist unions.[106]

The *Ständestaat* also continued existing fiscal policies, and the size of its budget remained almost unchanged. Expenditures, which had stood at 2.2 milliard in 1934, fell only slightly to 2 milliard in both 1935 and 1936.[107] Defense spending was increased, whereas less was spent on education and productive investments, the latter making up only 5 percent of expenditures in 1934 and 1935 and merely 1.8 percent in 1936.[108] Although the Vienna municipal food tax was canceled, other taxes were increased or extended, and while revenues from indirect taxes reached a new high, proceeds from income and wealth tax dropped. The government thus kept running a deficit of 10.4 percent in 1934, 7.6 percent in 1935, 1.6 percent in 1936,

102 Kernbauer, *Währungspolitik*, 398, 401; Sandgruber, *Ökonomie und Politik*, 390–91.

103 Mattl, "Die Finanzdiktatur," 141.

104 Jobst and Kernbauer, *The Quest*, 188; Kernbauer, "Österreichische," 568; Sandgruber, *Ökonomie und Politik*, 391.

105 Though the government offered 10 million Schilling in support to industry in direct export subsidies for about thirty-five groups, including timber, iron, paper, and textiles. See Enderle-Burcel, "Planwirtschaft," 38; Handler, "Two Centuries," 67; Mattl, "Die Finanzdiktatur," 139.

106 Kernbauer, "Österreichische," 568.

107 Austria—Public Finances, Second Report by the Financial Organisation of the League of Nations November 1936–March 1937 (Geneva: League of Nations, 1937).

108 Mattl, "Die Finanzdiktatur," 138; Stiefel, "Utopie und Realität," 412.

and 6.9 percent in 1937, which was smaller than most countries.[109] Sticking to small, balanced budgets increased unemployment and reduced consumption, while holding on to price and exchange-rate stability damaged the critical export trade. Foreign loans were issued not to finance employment programs, but largely to consolidate foreign debt and support currency stability and ailing banks.[110] The success of pre-Keynesian policies, not least in Germany, ultimately inspired a change of course in Austria, supported by the Association of Austrian Industrialists.[111] Belatedly, the government announced an interventionist employment program of 300 million Schilling in February 1938 and an activist department for industrial affairs.[112]

The failure of the Austrian *Ständestaat* to change course in time and generate the promised economic recovery did not, however, rekindle the debate about Austria's economic viability. In favor of joining Germany, politicians and economists after World War I had argued that their new country was economically unviable since it lacked sufficient coal and food production or a large export industry.[113] Hyperinflation at first affirmed their analysis, but stabilization, completed successfully with the help of the League of Nations by 1926, proved in fact that Austria, in the words of former Chancellor Seipel, "was able to live."[114] Distancing the *Ständestaat* from Nazi Germany, Dollfuss stressed the viability of his country, and Schuschnigg, addressing the League of Nations in 1934, argued that Austria could live and continuously underlined this position

109 Aiginger, "A Comparison," 32; Tálos, *Herrschaftssystem*, 320.

110 Mattl, "Die Finanzdiktatur," 139.

111 Weber, "Staatliche Wirtschaftspolitik," 549.

112 Sandgruber, *Ökonomie und Politik*, 394.

113 Norbert Schausberger, "Österreich und die Friedenskonferenz. Zum Problem der Lebensfähigkeit Österreichs nach 1918," in *Wissenschaftliche Kommission zur Erforschung der Geschichte der Republik Österreich. Veröffentlichungen Band 11: Saint-Germain 1919*, eds. Isabella Ackerl and Rudolf Neck (Vienna: Verlag für Geschichte und Politik, 1989), 229–64; Marion Aichinger, "Die Diskussion um die Lebensfähigkeit der Ersten Republik (insbesondere von Gustav Stolper und Friedrich Hertz) 1919–1931" (MA diss., University of Vienna, Vienna, 1990).

114 "Altkanzler Dr Seipel in Paris," *Reichspost*, June 3, 1926, 3–4.

in his speeches and interviews.[115] Indeed, by 1937, 84 percent of Austria's imports were covered by exports, and the remainder was covered through growing income from tourism or other invisible exports. Foreign debt had been reduced, and so had the dependence on foreign credit so that in terms of trade and capital flows, Austria seemed viable indeed.[116] But all this had been achieved by reducing imports, protecting agriculture, and without finding a way to significantly reduce unemployment, so that the question now was whether Austria by itself, albeit viable, could ever be prosperous.[117]

Austrian governments' failure to stimulate the economy coupled with a series of banking crises meant that the Great Depression in Austria was longer and more severe than in most other countries, and historians agree that the dire economic crisis Austria experienced during the Great Depression accentuated the weakness of parliamentary democracy and strengthened the call for fascist rule.[118] In 1933, Germany had limited the amounts of money its visitors could carry into Austria to 1,000 mark, which had severely hurt tourism. Under pressure from Italy and to have the rule lifted, Austria made concessions to Germany in July 1936, freeing imprisoned Nazis and appointing two national-socialist ministers. In February 1938, Schuschnigg, threatened by Hitler with military intervention, agreed to appoint Austrian Nazi leader Arthur Seyss-Inquart Minister of the Interior. Schuschnigg also announced a referendum on joining Germany, provoking a German ultimatum, upon which he resigned in favor of Seyss-Inquart. On the eve of the planned referendum, on March 12, 1938, German forces crossed the border into Austria and incorporated the country into the Third Reich.[119] Economic misery was not the only reason for the failure of

115 Elke Russ, "Das Problem einer österreichischen Nation und die Frage der wirtschaftlichen Lebensfähigkeit der Ersten Republik im Spiegel zeitgenössischer Politikeraussagen" (MA diss., University of Vienna, Vienna, 1991), 147.

116 Kurt W. Rothschild, "Staatengrösse und Lebensfähigkeit. Das österreichische Beispiel" *Zeitschrift für Nationalökonomie* 19, no. 3 (1959): 305.

117 Berger, "The Austrian Economy," 282–83; Maderthaner, "12 February," 49; Matis, "An Economic Background," 42, 59.

118 Enderle-Burcel, "Planwirtschaft," 32; Matis, "An Economic Background," 42.

119 Vocelka, *Österreichische Geschichte*, 107–9.

Austrian democracy and sovereignty, but the success of Germany's expansionist policy made joining it attractive. In Marienthal, formerly a bastion of Socialism, workers did not resist the *Anschluss* as many of its laborers not only welcomed the new regime but would go on to become staunch supporters of National Socialism.[120]

120 Reinhard Müller, *Marienthal: das Dorf—die Arbeitslosen—die Studie* (Innsbruck: StudienVerlag, 2008), 193–94.

Chapter 4

POLAND

FOREIGN CAPITAL AND ECONOMIC NATIONALISM DURING THE GREAT DEPRESSION[1]

Jerzy Łazor

In a caricature printed on Christmas Eve 1934 by the Warsaw daily *Express Poranny*,[2] a man stares surprised at a swarm of cockroaches surrounding a black box on a wall. The title reads: "A French infestation near the electric metre," a play on *Francuz*, a Polish word both for Frenchman and cockroach (then written without the capital letter). The caricature was part of a conflict between the city of Warsaw and the local power plant, owned by *Compagnie d'Électricite de Varsovie*, a joint-stock company based in Paris.[3] After sputtering on for a decade, the dispute became harsher as the Great Depression affected Poland. In 1934, a local court put the power plant under compulsory administration, defying an international arbiter. Two years later, the city took the company over, with talks continuing into 1939. The two dates, 1934 and 1936, also mark turning points in relations between the Polish government and two other companies: a French-owned textile producer *Towarzystwo Zakładów Żyrardowskich S. A.* (Żyrardów Works),[4]

1 This work was supported by the National Science Centre, Poland Grant No. 2018/31/D/HS3/00405.

2 Express Poranny, December 24, 1934, found in Archives diplomatiques, La Courneuve [henceforth: AdC], CPC PL, 431, press cuttings, 157.

3 "Compagnie d'Electricité de Varsovie," *The Data for Financial History (DFIH) Database*, Paris School of Economics, accessed December 14, 2023, https://dfih.fr/issuers/2699.

4 Leszek Koziorowski, "Towarzystwo Akcyjne Zakładów Żyrardowskich Hiellego i Dittricha," *Historia Polskich Spółek Akcyjnych*, accessed December 14, 2023, http://www.historiafabryk.pl/projekt/baza-spolek-akcyjnych/towarzystwo-akcyjne-zakladoacute-w-zyrardowskich-hiellego-i-dittricha.html.

and a German-controlled coal and heavy industry trust from Upper Silesia, *Wspólnota Interesów Górniczo-Hutniczych* (Mining and Metallurgy Community of Interests).[5] Like the power plant, they were first put under compulsory administration, then taken over by the state. All three companies were the target of prolonged press campaigns, partially inspired by the authorities. Żyrardów also saw much publicized arrests of its foreign managers. This series of attacks was enough for the German minister in Warsaw to complain to the French ambassador—a rare occurrence.[6] During these conflicts, in 1935, Polish military authorities moved against the most successful high-technology foreign investment in their country, taking over most of the Franco-Czechoslovak aviation producer *Polskie Zakłady Skody SA* (Polish Škoda Works) near Warsaw.[7]

The multiple moves against foreign-owned enterprises contradict earlier Polish policies focused on attracting foreign direct investment (FDI). Back in the 1920s, the authorities wished "to encourage and call upon allied capital to cooperate in the reconstruction and further development of the Polish economy and finances" and promised "treatment both loyal and friendly."[8] Subsequent governments saw foreign investment as a solution to the country's postwar reconstruction woes and a necessary tool of development. Their pro-investment approach influenced conservative monetary policy and stood behind a series of expensive international agreements. The mantra was repeated by much of the economic establishment.[9]

5 Leszek Koziorowski, "'Bismarckhütte' S.A.," *Historia Polskich Spółek Akcyjnych*, accessed December 14, 2023, http://www.historiafabryk.pl/projekt/baza-spolek-akcyjnych/towarzystwo-akcyjne-zakladoacute-w-zyrardowskich-hiellego-i-dittricha.html.

6 Archives diplomatiques, La Courneuve [henceforth: AdC], Correspondance politique et commercial, 1918–1940, Pologne [henceforth: CPC PL], 400, Jules Laroche to Louis Barthou, March 21, 1934, 167v.

7 "Francusko-Polskie Zakłady Samochodowe i Lotnicze S.A.," *Historia Polskich Spółek Akcyjnych*, accessed December 14, 2023, http://www.historiafabryk.pl/projekt/baza-spolek-akcyjnych/towarzystwo-akcyjne-zakladoacute-w-zyrardowskich-hiellego-i-dittricha.html.

8 Zbigniew Landau and Jerzy Tomaszewski, "Misja Prof. A. Benisa," *Teki Archiwalne* 6 (1959): 61.

9 Jan Kofman, "Koła wielkoprzemysłowe a kwestia kapitałów obcych w okresie 1920–1939," *Kwartalnik Historyczny* 82, no. 2 (1975): 303–20.

The policy was mostly a failure. Interwar capital markets were significantly less bullish than before 1914, and Poland was broadly considered a problematic market. It offered low security due to border disputes with all of its neighbors and an unstable political situation. Its governments' statist policies also served as a deterrent. As a result, foreigners rarely put money into greenfield investments, preferring to take over existing companies. France became the most important owner of industrial enterprises in the country, ahead of Germany and the United States. New foreign investment into the Polish economy was limited. In parallel developments, since late 1918 successive Polish governments hoped to borrow money from abroad. Some politicians and commentators imagined that the government would serve as a conduit for foreign money: take out loans and invest them into the economy. Polish negotiators found little beyond expensive military credits and small loans obtained by leasing state-owned enterprises and resources. Only in 1927 did Poland's dream of getting a "big loan" materialize with the American-led stabilization loan. Nonetheless, rather than for development, it was mostly used to bolster the country's gold currency.[10]

By 1929, foreign ownership accounted for some 40 percent of all share capital in joint-stock companies, with an even bigger role played in limited liability firms. In some sectors, such as oil production, coal mining, metallurgy, electricity production, or insurance, it achieved almost complete dominance; in many others it remained a powerful force, controlling the biggest and most profitable companies. Foreign-controlled firms transferred a total of 1.3 billion Polish złoty in profits between 1924 and 1929, or over half of the value of foreign capital located in joint-stock companies in 1929. While these numbers were worrying, until the Great Depression,

10 Rudolf Nötel, "International Credit and Finance," in *The Economic History of Eastern-Europe 1919–1975, v. II. Interwar Policy, The War, and Reconstruction*, eds. Michael Charles Kaser and E. A. Radice (Oxford: Clarendon Press, 1986), 170–295; Jari Eloranta, Stefan Nikolić, and Flóra Macher, "Between Disintegration and Convergence, 1918–1939: Flows of Capital, Goods, and Labor," in *The Economic History of Central, East, and South-Eastern Europe: 1800 to the Present*, ed. Matthias Morys (London and New York: Routledge, 2021), 216–42.

Polish commentators broadly accepted such transfers as justified returns on invested capital.[11]

The moves against foreign capital during the Depression formed part of the country's shift toward economic nationalism, "a structurally determined response of the underdeveloped economies and societies to crisis and to the very fact of their underdevelopment."[12] It included an increasingly autarkic trade policy, exchange controls (introduced in 1936), fiscal expansion (after 1936), and the further growth of state enterprise, including the creation of the Central Industrial District in southern Poland. This shift, which intensified after 1936, was overseen by high-ranking *Sanacja* officials, who considered economic independence and the central role of the state as the foundations of the country's political and economic strategy.[13] Within this response, exchange control and increased government supervision over foreign trade were a reaction to the perceived unequal character of the exchange of goods, and control over foreign investment—to the unequal character of capital flows.

While seen against this background, the stories of Żyrardów or Škoda suggest a coherent policy toward FDI, reality was more complex. As I argue in this chapter, the takeovers appeared in different contexts and their motivations had little in common. Rather than being guided by any theoretical program, they can be seen as *ad hoc* reactions to ongoing conflicts and reflections of the general Polish economic and political climate, which favored state rather than private solutions.

The rest of this chapter is divided into four parts. I start by covering the impact of the Great Depression on Poland, which provides context for government actions against the four companies. Armed with this knowledge, I look at four major conflicts with foreign capital. Analyzing the problems of *Wspólnota Interesów* allows

11 As in all matters related to quantifying foreign capital operating in the county, the numbers are a rough estimation. See Zbigniew Landau and Jerzy Tomaszewski, *Kapitały obce w Polsce 1918–1939: materiały i dokumenty* (Warszawa: Książka i Wiedza, 1964), 15, 18.

12 Henryk Szlajfer, "Editor's Introduction," in *Economic Nationalism in East-Central Europe and South America*, ed. Henryk Szlajfer (Genéve: Librairie Droz, 1990), 9.

13 Jan Kofman, *Economic Nationalism and Development: Central and Eastern Europe between the Two World Wars* (London and New York: Routledge, 2018).

a look into the complex German position in Poland, and the use of Polish holdings by foreign owners to bolster their domestic businesses during the Great Depression. The story of Żyrardów and the Warsaw Power Plant shows how the Depression served as a catalyst for much longer conflicts and illustrates the difficulties of attributing nationality to foreign capital. Finally, the example of Škoda Works demonstrates how a push for state-owned solutions by the Polish military, coupled with geopolitical struggles, cut short one of the most successful foreign investments in the country.

4.1 The Great Depression in Poland

Poland was hit particularly hard by the Great Depression. Its fall in industrial production was comparable to that of developed countries, and the recession lasted longer, as in rural states. While there are no reliable estimates of interwar Polish GDP, industrial production per capita likely fell by approximately 40 percent between 1928 and 1932, with net investments going into the red in 1932–35. Between 1929 and 1933, the number of industrial firms fell by almost 30 percent, even more among the largest companies. Total hours worked in industry fell by almost 50 percent, although industrial unemployment did not increase by a corresponding factor due to the spread of part-time employment.[14]

Industry, while being the most dynamic sector in the interwar period, was likely responsible for only about a third of Polish gross national income during the Depression. The majority came from agriculture, which also employed most of the Polish population.[15] In the early 1930s, the latter sector suffered particular difficulties, with the prices of agricultural products falling significantly more than those of industrial ones. Combined with considerable debt, this produced poverty and a shrinking of the domestic market.

14 These are rough estimates. See: Zbigniew Landau, "Sytuacja przemysłu polskiego w latach kryzysu gospodarczego (1930–1935)," *Przegląd Historyczny* 68, no. 2 (1977): 289–311, 291–93, 296, 298, 302.

15 Zbigniew Landau, "Badania nad dochodem narodowym II Rzeczypospolitej i ich przydatność do analiz historyczno-gospodarczych," *Przegląd Historyczny* 64, no. 3 (1973): 529–47, 545.

As in other countries, large landowners reacted to the crisis by reducing production, while smallholders, who constituted the vast majority of producers, increased sales to compensate for the fall in agricultural prices, only exacerbating the problem. In economic terms, rural households experienced a stunning 65 percent fall in incomes between 1928–29 and 1934–35, closely related to a similar fall in prices of agricultural products. By the end of the Depression, overall production fell and investment ground to a halt.[16]

With the collapse of global trade, Poland tightened its already protectionist trade policy. Initially, this was done through a series of duty increases, including a retaliatory tariff against Germany (1932). After long deliberations, an entirely new trade tariff, based on the League of Nations' nomenclature, came into force in October 1933, further increasing duties and forcing a renegotiation of existing trade deals. Nonetheless, foreign trade was increasingly based on outright bans and import quotas allotted to specific countries, sometimes tied to Polish exports. As a result, Warsaw reduced its imports by almost three-quarters between 1929 and 1934, and the country's balance of trade remained positive throughout the depression.[17]

The balance of trade remained a key element of Polish policy due to the country's long adherence to the Gold Standard, lasting until 1936, and the energy put by Warsaw into defending its gold reserves. These were under strain both due to Poland's indebtedness and the significant role of FDI in its economy. Faced with the global recession, some foreign-owned companies decided to shut down production in Poland, while others used accounting tricks to siphon funds abroad.[18] As financial markets in Central Europe melted after spring 1931, a banking crisis erupted in Warsaw in June 1931, further exacerbating the state of the złoty. The country lost a sixth of its

16 Mieczysław Mieszczankowski, *Rolnictwo II Rzeczypospolitej* (Warszawa: Książka i Wiedza, 1983), 261–91.

17 Zbigniew Landau and Jerzy Tomaszewski. *Gospodarka Polski międzywojennej 1918–1939. Vol 3: Wielki kryzys 1930–1935* (Warszawa: Książka i Wiedza, 1982), 360–64.

18 However, the share of foreign owners in the economy rose in the early 1930s due to failing domestic companies being taken over by outside creditors.

gold reserves in 1932 alone and continued to lose more until forced to introduce exchange control in April 1936.[19]

The economic and social costs of supporting the overvalued złoty were steep. Polish newspapers from the period are a harrowing read, with each issue bringing news of suicides, replete with personal details. The closing of emigration opportunities worldwide and the forced returns of some migrants put additional pressure on the labor market.[20] As employment opportunities were few, internal migrants traveled to Warsaw and the newly built city of Gdynia, looking for work. Throughout the country, tensions rose, leading to bloody strikes, increased civil disobedience, and even a minor rural rebellion.[21]

The Depression also brought problems to Poland's sizeable national minorities, which accounted for about a third of the country's population. While the exact data is debatable, the Ukrainians formed the largest group, with some 13.8 percent of the total population, with the Jewish minority in second place (8.5 percent), Belarusians in third (3.1 percent), Poleshuks in fourth (2.5 percent), and Germans in fifth (2.4 percent). Other groups were smaller. According to Włodzimierz Mędrzecki, a further 4.5 percent had transitional identities, stretched between minorities and the dominant Polish group.[22]

19 Cecylia Leszczyńska, *Polska polityka pieniężna i walutowa w latach 1924–1936: w systemie Gold Exchange Standard* (Warszawa: Wydawnictwo Uniwersytetu Warszawskiego, 2013); Nikolaus Wolf, "Should I Stay or Should I Go? Understanding Poland's Adherence to Gold, 1928–1936," *Historical Social Research* 32, no. 4 (2007): 351–68; Ben Bernanke and Harold James, "The Gold Standard, Deflation, and Financial Crisis in the Great Depression: An International Comparison," in *Essays on the Great Depression*, ed. Ben Bernanke (Princeton, NJ: Princeton University Press, 2000), 70–107.

20 Anna Ambrochowicz-Gajownik, "Reemigracja z Francji do Polski w Latach 1934–1936. Zarys Problemu," *Echa Przeszłości* XXIV/2 (2023): 141–57.

21 Piotr Cichoracki, Joanna Dufrat, and Janusz Mierzwa, *Oblicza buntu społecznego w II Rzeczypospolitej doby wielkiego kryzysu (1930–1935). Uwarunkowania, skala, konsekwencje* (Kraków: Historia Iagellonica, 2019).

22 Dan Gawrecki, "The Determination of Nationality in Selected European Countries up to 1938," *Prager wirtschafts- und sozialhistorische Mitteilungen—Prague Economic and Social History Papers* 22, no. 2 (2015): 27–54; Włodzimierz Mędrzecki, "Liczebność i rozmieszczenie grup narodowościowych w II Rzeczypospolitej w świetle wyników II spisu powszechnego (1931 r.)," *Dzieje Najnowsze* 15, no. 1–2 (1983): 231–52, 243–44.

The Depression did not affect the minorities in the same manner. The Ukrainians, Poleshuks, or Belarusians, who mostly worked in agriculture and occupied small holdings in regions dominated by large Polish landowners, suffered from a dramatic fall in income and expenses.[23] On the other hand, the Jewish population was predominantly urban, split almost equally between people living in large cities and those in small towns, with the two groups affected differently by the Depression.[24] The case of the German minority was even more complex—while the majority worked in agriculture, representing some of the richest rural producers in Poland, some regions, such as Polish Upper Silesia, the Bielsko-Biała Basin, and Łódź, saw most Germans working in industry and mining. In both cases, the Germans had significant holdings, and were decidedly richer than the other minorities.[25]

The Depression, a move toward authoritarian rule in Poland, and the broad pauperization of society brought rising tensions with some minorities. In the case of Ukrainians, organized sabotage against the Poles in 1930 led to reprisals ("pacification") in the same year, ordered personally by Józef Piłsudski. The conflict intensified in 1934, after a series of political assassinations. Attempts at cooperation with the Poles by other parts of the Ukrainian minority led to a temporary agreement in 1935, which did not change the overall trajectory of mutual relations.[26] Among the German minority, the hardships of the Depression were coupled with rising anxiety due to the increasingly authoritarian regime in Warsaw. However, the 1934 nonaggression treaty between Germany and Poland improved relations between the minority and the state, even if it continued to

23 Jerzy Tomaszewski, *Ojczyzna nie tylko Polaków. Mniejszości narodowe w Polsce w latach 1918–1939* (Warszawa, Młodzieżowa Agencja Wydawnicza: 1985), 52–95; Cf. Mieszczankowski, *Rolnictwo*, 413

24 Antony Polonsky, *The Jews in Poland and Russia*, vol. III, 1914 to 2008 (Oxford and Portland: The Littman Library of Jewish Civilization, 2012), 98–99.

25 Janusz Żarnowski, *Społeczeństwo Drugiej Rzeczpospolitej: 1918–1939* (Warszawa: Państwowe Wydawnictwo Naukowe, 1973), 378–97.

26 Roman Wysocki, *Organizacja Ukraińskich Nacjonalistów w Polsce w latach 1929–1939. Geneza, struktura, program, ideologia* (Lublin: Wydawnictwo Uniwersytetu Marii Curie-Skłodowskiej, 2003), 128–34, 299–312; Andrzej Chojnowski, *Koncepcje polityki narodowościowej rządów polskich w latach 1921–1939* (Wrocław: Zakład Narodowy im. Ossolińskich, 1979), 173–81, 201–5.

suffer from the Depression.[27] The Jews experienced increased economic anti-Semitism and competition from Polish traders, which undermined the most important form of economic activity of the group. By the end of the Depression, the ruling Sanacja moved to the right, with more radical anti-Semitic attitudes prevailing after the death of Piłsudski in 1935. By this time, the government condoned economic boycotts and an increased support for migration and Zionism.[28]

4.2 Polonizing a German Company?

Moving to conflicts with specific companies, let us start with the story of the German- and American-owned trust *Wspólnota Interesów Górniczo-Hutniczych*, which began with property changes after the Great War.[29] The trust had been created in 1929 by two major firms, which had mines and foundries in Polish Upper Silesia, but were controlled by foreign (mostly German) capital: *Katowicka Spółka Akcyjna dla Górnictwa i Hutnictwa* and *Górnośląskie Zjednoczone Huty Królewska i Laura, Spółka Akcyjna Górniczo-Hutnicza.*[30] Through shrewd investment and financial speculation, the German industrial magnate and Nazi supporter Friedrich Flick won control over both companies.[31] Together, the new trust was the largest

27 Winson Chu, *The German Minority in Interwar Poland* (Cambridge: Cambridge University Press, 2012), 166–71.

28 Ezra Mendelsohn, *Żydzi Europy Środkowo-Wschodniej w okresie międzywojennym*, trans. Agata Tomaszewska (Warszawa: Wydawnictwo Naukowe PWN, 1992), 104–14; Kinga Czechowska, *Polska dyplomacja wobec "kwestii żydowskiej" w latach 1932–1939* (Gdańsk and Warszawa: IPN, 2023).

29 Jochen Böhler, *Civil War in Central Europe, 1918–1921. Reconstruction of Poland* (Oxford: Oxford University Press, 2018), 104–5.

30 Jerzy Jaros, *Historia górnictwa węglowego w Zagłębiu Górnośląskim w latach 1914–1945* (Katowice and Kraków: Państwowe Wydawnictwo Naukowe, 1969), 170–74; Leszek Koziorowski, "Górnośląskie Zjednoczone Huty 'Królewska i Laura' S.A.," *Historia Polskich Spółek Akcyjnych*, accessed December 14, 2023, http://www.historiafabryk.pl/projekt/baza-spolek-akcyjnych/goacute-rnoslaskie-zjednoczone-huty-quot-kroacute-lewska-i-lauraquot-s-a.html.

31 Mariusz W. Majewski, "The History of Joint-Stock Companies in the Second Polish Republic as Exemplified by Wspólnota Interesów Górniczo–Hutniczych SA (Mining and Metallurgy Community of Interests Joint Stock Company)," *Studia Historiae Oeconomicae* 36, no. 1 (December 1, 2018): 43–69; David de Jong, *Nazi Billionaires: The Dark History of Germany's Wealthiest Dynasties* (London: Mariner Books, 2022).

producer of coal, pig iron, and steel in the country. To protect his holdings from the Poles, Flick cooperated with American investors through the Consolidated Silesian Steel Corporation.[32]

The position of *Wspólnota Interesów* was influenced by the changing international climate after the Great War. Before 1914, the nationality of investors was not a significant factor in policy toward FDI, but this changed after the forced requisitions of the war, with governments taking note of the citizenship and ethnicity of factory owners.[33] In Poland and other states created from the fall of empires in Central and Eastern Europe, the issue had even greater importance. Companies with headquarters in Berlin or Vienna, which before the war had been domestic on the territories of these future countries, suddenly became foreign. Others remained domestic but were owned by national minorities, looked upon with suspicion if not outright hostility. Because of festering border conflicts, both types of firms were seen as potentially destabilizing. Directly after the war, a wave of "nostrification" swept the region, as governments tried to take over companies owned by citizens of the former central powers. Their success was limited.

One area where the process seemed to hold much promise, thanks to provisions in the Versailles Treaty, was Upper Silesia. The prospect of mass takeovers in Germany's second industrial basin allowed the Poles to try to bribe Entente governments with concessions for political support in their conflict with Berlin over the province. However, while Warsaw managed to take control of the majority of Upper Silesian industrial territories, it was ultimately barred from takeovers of private companies until 1937. As a result, the most important enterprises remained in Germany—either owned by foreign citizens or members of the local minority. The Polonization of these companies through labor regulations, political influence, and

32 Jerzy Tomaszewski, "German Capital in Silesian Industry in Poland between the Two World Wars," in *International Business and Central Europe, 1918–1939*, eds. Phillip L. Cottrell and Alice Teichova (Leicester and New York: Leicester University Press and St Martin's Press, 1983), 228–47, 237.

33 Alfred Reckendrees, Boris Gehlen, and Christian Marx, "International Business, Multinational Enterprises and Nationality of the Company: A Constructive Review of Literature," *Business History* 64, no. 9 (2022): 1567–99.

more forceful policy remained at the heart of economic conflicts in the province.[34]

German-owned companies in Upper Silesia, such as the constituent parts of *Wspólnota Interestów*, were often small fragments of much greater industrial conglomerates. When the Great Depression started, their owners were more interested in supporting their domestic companies. In the case of Flick, this meant that money from Polish enterprises was transferred to Germany, generally through legal, if somewhat spurious, channels. As a result, the companies ran losses in Poland, amounting to 180 million złoty, which put them on the verge of bankruptcy and made them significantly indebted to Polish and Upper Silesian authorities.[35]

In reaction, in late 1933 the Poles decided to buy out *Wspólnota Interesów* and start a criminal investigation into tax fraud allegations against the trust.[36] In the following year, the companies were subjected to compulsory administration, and with a loan from the Polish state-owned Bank of the National Economy (*Bank Gospodarstwa Krajowego*), put back on their feet. By 1936 the Poles signed an agreement with the Germans, purchasing their shares. Soon, the firms were reformed into a single state-controlled joint-stock company, the *Wspólnota Interesów Górniczo-Hutniczych SA*.

The story of Flick's trust seems like a case of forced Polonization of a German company undertaken by the state. Indeed, during the Great Depression such takeovers led to a significant fall in the importance of German capital in Upper Silesia.[37] However, as documents from the case show, the Poles acted in this manner primarily to avoid a major employer from going under during the Depression, with potentially disastrous consequences for the Polish economy. Moreover, state authorities were reluctant to take the company over, and would have preferred private investors. But with a dearth of private capital, it became yet another example of Poland's "forced

34 Mieczysław Grzyb, *Narodowościowo-polityczne aspekty przemian stosunków własnościowych i kadrowych w górnośląskim przemyśle w latach 1922–1939* (Katowice: Uniwersytet Śląski, 1978).

35 Majewski, "The History," 58, footnote 18; Tomaszewski, "German Capital," 237.

36 Grzyb, *Narodowościowo-polityczne aspekty*, 193–94; Majewski, "The History," 58.

37 Chojnowski, *Koncepcje*, 167.

statism," with authorities taking over failing companies for economic rather than political reasons.[38]

4.3 The Great French Affairs

If the Community of Interests presents a story of enmity between the Poles and German capital, the cases of Żyrardów and the Warsaw power plant offer a more nuanced picture. Both companies' owners ostensibly came from France—Poland's key interwar ally and the biggest provider of foreign capital—yet their relations with the Poles were mired in long conflicts stemming from the consequences of the Great War.

The Russian evacuation in 1915, followed by compulsory administration under German rule, greatly affected both companies, and their owners were not immediately interested in returning after the war due to high reconstruction costs. Polish authorities, which assumed control over both in 1918, invested heavily to get production back on track. As this was happening, a capital group headed by the French mogul Marcel Boussac bought Żyrardów's shares from their Czechoslovak owners for a pittance, becoming the largest shareholder. This allowed the French to assume control over the company in 1923, after the factory had already been rebuilt. The Polish government's failure to force the new owners to pay back for postwar reconstruction caused a parliamentary crisis in Warsaw.[39] The matter continued to fester throughout the 1920s, and despite losing in Polish courts, the French refused to pay. With the support of Paris, they were able to reach an advantageous agreement with the Poles in 1932, seemingly ending the dispute.[40] By this time, however, the locus of conflict had changed. After a workers' strike in 1926 and a memorandum published by local authorities in the

38 Zbigniew Landau and Jerzy Tomaszewski, *Kapitały obce w Polsce 1918–1939: materiały i dokumenty* (Warszawa: Książka i Wiedza, 1964), 317–32.

39 Basic chronology of the conflict based on Zbigniew Landau and Jerzy Tomaszewski, *Sprawa żyrardowska. Przyczynek do dziejów kapitałów obcych w Polsce międzywojennej* (Warszawa: Książka i Wiedza, 1983).

40 Archiwum Akt Nowych, Warsaw [henceforth: AAN], Ministerstwo Spraw Zagranicznych [henceforth: MSZ], 3855, Chłapowski to Herriot, August 12, 1932, 1–3.

following year, Polish public opinion increasingly focused on the wrongdoings of the new owners: exploitation of workers and window dressing. When a former clerk at the company killed its director in April 1932, the press erupted with hundreds of articles on the "evil" in Żyrardów, which treated workers like "slaves," and Poland like a "colony."[41] Tabloids in particular were quick to focus on the actions of foreign capital: "We know that it is not the crisis that plays the most ruinous, destructive role here, that foreign capitalists are not truly fair. These people have no heart for either the Polish worker or the Polish clerk, and treat both like natives from Tonkin or Madagascar."[42]

The French majority owners of the Warsaw power plant reluctantly returned to the firm in 1924, without additional compensation for the period of the war and Polish administration.[43] They agreed to do so, because the overvalued złoty after the 1924 stabilization seemed to promise high returns. However, as Poland suffered from a financial crisis in 1925 and 1926, leading to the so-called second inflation, the French reconsidered their position. They asked for a prolongation of their prewar concession by 20 years, valorizing electricity tariffs, and setting them in gold, to avoid losses in the future.[44] When Warsaw municipal authorities refused, the French demanded international arbitration based on a 1922 Franco-Polish treaty on prewar rights. The Poles continued to lose before the arbiter, who, in 1933, finally awarded the French everything they asked for, including compensation, despite the company's record profits and high dividends, and the Poles having financed reconstruction

41 I explore this in more detail in: Jerzy Łazor, "'A Colony of Alien Capital': French Investments, Polish Identity, and a Story of Murder in 1930s Warsaw," *Slavic Review* 81, no. 1 (Spring 2022): 122–41.

42 "Słyszeliście strzały na Mazowieckiej? Kto wiatr sieje—zbiera burzę," *Dobry Wieczór! Kurjer Czerwony*, April 28, 1932, 3.

43 I explore this conflict in more detail in Jerzy Łazor, "French Capital, the Warsaw Power Plant, and the Birth of Interwar Polish Economic Nationalism" (forthcoming).

44 AdC, CPC PL, 280A, CEV to Magistrat de la Ville de Varsovie, October 27, 1926, 114–15v; AdC, CPC PL, 427, Arbitrage. Compagnie d'Électricité de Varsovie contre Ville de Varsovie. Stenographie des audiences des 2 et 3 Juillet 1931 tenues à Amsterdam, n.p.

(the verdict was followed by a further decision in December 1934).[45] Warsaw viewed this as unjust, but, as documents show, the Poles would have likely challenged even a less one-sided verdict.[46] As the company was reporting profits, municipal authorities had already decided to take over the power plant and sell it to a new bidder on better conditions for the city. In essence, the Poles were hoping to redress the prewar concession, granted by Russian authorities, which gave the French disproportionate privileges.

These events provoked the first significant discussion about foreign capital in Poland. Many commentators, like the writer and translator Paweł Hulka-Laskowski, focused on the unequal and unstable character of capital exchange. "The profits are someone else's, the losses ours," he wrote, commenting on foreign investors siphoning money back to their homelands while letting workers go and making them dependent on the Polish government.[47] Others likened French actions to colonialism, with Żyrardów's owners portrayed as immoral exploiters. At first, the government distanced itself from attacks on FDI. This changed in late 1932, when the first article challenging the policy of capital imports appeared in the governmental *Gazeta Polska*. It was penned by Wacław Fabierkiewicz, head of the Department of Tariffs in the Ministry of Treasury.[48] He was the leading theoretician of the so-called First Economic Brigade (*Pierwsza Brygada Gospodarcza*), a group of Sanacja officials arguing for an increased role of the state in the Polish economy, a forerunner of the economic nationalism of the 1930s. The group was led by Stanisław Starzyński, who, as acting president of Warsaw, pursued actions against the Warsaw power plant. Other attacks followed in 1933 and 1934, most notably against Żyrardów.[49] A leading Sanacja

45 AdC, PL 1918–1940, 428, Arbitrage de M. Asser. Compagnie d'Électricité de Varsovie contre Ville de Varsovie. Décision du November 24, 1932, n.p.; AdC, CPC PL, 427, Dividendes & tantièmes verses par la Compagnie d'Électricité de Varsovie depuis la repreise de son explitation fin 1924, [1932], 239; AdC, CPC PL, 429, Compagnie d'Électricité de Varsovie contre ville de Varsovie. Sentence Arbitrale du 20 Juin 1933, 21.

46 AAN, MSZ, 3853, Notatka w sprawie elektrowni warszawskiej, November 9, 1932, 154–55.

47 "Faktografja żyrardowska," *Wiadomości Literackie*, June 5, 1932, 1.

48 "Punkt ciężkości," *Gazeta Polska*, December 20, 1932.

49 Kofman, "Koła," 304.

publicist Ignacy Matuszewski explicitly argued that the affair was "a matter of ethical standards of capital activity in Poland. Using this example, we must show ourselves and the world what is allowed and what is not allowed, what is permissible and what will not be. Due to its vividness, the Żyrardów case has become a symbol. A symbol of capitalist morality in Poland . . . Today, its solution largely determines whether we will have a healthy, honest, solid industry in Poland—or a speculative, thieving, poaching one."[50]

The discussion resulted in a new official policy of "loyal cooperation" with foreign capital, which crystallized in government circles in 1934.[51] Investors from abroad would be treated like domestic ones and allowed "normal" profits, provided that their companies submitted to strict control and surveillance by central authorities and ceased abusing their position. If they failed to follow these rules, they would be prosecuted without remorse.

As Jan Kofman rightly observed, this approach missed the mark, since it focused on morality rather than policy and incentives, and was unlikely to bear fruit.[52] Nonetheless, these matters were treated as important, with decisions on major conflicts depending on input from the highest Polish officials.

By 1934, Warsaw's relationship with Paris changed as well. In the previous decade, France had been Poland's primary ally and main provider of foreign capital. By the early 1930s, relations between the two countries rapidly deteriorated.[53] In November 1932, the pro-French foreign minister August Zaleski was replaced by Józef Beck, who had as little love for Paris as the French had for him. The relationship took a further hit with Hitler's ascension to power in Germany.

50 Ignacy Matuszewski, "Parszywa umowa," *Gazeta Polska*, August 8, 1934, 1.

51 AdC, CPC PL, 431, Bressy to Laval, December 24, 1934, 154v.

52 Kofman, "Koła," 312.

53 For a thorough investigation of this process, cf. Piotr Stefan Wandycz, *The Twilight of French Eastern Alliances, 1926–1936: French-Czechoslovak-Polish Relations from Locarno to the Remilitarization of the Rhineland* (Princeton, NJ: Princeton University Press, 1988); Jerzy Łazor, *The Political Economy of Interwar Foreign Investment: Economic Nationalism and French Capital in Poland, 1918–1939* (London and New York: Routledge, 2024, forthcoming), ch. 2.

It was at this lowest point of Franco-Polish relationship in 1934 that Polish courts put both French-owned companies under compulsory administration. In the case of Żyrardów, this was followed by arrests of French managers, while the decision concerning the power plant was taken in defiance of international arbitration. Despite intermittent discussions between the various engaged parties, the following year did not see any meaningful changes in the situation of the two companies, and in 1936 both were taken over by Polish authorities.

The mechanisms of the two takeovers were different, and they shed light on otherwise obscure Polish motivations. In the case of Żyrardów, the initial attacks in 1934 were the result of internal power struggles within the ruling Polish Sanacja, which explains the violence of the press campaign in August, started by *Gazeta Polska*.[54] Their political character was made even more obvious in 1936, when much of the anger at Boussac quickly disappeared as soon as the French made an amicable solution to the conflict a prerequisite for a large military loan. An agreement was thus quickly reached, and Warsaw paid for the company's shares while dropping criminal charges against its managers and suppressing press coverage. Attacking Żyrardów proved a useful political tool during the Great Depression, but was abandoned when it outgrew its usefulness.

The case of the power plant also combined the political and the economic. It was pursued relentlessly by Warsaw municipal authorities with full support of central Sanacja authorities, which saw it as proof of Poland casting off its shackles. The second half of the 1930s saw dozens of letters exchanged between Warsaw and Paris, as well as many negotiations concerning the company's future. However, as the owners of Compagnie d'Électricite de Varsovie lacked the political clout to have their goals linked by Paris to other major negotiations with Warsaw, no solution seemed forthcoming. However, just before the war, the Poles found a powerful argument. Apparently, while the company declared it had been mostly French-owned before the war, the Poles discovered that in 1914 it was a predominantly German enterprise, with French coinvestors used as

54 I explore this in more detail in Łazor, *The Political Economy*, ch. 7.

a front.[55] As a result, the company could not profit from the Franco-Polish agreement from 1922, and thus from international arbitrage. Its reaction proved that the revelations were true. The Poles were able to sign an agreement in July 1939, formally buying the rights to the company for a small price.[56] This marked the end of the longest conflict with foreign investors in interwar Poland.[57]

4.4 An Investment Cut Short

The engagement of Škoda in Polish airplane engine production was the result of Warsaw's attempts to create its own aviation sector based on foreign capital and technology.[58] Initially, due to the strength of the Franco-Polish relationship, this was done through *Francusko-Polskie Zakłady Samochodowe i Lotnicze SA* or *Frankopol* (Franco-Polish Automobile and Aviation Works), which in May 1921 signed a 10-year contract with the Polish government for the delivery of planes and the construction of a factory.[59] However, the French saw little reason to create competition for themselves in Central and Eastern Europe, and after signing the contract, they kept stalling and defrauded money provided by the Poles. Ultimately, Warsaw annulled the agreement and, after the May 1926, started looking for

55 AAN, MSZ, 3860, Elektrownia Warszawska. Przyczynek do materiałów wskazujących niemiecki charakter tow. "Compagnie d'Électricité de Varsovie," [1939], 159–66.

56 AAN, MSZ, 3860, Copy of a notarial deed no. 2079/39, July 31, 1939, 185–221.

57 The beginning of World War II meant that the Poles never paid the French shareholders. As a result, the matter was only truly settled with the Franco-Polish indemnization agreement in 1948; Dariusz Jarosz and Maria Pasztor, *Conflits brûlants de la Guerre froide: les relations fran polonaises de 1945 à 1954* (Panazol: Lavauzelle, 2005), 104–6.

58 The story of Franco-Polish cooperation in aviation is explored in detail in: Mariusz W. Majewski, "Druga próba uruchomienia produkcji silników lotniczych Polskie Zakłady Škody (1926–1935)," *Annales Universitatis Paedagogicae Cracoviensis. Studia Historica* 4, no. 28 (2005): 148–65; Mariusz W. Majewski, "Początki produkcji silników lotniczych w II Rzeczypospolitej (1921–1926)," *Annales Universitatis Paedagogicae Cracoviensis. Studia Historica* 2, no. 17 (2003): 201–21; Wojciech Mazur, *Pod wiatr. Francja i lotnictwo wojskowe II Rzeczypospolitej (1921–1938)* (Kraków: Ksiegarnia Akademicka Publishing, 2015). I place it in context in Łazor, *The Political Economy*, ch. 4.

59 AAN, Prokuratoria Generalna, 71, Agreement from May 31, 1921, 1–6.

new investors to take over the failed factory in Warsaw.[60] To Paris's surprise, it ended up picking the Czechoslovak company Škoda from Plzeň, which in the interwar period was the most important French holding in Poland's southern neighbor.[61] It took over Frankopol's plant and soon started production, with employment growing to over 1,500 workers by February 1929.[62]

Despite limited experience in aviation, the new company was a success. It first manufactured licensed French and American engines and soon diversified its production, becoming the most important private producer in the Polish so-called combustion engine, automobile, and aviation sector. However, as Mariusz W. Majewski described, the success brought problems.[63] Polish military authorities were annoyed that the company imported components rather than purchased them domestically. However, when Škoda attempted to do so, Polish producers repeatedly failed to meet quality requirements needed for airplane engine production—an interesting confirmation of the difficulty of high-tech FDI in underdeveloped economies. The Poles also never truly saw it as a domestic firm. In a telling example, when the company's letter to the Polish General Staff mentioned its "civic duty" to help Polish aviation become independent, the words were underlined by one of the officers.[64] With growing Czechoslovak-Soviet cooperation, the Poles started viewing Škoda as a security problem, and moved against it, causing the Czechs to sell their factory and associated intellectual rights.

60 Centralne Archiwum Wojskowe, Rembertów [henceforth: CAW], Biuro Administracji Armii Ministerstw Spraw Wojskowych [henceforth: BAA], I 300.54.123, Krzemiński to Żeligowski, March 3, 1926, 567–74; Jerzy Gołębiowski, *Sektor państwowy w gospodarce Polski międzywojennej* (Warszawa and Kraków: Państwowe Wydawnictwo Naukowe, 1985), 113–14; Majewski, "Początki produkcji," 214–17.

61 Alice Teichova, *An Economic Background to Munich: International Business and Czechoslovakia 1918–1938*, Soviet and East European Studies (London: Cambridge University Press, 1974); Jonathan A. Grant, *Between Depression and Disarmament: The International Armaments Business, 1919–1939* (Cambridge: Cambridge University Press, 2018).

62 CAW, I Oddział Sztabu Generalnego [henceforth: IOSG], I 303.3.545, Ministerstwo Spraw Wojskowych to Szef Sztabu Generalnego, January 7, 1927, 47–48; CAW, BAA, I 300.54.312, Polskie Zakłady "Skody," February 8, 1930, n.p.

63 Majewski, "Druga próba."

64 CAW, IOSG, I 303.3.545, Polskie Zakłady Skody SA to IOSG, June 11, 1931, 277.

The story of Škoda thus reflects the security component of Poland's growing support for state enterprise. Moreover, it showcases an important undercurrent of Polish policy. After the May 1926 coup, the Polish military increased its influence over politics and the economy. The process was enhanced through the practice of revolving doors. It was standard practice for officials who took part in the setting up of state enterprises to get posts in the new companies, or places on their boards. As the new positions would come with high salaries, the result was a systemic bias against engaging with private capital instead of setting up state-owned firms.[65] While in the case of Škoda, the Poles took over a foreign-owned company, partially due to the policy of the country where the owners were located, this detail was largely incidental. The same fate awaited other private aviation manufacturers in Poland, as the authorities pursued a powerful, consolidated state-owned sector. It was thus a story of expanding state enterprise, not a reflection of wider antiforeign policy.

4.5 Conclusion

Within a year, the Polish government and Warsaw municipal authorities took over four foreign-owned businesses, following long press campaigns against three of them. This in itself suggests a coordinated policy change, with the Great Depression pushing Warsaw toward economic nationalism. However, a study of the four cases suggests that there was not a single economic mechanism that made the Poles push for nationalization. The conflicts were distinct in all but timing, and the so-called policy of loyal cooperation, which would ostensibly explain Polish actions, was not followed in all four cases and was formulated after decisions against most of the companies had already been taken. Ultimately, there was little coherence to Polish policy, which mostly evolved through reactions to events and through internal political conflicts within the power apparatus in Warsaw.

65 Polish Institute and Sikorski Museum, London, Depositions concerning the Polish 1939 Campaign, B.I. 116/50, Zeznania Inż. L. Małeckiego, February 14, 1940, 705, 710; Cf. Łazor, *The Political Economy*, ch. 5.

It is nonetheless notable that such distinct conflicts produced the same result—arguably due to a systemic tendency in Poland, with its power hierarchy based on proximity to Józef Piłsudski, and later to his closest military collaborators. The increasingly centralized political decision-making was reflected in the economic sphere. The state was seen as the answer to most economic and social problems, and its expansion was considered natural. Coupled with the consequences of the Great Depression, the weakness of private investors, and the practice of revolving doors, this produced a swelling up of the state sector. It also fueled a bias against FDI. The head of the *Polskie Zakłady Optyczne* (PZO), a highly successful optics manufacturer that cooperated with French capital, complained that he had "never received any recognition from authorities for introducing reliable foreign capital into the country." On the other hand, he "often heard accusations that the factory was French, that the French were squeezing Poland dry, etc."[66] This bias was not rooted in any theoretical reflection on the role of foreign capital in development—indeed, PZO, like Škoda, was a rare example of loyal, high-technology FDI in Poland. Foreign owners were less likely to be as influenced by the government as domestic ones, and the resulting friction made them less desirable in some sectors.

66 Polish Institute and Sikorski Museum, London, Depositions concerning the Polish 1939 Campaign, 710.

PART TWO

Business Networks during the Great Depression

Chapter 5

CZECHOSLOVAKIA

"THE LAST STRAW": BAT'A AND ENDICOTT-JOHNSON DURING AND AFTER THE GREAT DEPRESSION

Zachary Doleshal

On June 1, 1929, the Bat'a Company newspaper ran a front-page story on how the firm and the shoe industry worldwide were going to deal with a growing tariff crisis and a worldwide slowdown in sales. Remarkably for the Czech-speaking employees of the Bat'a Company, the story included a reproduction in English of an open letter from George F. Johnson, the co-owner and General Manager of the US company Endicott-Johnson (from here: EJ), one of the largest shoe manufacturers in the world, to his employees on the same topic. Johnson's letter celebrated the workers of EJ, who had recently expressed loyalty to the company in a Home Coming Celebration, where thousands of employees and their families gathered to salute the "big family" of EJ at a time when "we (managers) have been forced to ask you to give up something." This something was a cut in wages and a reduction in health-care services.[1] Bat'a used Johnson's letter to stress to workers that hard times would be overcome through loyalty and sacrifice. Bat'a too was starting to see storm clouds on the horizon.

The letter provides evidence of a tight connection between two firms on the cusp of the Great Depression. Indeed, these items were but two pieces in a decades-long interaction between the companies that began in 1919, when the chief executive of Bat'a, Tomáš Bat'a, visited the company towns of EJ. From then to the mid-1930s, EJ

1 "K situaci", *Sdělení*, Zlín, June 1, 1929, 1. Gerald Zahavi, *Workers, Managers, and Welfare Capitalism: The Shoeworkers and Tanners of* Endicott Johnson, 1890–1950 (Urbana, IL: University of Illinois Press, 1988), 133–34.

and Bat'a were friendly travelers on a shared path. Initially, EJ was the larger and more developed firm, but Bat'a caught up, and, by 1928, EJ was sending employees to Zlín to learn Bat'a's methods. The companies shared similar historical trajectories and similar business philosophies. They both had grown into major industrial producers of footwear during World War I, and they had become fascinatingly similar operations in different contexts in the 1920s. At the beginning of the Great Depression, they were two of the most outstanding examples of welfare capitalism in the world.[2] So perhaps it is not surprising that they had had contact and a friendly ongoing correspondence. What is surprising, though, is that this friendship unraveled in the aftermath of the Great Depression. By 1938, George F. Johnson was writing to his workers that the lowering of tariffs on shoe imports from Czechoslovakia would be the proverbial "last straw" for EJ. "Be not deceived. We have been exploited and swindled."[3]

Using sources from the Bat'a Archive in the State Archive of Zlín, the George F. Johnson Collection at Syracuse University, the E-J Collection at Binghamton University's Special Collections, the National Archives of the United States and the Czech Republic, as well as secondary literature, this article investigates the complex interactions between these companies from 1919 to 1940 for the first time.[4] Their trans-Atlantic relationship helps to illustrate how the Great Depression and World War II profoundly changed globalization and welfare capitalism. Although the stunning collapse of the global economy and the attendant isolationist trade policies pulled back the rapid development of intercontinental networks, it did not stop them altogether. As with most economic crises, the Great Depression sharpened business strategies and highlighted differences as companies sought to survive. In the shoe business,

2 Stuart Brandes, *American Welfare Capitalism, 1880–1940* (Chicago, IL: University of Chicago Press, 1976).

3 George F. Johnson, "The Last Straw Which Broke the Camel's Back," March 11, 1938, George F. Johnson Papers, Box 15, Syracuse University Library Manuscript Collections.

4 For Bat'a, see Martin Jemelka, Kimberly Zarecor, Vít Strobach, Ondřej Ševeček, Martin Marek, Petr Sczepanik, Annett Steinführer, Bohumil Lehar, Jan Beranek, Kirstin Gust, Katrin Klingan, and Zdeněk Pokluda. For EJ, see Gerald Zahavi's *Workers, Managers.*

these two titans, Bat'a A. S., Zlín, and Endicott-Johnson, New York, fought to survive the economic collapse with similar ideologies, but with starkly different attitudes about globalization.

Such a comparison reveals fascinating insights. The first, which Bat'a and EJ not only survived the Depression but maintained remarkably high employment rates from 1930 to 1935, exemplifies the elastic strength of welfare capitalism. The second, which their strategies diverged because of geography and personality, connects to a larger literature on globalization and free trade. Bat'a accelerated globalization during the Depression, pioneering a model of global expansion in textile manufacturing. EJ looked to strengthen its position in the large internal market in the United States by leaning into protectionist legislation and staying put in its retail operations. Bat'a's strategy, while being far from smooth, worked in the long run. It remains a major player in the shoe industry worldwide. EJ sputtered to an ignominious closure in 1995. Third, such a conclusion was far from inevitable. During World War II, EJ had the advantage and Bat'a came dangerously close to collapse. There was little inevitable about the transnational corporation.

5.1 The Early Development of the Companies

Bat'a's Zlín and the cities of EJ emerged out of areas that were rural, underdeveloped, and largely out of the way. The geographic contours of both areas consist of river valleys with hills. Before they became "ideal industrial cities," small farms dotted both landscapes as did temperate forests. Neither place was close to traditional centers of large-scale shoe production—though Zlín did have a long tradition of small-scale shoe making.[5] And neither place was particularly important strategically or economically to the large states that governed them—though nearby Broome County, New York, was a bit larger and more economically diverse than Zlín was in the 1880s.[6] From this comparison, one can conclude that these large company towns needed a relatively blank slate—their development

5 Zdeněk Pokluda, *Sedm století zlínských dějin* (Zlín: Klub novinářů, 1991), 11–12.

6 H. P. Smith, *History of Broome County* (Syracuse, NY: D. Mason, 1885), 266.

just as at odds with an organically developed town as the modern landscapes of Norman bel Geddes or Le Corbusier.

Aside from room to grow, conflict was of central importance to both companies, as their founders' philosophies sprang from the often-violent conflicts between labor and capital that marked the turn of the twentieth century. In the United States, there were some 23,000 strikes between 1880 and 1900.[7] In the Austro-Hungarian Empire, organized labor was slightly slower to develop, but proved robust. Between 1897 and 1900, there were 1,115 strikes across the Austrian side of the Empire.[8] By 1906, the major labor unions on the Austrian side were strong enough to issue a general strike in order to pressure the government to enlarge the franchise, which it did. Moreover, since its founding in 1889, the Social Democratic Party of Austria continued to gain ground everywhere in the Austrian half of the empire with promises of a legal social revolution. Welfare capitalism was born out of such conflict between labor and management—it was one possible solution to the systemic discord in industrial capitalism.

Discord was what led the precursor to EJ, The Lestershire Manufacturing Company, to move 2 miles away from the city of Binghamton in 1888. There, the company promised a model industrial town to its workers, with clean streets, new homes, and easy access to the new factory. The project proved to be more about land speculation, as workers were required to purchase land with the company-controlled real estate group to continue their employment.[9] Still, the move offered both the promise of a welfare company and a large undeveloped area in which to expand.

The people who populated this area that would become Johnson City were involved in agriculture, and many of them were quite poor. Such a situation proved ideal for shareholders. Indeed, the major reason EJ took root in Broome County was that Henry B. Endicott, a major shareholder from Massachusetts, saw the labor

7 Brandes, *American Welfare Capitalism, 1880–1940*, 1.

8 Josef Steiner, *Utrpení sociální demokracie československé a postup strany v Rakousku* (Prague: Nakl. Tiskoveho družstva československé strany socialne demokratické, 1902), 116.

9 Zahavi, *Workers, Managers*, 3.

situation there as "desirable."[10] Convinced of a supply of cheap labor, Endicott bought into the Lestershire Manufacturing Company and then bought the other partners out in 1893. The same year, George F. Johnson, a foreman who had risen to become general manager, borrowed enough money from Endicott to buy half of the company and took over management of the new factory.[11]

Bat'a opened its operations in 1895 when the Bat'a siblings Antonín, Tomáš, and Anna used an endowment from their father to go into the family business of shoemaking in the small town of Zlín. After inventing a popular type of light canvas shoe, the company took off and expanded into the eight largest shoe company in Austria-Hungary by 1900.[12] This expansion led Bat'a into a search for up-to-date machinery, which simply did not exist in Austria-Hungary. On this search, Tomáš came to quickly understand that American machinery was state of the art, especially Matzeliger's lasting machine and Goodyear's welt sewing machine, as were American manufacturing techniques. Bat'a shoes at the turn of the century were largely made by hand with the one major exception of sewing machines. Such a discovery led Tomáš to the United States in 1905, where he lived and worked in Lynn, MA, the cradle of industrial shoemaking. There he witnessed and participated in a fundamentally different organizational approach to shoemaking. When he returned home to Moravia, he became a revolutionary Americanizer.

It took him a while until his company could afford all the machinery he wanted, but Tomáš was certain that shoemaking would be centered on machines, highly stratified in its labor, and standardized in its production. Of these principles, EJ was well aware. At least as early as 1914, the EJ factories were using the latest in industrial technology and had implemented a hierarchy of labor that had skilled workers, such as machinists, lathe makers, and tanners, above the majority of employees who were stitchers, sewers, and cutters, with higher wages and better living quarters. Management

10 George Lyman and Henry B. Endicott, *Henry B. Endicott: A Brief Memoir* (Boston, Mass.: McGrath-Sherrill Press, 1921), 10.

11 Endicott, *Henry B. Endicott*, 4.

12 Hodáč Collection, "Centralisace kapitalu," Státní Okrésní Archiv-Zlín (SOkA Zlín), Baťa Fond I-3 č. 20 k.19.

owed personal loyalty to the chief executive through family connections and personal relationships. The beginnings of both companies were marked by the strong and ambitious managerial personalities of Tomáš and George F., who knew that the future of shoe manufacturing was building up economies of scale so that the expensive machinery now on offer could be harnessed to make inexpensive shoes at a large volume. Both men knew the hub of the shoe industry intimately, and they knew that it did not need a majority of skilled craftsmen on payroll.

Therefore, the expansions of the companies between 1900 and 1914 relied on the hiring of unskilled workers. These workers were largely pulled in from the surrounding countryside, the adolescent children of local farmers. The EJ Company took in thousands of agricultural workers from the Susquehanna Valley and the rural areas of New York.[13] Bat'a took in approximately 2,000 agricultural employees from the Uherské Hradiště and the Valašsky regions of rural Moravia, many quite desperate.[14] What is particularly interesting is that both companies began rapidly expanding their payrolls with former agricultural workers around the same time—between 1905 and 1914. This suggests that the dramatic shift in industrial organization and mechanization coincided with a major shift in agricultural labor patterns.[15] From 1900 onward, New York State, for example, witnessed a steady decline in the number of small to middling family farms.[16] Meanwhile, Moravia witnessed whole villages immigrate to North America. Both companies took advantage of the increasingly marginal returns of family farming as they led their industries into a highly disruptive industrial model of production.

13 Zahavi, *Workers, Managers*, 6.

14 Between 1870 and 1910, some 3.5 million people emigrated from the Austrian Empire. Entire villages in Moravian Wallachia left. Faßmann, Heinz, and Rainer Münz, *Einwanderungsland Österreich?: historische Migrationsmuster, aktuelle Trends und politische Maßnahmen* (Vienna: Jugend & Volk, 1995), 20.

15 Leslie White, *Modern Capitalist Culture* (New York: Routledge, 2016), 184.

16 Leon Truesdall, *Farm Population of the United States* (Washington, DC: U.S. Government Printing Office, 1926), 43.

5.2 Shoes and the State

World War I brought a boom to both EJ and Bat'a with massively important contracts for military footwear, which in turn led to an expansion in employees and factory buildings. The contracts allowed EJ and Bat'a to further develop their company towns. In Zlín, new Lynn-inspired factory buildings, boulevards, and cars led one observer to remark that Bat'a had created an American Moravia—a new ideal for the future of the country.[17] Meanwhile, EJ's workforce doubled during the war.[18]

Yet the contexts of the companies' World War I experiences proved significantly divergent. Bat'a ended up using Russian prisoners of war and Austrian gendarmes to oversee not only the Russians but other increasingly disgruntled workers as well. Zlín experienced a serious housing and food shortage—with many workers sharing beds in shifts.[19] Broome County meanwhile built to keep up with its growing population at a quick pace. Wages increased at EJ, and its expansion led to the development of the two company towns of Johnson City and Endicott. While some wartime shortages entered everyday life, they were far from the deprivations of late war Moravia, where many were desperate for food.[20] Immediately after the war, Bat'a experienced the economic shock of the loss of the large internal Austro-Hungarian market alongside the political confusion at the dissolution of the Empire, which led to a serious economic crisis. No such shockwaves were felt in Broome County.[21]

The lessons learned from World War I were therefore different. EJ's welfare capitalism reached maturity during the immediate postwar years with "the square deal." This was the idea that a worker joined a "happy family" when going to work for EJ with

17 Zachary Doleshal, *In the Kingdom of Shoes: Bat'a, Zlín, Globalization, 1894–1945* (Toronto: University of Toronto, 2021), 52.

18 Zahavi, *Workers, Managers*, 38.

19 Letter to the district office in Uherské Hradiště from F. Štěpanek, October 13, 1917, Různé policejní záležitosti 1911–1918, SOkA AMZ č.954.

20 See Rudolf Kučera, *A Rationed Life: Science, Everyday Life, and Working-Class Politics in the Bohemian Lands* (New York: Berghahn, 2016).

21 *Partners All: A Pictorial Narrative of an Industrial Democracy* (New York: Huntington Corp., 1938), 6–10.

"Medical and Hospital Service," with "privileges of many kinds."[22] Chief among these privileges was access to own affordable housing close to the factories. Workers also participated in a profit-sharing plan. All of this was created within the company by 1921. The vision was of a paternalistic corporation where managers had personal contact with the employees—at work and in the neighborhood.

Tomáš Bat'a in 1918 had similar ideas of housing and personal contact, but no discernible ideology. He was embracing American ideas in a world of deep uncertainty. As he wrote to his workers in May 1918, "Nothing is as pressing today as is the issue of housing. To add to it will be serious supply concerns . . . and next to the needs of the body will be the needs of the soul. To manage all of this is beyond one person but requires everyone to help that believes in the factory."[23] As Bat'a expanded from 400 employees in 1914 to between 4,000 and 5,000 by the end of World War I, it faced a growing communist-led labor movement, new borders to negotiate, and a grinding halt to the leather trade. Its leadership was looking for help.

5.3 Bat'a and EJ from 1919 to 1923

It was then, in the immediate postwar period, that the EJ model became known to Tomáš Bat'a. In 1919, as his company faced a major crisis, he returned to the United States in hopes of finding further inspiration. The EJ complex was one of his two places of travel—the other being the Ford factories in Michigan. Tomáš's visit to EJ has only one source, from chief company propagandist Antony Cekota, who wrote the following:

> Here in the Susquehanna Valley, wider but greatly resembling the valley of Drevnice, (Tomas) found shoe factories and buildings like his own, surrounded by workers' houses, schools, parks and sports fields, bearing a resemblance to the private clubs of the American middle class. There were

22 Zahavi, *Workers, Managers*, 40.

23 Quote of T. Bat'a taken from the Hodač Collection, Bat'a Fond I/3 č. 20 k.15 SOkA Zlín.

> the Endicott Johnson Hospital, Dental Clinic and Library . . . The whole enterprise struck him as a rather peculiar one with its clusters of factories and residences spread over an area of more than thirty miles.[24]

According to Cekota, Bat'a was not impressed with the EJ methods of production, which he had already implemented and improved upon, but by its methods of social organization. EJ proved to offer the most progressive model on how to keep labor unions away. His other visit to Highland Park, Michigan, showed him a more invasive technique of social control in Ford's Sociology Department. There, company agents inspected a wide variety of employee habits, thoughts, and behaviors in order to award them full wages and benefits.[25] Taken together, EJ and Ford deeply impressed Tomáš, who was convinced by the loyal returns made on social welfare investment. From then on, Ford and George F. Johnson became two of the most important sources of inspiration for Tomáš, largely replacing his previous idol, Thomas Edison.

Tomáš Bat'a returned home in the fall of 1919 to not only a significant economic depression, but a hostile city council with a majority of council members of the communist persuasion. The mayor of the town, František Novák, did his best to discredit the firm while he was in office, publicly stating that the firm was swindling its workers by "selling produce on the black-market at the border."[26] Such hostility persuaded Tomáš to launch his own political party in 1923 and formally take control of the town, which he did. Meanwhile, EJ never felt the need to run a slate of company candidates. Instead, the company preferred an indirect influence in political affairs by funding political campaigns and largely controlling the finances of Endicott and Johnson City through donations and tax payments. The company did hire Pinkerton detectives to investigate potential troublemaking employees, but they found little evidence of discontent.[27] Bat'a's takeover of the city offices after 1923 gave the company

24 Cekota, Zlín, 149.

25 Stephen Meyer III, *The Five Dollar Day: Labor Management and Social Control in the Ford Company, 1908–1921* (Albany, NY: SUNY Press, 1981).

26 "Našim zaměstnancům!," October 16, 1920 (SOkA-Zlín Bat'a Fond, č.383).

27 Zahavi, *Workers, Managers*, 135.

more direct control over its workforce. After all, the company used the city police to help keep watch over ideological enemies. Once the Personnel Department started using social inspectors along the same lines as Ford—Bat'a had a range of company and city men to keep track of the workers.

In Endicott and Johnson City, EJ used a less sophisticated surveillance network, one that relied on the reports of "loyal" employees and their families. Chiefly, rumors and memberships in a variety of clubs helped the company sort out who was potentially a "subversive." The EJ philosophy on managing dissent remained a thoroughly paternal one, with the Johnson family maintaining close personal knowledge of employees. Instead of police inspectors, EJ had clam bakes and Fourth of July parades to sniff out potential troublemakers among the employees.[28] As such, EJ would never reach the heights of Bat'a's surveillance network.[29]

As it took over municipal affairs in Zlín, Bat'a's economic situation also stabilized in 1923. The Czechoslovak economy was growing at the impressive pace of a 6% year on year average from 1923 to 1928.[30] Shoe sales across Czechoslovakia, however, fell considerably in 1923 from 129 mil. Kč to 62 mil. Bat'a, though, grew its sales in this same period from 15.4 mil Kč to 23.1 mil, which meant that the company accounted for over a third of the entire Czechoslovak shoe industry.[31] EJ experienced a fall in revenue as well in 1920, yet rebounded quickly to have its most profitable year in the history of the company in 1922 with a profit of $5.6 mil. The following 6 years remained robust.[32]

While warm correspondence and economic good times marked the two firms' relationship from 1921 to 1929, the mid-to-late 1920s also witnessed important moments of divergence between the

28 Kristina Knight, *Patriotism, Parades and Paternalism: How the Endicott-Johnson Corporation Controlled the Lives of Women in Johnson City and Endicott, New York, 1945–1965* (BA diss., Binghamton University, Binghamton, NY, 2006).

29 Petr Szczepanik, "The Aesthetics of Rationalization: The Media Network in the Bat'a Company and the Town of Zlín," in *A Utopia of Modernity: Zlín Revisiting Bat'a's Functional City*, ed. Katrin Klingan (Berlin: Jovis, 2009), 23.

30 Oldčich Krpec and Vít Hloušek, "Czechoslovak Tariffs in the 1920s: An Example of Historical Specificity in Economic Policy," *Slavic Review* 80, no. 3 (2021): 523–43.

31 B. Lehár, *Dějiny baťova koncernu* (Praha: Státní nakladatelství, 1960), 88.

32 Zahavi, *Workers, Managers*, 221.

companies. Between 1924 and 1930, Bat'a implemented three new components of its operations: a decentralized management and production process, an industrial school in Zlín, and an aggressive expansion into foreign markets. EJ did none of those things, remaining content with its large divisions, its public-school system, and large internal market. The result would be that Bat'a was becoming a transnational corporation with retail outlets across the globe, a cadre of trained managers from its own industrial school to run them, and a remarkably responsive system of management that allowed for lower costs and higher degrees of efficiency. The decision to go global had much to do with the context of the two companies. Simply, a small domestic market versus a big domestic market led to different strategies, and once governments around the world passed a cascade of tariff acts that choked export channels, these differences crystallized.

The impact of increasing tariffs can be gleaned from a letter Tomáš' sent to George F. at the end of 1929, which was faithfully reprinted (in Czech) in the company newspaper and captured the Bat'a position.

> You have a self-sufficient internal market in America that is ten times larger than what we have . . .
>
> The European shoe industry on the other hand is still small. It has only been a few years since one could buy factory made shoes. Few workers know how to do this kind of work and so for now we must educate them.
>
> Machines arrived to us relatively late, which meant that we are still learning how they function while your factories have them working at full speed. We have to bring in instructors for our unskilled people because they work much slower than yours.
>
> Your guarantee that Europe will never be a much of a rival to you in America is also in the context that the feet of your citizens are about three times weaker than our peoples' due to the differences in our standards of living—for us, the automobile is the exception.

> Here factories have to make specific adjustments to their production line in order to export to the American market, which is met with difficulty from the start.
>
> From these reasons you can see that our handicap is considerable and that it isn't necessary to worry oneself over European competition and to hide behind a Chinese wall against imports.
>
> I would like to raise the awareness of your American colleagues that humanity still needs billions of pairs of shoes a year . . .[33]

A year before the Smoot-Hawley Tariff Act of 1930, which raised tariff rates on a large number of imports into the United States, Bat'a was crafting an antitariff argument for his friends and colleagues in the United States. This argument, though, had no apparent effect.

Bat'a shoes had arrived in the United States market in 1927. Within 2 years, Bat'a was importing 300,000 pairs of shoes into the United States, which, while a tiny fraction of EJ's output, was enough to alarm the shoe industry. George F. Johnson did not view the arrival of Bat'a shoes as a friendly rivalry as Tomáš had hoped. Instead, he encouraged his congressman, John Clarke, to argue in favor of shoe tariffs, which Clarke did with force.[34] This political action resulted in the United States adding tariffs on shoe imports into the vast Smoot-Hawley Tariff Act, tariffs that remain in effect today. This meant that after 1930, most of Bat'a's exports to the United States faced a 30% average tariff. After the protectionist measure passed, EJ felt forced to delineate the difference between its industrial democracy and the Bat'a system. In a letter to employees in 1931, George F. Johnson began the process of setting one form of welfare capitalism apart from the other.

> I have had correspondence with Mr. Bat'a, in connection with Tariff laws. Naturally he objected to the efforts of American shoe manufacturers to close their markets to his

33 Tomáš Baťa, "Mr. T. Bat'a Wrote This Letter to Mr Johnson," December 1, 1929, Sdělení, 2.

34 G. F. Johnson letter to John Clarke, January 17, 1929. George F. Johnson Papers, Box 10, Syracuse University Library Manuscript Collections.

> products. He is a very intelligent, very remarkable and wonderful character, and has accomplished much. It is safe to assume that he has improved the conditions of his workers.
>
> What has been accomplished under his plan of procedure in his country, would be impossible to accomplish here. We haven't any "cheap labor", comparatipely [*sic*] speaking, in the first place. And in the second place, our people are quite independent, as a matter of right and justice.
>
> This is the United States of America, "the home of the brave and free". Personally I believe in that old-fashioned, somewhat obscure but still famous saying "that government is best which governs least." . . . The utmost freedom from restraint which may be granted—the most latitude which permits of the greatest self-expression—is the most desirable relation to establish. Therefore every effort should be made to see to it that we are permitted self expression, beginning with early childhood and only ending with death. Rules of Human Conduct or law which restrain natural behaviors and assume dictation of conduct do not build up character . . . So it is in our nation we have made very serious errors in an effort to "make people behave."[35]

The cornerstone of the difference in the firms' ideologies was for the first time given expression—the difference between Bat'a and EJ in the rhetoric of EJ was personal liberty.

As the firms grappled over tariff policy, a series of banks failed (most outstandingly the Austrian Credit-Anstalt), the New York Stock Exchange crashed, and the world economy spiraled downward. In the US shoe industry, labor productivity declined from 1929 to 1932 by about 8%.[36] In the cradle of modern shoe manufacturing, Massachusetts, the Depression accelerated a long-term overall decline in productivity and employment.[37] Overall, statistics

35 George F. Johnson as reprinted in "'Geo. F.' Renews Pledge to High Ideals of E.J.," *Endicott Bulletin*, June 9, 1931, 1–2.

36 Boris Stern, "Labor Productivity in the Boot and Shoe Industry," *Monthly Labor Review* 48, no. 2 (February 1939): 271–92.

37 "Footwear: Issue Supplementary Report on Boot, Shoe Industry in Mass.: I. Summary Well-Substantiated Facts," *Women's Wear Daily* 49, no. 116 (December 13, 1934): 16.

compiled by the Federal Reserve Board in 1932 showed a 22% decline in employment in the industry. The reason for the sizable difference in employment decline versus productivity has much to do with the vast differential between large, machine-based factories and the many more numerous smaller handicraft operations. Scale mattered a great deal to businesses during the Depression, and those in the boot and shoe industry that were at the forefront of technological efficiency did not collapse.[38]

The Czechoslovak economic story of the Great Depression parallels that of the United States in that it too had its most painful collapses in smaller, less technologically developed businesses. Yet Czechoslovakia had features to its political economy that made its overall experience unique. The general historical consensus on the Great Depression in Czechoslovakia is that it found its bottom a little later than that of most of the industrial world, stayed in it a bit longer, and its ethnicities experienced uneven effects.[39] Such unevenness has been attributed to the way in which consecutive Czechoslovak governments implemented trade and industrial policies that benefited "Czech"-owned industries at the expense of the export-heavy light industries of the German-speaking minority. Upon its founding, Czechoslovakia implemented *nostrification*, which was a rather complicated process attempting to move capital and majority ownership in large businesses from Austria, Germany, and Hungary to Czechoslovakia. It was not particularly successful at doing this as most companies found easy ways around the law, but its nationalist favoritism set the tone for the interwar period.[40] This favoritism reached an apogee with the Law on National Defense in March 1936 and the subsequent major fortification and armament program, which was what formally took Czechoslovakia's economy

38 Bernard William Gibbons, "Recent Cost Schedule Variations in the Boot and Shoe Industry" (MA diss., Loyola University Chicago, Chicago, IL, 1935), 190.

39 V. Lacina, *Velká hospodářská krize v Československu, 1929–1934* (Praha: Akademia, 1984). A good overview in English can be found in Patrick Crowhurst, *A History of Czechoslovakia between the Wars* (London: Taurus, 2015).

40 Jaromír Balcar, "'Czechization' versus 'Germanization': Creating a National Homogeneous Economy in Czechoslovakia (1918–1945)," in *National Economies: Volks-Wirtschaft, Racism and Economy in Europe between the Wars* (1918–1945), eds. Christoph Kreutzmüller, Michael Wildt, and Moshe Zimmermann (Newcastle upon Tyne: Cambridge Scholars Publishing, 2015), 239–55.

out of its depression. The contracts related to the armament could not go to firms deemed "unreliable," which state officials mostly identified as German, out of reasons of state security.[41] While the law did not lead to mass dismissals of German-speaking employees, it did limit which firms gained lucrative contracts. The exact picture of the depression across the country is therefore highly variable. What is certain is the Depression had the effect of hardening imaginary lines in Czechoslovakia. Economic hardship intensified nationalist antagonisms, which were deeply ingrained in the cultural fabric of the post-Habsburg state.

However, one can go too far with such a focus on nationalist rivalries. Equally important for the overall picture is that the Great Depression unleashed a turn toward planning. As Antonie Doležalová has ably shown, the Depression "dynamized" thoughts among Czech public intellectuals that state planning and rationalization were key to fixing the problem.[42] As rationalization became a hot topic across print media, Bat'a, with its vertically integrated model, became a darling example of those who were pushing for state planning.[43] And, when looking at both EJ and Bat'a's numbers on productivity and employment, they might have had a point.

Employment and productivity numbers reveal a stunning exceptionalism for both companies during the Depression. Both experienced declines in personnel and productivity from 1929 to 1930. Bat'a's yearly shoe exports dropped from 2,736,000 pairs in 1928 to 1,729,000 in 1929.[44] EJ's net profits shrunk from 3,601,263 in 1928 to 765,267 in 1930.[45] Yet they were able to keep most of their skilled workforce, and, relative to the rest of the industry, would have exceptionally low layoff and quit rates throughout the 1930s. As one study found, "roughly, the layoff rates in the industry were twenty-four

41 Jaromír Balcar, "'Czechization' versus 'Germanization': Creating a National Homogeneous Economy in Czechoslovakia (1918–1945),", 251.

42 Antonie Doležalová, *A History of Czech Economic Thought* (Oxon: Routledge, 2018), 112.

43 Doleshal, *In the Kingdom of Shoes*, 88.

44 Lehár, *Dějiny baťova koncernu*, 131.

45 Zahavi, *Workers, Managers*, 221.

times the size of those in Endicott Johnson."[46] Gerald Zahavi found that between "January 1930 and April 1935, with a single exception in December of 1933, the company did not lay off any regular workers."[47] For Bat'a, employment and productivity numbers over the same period were less stable, yet more explosive over time. In 1929, the company let go of 54% of its entire workforce, which was 5,555 workers out of 10,295. Many of these were temporary workers hired on piece rates, whose firing and rehiring became routine in the years of the economic crisis. The bigger picture was that employment numbers more than doubled from 1929 to 1931, from 10,295 to 23,500, before dipping to 18,505 in 1932. The number of permanent employees went from 3,912 in 1929 to 7,224 in 1932.[48] These numbers clearly show massive growth. Indeed, when looking at export numbers for these years, a picture of just how well Bat'a handled the economic crisis compared to its domestic competitors becomes even clearer. In 1929, Bat'a exported 7,166,000 pairs of shoes, which was 50.7% of the total number of Czechoslovakia's shoe exports. By 1933, Bat'a exported 10,582,000 pairs of shoes, which was now 86% of all the shoe exports of Czechoslovakia.

Clearly, the Bat'a and EJ models had built companies that could withstand the stress of the Great Depression. What this meant for thousands of people was quite clear to them. Workers in both companies felt their employment in the 1930s kept them from the abyss of destitution. Genevieve Behill, who worked at EJ as a teenager in the late 1930s, remembered her time as such, "nowadays it's difficult to put yourself in that time—but we were doggone happy to have a job there."[49] A longtime Bat'a employee, Svatopluk Jabůrek, recalled life in the early thirties as such, "we had high wages. It was

46 William Patrick Burns, "A Study of Personnel Policies, Employee Opinion and Labor Turnover (1930–1946) at the Endicott-Johnson Corporation" (MA diss., Cornell University, 1947): 88-89, found in Zahavi, *Workers, Managers*, 61.

47 Zahavi, *Workers, Managers*, 130.

48 Lehár, *Dějiny baťova koncernu*, 176.

49 "Family Has Fond Memories of EJ," *Binghamton Sun*, November 12, 1990, 4. Found in Bartle Library Special Collections, Binghamton University.

just great. Even living in the company houses, for example, was extremely modern and nice."[50]

The companies' vigor came from a managerial commitment to community. In the middle of the economic crisis, Tomáš wrote a passionate and provocative 26-page article titled "How can we overcome the economic crises?" which was partially reprinted in the company newspaper.[51] For him, the crisis had much to do with the egotism, fear, and panic of the individual.

> Progress is only possible by increasing togetherness and cooperation and making sure that economic goals devoid of morality and social awareness always end in failure. For there is no way to protect labor, management, and profit unless the business's success provides a greater profit for the village, district, country, nation, and society. All of this applies doubly in times of crisis when egotism and personal fear and panic easily come before considering society. Everyone knows how confused people act when there is a fire, running about with tin mugs in their hands, when with calm and understanding the fire is simply put out.[52]

Throughout the piece, one can find the ethos of welfare capitalism. And with Bat'a's medical care, housing, relief, and company stores, it was doing just that. At EJ, family was the organizing principle of George F. Johnson's "square deal." On the eve of the Great Depression, the company offered extensive cradle-to-grave medical care, a progressive home ownership program, workmen's compensation, "old age and widow's pensions, sickness relief, burial funds, housekeeping assistance, and food, fuel, and clothing allowances to needy workers."[53] These were the bedrock principles of the two companies, and they were why they had such low worker turnover during the economic crisis.

50 Jaroslav Rudiš in conversation with Svatopluk Jabůrek, "It Was Extremely Modern and Nice," in *A Utopia of* Modernity, ed. Katrin Klingan (Berlin: Jovis, 2010), 138.

51 T. Bat'a, "Jak překonáme hospodařskou krisi?" December 1931. Hodač Collection. Bat'a Fond I/3 č.29 k. 19: 1–4.

52 Bat'a, "Jak překonáme hospodařskou krisi?" 7–8.

53 Zahavi, *Workers, Managers*, 48.

Yet, geopolitical context matters. Operating from a small market in the face of increasing worldwide tariffs forced Bat'a, but not EJ to explore the possibilities of globalization and the exportation of industrial manufacturing. The first Bat'a satellite factories were within Czechoslovakia, but the Bat'a Company launched satellite factories in eight different countries between 1931 and 1934. That Bat'a expanded in the face of the Great Depression is one of the most important stories in the history of modern industrial capitalism, for it illustrated the potential of globalization. Especially as it expanded into India in 1934, building the factory town of Batanagar just outside of Calcutta, the company could utilize cheaper labor and reach untapped markets.[54] As it embarked upon this global expansion, the top executives of the company steadily came to see that Zlín was certain to evolve into a hub of organizational and managerial expertise while manufacturing would expand to places of cheaper labor. All of the repercussions of this, of course, were not immediately apparent to the company, which still put great importance on the company town model being exported into desired markets.

What was clear, though, was that Bat'a needed to inculcate a national indifference in its management that would allow for flexible national identity. After all, management was being sent across the globe into nationalist contexts that routinely resisted Bat'a. As such, Bat'a employed a decidedly fluid national identification. Top-ranking Bat'a employees were the engines of this new identification. Dominik Čipera and Antony Cekota, the equivalent of Chief Financial Officer and the head of the advertising department respectively, consistently advocated cosmopolitanism and tried to inculcate it in the workforce and promote it in Czechoslovak society. Cekota declared, "Here in this rather provincial town are people who are worldlier than citizens of the largest cities. English is heard on the streets as well as German. There isn't a European language that isn't heard here. The words, business contracts, tariffs, balance sheets, courses, import, export, etc. are not only theoretical but a

54 Ondřej Ševeček, "The Case of Company Towns of the Bat'a Concern," in *Company Towns of the Bat'a Concern: History, Cases, Architecture*, eds. Ondřej Ševeček and M. Jemelka (Stuttgart: Franz Steiner Verlag, 2013), 33–35.

part of daily life. The cosmopolitanism of the people of Zlín is the direct result of not having political corruption and bad blood."[55]

EJ, meanwhile, was the site of significant immigration—the majority of the immigrants were from Czechoslovakia, in fact—and adopted a policy of multicultural nationalism for their large immigrant workforce. Never as intense as Ford's Americanization procedure, EJ nevertheless deployed a host of tactics, mostly "soft" cultural events, such as baseball leagues, mandatory July 4 parades, George Washington Birthday celebrations, and EJ's own invented "Loyalty Day," where workers marched through Binghamton under banners expressing fidelity to company and country. Their slogan was "cosmopolitan but all American." A certain kind of ethnic diversity was encouraged by EJ, through many gifts given to various religious organizations. But the strategy was quite clear; immigrants were to be made into loyal Americans through cultural events and public expressions of loyalty. [56]

The Bat'a Company became a massive multinational corporation in a small state, while EJ grew to be a large corporation among many in a massive state. This fact had profound effects on the ways in which the companies dealt with national and company identification. Primarily concerned with the American market, EJ did not expand into all corners of the globe like Bat'a. The result was that EJ took a multinational workforce and championed its Americanness, while Bat'a took a multinational workforce and championed its internationalism. Both firms organized massive shows of loyalty, but the differences between them are revealing. EJ workers marched on July 4 and George Washington's birthday, while Bat'a workers' big event was on May 1, an international socialist holiday that Bat'a took over as its own. Bat'a thought globally. EJ thought locally.

Interestingly, their differences over tariffs and globalization did not prevent the companies' executives from maintaining friendly relationships and relatively open lines of communication. The companies arranged three official visits to each other during the mid-1930s—Jan Bat'a, who took over as chief executive in 1932 after Tomáš perished in a plane crash, made his second visit to EJ in

55 Cekota, Zlín, 4.
56 "Cosmopolitan, but American," *EJ Workers' Review*, March 20, 1919, 6.

August of 1933 (his first was in 1921). Charles F. Johnson Jr. and six other managers came to Zlín in October of 1933. Two years later, chief operations manager George W. Johnson traveled to Zlín. While Jan surely learned a great deal from his first trip in 1921, such as the way in which the welfare system worked for EJ, it is unclear whether he gained much from his second visit. The EJ executives, however, seemed to have picked up the practice of embedding competition into the workplace from Bat'a—just 2 months after George W's visit, EJ introduced worker competition events.[57]

Such goodwill did not last into the late 1930s. The Great Depression began to strain the generosity of EJ—especially problematic was the cost of healthcare—and sour its attitude toward Bat'a. The most pressing cause for the renewed conflict between the two welfare capitalists was a proposed trade treaty with Czechoslovakia. Upon hearing of the treaty, George F. Johnson listed the major threats to the company as such, "hanging over us is the threat of the CIO or the American Federation of Labor." And, "the Czechoslovak threat of invasion in our own market, with politicians negotiating what they call a reciprocity agreement . . . they come in here now, with their shoes made with 50 to 60% cheaper labor than ours, and sell certain patriotic(?) merchants, who in turn can sell this foreign stuff to patriotic(?) citizens" (his own parenthetical remarks).[58] EJ once again sought political help to stop Bat'a from entering the American market.

The issue led to a showdown in Washington DC as representatives from the two companies faced each other in front of the Committee on Reciprocity Information in October of 1937. There, Bat'a representatives tried to assure legislators that they offered no unfair competition by praising the quality of EJ shoes. In turn, EJ representative Charles F. Johnson Jr. claimed that they had recently lost a $350,000 order to Bat'a.[59] Remarkably, EJ, which had doggedly fought off all efforts to unionize its employees, found itself

57 George F. Johnson letter to George W. Johnson, December 10, 1936, George F. Johnson Papers, Box 14, Syracuse University Library Manuscript Collections.

58 George F. Johnson to E. H. Ellison, September 11, 1937, George F. Johnson Papers, Box 15, Syracuse University Library Manuscript Collections.

59 "Bat'a Shoe Co. Testifies in Favor of Czech Pact," *Endicott Daily Bulletin*, October 27, 1937, 1.

allied with the most powerful North American shoe manufacturers' unions. At the very same committee meeting, Powers Hapgood, an organizer for the United Shoe Workers of America, and Frank I. Miller of the National Boot and Shoe Manufacturers Association, lambasted Bat'a practices. Hapgood described the typical Bat'a employee as a "slave" who was "confined in dormitories under military discipline." Miller referred to the Bat'a system as "industrial feudalism" because of its decentralized management system that left each division competing against the other while Bat'a "relieves himself of all management costs."[60]

Shortly after the committee meeting, major shoe manufacturers, especially Endicott-Johnson, lobbied the Tariff Commission for a 50% raise in tariffs on shoe imports (this would have been on top of the average 30% tariff imposed by the Smoot-Hawley Tariff of 1930). They specifically mentioned "Czechoslovakian shoes" and Bat'a in particular. This attempt at protecting the internal American market was prescient in many ways. The companies argued that they could not compete with the cost of production abroad, a nod to their rising awareness that cheaper labor elsewhere would sink American shoe manufacturing. Bat'a replied that its shoes were not selling for less than their American counterparts on the American market. Their argument was that they were simply making quality shoes that were competitive.[61] Unlike in 1930, instead of a rise in tariffs, the US-Czechoslovakian Trade Agreement lowered tariffs on shoe exports by 50%. The Roosevelt administration, because of both political and economic motivations, effectively unblocked Bat'a, at least partially. Due to a restriction in the total amount allowed in, this only meant a net increase of around 600,000 pairs of shoes. Predictably, Massachusetts and Broome County politicians railed against the treaty.[62]

Their loss in 1938 did not stop EJ's lobbying efforts against Bat'a. EJ leaned on the new US Congressman from Binghamton, Edwin

60 "Warn of Pay Drop in Czech Duty Cut," *New York Times* (1923-Current File), October 28, 1937, 46, https://ezproxy.shsu.edu/login?url=http://search.proquest.com/docview/102136592?accountid=7065.

61 "Commission Considers a Higher Shoe Tariff," *Endicott Daily Bulletin*, December 17, 1937, 7.

62 "Shoe State Congressmen Assail Treaty," *Endicott Daily Bulletin*, March 8, 1938, 1.

A. Hall. Hall quickly gained notoriety for his aggressive attacks against the Bat'a Company, especially its industrial expansion into the United States. In 1938, after the infamous Munich Accord, the Bat'a Company embarked on an adventurous plan to move its headquarters to the United States. They bought some five square miles of land in Belcamp, MD, and began the arduous process of transferring headquarters. Congressman Hall sought to block their move by echoing the rhetoric first expressed by George F. Johnson in 1931, claiming that Bat'a "smacked of regimentation and mass dictation."[63]

In the midst of these fierce attacks on their operations in the United States, Bat'a launched a public relations campaign to save the reputation of the company. Dr. Joseph Schneider, Director of the Bat'a Department of Education, issued a statement in the midst of the controversy over the Belcamp plant and its Czech employees. "Whatever Bat'a does is being misinterpreted from a narrow angle, which tries to find some un-American activity at any cost. If nothing can be found even when looking through these glasses, Bat'a is wrapped into a mysterious cloak of 'paternalism'. What harm is there in an employer acting always to the benefit of his employees?. . . Much criticism comes from the unions . . . one cannot overlook the fact that a labor union is a special interest and sometimes more concerned with displaying its power than with promoting the general good."[64] Despite Schneider's public relations campaign, Bat'a stumbled in the court of public opinion, and then in the court of law.

Opening up their factory town in Belcamp, MD, Bat'a executives planned to move their philosophy and manufacturing process as a whole piece. However, the operation was plagued with difficulty. One of the first major issues concerned the company's desire to create a Bat'a industrial school for young women and men along the lines of the Bat'a School of Work in Zlín. Company employees fanned out in Belcamp neighborhoods and went to the area's high schools to distribute recruiting pamphlets for the school. They promised recruits a week of 40 hours of work at the factory, 10 hours

63 "Under Fire from Congressman Hall," *Endicott Daily Bulletin*, March 28, 1940, 1.

64 "Bat'a Shoe Issues Statement Answering Many Accusations," *Women's Wear Daily* 60, no. 18 (June 10, 1940), 18.

of instruction, room and board, and recreation. They would have to live in Bat'a dormitories and would be paid $12.63 a week, out of which $7 would be taken for room and board, and three dollars for entertainment and education. The other $2.63 would go into a Bat'a savings account for the adolescents. The area residents were alarmed by the idea and the recruiting tactics. Loud protests erupted at school meetings, and city officials fielded calls from outraged citizens. Bat'a had to abandon the school entirely.[65] Next, Federal Judge Calvin W. Chesnut enjoined Bat'a because of a violation of US child labor laws, and this shortly after the company pleaded guilty to a wage and hour violation charge. The wage charge forced the company to make restitution of $10,000 to its employees.[66] None of this was great public relations for the embattled firm. The Czech model of the ideal city as seen through American eyes seems to have become highly problematic. Bat'a had become saddled with the rhetoric of "mass dictation."

EJ meanwhile became a media darling in the late 1930s, and George F. became the "industrialist who shares his wealth." In the context of the New Deal, EJ became an iconic exception to the greed of industrialists and thereby came to be seen by many as a progressive force, even when the company came directly in the crosshairs of the National Labor Relations Board (NLRB).[67] Indeed, somehow, when the NLRB sent two inspectors to investigate the anti-union practices of EJ, they came up empty-handed and failed in their efforts to facilitate unionization. EJ agreed to hold an election on whether or not to unionize in late 1938, and the results went against the American Federation of Labor (AFL).[68]

65 "Digest of a Confidential Report of an Investigation by Agents of the Immigration and Naturalization Service into the History, Activities and Financial Transactions of the Bat'a Shoe Company," August 21, 1940, National Archives, Department of Justice Foreign Funds Control Docket Files, Records of the Office of Alien Property, Docket Files of Business Enterprises, Record Number 131, Container Number 902.

66 "Bat'a Concern Enjoined," *New York Times (1923–Current File)*, June 4, 1940, 36, https://ezproxy.shsu.edu/login?url=http://search.proquest.com/docview/105292960?accountid=7065.

67 Rose Feld, "Industrialist Who Shares His Wealth," *New York Times*, August 11, 1935, 8.

68 Leigh Plummer, "Endicott Johnson Workers May Vote Against AFL Union," *The New York Times*, December 6, 1938, 1.

Once the World War broke out in September of 1939, British authorities had the difficult task of determining what to do with the multinational behemoth that was Bat'a. There were conflicting accounts of Jan Bat'a's relationship with Nazi officials, and, given the national indifference of top management, the British had a hard time pinning down the company's allegiances. They gave Jan 5 months to make a public statement of support for the Allies and deposit 100,000 pounds in a government account, which he did not do. Instead, he carried out negotiations with the British through an intermediary and dallied. They put him and the Bat'a Company on the "Statutory List," also known as the blacklist of Nazi collaborators.[69]

Such a move emboldened EJ and the enemies of Bat'a, who moved the machinery of government to take down the company. An Immigration and Naturalization investigation into the Belcamp plant found that 100 "instructors" from Czechoslovakia were not simply instructing. Their visas were voided, and they and Jan Bat'a were expelled from the United States. Then, once the United States entered the war, American authorities carried over the British list and Bat'a's operations in the Americas, Asia, and Africa were put under the strictest surveillance and government oversight for the duration of the war.[70] The Baltimore Sun picked up the story and ran a series of articles on the company linking Bat'a to "the Nazi War Machine."[71] Bat'a would seem to have been sunk.

Surprisingly perhaps, given the 20-year relationship that existed between the companies, the EJ Company did not provide a lifeline to Bat'a when Nazi occupation unmoored it from its headquarters

69 Memorandum, Interdepartmental Committee on the Proclaimed List on May 21, 1946, National Archives of the United States, Department of Justice Foreign Funds Control Docket Files, Records of the Office of Alien Property, Docket Files of Business Enterprises #371-D, Record Number 131, Container Number 902.

70 "Digest of a Confidential Report of an Investigation by Agents of the Immigration and Naturalization Service into the History, Activities and Financial Transactions of the Bat'a Shoe Company," August 21, 1940, National Archives of the United States, Department of Justice Foreign Funds Control Docket Files, Records of the Office of Alien Property, Docket Files of Business Enterprises #371-C, Record Number 131, Container Number 902.

71 "Bat'a Maryland Plant Linked in US Files to Nazi War Machine," *Baltimore Sun*, July 20, 1941, 1.

when the latter was at its most vulnerable. When faced with the competition of Bat'a, and especially a Bat'a factory with hundreds if not thousands of American workers, EJ personnel throatily decried the firm's business practices and sought government intervention. Though they came from the same current of modernity, EJ felt threatened by the methods of its eastern bank. Beginning as early as 1931, there was wariness evident in the way EJ approached Bat'a. One could argue that this hostility toward Bat'a was a natural outcome of capitalistic competition. Indeed, there are multiple examples of shoe manufacturers protesting the competition of Bat'a throughout its global expansion. Yet Bat'a was a profound threat to the smaller shoe manufacturers, not a fully mechanized mass-scale operation like EJ. Indeed, it seems unlikely, given that the price of Bat'a Belcamp shoes was not undercutting that of similar American-made shoes, that EJ would have been at serious risk with a Bat'a headquarters in the United States. George F. Johnson knew this and advised his managers in 1937 that

> While we may not get our labor as cheap as Bat'a, I think we get everything else quite as cheap as he does, except what we have top pay for duty on quebracho and hides. In other words, I don't think we need to run away from Bat'a. If we use our hides, we will be able to compete even with Bat'a, by making wage adjustments when necessary, and handling our business in the good old-fashioned way, by savings and economical management.[72]

Interestingly, though, George F.'s private confidence did not stop him from mobilizing his considerable connections to ensure the failure of Bat'a in the United States, and to ensure that protectionist measures stayed in force, which they did. Bat'a scaled back its plans at Belcamp—in fact, its unique ability to vulcanize rubber was the only thing that kept the US government from shutting down its operations—and abandoned its dream of a permanent move to the United States. In what must have been a bitter irony, the

72 George F. Johnson to all Executives, December 4, 1937, George F. Johnson Papers, Box 15, Syracuse University Library Manuscript Collections.

Czechoslovak company that had heartily promoted the culture and business practices of the United States since 1905 was shut out of the United States at its most desperate hour. The last laugh, however, went to Bat'a.

While having a terrible time dealing with being blacklisted, maneuvering through Nazi occupation, and then losing all operations in Czechoslovakia, Poland, Yugoslavia, and Hungary to nationalization, Bat'a was able to maintain itself as a viable company during World War II and transition into the new postwar era. It was able to do so because of its global footprint; its factories and retail stores in South and Southeast Asia, Africa, Western Europe, Canada, Latin America, and the Middle East remained in company hands. The high tariffs of Smoot-Hawley grew less effective on the global shoe industry after World War II as manufacturing increasingly moved to the Global South. Thus, Bat'a survived and currently thrives in the world of shoe manufacturing and retail, selling some 150 million pairs of shoes a year.[73] Endicott-Johnson no longer exists.

This is not to say, though, that the idealized company town of Zlín was much better off than those of Broome County. Both sites became victims of the race for cheap labor in shoe manufacturing, and neither place manufactures shoes these days. Rather, what is to be taken from a comparison between these companies is that the welfare capitalism as practiced by Bat'a and EJ allowed for a remarkable shield for their workers during the Great Depression, and this shield was abandoned by both companies at different times and for different reasons. Their divergence in their approach to globalization foreshadowed the ways in which they would handle the macroeconomic transition to globalized manufacturing. A group of maverick Czech speakers from the margins of Moravia first discovered globalization's economic potential in the world of footwear. The Bat'a Company's willingness to export its company town model allowed it to find cheap labor and produce with that labor for local markets. By so doing, Bat'a pulled off a miraculous expansion amid

73 "About us." https://thebatacompany.com/ Last accessed October 12, 2023.

the Great Depression and then an even more impressive recovery in the face of geopolitical uncertainty. EJ fostered an emotional attachment to a specific location and was uninterested in the possibilities of cheap labor outside of the United States. Of course, what proved better for the workers of the world remains debatable.

Chapter 6

LATVIA

BETWEEN ECONOMIC RECOVERY AND THE GREAT DEPRESSION: MULTI-ETHNIC ENTREPRENEURSHIP, FRAGMENTATION, NATIONALIZATION[1]

Katja Wezel

In January 1932, the stock corporation Mineral Oil Works A. Oehlrich & Co. with a share capital of 2.5 million lats, was forced to initiate bankruptcy proceedings. Founded in 1874, it had until then been one of Riga's most successful companies. It had managed to re-emerge as a flourishing producer of oil products in the 1920s, even though Riga's industries had been shut down and its machinery deported to Russia during World War I. A document issued by the Riga Exchange Committee, in charge of the bankruptcy proceedings and creditors' meetings, sums up the company's problems in 1932:

> In the last year, the stock cooperation [A. Oehlrich & Co.] began to experience payment difficulties due to a lack of circulating funds, mainly as a result of the contract concluded three years earlier for the purchase of oil at fixed prices. However, through the ongoing struggle between U.S.S.R. and American Oil Companies, oil prices on the world market have fallen sharply, as a consequence of which the company has been subject to heavy losses because the

1 The archival work for this article was made possible by a stipend from the Alexander-von-Humboldt Foundation and a stay at the Latvijas Universitāte (LU) in Riga. The author would like to thank the Humboldt-Foundation and Ilgvars Misāns for their support. At the Historical State Archive of Latvia (LVVA), the author especially thanks Īra Zaneriba for her help in finding relevant files and providing access to archival documents.

> oil is expensive to purchase under the existing contract; on the other hand, the general economic crisis and the unexpectedly high credit restrictions by local banks have had an impact on the company.[2]

With the start of the Great Depression, companies such as Oehlrich suffered from the decline in world market prices, especially when they were buying their commodities under the conditions of old agreements for high prices. In an attempt to stabilize its own economy and its currency, Latvia's authorities stuck to the Gold Standard longer than most other states in Europe, which made the country's exports expensive and less competitive on the world market. Seeing inflation as their main threat, the government also severely limited options to obtain credit, while at the same time heavily restricting the influx of foreign capital and the possibilities of conducting business in foreign currencies.

This article will assess the revival of the economy in Latvia after World War I, its decline during the Great Depression, the reaction by the Latvian government, and the effects on large businesses and entrepreneurs. In doing so, the article will rely on primary sources from the Riga Exchange Committee, responsible for Riga's trade and for overseeing bankruptcy proceedings of members of the Riga Stock-Exchange Association. Other sources are from the Riga Association of Factory Owners; "Konzums," that is, one of the biggest cooperatives in interwar Latvia; files of companies that experienced financial difficulties, if available; documents from *Latvijas Kredītbanka*, the main loan provider in the mid-1930s; and contemporary statistical reports by state agencies and other institutions.

Latvia, one of East-Central Europe's newly emerged states in the interwar period, has so far received little attention from historians dealing with the Great Depression, or generally with Central and Eastern Europe's economic history in the interwar years. With the exception of the Latvian emigré economist Arnolds Aizsilnieks, whose seminal work *Latvijas saimniecības vēsture* covers the period

2 Rīgas Biržas komiteja (Riga Exchange Committee), Mineralelļu Fabrikas Akciju Sabiedrības "A.Oehlrich & Co" Valdes, Lugums, January 5, 1932, Latvijas Valsts vēstures arhīvs, LVVA 3143-1-1727, 1. Translation from Latvian by the author.

1914–45, the economic history of Latvia during the Great Depression has rarely been discussed in detail.[3] Aizsilnieks also coauthored a study on one of Latvia's most successful textile companies in interwar Latvia, *Rīgas Audums*; the study provides detailed information on the effects of Latvia's financial and economic policies during and after the Great Depression.[4] Economic historian Viesturs Karnups has focused on Latvia's trade policies with various countries during the interwar years and the devaluation of the lat in 1936.[5] Aivars Stranga's latest works on Latvia's authoritarian leader Kārlis Ulmanis and his economic policy, and on the fateful year 1939, discuss the effects of the Great Depression, which contributed to Latvia becoming an autocratic regime in 1934; but he focuses on the post-1934 period and not on the beginnings of the Great Depression in Latvia or the period running up to it.[6]

On November 18, 1918, the Latvian nation successfully put itself on the map of post-World War I Europe with its declaration of statehood. During the Latvian War of Independence (1918–1921), the Latvian government gained control over its territory, kicking out the Baltic German Landeswehr and German Freikorps units, as well as the Bolsheviks, who had installed a Soviet Republic in parts of the country. Latvia's statehood and democracy were manifested with the adoption of its constitution on June 20, 1922. This was followed by the introduction of a Latvian national currency, the lats, on August 3, 1922. In financial policies, interwar Latvia followed the example of France. The lat, established in 1922, was fixed to the gold franc and followed the rules of the Latin Monetary Union. The smaller Latvian coins "santimi" were named after the French

3 Arnolds Aizsilnieks, *Latvijas saimniecības vēsture, 1914–1945* (Sundbyberg: Daugava, 1968).

4 Nicholas Balabkins and Arnolds Aizsilnieks, *Entrepreneur in a Small Country. A Case Study against the Background of the Latvian Economy, 1919–1940* (Hickville, NY: Exposition Press, 1975).

5 Viesturs Pauls Karnups, *The Little Country That Could. Latvian Economic Relations and Foreign Trade with Various Countries in the Interwar Period* (Riga: University of Latvia, 2022).

6 Aivars Stranga, *Kārļa Ulmaņa Autoritārā Režīma Saimnieciskā Politika, 1934–1940* (Rīga: Latvijas Universitāte, 2017); Aivars Stranga, *Latvija: Neatkarības pēdējais celines. 1939. gada 23. Augusts–1940. gada 17. Jūnijs* (Rīga: Mansards, 2022).

"centimes."[7] On September 7, 1922, Latvia established its national bank.

Article 2 of the Constitution of Latvia stressed that "the sovereign power of the State of Latvia is vested in the people of Latvia," and thus avoided any ethnic connotations. However, the statements and actions of many Latvian statesmen at the time made it clear that a crucial aim of this state would be to overcome the former domination by the Baltic German minority, which had held key positions in the country and the capital city Riga until World War I. Latvians should now obtain their rightful place in their own state and the power to rule themselves.[8] This was particularly hard to achieve in the economic sphere. Although a number of Latvian entrepreneurs had successfully established their own companies during tsarist Russia's belated industrialization, ethnic Latvians were a minority in the economic sector.

Latvians were a people of farmers, not industrialists or traders. It became one of the main goals of Latvia's post-World War I governments to remedy this and give Latvians more influence in running their own economy. With the aim of strengthening the role of ethnic Latvians in business, the government of Latvia set out to diminish the influence of the country's ethnic minorities. The result of this policy was a fragmentation of the economic sphere. These policies were sharpened after the start of the worldwide depression in 1929 and even more so after the coup d'état of Kārlis Ulmanis on May 15, 1934, when his policy "Latvia for the Latvians" won over. At the same time, especially during the 1920s, continuities with regard to business connections from the tsarist period were also traceable in Latvia's economy, leading to an alternation of continuities, fragmentation, discontinuities, and the creation of new barriers. In this chapter, I will address these different policies implemented in Latvia, particularly in Latvia's capital and economic power center Riga during the 1920s and as a result of the Great Depression.

7 Aizsilnieks, *Latvijas saimniecības vēsture*, 180.

8 Per Bolin has analyzed the politics of making Latvia more Latvian in his monograph about the University of Latvia in Riga. See Per Bolin, *Between National and Academic Agendas: Ethnic Policies and "National Disciplines" at the University of Latvia, 1919–1940* (Södertörn: Huddige Södertörns Högskola, 2012).

For the term "fragmentation," I follow the definition of Klaus Richter in his recently published monograph, where he argues that fragmentation describes "a gradual process of breaking and reconfiguring networks of economic, political, social and cultural exchange."[9] Under continuities, I understand policies and actions that would result in keeping business practices and trade connections from the Russian Empire alive—practices, which were extremely important for the renewal of Latvia's trade after 1920. Discontinuities were manifold in a new state such as Latvia, but it is important to also point toward continuities, that is, practices where actors chose or were forced to rely on old traditions. Finally, the economic problems of the interwar years and the Great Depression led to the creation of new barriers in trade and finances. Aiming to make Latvia more self-sufficient and to keep the national currency strong and stable entailed a number of measures, which reduced the scope of action for entrepreneurs.

6.1 Latvia's Economic Recovery after World War I

After World War I, Latvia faced numerous problems. For one, the country was depopulated because of war casualties, flight, and deportations during the war. The territory of Latvia lost 1 million people, and its population decreased from 2.6 million in 1914 to 1.6 million in 1920.[10] The loss of human capital was a crucial problem. In percentage terms, the capital Riga experienced even higher losses. Whereas the census of 1913 had counted 472,068 residents, by 1920 Riga's population had decreased to 166,536 inhabitants.[11] War casualties were only a small part of the population losses. Many residents had fled or were evacuated and did not return to Latvia for political or economic reasons. Tsarist war policies led to the evacuation of 500 industrial enterprises from Latvia to Russia; 200,000 skilled workers were resettled with their companies and some of

9 Klaus Richter, *Fragmentation in East Central Europe. Poland and the Baltics, 1915–1929* (Oxford: Oxford University Press, 2020), 3.

10 Balabkins and Aizsilnieks, *Entrepreneur in a Small Country*, 30.

11 "Rigas civiliedzīvotaji pēc tautības īstā pilsētas novadā 1867.–1920. g.," in *Rigas pilsētas statistiskā gada grāmata 1920–1922* (Riga: Müllera drukatava, 1923), 12.

them never returned.[12] A part of the former Baltic German landowners and also German farmers with medium-sized farms, who had only been settled in Latvia after the 1905 Revolution, left Latvia as a result of the land reform.[13] The reform distributed Latvia's farmland among Latvian peasants while the former owners were expropriated without compensation.[14]

The new Latvian state and especially its largest port and formerly key industrial center, Riga, suffered enormous difficulties after the war. Riga had been right on the frontline between 1915 and 1917, resulting in the evacuation of almost all of its industries. Between September 1917 and November 1918, Riga was occupied by the German army, and from December 1918 to May 1919 it was taken over by Bolshevik forces. Hence, its economy was in ruins when the first national government finally established self-rule over Latvia's territory and drove out the last remnants of the Bolshevik forces in eastern Latgale in the winter of 1920/21.

Latvia's state founders envisioned Latvia primarily as an agrarian society with (ethnic) Latvian farmers generating a surplus that would be exported through the country's ports. To revive trade and the economy, the resurrection of Latvia's ports, and especially its biggest and formerly most successful port of Riga, was of utmost importance. To achieve this, the national Latvian government was even willing to work together with the city's previously leading Baltic German community, whose economic representatives were organized in the powerful Riga Exchange Committee (Germ. *Rigaer Börsen-Comité*, Latv. *Rīgas Biržas komitēja*), which functioned both as a representation of entrepreneurs trading at Riga's Stock-Exchange and as a Chamber of Commerce. It was not only an economic but also a political institution. Since 1816, it had effectively

12 Aivars Stranga and Gatis Krūmiņš, "Von der Marktwirtschaft über die Staatswirtschaft zur Planwirtschaft 1918 bis 1990," in *Lettland 1918–2018. Ein Jahrhundert Staatlichkeit*, eds. Ivars Ījabs, Jan Kusber, Ilgvars Misāns, and Erwin Oberländer (Paderborn: Schöningh, 2018), 183.

13 Michael Garleff, "Die Deutschbalten als nationale Minderheit in den unabhängigen Staaten Estland und Lettland," in *Deutsche Geschichte im Osten Europas. Baltische Länder*, ed. Gert von Pistohlkors (Berlin: Siedler Verlag, 1994), 490.

14 Erwin Oberländer, "Stärken und Schwächen des neuen Staates," in *Lettland 1918–2018. Ein Jahrhundert Staatlichkeit*, eds. Ivars Ījabs, Jan Kusber, Ilgvars Misāns, and Erwin Oberländer (Paderborn: Schöningh, 2018), 31.

been responsible for running and modernizing the harbor of Riga. The port had suffered during the blockade in World War I. Four years of nonuse left its marks as the port was always prone to sand up. Russian war authorities had evacuated the port's ice-breaker, its power shovels, and other machinery that might have been used for reconstruction.

To get the ports up and running again became a primary task for the government after the War of Independence was won. In 1922, the Riga Exchange Committee received a loan from the Latvian government for the repair and modernization of Riga's port and shipping facilities.[15] The Latvian government also helped recover the power shovels, which were owned by the Exchange Committee but which the Russian government had evacuated during the war. They were located in the bay of Haapsalu, now independent Estonia.[16] Taking into account that in 1922, the Riga Stock-Exchange Association and its executive Exchange Committee were still largely dominated by Baltic German entrepreneurs and merchants, this level of support by the Latvian government was quite extraordinary. However, the Latvian government had basically no choice: It did not possess any infrastructure needed to dredge the ports on its national territory. By recovering the old possessions of the Exchange Committee and bringing them to Riga, the Latvian government also supported the recovery of its national economy.[17] In return, the Riga Exchange Committee agreed that its power shovels could also be used to remove sand from the shipping passages in Ventspils and Liepāja.

In the last decade before the war, Riga had emerged as the port with the highest sales volume in the Russian Empire.[18] This success of the Riga port was based not only on a high number of agricultural exports, such as timber, flax, grain, and eggs, but also on

15 Loan Agreement, Pagarinajums. Parada Sihme, January 18, 1922, LVVA 3143-1-1621, 313.

16 Ingenieurabteilung des Rigaer Börsenkomitee, letter from December 1, 1920, LVVA 3143-1-1621, 99–102.

17 See list of all evacuated power shovels and other shipping equipment, October 30, 1920, LVVA 3143-1-1621, 77.

18 Katja Wezel, "The Most Successful Trading Hub in Late Imperial Russia: Using Historical GIS to Map Riga as a Global Port City," *Zeitschrift Für Ostmitteleuropaforschung* 70, no. 3 (2021): 389–415.

an increasing number of imports for Riga's native industries which thrived in the period up to World War I. While Riga stayed an export-oriented port with a positive trade balance, imports slowly caught up. After World War I, the situation was reversed: cut off from the Russian hinterland, Riga's export numbers dwindled, while Latvia needed imports, especially foreign machinery, to jump-start its economy. This led to a constant trade deficit with imports exceeding exports throughout the 1920s. However, the shipping traffic increased steadily. The number of ships entering the ports of Latvia (Riga, Liepāja, and Ventspils) rose by a factor of 2.5 between 1920 and 1928—from 1,679 ships with a net tonnage of 479,801 tons in 1920 to 4,335 ships with 2,014,962 tons in 1928.[19] Compared to 1913, when all Latvian ports together had received 5,289 ships with an overall tonnage of 3,591,195, these numbers were still considerably lower.[20] Yet, they were nevertheless substantial, considering how the territories that Latvia's ports were serving had shrunk. Over the course of the 1920s and 1930s, the Latvian economy slowly managed to reduce the passivity of its trade balance. The trade deficit, which had amounted to Ls 100,995,000 in 1925, fell to just Ls 49,357,000 in 1928.[21] Only in 1932, when Latvia was still struggling with the effects of the Great Depression, did its trade balance turn active.[22] It was slightly passive again in the years 1933–36, before Latvia achieved a trade surplus in 1937, which it continued to keep until the outbreak of World War II.[23]

After the signing of the Latvian-Soviet Trade Agreement on June 2, 1927, transit import and export also increased. The main commodities exported from the Soviet Union via Latvia in the first year after the signing of the Latvian-Soviet trade agreement were timber, flax, lentils, eggs, and poultry—mirroring the goods that had

19 Referat verlesen vom Syndikus des Rigaer Börsenkomitees W. Held in der Festsitzung der Rigaer Stadtverwaltung, October 11, 1929, in LVVA 3143-1-1631, 398.

20 For comparative numbers from the imperial Russian period, see "Kuģu kustiba Latvijas ostās 1902–1923," in *Latvijas Ārejā Tirdznieciba un Kuģu Kustiba 1923*, ed. Valsts Statistiskā Pārvalde (Riga: Valsts Statistiskā Pārvalde, 1924), 123.

21 LVVA 3143-1-1631 (see footnote 15), 397.

22 Tab. 1. "Ārēja tirdzniecība 1921.–1938. g.," in *Latvijas Ārējā Tirdzniecība un Tranzits 1938*, ed. Valsts Statistiskā Pārvalde (Riga: Valsts Statistiskā Pārvalde, 1939), IX.

23 Tab. 1. "Ārēja tirdzniecība 1921.–1938. g."

already been exported from Russia via Latvia's ports before the war.[24] Important Soviet imports via Latvia were machinery, fertilizers, wool, and lead.[25] Most of the transit exports went via rail to Riga and from there by ship to Western Europe. For imports, the Latvian ports played a less significant role than for exports, since import commodities went more often by rail to the Prussian border town of Eydtkuhnen and continued from there by railroad to the Soviet Union.[26]

The new Latvian government also supported the recovery of the industrial sector, although what counted as an "industrial enterprise" differed from the prewar years. By 1923, Latvia overall had 2,032 industrial establishments employing 44,100 workers. The number rose to 5,977 industrial establishments with a total of 117,200 employees in 1938.[27] This looks like a remarkable increase. Still, in comparison to the fact that in 1913 the city of Riga alone had 372 industrial enterprises employing more than 86,000 people, it becomes obvious that, first, the prewar levels of economic development could not be reached and, second, most industrial enterprises and trading businesses in Latvia after World War I remained rather small with only a few employees.[28] According to Balabkins and Aizsilnieks, the average industrial firm in interwar Latvia employed only 17 people.[29] By counting more businesses as industrial enterprises, including those that had been regarded as crafts prior to World War I, the Latvian government was able to count more ethnic Latvians as business owners. The same happened in the trading sector. As the Latvian political scientist and contemporary observer Bilmanis (Bihlmans) explained in his 1926 handbook about the political and economic foundations of the Baltic republic

24 Ein Jahr Handelsvertrag zwischen Lettland und der Union der Sozialistischen Räterepublik, in LVVA 3143-1-17, 21.

25 Ein Jahr Handelsvertrag zwischen Lettland und der Union der Sozialistischen Räterepublik, 21.

26 "Der russische Eisenbahntransit über Lettland," *Rigaer Wirtschaftszeitung*, April 2, 1927.

27 Balabkins and Aizsilnieks, *Entrepreneur in a Small Country*, 58

28 For prewar numbers see: Die Industrie Rigas 1913, in LVVA 2765-1-84, 47. The number of employees varies between 85,432 and 87,606. See also the number of employees and turnover of Rigas industrial enterprises in the year 1913, in LVVA 2765-1-84, 10.

29 Balabkins and Aizsilnieks, *Entrepreneur in a Small Country*, 59.

of Latvia: "In Latvia, anyone can trade after purchasing the appropriate trading certificate, so it is understandable that the number of traders has increased considerably."[30]

With their aim to empower ethnic Latvians, nationalists increasingly fought on two fronts: against the former German-speaking elite, which was portrayed as "the Germans" even though many of them had roots in the territory of Latvia going back several centuries, and against the Jewish minority, which was very active in the trade sector and industries. During the 1920s and 1930s, right-wing Latvian newspapers directed their rhetorical attacks mostly against "the Germans." This was a consequence of the hostilities and the economic, social, and ethnic struggles that had manifested themselves during the Revolution of 1905–7, when Baltic German landowners and industrialists had been the main representatives of power against whom the Latvian workers and farmers stood up.[31] In the 1920s and 1930s, the memory of this revolution and its military repression still lingered and strongly resonated with those in power (Table 6.1).

The distinctions along lines of ethnicity were therefore extremely sharp during the interwar era, especially in the economic sector. As Balabkins and Aizsilnieks, describing the economic sphere of interwar Latvia, argued:

> A disproportionate number of one-man proprietorships in industry belonged to Latvia's Jews and Germans [. . .]. Another revealing feature of Latvia's industrial corporations is the fact that the bulk of the shares outstanding belonged to foreigners [. . .]. Usually the balance of stock not owned by foreigners was held not by ethnic Latvians but by Latvia's Jews and Germans. And ethnic Latvians resented this very much.[32]

30 Alfred Bihlmans. *Die politischen und wirtschaftlichen Grundlagen der Baltischen Republik Lettland. Ein Handbuch für Journalisten, Politiker und Wirtschaftler* (Bibliothek des baltischen Ostdienst-Verlages für Wirtschaft und Recht, Riga, Lettland Nr. 18/1926), 83.

31 Arnolds Spekke, *History of Latvia. An Outline* (Riga: Jumava, 2006 [1948]), 288.

32 Balabkins and Aizsilnieks, *Entrepreneur in a Small Country*, 61.

Table 6.1 Census Data for Language Groups/Nationalities of Latvia in Percent

Ethnicity (tautība)	*1897*[a]	*1920*	*1925*	*1930*
Latvian	68.3	74.89	75.42	75.25
German	6.2	3.75	3.96	3.78
Russian	12	10.19	10.23	10.4
Polish	3.4	3.37	2.78	3.12
Jewish	7.4	5.13	5.33	5.1
Lithuanian	1.4	1.65	1.29	1.4
Estonian	0.9	0.56	0.44	0.41
Others	0.4	0.46	0.55	0.54

[a] In the all-Russian census of 1897, the population was not asked for their nationality or ethnicity but "which is the language most commonly used in your household," in addition to accounting for their faith. All Latvian censuses after 1920 registered the self-proclaimed nationality.

Source: Table after "Latvijas iedzīvotāju nacionālais sastāvs," in Marģers Skujenieka, *Treša Tautas Skaitīšana Latvijā 1930. gadā* (Riga: Valsts Statistiskā Pārvalde, 1930), 68.

Ethnicity (Latv. *tautība*) became a strong argument in Latvian politics. By implementing policies that would help empower ethnic Latvians, the government continuously ethnified the political and economic spheres, thereby hindering the process of creating one single people of Latvia. Instead of getting rid of ethnic boundaries, Latvian politicians manifested them and thereby promoted fragmentation. In the early 1930s, the economic crisis further magnified existing particularization and divisions between Latvia's ethnic groups.

The traditional economic institutions on the territory of Latvia, in particular the Riga Exchange Committee with its strong independent position and responsibility for the trade of Latvia's largest port, were not to the liking of the Latvian government. The Latvian Ministries of Trade and Finance were eager to gain more influence and become the primary actors in Latvia's (and Riga's) trade. In July 1920, the chair of the Riga Exchange Committee, a Baltic German, complained in a letter to the "information office of minorities" about the policies and laws that the Latvian government was seeking to implement in order to regulate the stock-market.[33]

33 Letter of the Rigaer Börsen-Comité to the Information Office of Minorities, July 31, 1920, LVVA 3134-1-16, 170–72.

He expressed his fear that "the main motivation behind the actions of the Latvian government is their desire to win significant leverage about the assets of the Stock-Exchange Association and the Exchange Committee."[34]

That a complete takeover and nationalization of the Riga Exchange Committee by the Latvian Finance Ministry could be prevented, at least until 1939, was also due to the fact that Riga's merchants and entrepreneurs quickly reoriented themselves and found a person whom they felt represented the interests of ethnic Latvians (and thus appeased the Latvian government), but who was also well respected among Riga's polyethnic and largely German-speaking business community. In 1921, the Riga Stock-Exchange Association elected Jānis Zēbergs (Johann Seeberg) as the new chair of the Riga Exchange Committee. Zēbergs was trusted and well-connected both among the Latvian- and the German-speaking communities. This clearly helped the Exchange Committee to survive in the early years of the Latvian republic. Zēbergs was born in 1871 in Cērkste and studied at the Riga Polytechnical Institute before becoming a leading figure in the Baltic German shipping company Helmsing and Grimm. After briefly serving as minister of trade and industry in newly independent Latvia in 1919, he became a member of the supervisory council of the newly founded Bank of Latvia in 1922, while also chairing the Riga Exchange Committee.[35] In 1923, he became coowner of the well-known Baltic German Helmsing and Grimm shipping company.[36] It is clear from the obituaries published on the occasion of Zēbergs' death in 1927 (and the fact that both a Latvian and a German pastor spoke at his funeral) that Latvians *and* Baltic Germans regarded him as one of their own.[37]

With the new Statute of the Riga Stock Exchange, adopted on March 7, 1924, the Latvian government ensured that ethnic Latvians would have the majority in this important institution.

34 Letter of the Rigaer Börsen-Comité to the Information Office of Minorities, 171.

35 Ineta Lipša, *Latvijas Bankas Vēsture, 1922–1940* (Riga: Latvijas Banka, 2022), 64.

36 See Firmeninhaber seit der Gründung, in family file Helmsing, Deutsch-Baltische Genealogische Gesellschaft Darmstadt, unnumbered.

37 See "Jahnis Seebergs," *Latwis*, September 6, 1927, and "Die Beehrdigung Konsul J. Seebergs," *Rigasche Rundschau* September 19, 1927. See also bilingual invitation card for the funeral service of Jānis Zeebergs/Johann Seeberg, LVVA 3143-1-27, 245–46.

The new law stipulated that two-thirds of the members of the Exchange Committee had to be citizens of Latvia with Latvian ethnicity [*latviešu tautības Latvijas pilsoņiem*].[38] With this change, the *Börsen-Comité* became the *Biržas komiteja* because the majority of members had to have Latvian ethnicity (*tautiba*). The Exchange Committee was enlarged to twenty (instead of the former fifteen), of which twelve had to be ethnic Latvians. The revision of the statute meant that Latvians were actually overrepresented in Riga's leading institution of trade. They did not make up two-thirds of Riga's merchants and entrepreneurs because trade and industries were dominated by Germans and Jews. Yet, the new Statute on the Riga Stock Exchange contributed to the reconfiguration of Riga's economic networks and—since Riga was Latvia's capital of trade and the main economic center of the country—by extension also to the gradual replacement of the former Baltic German elite with a new ethnic Latvian elite. In exchange for the empowerment of Latvian entrepreneurs, the Latvian government, at least at this point, dropped its initial plan to have permanent and mandatory members of the Finance Ministry as associates on the Exchange Committee. Therefore, the Riga Exchange Committee continued to be a relatively independent institution with its members voted into office by the Riga Stock-Exchange Association.

6.2 Continuities—Latvia's Timber Industry and Butter Exports

Despite the economic fragmentation resulting from new borders and destruction through war, evacuations, and population decline, continuities from the tsarist period still played a considerable role in Latvia's economy and its postwar recovery. In the following, I will focus on two main export commodities of interwar Latvia: timber and butter. I will look at the developments of exports until right before the Great Depression and later assess their impact on the economic recovery in the late 1930s. Both commodities had already been key commodities of export for Latvia's ports in the

38 See the published version of the law in *Valdības Vēstnesis*, March 8, 1924, LVVA 3131-1-17, 220–21.

tsarist period. Sawmills and the wood-producing industry belonged to the industrial sector, whereas butter became Latvia's most successfully promoted agricultural export item in the interwar period. Thus, these two commodities also allow us to reflect more broadly on the recovery of Latvia's exports in the postwar period and the developments after the Great Depression.

In 1929, the timber and lumber industry was still Latvia's largest industrial sector, employing 20 percent of all industrial workers.[39] Being a sector that required comparatively small investments and machinery to operate, it had recovered relatively easily from the war evacuations during the 1920s. The number of businesses grew; however, the total number of workers in each enterprise shrank (compared to the tsarist period). Whereas 99 companies in the wood processing industry employed 11,304 workers on the territory of Latvia in 1910, there were 343 companies with a total of 10,000 workers in 1925.[40] Before World War I, the average steam-powered sawmill had more than 100 employees, and several employed more than 200 workers. Meanwhile, in 1925, the average number of workers in any wood-producing company in Latvia was only 29.[41] Latvia's sawmills also used rather old and inefficient log-cutting saws. Yet, since the government of Latvia owned most forests and sold only small woodlots at annual auctions, it was not economically viable for entrepreneurs to invest in modern equipment.[42]

While the large Russian hinterland was gone and the railroad infrastructure designed to connect Riga with central Russia was less useful, the well-established production cycles of floating timber on the river Daugava and its tributaries still worked. In addition, decisions about railroad construction in the Russian Empire had led to an alignment of the railroad lines with Latvia's main ports: all three of them, Riga, Ventspils, and Liepāja, had railroad connections, which also allowed for the transport of commodities within Latvia, at least from East to West. While a number of railroads and bridges had been destroyed during World War I, these at least had to be

39 Balabkins and Aizsilnieks, *Entrepreneur in a Small Country*, 59.

40 Bihlmans, *Die politischen und wirtschaftlichen Grundlagen*, 76.

41 Bihlmans, *Die politischen und wirtschaftlichen Grundlagen*, 76.

42 Balabkins and Aizsilnieks, *Entrepreneur in a Small Country*, 60.

repaired only and not built from scratch. Latvia's timber merchants also had well-established personal contacts abroad from before the war, especially on the all-important London market.[43] The United Kingdom had long been Latvia's main trading partner. Its building boom in the 1920s led to an increasing demand of timber.[44] British merchants knew and trusted their counterparts in Latvia. Even though the timber industry was now operating in a newly independent country, name recognition with old trading partners still worked.

A good example of continuities with the postwar era is the business of the Baltic German entrepreneur August Edgar Grube (1874–1930), who had started his timber trading company in 1907. Before World War I, he was also the head of the timber delegation within the Riga Exchange Committee and one of Riga's major timber merchants.[45] He appears to have successfully revived his timber export company "A. E. Grube" after World War I, most likely due his personal business connections from before the war. From 1919 to 1924, Grube served as director of the Riga Bourse Bank, which was one of the few banks operating in postwar Latvia whose exchange bills and creditworthiness were known abroad and accepted by foreign merchants and companies in the early 1920s. Grube was one of only two Baltic Germans elected as a member of the supervisory council of the Bank of Latvia, serving from 1928 to 1929.[46] His connections abroad and his experience in the banking sector likely played a role in the decision to take him on board the supervisory council, although he was a member of the Baltic German community and therefore not the kind of person the Latvian government wished to empower. Still, despite his numerous professional achievements, Grube's company faced financial difficulties in 1929. On October 20,

43 Cf. the life story of Mendel Berlin, father of the philosopher Sir Isaiah Berlin, who was born in Riga: Mendel Berlin, "For the Benefit of My Son," in *The Book of Isaiah. Personal Impressions of Isaiah Berlin*, ed. Henry Hardy (Woodbridge, NJ: Boydell Press, 2009), 309.

44 Martin Bemmann, "Im Zentrum des Markts. Zur Rolle Großbritanniens im internationalen Holzhandel der 1930er Jahre," *Vierteljahresschrift für Sozial- und Wirtschaftsgeschichte* 99, no. 2 (2012): 151.

45 See the report of the timber delegation to the *Riga Börsen-Komitee*, May 12, 1911, signed by A. E. Grube, LVVA 3143-1-201, 312.

46 Lipša, *Latvijas Bankas Vēsture*, 73.

1929, Riga's newspapers started to report about Grube's bankruptcy.[47] This was not yet a result of the worldwide Great Depression, which only began after the Wall Street Crash on October 24, 1929, but rather a consequence of dramatically falling prices in the timber market due to increasing competition. With its first 5-Year Plan (1928–32), the Soviet Union claimed Russia's old role as a major European timber supplier and started to flood the market with cheap timber, especially on the London market.[48] This put pressure on all timber-exporting countries around the Baltic Sea, including Latvia. The timber trade confirms the argument made by other economic historians that Eastern Europe was already sliding into a recession well before the Wall Street Crash occurred.[49] Grube died shortly after his company went bankrupt in 1930. Latvia's timber industry recovered in the mid-1930s although it did not regain its high export numbers from 1928. In the 1930s, the textile industry became Latvia's most successful sector in terms of exports.

Another important continuity to the imperial period was the export of butter through Latvia's ports, especially Ventspils and Riga. Between 1901 and 1902, Riga, as the first port in the Russian Empire, constructed a cold store in its harbor, financed by the London Society Union.[50] This enabled the establishment of the Siberian butter trade through the Riga port handled by the company Helmsing and Grimm.[51] By 1906, Riga held the top position in Russia's butter exports, with 59.5 percent of butter being exported through its port.[52] After that, Riga's position as a butter exporter

47 "Bankrots par 80 miljoneem," *Rīga*, October 20, 1929. See also "Zum Bankrott der Firma A. E. Grube," *Rigasche* Rundschau, October 23, 1929.

48 Bemmann, "Im Zentrum des Markts," 157. Elina Kuorelahti, *The Political Economy of International Commodity Cartels. An Economic History of the European Timber Trade in the 1930s* (London: Routledge, 2021), 28.

49 Patricia Clavin, *The Great Depression in Europe, 1929–1939* (Basingstoke: Palgrave Macmillan, 2000), 4.

50 Arnolds Papst, *Hafen von Riga* (Riga: Buchdruckerei von W. F. Häcker, 1908), 37.

51 See the letter of Helmsing and Grimm to the Riga Exchange Committee, January 19, 1902, informing the Exchange Committee about the approval of exporters and importers of Siberian butter to handle large quantities of butter and export them via the Riga port, LVVA 3143-1-1470, 56.

52 Bruno von Schrenck, *Beiträge Zur Statistik der Stadt Riga und ihrer Verwaltung* (Riga: Müllersche Buchdruckerei, 1909), 144.

declined because the shareholders of the Moscow-Windau [Moscow-Ventspils] Railroad successfully redirected most of the Siberian butter trade through the port of Ventspils.[53] Still, both ports had the facilities and the connections to enable a revival of the butter trade in interwar Latvia, and they used these opportunities during the 1920s and 1930s. The existing infrastructure—direct railroad access to the port and cooling facilities—allowed Latvia to export butter produced by its dairy farmers to consumers in Western Europe. Butter became one of Latvia's most sought-after products, which is remarkable since the butter trade out of Riga and Ventspils had initially relied entirely on butter from Siberia.[54] Pre-World War I production levels for Latvian butter had still been relatively small, even though they had increased in the last 3 years before the war.[55] During the 1920s, Latvia's dairy farmers stepped up and production levels for butter rose significantly.

Most Latvian farmers were organized in cooperatives. The cooperative movement in Latvia dated back to the late nineteenth century. The first cooperative Latvian dairy society had been founded in Spāre in 1909.[56] By 1914, there were already 95 dairy societies in the territory of Latvia producing butter.[57] After the war, the dairy societies were revived, also pushed by the new Law Governing Cooperative Societies and their Unions, already adopted by the provisional Latvian People's Council in 1919.[58] It stipulated that the establishment of a cooperative society required no permission from the government. The number of dairy societies increased

53 Wilhelm Lenz, *Die Entwicklung Rigas zur Großstadt* (Kitzingen a.M.: Holzer-Verlag, 1954), 66. See also Lidija Malahovska, *Latvijas transporta vēsture 19. gs. otrā puse—20. gs. sākums* (Riga: LV fonds, 1998), 181.

54 See Report on the Russian Butter Trade, by the British Consul in Riga Arthur Woodhouse, October 14, 1904, in FO 65-1692, 80: "Now, all butter exported from Riga is produced in Siberia and special arrangements have been made for its transport, storage etc."

55 In 1912, butter produced in Latvia was first exported to the United Kingdom, Germany, and the United States. See Stranga and Krūmiņš, "Von der Marktwirtschaft über die Staatswirtschaft zur Planwirtschaft," 184.

56 Arnolds P. Aizsilnieks, *The Cooperative Movement in Latvia* (Bonn: Baltisches Forschungsinstitut, 1962), 11.

57 Arnolds P. Aizsilnieks, *The Cooperative Movement in Latvia*, 11.

58 Arnolds P. Aizsilnieks, *The Cooperative Movement in Latvia*, 18.

significantly between 1922 and 1927. Whereas there had been 84 dairy societies in Latvia in 1922, their number rose to 465 in 1927, producing 11,000 tons of butter.[59] By 1929 the market was consolidated, and the number of dairy societies slightly decreased to 450, producing 15,000 tons of butter a year. The value of butter exports rose from Ls 2.8 million in 1922 to Ls 58.8 million in 1929.[60] By 1929, the export of butter made up 21.46 percent of Latvia's overall exports.[61] In the case of the butter exports, continuities with the tsarist period, such as the use of existing trade facilities and structures of Latvia's ports with partners in Western Europe, played just as important a role as the re-orientation of the Latvian economy to foster agricultural production and export.

6.3 Latvia and the Great Depression

When the Great Depression started, Latvia started feeling its effects in trade numbers with a certain delay. In 1930, numbers for exports and imports saw only a moderate decline. Compared to 1929, the combined value of exports and imports in 1930 was only 13 percent lower. However, by 1932—the nadir for Latvia's trade—the value of goods shipped by sea, exports and imports combined, declined by 70.5 percent in comparison to 1929.[62] The value of exports and imports in 1932 was even lower than the value of shipments in 1922, the first year when interwar Latvia started to record its overall trade numbers. The numbers were dramatic for both imports and exports, but especially for exports, considering that the revenues from the export of agricultural products were the main source of income for Latvia.

Latvia's wood-processing industry was hit particularly badly by the Great Depression. In addition to the worldwide recession,

59 For these and the following numbers, see table "Piensaimnieku sabiedrības," in Aizsilnieks, *Latvijas saimniecības vēsture*, 362.

60 Aizsilnieks, *Latvijas saimniecības vēsture*, 363.

61 Tab. 6 "Lauksaimniecības ražojumu un pārējo preču eksports 1921.–1930. g.," in *Latvijas Ārējā Tirdzniecība un Tranzits 1930. g.*, ed. Valsts Statistiskā Pārvalde (Riga: Valsts Statistiskā Pārvalde 1931), XII.

62 See table "Ārējās tirdzniecības (eksporta un importa) kopvērtība pa jūras ceļu," in *Rīgas Biržas Komitejas 1933. gada darbības pārskats* (Riga: Izdevējs, 1934), 121.

which led to a standstill in construction businesses and a significant decrease in the demand for timber, the timber prices were already in the process of falling due to the competition from low-priced Soviet timber exports. The slump in the timber industry explains the high number of bankruptcy cases among Riga's sawmills, naturally Latvia's center for the wood-processing industry and timber exports because of the importance of the river Daugava for the transport of timber. Whereas in 1927 Riga had 20 operating sawmills and other wood producers organized in the Riga Association of Factory Owners, the number of registered wood-producing industries in 1932 fell to just six.[63] Several sawmill owners and exporters of timber products in Latvia went bankrupt or were forced to close down between 1929 and 1932. The workforce in the Latvian timber industry almost halved: Whereas the wood-producing businesses still employed 9,131 workers in 1930, the number of employees decreased to 5,404 in 1932.[64] In the case of the timber industry, the effects of the Great Depression magnified an already existing problem due to the oversupply of timber as a result of Soviet overproduction.

The economic downfall hit even companies that had already operated in the tsarist period and had long-standing customer relationships with firms in the United Kingdom. On May 11, 1932, the well-established Jewish-run Bolderaja Flooring Mills and Timber Cooperation Philipp Schapiro with creditors in London, Glasgow, and Exeter had to ask the Riga Exchange Committee to install a bankruptcy commission:

> Since we are mainly engaged in the export of boards, and since we are producing these goods in large quantities in our enterprise, the fall of the English currency has meant that our enterprise has had to suffer heavy losses. A series of unfavorable circumstances forced us to resort to the

63 See membership lists of the Riga's Association of Factory Owners (Rigaer Fabrikantenverein) 1927 and 1932, in LVVA 2765-1-436, 104, 125.

64 Tab. VIII Rūpniecības uzņēmumi 1930.–1932. g. pēc nozarēm [Industrial enterprises 1930–1932 by industry], in *Rīgas Pilsētas statistiskā gada grāmata 1931–1932* (Riga: Rīgas pilsētas Statistiskā biroja publicējums, 1933), 104.

> establishment of a [bankruptcy] administration for our company.[65]

For this timber business, the United Kingdom's decision to devalue its currency had almost immediate consequences. On September 21, 1931, the British Parliament voted in favor of dropping out of the Gold Standard and the Bank of England transitioned to a flexible exchange rate.[66] In relation to the lat, the sterling pound lost about 40 percent of its value.[67] For Latvia, this financial decision by its biggest trading partner had a significant impact: For the United Kingdom, imports from countries like Latvia that stayed in the gold bloc were now far more expensive. The Scandinavian countries soon followed the UK's example by also devaluing their currencies and leaving the Gold Standard.[68] As a result, their products, often similar to Latvia's (such as Swedish timber, Danish butter, etc.), were cheaper and more competitive on the global market. Still, the Latvian government, afraid of inflation and focused on a stable currency, kept the lat pegged to the Gold Standard.

In order to keep the influx of foreign currency low, the Latvian government heavily restricted the use of foreign currency for payments after the devaluation of the pound sterling and other currencies that followed the lead of the United Kingdom. It installed a Currency Board (*Valūtas Kommisija*) at the Ministry of Finance to oversee transactions with foreign currencies.[69] Importing goods and materials from abroad became a hideous task, as entrepreneurs first had to receive an import license from the Latvian Import Regulation Commission and then ask the Currency Board for permission to change the necessary amount into foreign currency. Whenever they wanted to pay creditors abroad, for instance for obligations that

65 Bolderaa Flooring Mills & Timber Co. Philipp Schapiro Ltd., "Rigas Biržas Komitejai Bolderajas Ēvelēšanas un Kokrūpniecības akc. sab., bij. Filips Šapiro," May 11, 1932, in LVVA 3143-1-1735, 1. Translation from Latvian by the author.

66 James Ashley Morrison, "Shocking Intellectual Austerity: The Role of Ideas in the Demise of the Gold Standard in Britain," *International Organisation* 70, no. 1 (2016): 177.

67 Karnups, *The Little Country That Could*, 211.

68 Karnups, *The Little Country That Could*, 211.

69 Karnups, *The Little Country That Could*, 211.

were agreed upon in a foreign currency, Latvian companies had to receive authorization from the Currency Board.

The use of the lat for foreign transactions was restricted as well, as a complaint by the owner of the machinery factory G. Waldispühl in Riga, P. Reichert, shows. The company used to export water turbines, milling machinery, and machinery parts to Lithuania. However, by 1934, these business transactions had become almost impossible:

> My export there [to Lithuania] has almost completely stopped in the last two years, while it used to be very lively. The main reason for this decline are our export regulations, which do not allow payment in lats for export transactions. [In the past] this method of payment allowed me to compete against the other countries trading in Lithuania due to the existing exchange rate difference. The former way to avoid the problem included the Lithuanian buyer coming here, paying us in lats and taking care of the transport himself. But this is now also prohibited.[70]

This example shows how the Latvian government's rules for financial transactions with foreign customers, designed to hinder an outflow of the Latvian currency, severely interfered with the selling products abroad.

One of the large-scale effects of the Great Depression was the general decline in prices for agricultural produce, which dropped significantly and drove farmers around the globe into ruin.[71] For an agrarian country like Latvia, whose economic well-being depended on the export of agricultural produce, this was bad news. The prices for Latvia's leading export, butter, went into a downward spiral. In September 1929, prices for unsalted Latvian butter (first class) for export still ranged from Ls 3.67 to 4.04 per kg; by May 1930, they

70 Letter from the G. Waldispühl Machinery factory to the Riga Association of Factory Owners, "G. Waldispühl, Riga vorm. Ferd. Meyer & Co. Maschinenfabrik, Eisen- und Metallgiesserei. An den Rigaer Fabrikantenverein," September 29, 1934, in LVVA 2765-1-589, 65. Translation from German by the author.

71 Clavin, *The Great Depression in Europe*, 100.

were down to Ls 2.86 to 2.96 per kg.[72] But the price decline was only one issue. After the devaluation of the pound sterling, Latvia's butter was too expensive even at the lower price, which resulted in a dramatic decline in butter exports. In 1929, Latvia had exported butter with a value of Ls 58.7 million, equivalent to 21.46 percent of the exports.[73] The butter exports declined to Ls 14.3 million in 1934, equivalent to 16.9 percent of Latvia's exports. It took until 1938 before they almost reached the level of 1929 again: In 1938, Latvia exported butter valuing Ls 54.2 million, which accounted for 23.9 percent of the overall value of Latvia's exports.[74]

On September 28, 1936, Latvia—as almost the last state in Europe—finally devalued its currency.[75] Two days earlier, France had left the Gold Standard and decided to join the devaluation policy.[76] This decision about the devaluation of the lat was not communicated in advance and hit a number of businesses in Latvia hard. Many companies had outstanding debts for raw materials and machinery in foreign currencies, often in pound sterling, which overnight almost doubled in value. The pound sterling had been Ls 15.58 before the devaluation, whereas it cost Ls 25.22 after.[77] Due to a restrictive loan policy of Latvian banks, another outcome of the focus on a stable lat, many merchants and entrepreneurs in interwar Latvia had no access to long-term loans. Latvia's private banks took very high interest rates, and the state-owned bank primarily supported farmers organized in agricultural societies and

72 Cf. Centralās Savienības "Konzums" Exportsviesta Nodaļa Ziņojums, Riga, September 3, 1929, in LVVA 5172-1-197, unnumbered; and Centralās Savienības "Konzums" Exportsviesta Nodaļa Ziņojums, Riga, May 12, 1930, in LVVA 5172-1-195, unnumbered.

73 "Lauksaimniecīvas ražojumu un pārējo preču eksports," in *Latvijas Ārējā Tirdzniecība un Tranzits 1930*, ed. Valsts Statistiskā Pārvalde (Riga: Valsts Statistiskā Pārvalde, 1931), XII.

74 Tab. 8. "Imports un eksports 1934.–1938. g. pēc galvenām precēm," in *Latvijas Ārējā Tirdzniecība un Tranzits 1938*, ed. Valsts Statistiskā Pārvalde (Riga: Valsts Statistiskā Pārvalde, 1939), XVIII.

75 "Gesunde Geld- und Kapitalmärkte im Goldblock nach der Abwertung," *Rigasche Rundschau*, November 4, 1936.

76 Karnups, *The Little Country That Could*, 214.

77 Balabkins and Aizsilnieks, *Entrepreneur in a Small Country*, 112.

cooperatives.[78] Thus, many industrial enterprises resorted to financing their purchase of raw materials and machinery either with short-term loans or by using the opportunities provided by foreign companies, whose bills did not have to be paid in full immediately but rather between 6 months and 2 years after delivery or installation.[79] This effectively gave many entrepreneurs short-term credit. When these short-term credits were called in, or bills by foreign creditors or customers had to be paid based on new rules such as after a currency devaluation, Latvia's entrepreneurs had no alternative options to refinance their businesses.

Between 1931 and 1936, several companies in Latvia experienced severe sales difficulties because of the overvalued lat and Latvia's restrictive financial policies. The candy and chocolate producer *Laima (Latv.* happiness) was one of them. Laima was founded in 1921, originally under the name "Maķedonija" by five Jewish entrepreneurs: Davids Moševičs (Moschewitsch), Gersons Preils, Ilja Kopilovs, Iljas Fromčenko, Josifs Zegals (Segal), and the Baltic German Jakobs Arens (Jakob Ahrens).[80] It became a stock corporation with the name "Laima" in 1925, still belonging to the same owners and financed primarily with Jewish and German capital. When the company became more successful and needed larger production facilities, Laima's owners bought the premises previously used by the company 4711 Eau de Cologne on Karoline Street (today Miera iela) in central Riga.[81] The Cologne entrepreneur Ferdinand Mülhens had used Riga as an entry into the Russian market and produced Eau de Cologne and other beauty products in Riga between 1880 and 1914.[82] During World War I, the factory premises changed owners and ended up under the ownership of Marietta Beaucamp, who lived in Kassel, Germany. She sold the premises to Laima.

78 Stranga and Krūmiņš, "Von der Marktwirtschaft über die Staatswirtschaft zur Planwirtschaft," 186.

79 Balabkins and Aizsilnieks, *Entrepreneur in a Small Country*, 105.

80 See Laima's shareholders' register, LVVA 4381-2-12, 1.

81 Vertrag zwischen "Laima" A/G, Karolinenstr. 22/24 nachstehend "Laima" genannt und Frau Marietta Beaucamp geb. Dumont in Kirchhain, Bezirk Kassel, LVVA 4381-1-2, 10–11.

82 Christoph Schmidt, "Über die Niederlassung der Firma '4711' in Riga 1880–1914," *Jahrbuch des Kölnischen Geschichtsvereins* 61 (1990): 137–49.

However, Laima's founders could only make a down payment of Ls 80,000. For the remaining Ls 95,000, the purchase contract foresaw payments in half-yearly installments of Ls 10,000, with a final installment of Ls 15,000 in July 1936.[83]

The fact that Laima's owners still bought additional premises for production in 1930 meant that they were not immediately affected by the depression. Still, when Latvia's biggest trading partner, the United Kingdom, started to devalue its currency while the lat stayed pegged to gold and was overvalued, it affected their day-to-day business and sales abroad, as this letter from a customer in South Africa in 1933 shows:

> The 23 Cases [*sic*] mentioned therein, duly arrived in good order, but landed at too high a cost to us on account for your increased price. This we recognise at the moment as something that cannot be helped, and we hope this will be remedied by your coming off the Gold Standard as Estonia has done. As things are at the moment, we are, strictly speaking not making on your lines, due to no fault of yours we admit. However we are making good progress in introducing the lines and getting a good grip, which we are determined to hold, so that we are ready to reap the full benefit when the money question is settled.[84]

Latvia's financial policies in reaction to the Great Depression—overvalued lat, restrictive loan policies, prohibitive regulations for the currency exchange—brought several formerly sound and flourishing companies to their knees. Even solid and economically viable businesses were suddenly on the verge of bankruptcy and could only survive with new loans.

When Kārlis Ulmanis staged his coup and installed himself as an autocratic leader on May 15, 1934, the bad performance of Latvia's economy was one of his key arguments for the takeover.[85] This was despite the fact that by 1934, the economy was already showing signs

83 See the purchase contract for the premises of Laima, LVVA 4381-1-2, 10–11.

84 Letter from "The Continental Chocolate Supply Co., Cape Town," to Laima Ltd., August 4, 1933, LVVA 4381-2-29, 1.

85 Stranga, *Kārļa Ulmaņa Autoritārā Režīma*, 49.

of improvements, trade numbers picked up again, and the worst seemed to be over.[86] One of Ulmanis' solutions for a more prolonged economic upswing was to bring key industries under government control and turn them into state-controlled joint-stock companies.[87] As a side effect, this also suited his "Latvia for Latvians" policy, since the newly created state-controlled joint-stock companies were run by (ethnic) Latvians, whereas the formerly independent firms that were nationalized belonged predominantly to the country's minorities, that is, Germans and Jews.

To put his policy into practice, Ulmanis created Latvijas Kredītbanka, essentially a state-owned bank. Latvijas Kredītbanka received an initial capital provided by the state of 10 million lats, which was later increased to 40 million lats.[88] According to Ulmanis' biographer Dunsdorfs, Latvijas Kredītbanka did all the "dirty work" in the process of nationalizing Latvia's key enterprises.[89] On October 3, 1935, Ulmanis' government passed a law that allowed Latvijas Kredītbanka to liquidate all commercial and industrial companies that had taken loans but could not meet their financial obligations.[90] Latvijas Kredītbanka and its director Andrejs Berziņš had far-reaching powers and insights into almost all companies operating in Latvia. The Currency Board, for instance also informed Latvijas Kredītbanka when companies, for which the bank held shares, were authorized to make payments abroad.[91] Laima, whose owners still had obligations in Germany because of the purchase contract of their production premises, regularly had to ask for permission from the Currency Board to exchange and transfer money to Germany, which was sometimes denied or only given with delay.[92] Because of the difficulties in meeting their obligations and because of the overvalued Lat, which made it difficult to sell

86 Balabkins and Aizsilnieks, *Entrepreneur in a Small Country*, 73.

87 Stranga, *Kārļa Ulmaņa Autoritārā Režīma*, 124.

88 Balabkins and Aizsilnieks, *Entrepreneur in a Small Country*, 79.

89 Dunsdorfs, *Kārļa Ulmaņa dzīve*, 391, cited after Stranga, 125.

90 Balabkins and Aizsilnieks, *Entrepreneur in a Small Country*, 80.

91 See the letter from the Currency Board to Laima, November 5, 1936, in the files of Latvijas Kredītbanka, LVVA 4590-1-121, 37.

92 Herrn Landrat T. Beaucamp, Düren, Betreff Kapital-Rückzahlung, June 21, 1934, LVVA 4381-1-2, 39.

their products abroad, Laima's owners were forced to take out loans at Latvijas Kredītbanka.

Between 1936 and 1939, the Ulmanis government increasingly used the opportunity to nationalize enterprises that had got into financial difficulties. Until January 1, 1939, Latvijas Kredītbanka took over and transformed 31 commercial and industrial companies.[93] This is how Laima became Latvia's biggest and state-owned candy producer. Originally, there were several chocolate and candy producing companies in Riga.[94] The oldest was Riegert, founded by the Baltic German Theodor Riegert in 1870. While the majority of Riegert shares were taken over by Hamburg-based shareholders after World War I, the descendants of Theodor Riegert still owned the production premises in Riga, participated in Riegert's profits, and had a say in the company's affairs.[95] Both Riegert and Laima started to have difficulties in the mid-1930s due to Latvia's financial policies and as a result of the sudden devaluation of the lat in September 1936—even though they were still profitable companies. Both took out loans with Latvijas Kredītbanka. This opened the door for Latvijas Kredītbanka and eventually allowed the state-run bank to acquire the entire stocks of Laima and Riegert.[96] After the takeover in 1937, the two companies were merged and became the state-owned Laima chocolate and candy factory run by an ethnic Latvian directorate.

The policy of nationalization did not only affect businesses run by Latvia's Germans and Jews—Ulmanis aimed to establish one key state-run company in every sector, which would then be pushed by the government to succeed. Companies run by ethnic Latvians were also approached by Latvijas Kredītbanka, for instance, the textile manufacturer Rīgas Audums.[97] Yet, since Germans and Jews

93 Balabkins and Aizsilnieks, *Entrepreneur in a Small Country*, 82.

94 See history of Laima on the company website: "Par mums," Laima, accessed March 12, 2024, https://laima.lv/company.

95 See agreement "Konsortium zum Betrieb der Kakao- & Schokoladenfabrik Th. Riegert in Riga and list of Hamburg based companies and individuals with shares" in *Konsortium Riegert*, LVVA 4818-1-2, 2–4, and 6–7.

96 Balabkins and Aizsilnieks, *Entrepreneur in a Small Country*, 112.

97 The owner of Rīgas Audums, however, was skeptical of the advances of Latvijas Kredītbanka and did not take their offers for a loan. See Balabkins and Aizsilnieks, *Entrepreneur in a Small Country*, 112.

were overrepresented among Latvia's entrepreneurial class, their companies were targeted more often. Under the Ulmanis regime, Latvianization of the economy and bringing the entire economy under state supervision were two sides of the same coin.

Latvianization and nationalization also affected Latvia's institutions with the aim to make them, first, run by Latvians and bring them, second, under government control. This also led to the effective end of the Riga Exchange Committee. In July 1939, a new stock exchange law was implemented and the Riga Exchange Committee became the stock exchange board, placed under the wing of the Latvian Ministry of Finance.[98] The Riga Exchange Committee had to hand over all its assets—including the house of the Riga stock-exchange—to the new stock exchange board and the Ministry of Finance. The new chair of the stock exchange management board was no longer elected by the Riga merchant society but appointed by the Finance Minister. As part of the nationalization of the stock exchange, the long-serving vice-chair of the Riga Stock Exchange Committee, the Baltic German Eugen Schwartz, lost his position. The new stock exchange board had both an ethnic Latvian chair and vice-chair.[99] This new law was the icing on the cake of the Latvianization policies of the country's autocratic leader Ulmanis in the financial and economic sector. The takeover of the once powerful Riga Exchange Committee shows that the policies of the Ulmanis regime were not only directed against independent entrepreneurs but also against independently operating economic institutions. In Ulmanis' state, the core of economic activity was to be in state hands.

6.4 Conclusion

To recover from the losses of World War I, the Latvian government used long-established trade relations, personal connections of its business community, and the country's existing infrastructure, especially its ports, to make independent Latvia an export-oriented agricultural economy. The focus was on the export of agricultural

98 "Die Börsenwahlen vollzogen," *Rigasche Rundschau*, July 28, 1939.
99 "Antritt des neuen Börsenvorstandes," *Rigasche Rundschau*, August 1, 1939.

commodities harvested and produced by (ethnic) Latvian farmers, who were usually organized in cooperatives. Latvia's industry recovered as well, albeit on a much smaller scale. Still, especially in the capital Riga, which had become a highly industrialized metropolis in the 30 years before World War I, about half of its industrial workforce could be revived. This allowed interwar Latvia to become not only an exporter of agricultural products but also of manufactured goods such as textiles or candy.

The government of the newly created nation-state of Latvia implemented policies to strengthen its independent statehood and to empower ethnic Latvians, especially in the economic sector, which initially was dominated by the German and Jewish minorities. Side effects of these policies were economic and social fragmentation. New barriers in the form of customs and duties, as well as restrictive loan policies, hindered the development of the industrial sector. During the Great Depression, the Latvian government implemented a number of financial policies that were designed to safeguard the Latvian currency but which created high obstacles for independent entrepreneurs. Restrictive financial policies during the Great Depression and the belated devaluation of the lat further escalated the problems for large industrial enterprises, especially for Latvia's mostly German and Jewish entrepreneurs. It also further increased the ethnic fragmentation of the economic sphere. The desire to turn Latvia's economic sector into one run by ethnic Latvians paved the way for a policy of nationalization. After the authoritarian takeover by Kārlis Ulmanis, more and more businesses were taken over by Latvia's state-run bank. The result was an increase in state-owned companies and the disempowerment of Latvia's formerly independent economic institutions. This was by no means a singular Latvian phenomenon. Latvia's government rode on a wave dominant in Europe at the time. However, illiberal tendencies clearly dictated the economic policies of interwar Latvia after the Great Depression, even before the country was occupied by Soviet troops in 1940.

PART THREE

Changing Relations between State and Society

Chapter 7

ESTONIA

"IS THIS THE ESTONIA WE WANTED?" HOW THE INTERWAR SLUMP RESHAPED ESTONIA'S SOCIETY

David Feest

It is widely accepted that the Great Depression was one of the most important—possibly even the primary—factors contributing to the decline of the young democracies in East-Central and Eastern Europe into totalitarianism. However, it is still not always evident how the connection works in detail. This article attempts to identify some connections between the decline in confidence in democratic processes and free markets, using Estonia as a case study. The economic crisis's destructive power grew in tandem with another crisis: The collective fear that the project of establishing a state to represent Estonians was on the verge of failure. It was also a time to look back and compare the reality with the ideals Estonia had started its statehood some 20 years earlier. The historian Jaak Valge has formulated succinctly that in the early 1930s, many Estonians had an "is-this-the-Estonia-we-wanted?-feeling."[1] This feeling was closely connected to the question of how independent Estonians had really managed to become. Karsten Brüggeman described in an article that in the early times of the Estonian Republic, the concepts of "foreign rule" and "own rule" were the subject of "semantic wars."[2] By 1931, the Estonian national state was undeniable, but whether it was really the embodiment of the Estonians' "own rule" was up for grabs.

1 "Kas-me-sellist-Eestit-tahtsime-tunne," Jaak Valge, *Eesti parlament 1917–1940. Poliitiline ajalugu* (Tallinn: Eesti Rahvusraamatukogu, 2019), 296.

2 Karsten Brüggemann, "'Foreign Rule' during the Estonian War of Independence 1918–1920: The Bolshevik Experiment of the 'Estonian Worker's Commune'," *Journal of Baltic Studies* 37 (2006): 215.

The Estonian Republic was born in crisis. When it was declared in 1918, there were numerous reasons to doubt its sustainability. Until February 1920, it remained in a war against Soviet Russia, a conflict that could have quickly extinguished aspirations for freedom. Economic challenges also threatened independence, as self-determination found limits within budget constraints. While securing foreign credits was a significant concern during the republic's initial years, many people simultaneously feared excessive reliance on foreign countries.

Internally, the multi-ethnic nature of the country further raised questions about the degree of Estonia's independence. The Baltic German minority, which had wielded local power for centuries, was reluctant to relinquish its authority and privileges. It is true: In the representational democracy, its political influence had shrunk just about to the percentage of people it had in the population, a mere 3 percent. Also, during one of the most radical land reforms in Europe, the landed gentry had been forced to give up most of their lands for the sake of Estonian so-called "settler" peasants. However, in the industry, the minority still controlled most of the economic assets. For some Estonians, this supremacy was deeply worrying.[3]

7.1 1924: From Crisis to Recovery

Roughly speaking, from 1918 to 1930, the Estonian economy ran through two stages. In 1920, the country's position had improved compared to 2 years earlier. A peace treaty with Soviet Russia brought the country into possession of its share of the Russian Imperial Gold inventory, and semilegal trade with Soviet gold added still more. Meanwhile, eastern trade seemed to function as a logical continuation of the Russian Empire's inner market. However, in the long run, this success caused serious problems. In 1924, the Baltic German banker Klaus Scheel explained to a representative of the League of Nations: "Unfortunately, Estonia began with two good years in 1920–21 [. . .] They earned a lot of money for two

3 "Majanduslise ülewõimu pärast," *Päewaleht* (August 9, 1924): 3. Vesa Vasara, "Die deutschbaltische Minderheit in Estland in der Zwischenkriegszeit: Wirtschaft und Finanzen," *Zeitschrift für Ostmitteleuropaforschung* 44 (1995): 581–82.

years and were surprised that it did not continue that way. They spent more than they should have and ran into debt."[4] Indeed, most of the political and economic elites did not see the end of Russian trade coming; the banks, as well as the state, continued investing in enterprises that were engaged in it long after it had stopped being profitable, and the issuing bank "Bank of Estonia" subsidized this policy by secretly using the country's gold reserves in an attempt to stabilize the currency. Eventually, it failed, and the country experienced severe inflation. For the head of government, Konstantin Päts, this scandal was the preliminary end of his career. The bank he cofounded—the Harju Pank—went bankrupt, and he disappeared from the stage of high policy for the next 5 years.[5]

The minister of finance, Otto Strandmann, who took office in 1924, pursued a policy that was directly opposed to his predecessor's policy of borderless loans. Instead of relying on the eastern markets and large industries, the economic focus was shifted to producing agricultural goods (especially dairy products) for the Western market, following the Danish model.[6] Concerning monetary policy, Strandmann was very much in agreement with the concepts of orthodox economic policy which the League of Nations had designed to facilitate East-Central Europe's recovery. Strict budget discipline was to help return to a balanced budget and reintroduce the Gold Standard that had the reputation of having secured the stability of Europe's economy before the war.[7] Under Strandmann's auspices, Estonia adjusted the monetary value of the Eesti Mark

4 Entretien avec M. Klaus Scheel, Directeur de la Banque Scheel et Co. 23. Janvier 1925, *Files of Sir James Arthur Salter—Esthonia—Records of Interview during journey to Esthonia and notes* (League of Nations Archives (LONA), S122/72/6, n.d.).

5 Jaak Valge, *Lahtirakendamine: Eesti Vabariigi majanduse stabiliseerimine 1918–1924* (Tallinn: Rahvusarhiiv, 2003), 135–43; Jaak Valge, "Es ist nicht alles Gold, was glänzt. Das Gold der Bolschewiki in Estland 1920–1922 und die Folgen," in *Estland und Russland. Aspekte der Beziehungen beider Länder*, ed. Olaf Mertelsmann (Hamburg: Verlag Dr. Kovač, 2005), 167.

6 Anu Mai Kõll, *Peasants on the World Market. Agricultural Experience of Independent Estonia 1919–1939* (Stockholm: Almqvist & Wiksell International, 1994), 70.

7 Patricia Clavin, *The Great Depression in Europe, 1929–1939* (New York: St. Martin's Press, 2000), 44; Nathan Marcus, Stefan Nikolić, and Tobias Straumann, "Economic Policy 1918–1939," in *The Economic History of Central, East and South-East Europe: 1800 to the Present*, ed. Matthias Morys (London and New York: Taylor & Francis, 2021), 192.

(*Estonian Mark*) to the inflation rate. Although the new currency, Eesti Kroon (*Estonian Crown*), was introduced as legal tender as late as September 1928, it was used as a unit of account from 1924 on. It was pegged to the Swedish krona with a precisely defined gold content. As opposed to previous years, loans obtained by private enterprises would not diminish over time due to inflation but had to be paid back at total value. This measure was an essential prerequisite for stopping inflation.[8] The currency's exchange rate was stable in the second half of the 1920s. In this respect, Estonia's development was similar to most other East-Central Europe countries.

Currency reform was also a precondition for a substantial loan. It was backed by the League as part of the Ter-Meulen program, which was intended to help small countries organize short-term commercial loans. The loan also signified an increased scrutiny of Estonian affairs by the League of Nations. In 1925, a delegation of the League visited Estonia to acquaint themselves with the local conditions. Such preparations raised suspicions among many Estonians. "This will turn us into Austria!" the politician and diplomat Friedrich Akel privately expressed his concerns.[9]

An incident during the negotiations with the League illustrates that even politicians supportive of the loan and the accompanying currency reform were uneasy about the foreign meddling in Estonia's economy that came with it. Minister of Finance (1924–27) Leo Sepp, who had previously directed the Estonian Bank from 1921 to 1924, strongly objected to the Financial Committee's plans to appoint an "advisor" to the Bank for the next 3 years. He argued that this could convey the impression of foreign control and that Estonia could rectify its errors independently. The conflict was resolved when the commission explicitly stated that the new functionary would only

8 Villu Zirnask, *Eesti Panga lugu* (Pärnu: Eesti Pank, 2019), 101.

9 Eduard Laaman, "Meie Vastus. Eduard Laamani päevik, II," *Akadeemia* 14 (2013): 1773. Austria had been the subject of the League's first reconstruction scheme in 1923, followed by others for Hungary in 1924 and Bulgaria in 1926 and 1928, as well as in 1925 and 1927 for Greece. Rudolf Nötel, "International Credit and Finance," in *The Economic History of Eastern Europe 1919–1975*, eds. Michal Charles Kaser and Edward Albert Radice (Oxford: Oxford University Press, 1986), 193.

provide advice, not exercise control.[10] Meanwhile, the Estonian press made clear that Estonia was not in the deplorable state Austria had been in when it accepted the League's help but was seeking assistance to prolong its successful financial development.[11]

What made matters worse was that from May 1926 on, the League was processing a petition by an organization of Baltic German former large landowners against the 1918 land reform. Also, the proposed head of the delegation to Estonia, the Swedish banker Marcus Wallenberg, who had been the chairman of the powerful Financial Commission of the League from 1920 to 21, was rumored to have commercial interests in the old Baltic German Estates. Eventually, Wallenberg was not chosen for the job, but the suspicion remained that Baltic Germans might use the League to further their interests.[12] To make matters worse, the negotiator for the German side was a Baltic German with close connections to Wallenberg—the banker Klaus Scheel. Instead of achieving "our rule," in economic issues "foreign (or at least non-Estonian) rule" seemed to prevail.

In fact, the League politics in Estonia did not differ from the course it pursued in other countries: it enforced an orthodox financial policy.[13] A central demand was the separation of the respective central banks from the state. Instead of being willing financiers of the state's economic policy, the banks were to make the stabilization of the currency their main task and operate independently from the government. Most East-Central European countries—some rather grudgingly—gave in to this demand.[14] The same was also true for

10 Otto Karma, *Eesti Vabariigi majanduspoliitika: kaks aastakümmet 1919–1939* (Tallinn: Umara, 1999), 78.

11 Vahur Made, *Estonian Banking and Currency Reform Loan of 1927: A Case Study of the Estonian Economic Cooperation with the League of Nations* (Tallinn: Eesti Kõrgem Kommertskool, 1998), 13.

12 Vahur Made, *Estonian Banking and Currency Reform Loan of 1927*, 9. On the Financial Commission see Nötel, see n. 9, 193.

13 Richard J. Evans showed in 1977 that the League did not pursue hidden political goals but was interested in creating economic stability. Richard J. Evans, "The League of Nations and the Financial Reconstruction of Europe, 1924–1930," *Past & Present* 76, no. 1 (1977): 125–49; see also Patricia Clavin, *Securing the World Economy: The Reinvention of the League of Nations, 1920–1946* (Oxford: Oxford University Press, 2013).

14 Marcus, Nikolić, and Straumann, see n. 7, 192, 208, note 17.

Estonia, where the *Eesti Pank* had previously existed in a limbo between private and state interests. Although selling the bank to private owners by turning it into a joint stock company did not work as expected—some two-third percent had to be bought by the state—the bank was now clearly engaged in monetary rather than fiscal policy. The economy as a whole was not at the center of the bank's attention; it was only the currency.[15] The loan was issued in 1928. From 1927 to 1930, Walter Williamson, the financial expert at the League, served as a counselor at the *Eesti Pank*. Despite the initial reservations, Estonia remained the only party consistently adhering to the full service of its League loan until July 1940.[16]

In hindsight, it is easy to state that this policy, in the long run, turned out to be too inflexible to prepare the country for the challenges of the late 1920s and early 1930s. However, in the short run, despite the hardships the strict policy of a balanced budget caused, it provided the country with a stable currency that made it more attractive for foreign capital. Switching from industrial to agrarian production, Estonia profited from the relatively favorable food export prices. Its exports mainly went to Germany and England. In 1926 and 1927, it achieved an export surplus, which set it apart from most other East-Central European countries, except for Czechoslovakia.[17] For Estonians, the development of the country's economy from 1925 could be experienced as a transition period from the chaotic first years of the republic to integration into a stabilizing European economic system. By joining the Gold Standard, they felt they had entered a world of reliability, well-earned by fiscal self-discipline and hard work. Also, the relation to Williamson, who had initially been regarded suspiciously as a watchdog, was amiable, symbolizing the young republic's positive attitude toward the United Kingdom. The fact that Estonia was exporting bacon to England seemed like symbolic proof that the transition from east trade to west trade had been accomplished.

15 "Mis saab Eesti pangast?," *Järva Teataja* (September 6, 1929): 3. Zirnask, see n. 8, 115–20.

16 Made, see n. 11, 11. Clavin, *Depression*, see n. 7, 33.

17 Maie Pihlamägi, *Eesti industrialiseerimine 1870–1940* (Tallinn: Ajaloo Instituut, 1999), 196. "Estonia's Foreign Trade in 1927," *Scheel's Review* 8, no. 1 (1928): 10. Marcus, Nikolić, and Straumann, see n. 7, 194.

Despite this success story, Estonia's economy faced several issues that had already become apparent before the crisis exacerbated them manifold. The example of Estonia shows that despite the successful currency stabilization, paying back loans represented a serious burden. Over 70 percent of foreign capital was not used productively, but spent to service loans.[18] In addition, the *Eesti Pank* had large outstanding bills and loans.[19] Also, since many countries from East-Central Europe tried to profit from the good situation on the agricultural markets, the danger of overproduction leading to a decline in prices loomed on the horizon.[20]

The most crucial difficulties, however, originated from the entire European economic system and the position East-Central Europe had in it. While the prewar Gold Standard system had largely relied on a notion of collective responsibility, stabilization now had to be achieved at a national level. As per Patricia Clavin's analogy, with the decline of Britain's power, the "team of states" lacked a captain to reinvigorate the team spirit. Instead, the individual decisions of European countries to overrate or underrate their currency led to expensive exports for the first and an export advantage for the second. There was no control to compensate for the differences and restore the balance of the system. In a kind of prisoner's dilemma, individual rationality took precedence over collective rationality, leading to the least favorable outcome for everyone. Unsurprisingly, domestic producers soon demanded protection from cheap imports in practically all of East-Central Europe instead of trusting the market's balancing mechanisms.[21] Accordingly, Estonia's economic turmoil originated from systemic factors, and it was tied to this system by the Gold Standard.[22]

18 Clavin, *Depression*, see n. 7, 86.

19 "The Financial Situation of Estonia in 1927," *Scheel's Review* 8, no. 1 (1928): 1–10.

20 Kõll, see n. 6, 89.

21 Clavin, *Depression*, see n. 7, 44, 55f.

22 Barry Eichengreen, *Golden Fetters. The Gold Standard and the Great Depression* (New York: Oxford University Press, 1996), 14.

7.2 The Slump of 1931–33

Prior to the onset of the crisis, there were indications of impending difficulties. Estonian bonds were already falling in the second half of that year and more dramatically from February to March 1929. At that time, the Finance Committee began to worry about the repayment of Estonia's foreign loans.[23] Despite this, Aleksander Oinas, minister of finance from December 1928 to July 1929, claimed that the situation had already improved. He suggested that local production should be supported so the foreign trade balance would not become too negative.[24]

Even when things got worse the following year, the former finance minister and now chairman of the "Chamber of Commerce and Industry," Sepp, remained optimistic that the country could pull itself out of the crisis by cutting wages and industrial spending, closing idle plants and offices, and lowering taxes to draw in foreign investment. Sepp reminded his fellow citizens: "We are not sitting by the honeypot, where foreign capital is eager to penetrate, but we must accept all foreign capital offered to us."[25]

In 1931, Estonia's economy was hit even harder. Germany's economic collapse resulted in the loss of one of its most important business partners. Even worse, Estonia's reserves were directly affected when England decided to abandon the Gold Standard and devalued the Pound Sterling on September 31, 1931. At the Genoa conference in April 1922, the League of Nations had decided that, given the shortage of gold, countries could supplement their gold reserves with currencies backed by gold.[26] Following Williamson's advice, the *Eesti Pank* had extensively used this possibility. Now, due to the Sterling devaluation, the *Eesti Pank* lost about one-third of its coverage.[27] Meanwhile, export prices fell by 25 percent compared to the

23 Made, see n. 11, 15.

24 "Millal paraneb meie majanduslik seisukord?," *Uudisleht* (February 5, 1929): 4.

25 Zirnask, see n. 8, 121.

26 *Genoa Conference, received May 3, 1922—Genoa Conference 1922—Report of the Financial Commission* (LONA, R1609/40A/20486/20196, 1922), 9; Clavin, *Depression*, see n. 7, 48.

27 Valge, *Parlament*, see n. 1, 271.

previous year, while import prices decreased only by 20 percent. In 1932, the turnover was three times less than in 1928.[28]

The decrease quickly affected the banking sector, which had not been healthy in the first place. It was no exception since most other European countries suffered similar problems. Their liquidity reserves were shrinking, their hidden reserves had been eaten up by inflation, and smaller banks were merged into bigger ones.[29] Of 27 joint stock banks in Estonia in 1924, only 19 were left in 1929.[30] Even before the crisis, not all of them had seemed viable to foreign observers who had often noted their lack of viability, and by 1935, their number had diminished to 13.[31] These surviving banks were in a bad state: The unfavorable ratio of deposits to bonds in the big Estonian banks was a well-known fact publicly discussed in the daily press.[32] It made them especially ill-prepared for the challenges of the world market. In 1929, decreasing timber prices got the *Tartu Pank*, which played a key role in the financing of this industry, into serious problems. It was forced to reorganize itself by selling the majority of its shares to the "British Overseas Bank Ltd."[33] In November 1930, the *Diskonto Pank*, vital for the leather and shoe industries, went bankrupt. At the beginning of 1931, the *Eesti Kommertspank* and the *Krediit Pank* were insolvent. In the same year, the bank *G. Scheel & Co*, which was central for the machinery, textile, paper, and oil shale industries, ran into severe difficulties and had to be closed for 3 months by a state moratorium.[34]

28 Pihlamägi, see n. 17, 196–97.

29 Cp. for instance the German example: Harold James, "Banks and Bankers in the German Interwar Depression," in *Finance and Financiers in European History, 1880–1960*, ed. Youssef Cassis (Cambridge: Cambridge University Press, 2002), 221–22.

30 Oskar Sepre, *Eesti kodanlik riik monopolide teenistuses* (Tallinn: Eesti Riiklik Kirjastus, 1963), 76–77.

31 *Sonderberichte des "Ost-Express," Nr. 4 (90)* (BArch 31.01/19658. Nr. 2199, 1929), 4; Sepre, see n. 30, 76–77.

32 "Suurpankade seisukord juulis," *Kaja* (August 31, 1930): 2.

33 Karma, see n. 10, 105.

34 Zirnask, see n. 8, 122; Karma, see n. 10, 105. Jaak Valge, "Okkaline devalveerimine: Eesti krooni kursi ümberhindamine aastail 1931–1933," *Akadeemia* 8 (1997): 1610; David Feest, "Klaus Scheel, Estlands ungekrönter König. Eine biografische Skizze," in *Individuum und Gesellschaft in Ost- und Nordosteuropa*, ed. Joachim Tauber (Lüneburg, 2017), https://www.ikgn.de/cms/index.php/downloads1/send/55

The Estonian farmers especially felt the sudden fall of export prices. Sixty percent of the Estonians received their primary income from agriculture, where prices plummeted. In 1932, prices for agricultural products had fallen to less than half of their level of 1929, causing the total value of the market to shrink by the same percentage.[35] In addition, especially the farmsteads founded during the land reform of 1919—the so-called "settlers"—were still paying back their loans. Among them were many that had actively pursued the turn to an export-oriented production in the second half of the 1920s. Now, they had lost their markets.[36] Thus, the success story of the second half of the 1920s had turned into a tragedy, especially for those who had been essential clients of the new nation-state. For many, this was an expression of a completely misguided development. In 1931, Rudolf Penno from the Settlers' Party complained about the injustice of the Scheel Bank being protected from bankruptcy by a moratorium while overindebted farmers were forced to auction off their farms.[37] Another group that had emerged during the years of independence and was important for its stability was the urban middle class, working for the state or private enterprises. The crisis put their whole new social status into question—and, with it, the achievements of the Estonian nation-state. Finally, industrial workers were gravely affected when, from 1929 to 1932, their working hours were cut by a quarter.[38] In 1933, the number of unemployed had risen from 10,000 in 1932 to 25,000.[39]

Such hardships turned the mood against the free, international markets and those who were involved in them. The crisis enhanced a feeling that the liberal markets were a playground for the foul play of the rich and powerful. In this vein, promoting production for the domestic market had a two-sided character. On the one hand, it

-individuum-und-gesellschaft-in-ost-und-nordosteuropa/1251-feest-klaus-scheel-estlands-ungekroenter-koenig (accessed February 2, 2019), 54–57.

35 Valge, *Parlament*, see n. 1, 297.

36 Valge, *Parlament*, see n. 1, 297.

37 "Pangale moratoorium, põllumehele oksion," *Lääne Hääl* (October 10, 1931): 1.

38 Cp. Toomas Varrak, "Estonia: Crisis and 'Pre-Emptive' Authoritarianism," in *Authoritarianism and Democracy in Europe, 1919–39. Comparative Analyses*, ed. Dirk Berg-Schlosser and Jeremy Mitchell (Basingstoke: Palgrave Macmillan, 2002), 135.

39 *Eesti arvudes 1920–1935* (Tallinn: Riigi Statistika Keskbüroo, 1937), 240.

was an act of necessity. All over Europe, countries followed a course of so-called "import substitution industrialization," trying to produce as many products domestically as they had formerly imported. "Of course, complete self-sufficiency—i.e. complete economic independence from other countries—can only be realized in dreams," a brochure by the "Homeland Industry Propaganda Group" read in 1933, "but the current economic crisis also teaches us that economic independence must be extended to all necessary commodities in order to safeguard them."[40] On the other hand, the promotion of a "substitution industry" often had a patriotic ring to it, stressing the ability of Estonia to free itself from the constraints of international business. One article in the brochure declared: "We have to get to the point where we can proudly say—*as an Estonian, I use products of Estonian origin.*"[41]

Appeals to patriotic solidarity were also a dividing factor. Accounts of corruption and machinations between political and economic elites not only destroyed the trust in free markets.[42] They often gained an ethnic character, drawing a clear line between "us" and "them." A corruption scandal, which earned the textile manufacturer Issaak Citroén/Tsitron a 2-year prison sentence in 1932, was tailor-made for anti-Semitic explanations. Also, Scheel was, albeit incorrectly, often portrayed as a Jew who was steering the fate of Estonia's economy in the interests of Jewish international circles.[43] Others suspected the German state to be behind him.[44] Some feared that the Estonian national consciousness was not yet developed enough to counter such alleged machinations. In November 1932, an article in the patriotic newspaper *Sakala* bemoaned that the Estonian had always remained a "slave," heeding the call of "foreign

40 V. Kupffer, "Majanduslik rippumatus on riikliku iseseisvuse alussambaid," in *15 aastat Eesti tööstust—kaubandust—pangandust*, ed. Ernst Seim (Tallinn: Kodumaa Tööstuse Propaganda Toimkond, 1933), 7–8.

41 Ernst Seim, "Oleme hääd Eestlased!," in *15 aastat Eesti tööstust—kaubandust—pangandust*, ed. Ernst Seim (Tallinn: Kodumaa Tööstuse Propaganda Toimkond, 1933), 61.

42 Karma, see n. 10, 105.

43 "Poliitilike Lawakunst," *Waba Maa* (October 30, 1932).

44 *Riigikogu IV koosseis. IX istungjärk. 220. koosolek 9. veebruaril 1932* (Tallinn: Riigikogu, 1932), 3737.

influencers."[45] Such comments conveyed the impression that the national project had come to a standstill and that foreign forces controlled the republic. Eventually, the question of whose interest the nation-state in its present form actually served connected the economic crisis to the one of "our rule."

An immediate reaction to the failing of international market mechanisms was the state proving its will to act by enforcing regulations. The active involvement of the state in international trade was a development in all of Europe when governments tried to protect their national economies with tariffs, quotas, and currency control.[46] In Estonia, the cooperatives in charge of exporting agricultural goods had been under heavy state control from the mid-1920s on.[47] In late 1931 and 1932, a whole bundle of laws and decrees gave the government and the "Eesti Pank" thorough control over importing and exporting goods, foreign currency, and precious metals.[48] In addition, in 1932, a "Law of Authorizations" gave the government broad power to intervene in private enterprises and change the state budget.[49]

The "Law of Authorizations" was only temporary and aimed to remedy the current crisis. However, together with the other measures, it also led to a change in approach. Dealing with economic challenges was no longer limited to tightening the belt to maintain a balanced budget. Direct government control gained increasing significance in international trade to achieve the same end. This shift marked a new norm in addressing economic issues, surpassing the established practice of relying solely on gold parity and strict budget discipline.

45 "Tumedate püüete mängukannid," *Sakala* (November 1, 1932).

46 For Eastern Europe in particular, see György Ránki and Jerzy Tomaszewski, "The Role of the State in Industry, Banking and Trade," in *The Economic History of Eastern Europe 1919–1975*, ed. Michal Charles Kaser and Edward Albert Radice (Oxford: Oxford University Press, 1986), 22–24.

47 Kõll, see n. 6, 71.

48 Zirnask, see n. 8, 132–3; Karl Stern, "Valuutakontrolli rakendamine Eestis 1930. aastatel," *Ajalooline Ajakiri* 1, no. 159 (2017): 79–102.

49 Anu Mai Kõll and Jaak Valge, *Economic Nationalism and Economic Growth* (Stockholm: Alqvist & Wiksell, 1998), 42.

7.3 The Kroon Crisis

However, there was an alternative to the growing government control over exports and imports. Leaving the Gold Standard and devaluing the Kroon could have led to Estonian products becoming more attractive abroad and foreign currency flowing into the country using only the instruments of monetary policy. This possibility was the subject of very emotional discussions. These are textbook examples of how questions of monetary policy were embedded in broader disputes about corruption, dependence, and liberation. Today, most historians agree that such a devaluation would have been expedient in late 1931 already. When other countries like Sweden, Norway, and Denmark followed the British example by abandoning the Gold Standard and devaluing their currencies, countries such as Estonia suffered significantly due to their overvalued currencies. They were no longer competitive in the world market. The timely devaluation of the Kroon would most probably have changed this. The "reform farmsteads" and other export-oriented enterprises would have immediately felt the relief. In contrast, companies depending on imported raw materials would have suffered from higher prices but would have profited from the economy's overall recovery. It can be presumed that the winners would have outnumbered the losers.[50] Why was the option to devalue the Kroon dismissed until June 1933?

There are multiple answers to this question. First, the memory of the 1924 crisis was still fresh. People had been told for years that maintaining the Gold Standard was a prerequisite for stable economic conditions, and the economic recovery after 1924 confirmed this opinion. Maintaining the currency's value was seen as a safer bet than stimulating the economy while running the risk of new inflation. This opinion was backed by local experts, who believed that the 1929 stock market crash would not affect the country's economy and that the League of Nations loan would positively impact Estonia's credit and monetary conditions.[51]

50 Pihlamägi, see n. 17, 197; Valge, "Devalveerimine," see n. 34, 1615–16; Valge, *Parlament*, see n. 1, 299.

51 "Economic Review," *Scheel's Review* 11, no. 1 (1928): 2.

In addition to these reasons, devaluation was discussed as more than just a monetary policy measure. Politicians of various persuasions also presented it as an instrument of influential groups seeking influence and prosperity through it. Many believed that speaking out in favor of devaluation was part of a covert strategy to belittle the Estonian economy. The socialist Leopold Johanson linked it to the question of Estonian statehood. For him, the battle for stabilizing the Kroon was a battle for Estonian independence, and if Estonia lost economic life, it would also lose its independence.[52] In this way, supporting the Kroon had become a patriotic matter, which was soon discussed in terms of loyalty and betrayal. Not only the socialists demanded a kind of "pledge of allegiance to the Estonian Kroon."[53] Sepp, one of the fathers of the financial reform of 1927 and not a member of any political party, also used this term. In an article with the same title, he surmised that leading businessmen were trying to ruin the reputation of the Estonian economy abroad.[54] When the League's liaison man, the director of the National Bank of Belgium and former Minister of Finance Albert Jansson, visited Estonia in August 1932, there were rumors that he had been invited by the initiative of "some local circles and on private initiative."[55] This alleged misuse of the League for personal benefits fit well into the common conspiracy narrative: Jansson was a staunch supporter of devaluing the Kroon since, in his opinion, Estonia did not have the means to hold it at its current level.[56] Williamson shared this opinion. Such advice from abroad was not well received in Estonia. Although Johannes Zimmermann, the minister for Economic Affairs from 1929 to 1931 and 1932 and supporter of devaluation, tried to iron out misunderstandings, the League did not look good in this episode. It is hard to deny that Estonia had run into trouble despite strictly following the advice from Geneva. The 180-degree turn in the advice did little to strengthen the trust of the Estonians in the

52 Valge, *Parlament*, see n. 1, 338.

53 Valge, *Parlament*, see n. 1, 299.

54 L[eo] S.[epp], "'Truudusevanne' kroonile. Kahekeelsete pette-demonstratsioon. Rahvasteliidu nu ja nuandjad," *Waba Maa* (October 26, 1932): 4.

55 "Genfis kõneldi Eesti majandusliku kokkuwarisemise wõimalusest," *Päevaleht* (August 31, 1932): 3.

56 Karma, see n. 10, 112.

international organization. When, in autumn 1932, the League proposed sending a new advisor to Tallinn, "Eesti Pank" refused. It rightly pointed out that it had failed to keep all its reserves in gold due to foreign advice.[57] Sepp went beyond this by demanding that it was time to end the "insidious intrigues" surrounding the Kroon.[58]

Under these conditions, factual arguments for leaving the Gold Standard and devaluing the Kroon had little chance of being heard. Indeed, in November 1932, the Estonian parliament passed a law that made calls for the devaluation of the Kroon a criminal offense punishable by up to 7 months in prison.[59] Ironically, in 1933, while this law was in effect, the ever-worsening economic situation made the restrictive monetary policy unpopular among financial experts as well as in business circles. However, they would not be heard. Even when, from May 1933 on, the liberal cabinet of Jaan Tõnisson began seriously debating leaving the Gold Standard, such discussions could not be made public because of the new law. It took pressure from delegates of the "settlers" to finally enforce a decision. On June 28, early at 5:00 AM, the government passed a bill that devalued the Kroon by 35 percent. This bill ended Estonia's adherence to the Gold Standard.[60]

The devaluation of the Kroon did not lead to the chaos and panic its opponents had feared. On the contrary, in the context of a general recovery of world trade, it contributed to an upward trend in the Estonian economy. Estonia fared well compared to countries like Latvia, which did not leave the Gold Standard. Still, the positive aspects of the devaluation did not result in a complete return to a liberal market economy. On the contrary, it made Tõnisson—one of the most experienced and arguably also deserving Estonian politicians of his days—a hated man.[61]

57 Zirnask, see n. 8, 132.
58 S.[epp], see n. 54.
59 Zirnask, see n. 8, 135.
60 Zirnask, 138.
61 Valge, *Parlament*, see n. 1, 354.

7.4 Government Crises and Coup d'état

Why was the success of the devaluation not perceived as a call to return to a more liberal, market-oriented politics? It can be assumed that it was precisely the immediate connection of the slump experience, the Kroon question, to more general frustrations about Estonian politics that led to such a harsh judgment about Tõnisson's decision to devalue. The debate about the Gold Standard made the political crisis most visible.

Estonia had a parliamentary democracy system with a strong legislative branch. The head of state, calso, had the function offunctioned as prime minister and depended heavily on the parliament. Accordingly, the governments were short-lived in comparison to the parliament. From autumn 1919 to autumn 1932, eighteen different governments ruled Estonia. In the peak years of the crisis, 1932–33, six governments were in power.[62] In these 2 years, the country experienced five government crises. The debates about how to deal with the economic crisis were one important reason for the disunity. "The Estonian government crisis is, in fact, a Kroon crisis," Sepp wrote in 1932, "a final battle between Kroon strikers and Kroon keepers." [63] This economic crisis worsened the already fragmented state of the country. Attempts were made to form more stable governments by merging parties in late 1931. However, when debating the future of the Kroon, the groups within these parties remained deeply divided, as different interest groups had varying interests concerning import and export. Overall, the political elites appeared inefficient, discordant, and lacking transparency. The Kroon crisis considerably added to the general distrust in the parliamentary system. If confidence in the League of Nations had suffered from its change of mind with regard to the Gold Standard, so did the confidence in the Estonian political elites. In 1933, the idea of cutting the Gordian knot by establishing a presidential system gained ever more supporters.

One group that profited from this situation was the "Central League of Veterans of the Estonian War of Independence," which

62 Varrak, see n. 38, 117; Valge, *Parlament*, see n. 1, 307.
63 S.[epp], see n. 54.

had by that time become a political organization known under the short form "Vaps." Their central topic was the corruption of the leading class and the necessity to renew national unity and solidarity as Estonians had, in their opinion, practiced in the War of Independence.[64] It is telling that the Vaps members had no clear opinion about the devaluation of the Kroon but attacked politicians of other parties for being either for or against it.[65] For all its lack of precision, the Vaps' rhetoric promised a reclaiming of power by the Estonian people from the political and economic elites who only had their selfish interests at heart. This program can be interpreted as a populist right-wing vision of establishing "our rule." In terms of content, the main political doctrine of the Vaps organization was their hostility to the parliamentary system and political parties and a vague but hardly well-informed sympathy for Italian and German fascism.[66]

It was not least due to the pressure of the Vaps movement that within little more than a year, the government conducted three referenda to change the constitution and introduce a presidential system. The respective state elders, Tõnisson and Päts, organized the first two. Both failed. The third and most radical one was held in October 1933 on the initiative of the Vaps movement. A clear majority of voters approved it. At the prospect of losing the first presidential election scheduled for April 1934, Päts, together with the retired general and hero of the independence war, Johan Laidoner, took action. On March 12, they declared a state of emergency and arrested the leading figures of the Vaps movement. From then on, Päts form ruled by decree. This was the end of democracy in Estonia. Päts and Laidoner claimed that they prevented a fascist coup planned by the Vaps organization, but it seems unlikely. The Vaps had a realistic chance of winning the presidential elections, and there is no convincing evidence to support the claim that they planned to take over power by force in 1934. In any case, Päts used

64 On the Vaps movement, cp. Rein Marandi, *Must-valge lipu all. Vabadussjalaste liikumine Eestis 1929–1937. I legaalne periood 1929–1934* (Stockholm: Almquist Wiksell, 1991); Andres Kasekamp, *The Radical Right in Interwar Estonia* (London: Macmillan Press, 2000).

65 Valge, "Devalveerimine," see n. 34, 1619.

66 Kasekamp, see n. 64, 68–70.

the opportunity to implement his own vision of an Estonian state without political parties, a free press, and an independent parliament to control the executive.[67] While he proclaimed that Estonia needed a breathing space before it could return to democracy, he began reorganizing the state and economy to move it further away from the liberal foundations of the republic.

7.5 Corporatism in the State and Economy

It seems that Päts did not have a clear idea of the type of state he wanted to establish in 1934, nor a concrete program to reorganize its economy.[68] Still, some basic convictions that he had already expressed before the Estonian Republic was founded are visible in his politics after 1934. Päts had always sympathized with corporatist ideas and believed professional associations were better suited to represent different interest groups than political parties.[69] Now, the Italian model offered some guidance. Päts' convictions established a tight connection between economic and political forms of organization. Päts preferred corporatist arrangements to a free, individualistic play of forces in both spheres. He resorted to the classical image of the human body: Corporate organizations should work together harmoniously for the common good, like the organs of a human body, instead of engaging in selfish rivalry and competition.[70] To this end, in 1935–36, in addition to the existing "Chamber of Commerce and Industry" and "Chamber of Agriculture," Päts created another fifteen such chambers, mainly for professional groups.[71] Estonian state propaganda later presented the corporatist

67 Ajo Pajur, "Die 'Legitimierung' der Diktatur des Präsidenten Päts und die öffentliche Meinung in Estland," in *Autoritäre Regime in Ostmittel- und Südosteuropa 1919–1944*, ed. Erwin Oberländer et al. (Paderborn: Ferdinand Schöningh, 2001), 171, 178–85.

68 Ajo Pajur, "Die 'Legitimierung' der Diktatur des Präsidenten Päts und die öffentliche Meinung in Estland," 174, 183; Kll and Valge, see n. 49, 65.

69 Cp. Toomas Karjahärm, *Vabameelne opositsionäär Konstantin Päts* (Tartu: Rahvusarhiiv, 2018), 332.

70 Kõll and Valge, see n. 49, 50–51.

71 Kõll and Valge, 50–51.

form of organization as a "disciplined" or "organized democracy," replacing representative democracy.[72]

While this kind of centralization meant a clear break from the democratic system that had existed before, in the economic sphere, Päts can be said to have continued a course that was already dominant in the early 1930s. Protectionist and interventionist measures were prolonged, and the "Law of Authorizations" lost its temporary character. The state steered the economy more than before in favor of special branches such as military, agrarian exports (especially milk products) and industry.[73] Still, all these measures were hardly perceived as part of a new approach by the people but rather as a continuation of the old course. A more liberal alternative ceased to exist in public discussion, since people who might have spoken up against it were either silenced under the new laws of censorship or integrated into the new system. For instance, the eminent businessman and chairman of the "Chamber for Industry and Commerce," Joakim Puhk, in 1931, still predicted that the crisis would resolve itself over time and warned that the state should not intervene in favor of one or the other economic sector.[74] However, when in March 1935 a new "economic council" was founded, replacing the old parliamentary economic council and comprising the most important commercial corporations, Puhk was one of its members. Typically, for the economic elites of these years, Puhk did not think the parliamentary system was able to protect and further the interests of the economy and he was no opponent of state protection from foreign competitors. "It was only when state intervention was aimed at them, that they evoked the principles of free trade and free enterprise," the historian Anu-Mai Kõll has pointedly summarized the attitude of the "Chamber for Industry and Commerce."[75]

The new regime's economic policies also had a patriotic aspect, which was very much in accordance with the general increase in displays of ethnic unity. On the one hand, the tighter control over the economy could be understood as the protection of originally

72 Pajur, see n. 67, 205.

73 Kõll and Valge, see n. 49, 52–53.

74 Joakim Puhk, "Kriis laheneb ajajooksul iseennest. Üksikute majandusharude soodustamine pole õiglane," *Järva Teataja* (January 3, 1931).

75 Kõll and Valge, see n. 49, 63–64.

Estonian interests against the internationalist elites who considered the small country to play, at best, a subordinate role as a supplier of raw materials. On the other hand, the government supplemented its foreign trade policies with a politics of "nostrification" aimed at taking over Estonian control of the country's economy. Such aspirations were not new. The appropriation of assets considered "alien property" had been practiced in several states that had emerged from World War II, and such thoughts had also guided the Estonian agrarian reform in 1919.[76] Now, the Päts regime more strictly controlled the usage of foreign employees in Estonia and took care of the consistent enforcement of rules according to which the accounts of all companies were to be kept in Estonian.[77] In times when unemployment numbers were rapidly sinking and the Baltic German minority boasted not only Estonian citizenship but also Estonian language skills, such rules were highly symbolic. Nevertheless, they conveyed that Estonians were also beginning to establish "our rule" in economic matters.

Päts's authoritarian state was established under favorable conditions to make that claim seem convincing. It operated during a general economic upswing in Europe. In Estonia, production numbers rose steadily, although they never reached the peak of 1928.[78] Now Päts was in a good position to take the praise—more so since dissenting voices could not be heard anymore. The economic development also justified the authoritarian system as a whole. The liberal path, it seemed, had failed in every respect, while the tighter organization of society could also carry the project of Estonian liberation and self-government, which had been stuck halfway to a successful end.

In reality, the new economic stability came at the price of new dependencies. When the European economy fell apart into trade and currency blocs, Estonia consequently did not return to the Sterling bloc of countries that maintained a certain degree of free market economy.[79] Rather, the German market began to dominate

76 Ránki and Tomaszewski, see n. 46, 7.

77 Kõll and Valge, see n. 49, 75–77.

78 Pihlamägi, see n. 17, 196.

79 On the different blocs see Barry Eichengreen and Douglas A. Irwin, "Trade Blocs, Currency Blocs and the Reorientation of World Trade in the 1930s," *Journal of International Economics* 38, no. 1 (1995): 1–24.

Estonia's foreign trade: If in 1933 Estonia's exports to Germany had amounted to 21.2 percent of its total exports, it had risen to 35.6 percent in 1939, while the share of exports to England fell from 37.1 percent to 26 percent in the same time.[80] When preparing for war, the Nazi regime needed secure supply chains for foodstuffs as well as shale oil and was ready to pay considerably more than the world market prices. However, it paid for the products in the context of clearing arrangements, which meant that Estonia received a significant part of payments not in currency but in respective imports from Germany. By the end of the 1930s, Estonia—just as neighboring Latvia—was to a high degree chained to Germany.[81]

7.6 Conclusions

The Estonian example shows the ambiguous relation between the economic and political crisis. It suggests that the economic and political crises were connected by a common fear that the national project, empowering Estonians to liberate themselves from alien oppression and achieving a version of "our rule," was on the verge of failing. The crises seemed to show that people were no longer committed to these aims in both the economic and political realms. The discussion surrounding the devaluation of the Kroon proved very destructive. Firstly, it went far beyond questions of monetary politics and soon included moral judgments and even conspiracy narratives. A measure that could have brought a certain degree of relief was outright criminalized. Secondly, the discussion caused divisions even within political parties, contributed to frequent government changes, and eroded trust in the political system. The prolonged debates and contentious nature of the issue left a bitter taste in the mouths of many Estonians. Despite their success, Tõnisson's efforts to push through a liberal agenda in 1933 were met with resistance from the public mood. Economically, the push for liberalization lost

80 Magnus Ilmjärv, *Silent Submission. Formation of Foreign Policy in Estonia, Latvia and Lithuania. Period from Mid-1920s to Annexation in 1940* (Stockholm: Almqvist & Wiksell, 2004), 212.

81 Hans-Erich Volkmann, "Ökonomie und Machtpolitik. Lettland und Estland im politisch-okonomischen Kalkül des Dritten Reiches, 1933–40," *Geschichte und Gesellschaft* 2 (1976): 471–500, 476–7, 484; Köll and Valge, see n. 49, 44.

momentum, and the country moved toward increased regulation. Politically, the conflict had far-reaching consequences, ultimately leading to the elimination of parliament in the Päts coup. Unified corporate arrangements seemed to be a more fitting solution to achieve a rule that could be called "their own." Most overlooked the loss of freedom and agency it entailed.

Chapter 8

LITHUANIA

THE GREAT DEPRESSION, SOCIAL DIVISIONS, AND ECONOMIC NATIONALISM

Klaus Richter

Formerly a part of the Russian Empire's northwestern periphery, Lithuania emerged as an independent country after World War I. Like the other states that were constructed from the ruins of the Central and Eastern European empires, Lithuania was in the process of state-building and consolidation when the Great Depression hit. An agrarian reform, designed to redistribute land from the Polish-speaking nobility to the Lithuanian-speaking peasants, was still in progress, as was the integration of the formerly German Klaipėda region, annexed by Lithuania in 1923, as the new state's outlet to the sea. This chapter will argue that, although the Lithuanian economy displayed striking resilience, the crisis fundamentally fragmented Lithuanian society, in terms of both nationality and class, and reshaped the relationship between society and state. Lithuanian scholars have stressed the depression's transformative impact on Lithuania's state structures, society, and agriculture, emphasizing how the attitudes of peasants toward farming traditions changed and how ethnic Lithuanians increasingly moved into the commercial sector.[1] Yet we know little about what social and political developments drove these changes.

There is no consensus so far on how Lithuania fared during the depression relative to other countries. Several scholars argue that the country's economy weathered the storm remarkably well. Adomas Klimantas has stressed that Lithuania's GDP did not experience a

1 Zenonas Butkus and Norbertas Černiauskas, "Krizė keičia Lietuvą: 1931–1935 metų pokyčiai visuomenėje ir valstybėje," *Lietuvos Istorijos Studijos* 36 (January 14, 2016): 69–87.

noticeable dent during the depression and slightly converged toward Estonia.[2] According to Zenonas Norkus, the Great Depression did not dramatically change the Baltic States' position vis-à-vis the other European states: Both in 1929 and 1938, Lithuania ranked at the bottom with regard to per capita income, significantly below Estonia and Latvia.[3] Lithuanian industrial production increased steadily throughout the period of the Great Depression, recording its strongest growth from 1931 to 1932. In this regard, Lithuania showed similarities to other predominantly agricultural countries such as Denmark or Greece, whose small industries also registered relatively undisturbed growth. However, we need to bear in mind that Lithuania's industry was minuscule by European standards, did not satisfy domestic demands, and was thus hardly affected by the global depression.[4] Yet others have emphasized that nominal wages dropped sharply during the depression. The wages of carpenters, for instance, contracted by 43 percent between 1931 and 1934. In 1938, they were still below the 1913 level.[5]

Over the course of the 1920s, Lithuania successfully disintegrated from its former Russian markets and reoriented its trade toward Germany and, to a lesser degree, Britain. Not least, the dependence on Germany was due to Lithuania's international isolation as a consequence of the Polish-Lithuanian conflict around the city of Vilnius. Vilnius came under Polish rule after World War I, but Lithuanian governments never relinquished their claim on what they considered Lithuania's historical capital city. This meant that Lithuania was in a particularly precarious geopolitical position

2 Adomas Klimantas, "Lithuanian Economy, 1919–1940. Stagnant but Resilient. The First Inter-War GDP Time-Series Estimates and Their Implications," *Scandinavian Economic History Review* (September 27, 2023), https://doi.org/10.1080/03585522.2023.2259909: 16.

3 Zenonas Norkus, "The Economic Output Growth of Baltic Countries in 1913–1938: A Quantitative Cross-Country Comparison," *Journal of Baltic Studies* 50, no. 2 (2019): 184, 197.

4 Anicetas Simutis, *The Economic Reconstruction of Lithuania after 1918* (New York: Columbia University Press, 1942), 38.

5 Zenonas Norkus, Aelita Ambrulevičiūtė, and Jurgita Markevičiūtė, "Real Wages of Lithuanian Construction Workers from 1913 to 1939 (Measured in Subsistence and Welfare Ratios) in a Cross-National Comparison," *Lithuanian Historical Studies* 23, no. 1 (December 28, 2019): 41.

Table 8.1 Total Lithuanian Exports and Imports (in Million Litai)

	Britain Exports	Imports	Germany Exports	Imports	Total Exports	Imports
1930	65	24	200	151	334	292
1933	72	24	53	51	160	142
1937	97	59	35	46	207	214

Source: Statistikos biuletinis, 1 (1939).

across the interwar period and remained excluded from most initiatives that were designed to mitigate the economic impact of new borders drawn after the end of the war.[6] This made Lithuanian agriculture highly contingent on Central and Western European business cycles.[7] Accordingly, when Germany fell into depression, this had a disproportionate impact on Lithuania. Between 1930 and 1933, Lithuanian overall exports to Germany fell from 200 million to 50 million Litai. The government managed to offset some of the damage through a targeted expansion of agricultural exports to Britain, which rose at the same time from 65 million to 72 million Litai (Table 8.1). In 1932–33, Lithuania's exports lost 15 percent in value—only Czechoslovakia, Romania, and Ireland fared worse.[8]

Like most other countries in Eastern Europe, Lithuania was a predominantly agricultural country, with approximately four-fifths of the population living and working in the countryside. As such, Lithuania was severely hit by the global decline in agricultural prices. Yet scholars have stressed that key economic key policies across the 1920s had made Lithuanian agriculture, on the whole increasingly productive and resilient. This was especially true with regard to the 1919 land reform. Scholars have noted that the land reform created a swathe of small, unsustainable farms. Yet it also transformed thousands of hamlets into middle-sized farms and large estates into

6 See, i.a., Dangiras Mačiulis and Darius Staliūnas, *Lithuanian Nationalism and the Vilnius Question, 1883–1940* (Marburg: Verlag Herder-Institut, 2015); Alfred Erich Senn, *The Great Powers, Lithuania and the Vilna Question 1920–1928* (Leiden: Brill, 1966).

7 Similar concerning the Habsburg Empire's successor states: Patricia Clavin, *The Great Depression in Europe* (London: Macmillan, 2000), 81.

8 *World Economic Survey. Third Year, 1933–34* (Geneva: League of Nations, 1934), 195.

rationalized cooperatives organized in the state-supported cooperative federations *Lietūkis* ("Lithuanian Agriculture"), *Pienocentras* ("Milk Centre"), and *Maistas* ("Food").[9] These were turned into the backbone of Lithuania's national economy. Since the mid-1920s, the Lithuanian government pushed for a diversification of agricultural production, especially by promoting dairy production and pig-breeding. Before the war, no dairies had existed in Lithuania. On the eve of World War II, 200 dairies produced 20,000 tons of butter for export through the dairy cooperative *Pienocentras*.[10] This has traditionally been interpreted as a consistent move away from grain production. However, from 1927, Lithuania also doubled its wheat production, with areas for wheat cultivation increasing by 150 percent.[11] Not least, this expansion was a result of new protectionist tariffs, on the one hand, and considerable subsidy payments that allowed farmers to grow and sell wheat at competitive prices.[12]

The crisis of agriculture is reflected in cooperative sales, which had increased steadily across the 1920s. However, from 1931 to 1932, the sales of *Lietūkis*, the federation of agricultural cooperatives, fell by approximately 21.5 percent. Those of *Pienocentras* fell by the same margin from 1931 to 1933.[13] Economic historians have argued that Lithuania's economy started to recover from 1933. However, this seems optimistic. Cooperative sales point toward a later recovery: Pre-depression sales volumes were reattained only by 1935, and this was less due to a general recovery and largely the result of a dramatic expansion of the share of cooperatives in the overall national economy of Lithuania (from 1931 to 1939, the sales

9 Elena Dragomir, "Development Characteristics of Interwar European Periphery: The Cases of Romania and Lithuania's Agriculture," *Revista Română pentru Studii Baltice și Nordice* 2, no. 1 (2010): 53–68; Jolanta Valčiukienė, Virginija Atkocevičienė, and Vilma Sudonienė, "Changes of Land Users in Interwar Lithuania," *Land Portal* (December 2015), https://landportal.org/node/84366.

10 Valentine Gustaitis, "Lithuania: The First Twenty Years," *The Slavonic and East European Review* 17, no. 51 (1939): 606–617.

11 *Acte Final de la Conférence Internationale Préparatoire de la IIème Conférence Mondiale du Blé (Rome, 26 Mars–2 Avril 1931)* (Rome: International Institute for Agriculture, 1931).

12 *World Economic Survey. Third Year, 1933–34*, 100–1.

13 Simutis, *Economic Reconstruction*, 38.

of *Lietūkis* almost quadrupled).[14] A 1933 recovery also seems questionable if we look at social discontent rather than economic indicators.[15] Lithuania's depression had a significant political dimension. Given the importance of Germany as an outlet for Lithuanian foreign trade, the deterioration of Lithuanian-German relations after Hitler's rise to power severely prolonged the economic crisis. When the Lithuanian government put local Nazis from the Klaipėda region on trial in 1934–35 (Neumann-Sass Trial), Nazi Germany terminated its trade agreement with Lithuania, thus delaying the recovery of German-Lithuanian commercial relations. This additional blow to Lithuania's economy sparked socioeconomic unrest in the countryside, especially in Southern Lithuania (Suvalkija), where rural strikes broke out in the summer 1935 and continued until February 1936. State propaganda painted strikers as anti-Lithuanian agitators financed by Nazi money.[16] The strikers lost public support in the latter half of 1936, not least because of the onset of economic recovery following the German-Lithuanian trade agreement of August 5, 1936. The Lithuanian government sentenced 19 strikers to death, which undermined the moral foundations of Smetona's authoritarian dictatorship.[17]

Throughout the depression, Lithuania remained committed to the Gold Standard, and while this certainly did not aid its recovery, it seemed less a determinant of economic failure than for other members of the Gold Block. Lithuania pegged its currency to the Gold Standard in January 1922 and abandoned it in October 1935. These almost 14 years on the Gold Standard were extraordinarily long, both in comparison to its Baltic neighbors (Latvia less than 13 years, Estonia less than 7 years) and to the broader region (Poland, for instance, stuck to the Gold Standard until the collapse of the Gold Block in 1936, but had entered it only in 1926). Even more astonishingly, Lithuania did not introduce foreign-exchange

14 Simutis, *Economic Reconstruction*, 38.

15 Lina Paulauskaitė and Simona Rekašiūtė, "Pasaulinių ekonominų krizių įtaka Lietuvos ekonomikai," *Ekonomikos ir vadybos aktualijos* 10 (2011): 516.

16 Mindaugas Balkus, "1935–1936 m. Užnemunės ūkininkų streikas: Propagandos ir viešosios nuomonės apžvalga," *Lietuvos istorijos metraštis* 1 (2012): 103–118.

17 Sigita Černevičiūtė, "Mirties bausmės taikymo praktika: 1935–1936 m. Suvalkijos ūkininkų streikas," *Istorija* 92, no. 4 (2013): 22–31.

controls either. Yet there was certainly no lack of calls for an abandonment of the Gold Standard after Britain's departure in autumn 1931. Most of Lithuania's authorities, however, threw their weight behind it. Albinas Rimka, director of the Central Statistical Office (*Centrinis statistikos biuras*), militated against efforts "to cure the crisis with money" and remained convinced that Britain's departure represented an aberration rather than a solution and that British policymakers were already trying to find ways to "return to the Gold Standard in some way, without loss of honour." Rimka was confident that abandoning the Gold Standard would only benefit a small number of risk-taking individuals who were "up to their ears in debt." "It is a thousand times healthier, better and more decent if a certain element of the unhappily indebted should perish or be liquidated," he added, "than to risk undermining the confidence and the stability of the value of our money, just to relieve them a little."[18] Kazys Radušis, director of the Land Bank (*Žemės bankas*), stressed that, as a small state, Lithuania might have to abandon the Gold Standard in the long term, but could not do so before all Great Powers, most notably the United States, had done the same.[19]

The League of Nations noted in 1934 that Lithuania had weathered the European banking crisis well, despite holding on to the Gold Standard, which it attributed to the country's "comparatively simple economic organization." The League stressed that Lithuania was one of the few gold-standard countries where "improvement was noticeable."[20] Adomas Klimantas has stressed Lithuania's "unconventional pattern" of maintaining the Gold Standard while registering relatively undisturbed growth across the Great Depression, and links this to the country's exceptionally low trade-to-GDP ratio (performing even below Italy, which pursued a policy of autarky), and thus its relative protection from external shocks.[21] Yet as Lithuania's depression continued, the country lost its badge as a Gold-Standard poster child. In 1935, the *Economist* warned: "It is not an economic necessity to abandon the Gold Standard, but it is

18 Albinas Rimka, "Krizis ir pinigai," *Lietuvos ūkininkas* 23 (1932): 4.

19 "Ankieta krizės klausimais," *Tautos ūkis* 5 (1932): 129–135.

20 *World Economic Survey. Third Year, 1933–34*, 262–63.

21 Klimantas, "Lithuanian Economy, 1919–1940," 15.

no longer true, as it was last year, to say that Lithuania is in the best financial and economic position of the Baltic States."[22]

8.1 The Agricultural Crisis as a Never-Ending Crisis

Like elsewhere in East-Central Europe, the Great Depression was predated by a pre-existing agricultural crisis. In 1928, Lithuanian agriculture was devastated by a crop failure, forcing many peasants to take out loans to mitigate the damage.[23] From 1931 to 1932, grain exports slumped from 40,664 to 7,035 metric tons.[24] As a response to the agricultural crisis, the Lithuanian government introduced various relief measures to bolster prices for agricultural products, such as long-term low-interest loans, special support for cooperatives, support to improve the quality of products, and protective tariffs. In March 1931, the government increased import duties on all principal commodities by margins ranging from 20 to 100 percent. These measures were aimed at protecting traditionally export commodities, such as rye, wheat, and flax, and those products that had gradually moved to the core of Lithuania's economic policy across the 1920s: dairy products and bacon. When representatives of the League visited the Baltic states in 1934, they were impressed by both the scope and the success of the relief measures carried out through the state-supported, "very powerful" cooperatives, which had "succeeded in granting the peasants the best prices for their productions."[25]

A law from November 17, 1930, authorized the government to purchase wheat and rye at fixed prices through *Lietūkis*. On 19 July already, a law was passed with the purpose of maintaining domestic prices for bacon and ensuring that it remained competitive in the British markets, the almost exclusive destination for Lithuanian

22 "Lithuania," *Economist*, February 16, 1935.

23 Zenonas Norkus, Aelita Ambrulevičiūtė, and Jurgita Markevičiūtė, "Real Wages of Lithuanian Construction Workers from 1913 to 1939 (Measured in Subsistence and Welfare Ratios) in a Cross-National Comparison," *Lithuanian Historical Studies* 23, no. 1 (2019): 44–45.

24 Simutis, *Economic Reconstruction*, 43.

25 "Visit of M. Walters and M. Smets to Latvia, Estonia, Lithuania and Finland," May 1934, League of Nations Archive, R 5691 50/10472/1719, unnumbered.

Table 8.2 Exports of Bacon from Lithuania in 1,000 Pounds

1928	330
1929	696
1930	9,048
1931	40,028
1932	55,405
1933	47,125
1934	27,944
1935	18,971
1936	22,636

Source: Reed, "Hog Industry," 162.

bacon. This law put slaughterhouses under the control of the Ministry of Agriculture. Under the tutelage of the government-owned meat-trade cooperative *Maistas*, these had to pay fixed prices to farmers for hogs, and the Ministry would compensate for their losses. On January 1, 1932, the government passed an amendment that turned this arrangement into a legal monopoly on bacon exports for *Maistas*.[26] Not only did these laws successfully mitigate some of the pressures caused by the global decline in agricultural prices, they also significantly reduced the problem of larger surpluses, which plagued Lithuania's northern neighbor, Latvia.[27] Indeed, the laws triggered a boom. Bacon exports more than quadrupled in 1930 compared to the previous year and increased further in 1931 (see Table 8.2). They only dropped from 1934 with the introduction of British import tariffs, but remained consistently above the pre-crisis levels throughout the 1930s. *Maistas* vastly increased in size, with new meat-processing factories built in Tauragė, Panevėžys, and Šiauliai. By 1939, *Maistas* accounted for 90 percent of all meat exports and 25 percent of the total value of Lithuanian exports.[28]

26 Lynn Ramsay Edminster, Leo J. Schaben, and Myer Lynsky, *Agricultural Price-Supporting Measures in Foreign Countries* (Washington, DC: United States Department of Agriculture, Economic Research Service, 1932), 161–67.

27 Harry E. Reed, "The Hog Industry in the Baltic States," *Foreign Agriculture: A Review of Foreign Farm Policy, Production, and Trade* 2 (1938): 160.

28 "Maistas," *Visuotinė Lietuvių enciklopedija*, accessed November 14, 2022, https://www.vle.lt/straipsnis/maistas-1/.

Until 1932, Lithuanian commentators conceived of Lithuania as a country that had fared relatively better than other European states and had responded in a more level-headed way. Lithuania had refrained from enacting excessively protectionist measures and had remained observant of the most favored nation principle. But the waves of the crisis were about to crash: Merchants had warehouses of goods they could no longer sell and farmers were considering laying off farmhands on a large scale because of falling agricultural prices and rising costs for production.[29] In September 1932, extreme right-wing politician Augustinas Voldemaras, who had been the driving force behind Smetona's coup of 1926 (and was then ousted from government by Smetona in 1929), wrote that "the crisis has engulfed the whole world—there are no signs that it should end and normal times return."[30] The realization that Lithuania was caught up in the maelstrom of the global depression challenged the conviction that the small country was best served by adhering to the crisis-ridden liberal order. Voldemaras was no outlier in believing that the depression would result in state intervention at levels unprecedented outside the Soviet Union.[31] Like other European countries, the Lithuanian government attempted to mitigate the downturn by pursuing bilateral commercial treaties. However, not least due to the Vilnius conflict, only a few were successfully concluded.[32] In 1933, Stasys Kuzminskas, Director of the Economic Department of the Ministry for Foreign Affairs, publicly declared that treaties based on the most favored nation principle were "in decline" and in the process of being replaced by agreements based on a "compensation system." Kuzminskas tied the existence of the "small states" of East-Central Europe to such agreements, as purchasing power was their only means to safeguard sovereignty.[33]

29 Buvęs, "Krizės klausimu," *Tautos balsas*, March 24, 1932.

30 Augustinas Voldemaras, "Krizis ir jos pasakos," *Tautos balsas*, September 24, 1932.

31 Voldemaras, "Krizis ir jos pasakos."

32 Until 1934, Lithuania concluded such treaties with Denmark, Austria, Czechoslovakia, Switzerland, Latvia, and Britain. A Baltic customs union failed due to Polish opposition. *World Economic Survey. Third Year, 1933–34*, 207.

33 "Rapport Nr. 1 sur la Lithuanie au Directeur du B.I.T.," December 30, 1933, Internal Labour Organisation Archive, C 39-2-1, unnumbered.

The year 1932 represented the depression's peak in Lithuania in the sense that the downturn was so severe and sustained that it became increasingly difficult to imagine a way out. Fearing for their existence, peasants began to take out loans on the pretext of purchasing new machineries but used them to service existing debts. In winter 1931–32, many farmers had begun to run out of fodder for their cattle. Some districts were at risk of running out of summer seeds. Trade collapsed by 30 percent, in some districts 50 percent. Production in the leather industry fell by up to 40 percent. Auctions for unpaid debts soared.[34] To make matters worse, the Lithuanian government had banked on 2,000,000 USD it was still due to receive as part of a loan granted by the Swedish "matchking" Ivar Kreuger—however, after Kreuger's empire collapsed and Kreuger committed suicide, the loan was never paid out.[35]

Reviewing the year 1932, the editors of the center-left Lithuanian Peasant Party's newspaper *Lietuvos ūkininkas* ("Lithuanian Peasant") stressed that the year had seen "humanity standing on a swollen volcano." The depression had changed the "relationship between nations and states" forever, as governments had collapsed, new blocs of states were in the process of formation, the League was in decline, and a "spectre of a terrible war" loomed. Mankind, the editors lamented, "no longer guided its forces through reason and wisdom, through trust and understanding, but through concealed and open hatred, distrust and complacency."[36] When the newspaper asked Jonas Dobkevičius, director of the Chamber of Trade and Industry (*Prekybos ir pramonės rūmai*), about prospects of an end to the crisis, he conceded the crisis would continue as long as there were no markets for Lithuanian agricultural products. Not even the strictest control of *Lietūkis, Pienocentras*, and *Maistas* over exports could change this. The only way out of the crisis, Dobkevičius argued, was to slim down Lithuania's economy to the point where Lithuanian peasants could undercut the prices of the modern overseas producers and hope for the survival of a

34 "Lietuvos ūkis metų balandžio gale," *Lietuvos ūkininkas* 20 (1932): 5.

35 William H. Stoneman, *The Life and Death of Ivar Kreuger* (Indianapolis, IN: Bobbs-Merrill, 1932), 101.

36 "1932 metai," *Lietuvos ūkininkas* 1 (1933): 4.

cooperation-based international order: "For the time being we have no alternative but to shrink as much as possible." And even then, Dobkevičius cautioned, "it is difficult to say whether any recovery will be permanent."[37] This pessimism concerning the never-ending character of the depression was shared by most economic experts, who agreed that Lithuania, as a small country, was in no position to shape the further unfolding of the global slump. Jonas Lapėnas, director of *Maistas* and chairman of the Association for Economic Studies (*Ekonominių studijų draugija*), predicted "perhaps a dozen years of crisis."[38]

Over the course of 1933, the *Lietuvos ūkininkas* continued an anti-capitalist conversation on the roots and duration of the depression. The editors lamented that the "learned people" were coming up with "all sorts of plans, some of them very fantastic" that could never be implemented. The increasing protectionism, on the other hand, was too feeble a measure against the depression, which was "too vast, too complex." The depression, the editors claimed, had its roots in the economic challenges of the immediate postwar period, which were never fully addressed and had resurfaced in their full severity in 1929–30.[39] In summer 1933, the editors concluded that only the collapse of capitalism could end the depression: "Incidentally, all the measures devised by the capitalists only serve to line their pockets, but they will not eliminate the crisis. The crisis will last as long as the capitalist system lasts."[40]

8.2 Deepening Rifts in the Countryside

Although no one in Lithuania remained unaffected by the depression, it is fair to say that it affected Lithuanians unequally. The newspaper *Lietuvos ūkininkas*, with its comprehensive letters-to-the-editor section, provides us with insights into the specific experience of Lithuania's peasantry. Despite the land reform, 18.6 percent of farms were still smaller than 5 ha (and thus barely sustainable) and

37 "Kada Lietuvoj praeis ekonominis krizis," *Lietuvos ūkininkas* 4 (1933): 5.
38 "Ankieta krizės klausimais," *Tautos ūkis* 5 (1932): 129–135.
39 "Krizių metai," *Lietuvos ūkininkas* 17 (1933): 4
40 J. Budavietis, "Krizis ir ūkininkai," *Lietuvos ūkininkas* 27 (1933): 5

27.4 percent were between 5 and 10 ha.[41] Owners of these farms were particularly vulnerable to the lack of credit and the failure of buyers to pay for the purchase of agricultural goods. Jonas Frišenbrūderis, for instance, owned 8 ha of land, meaning his farm was only half the size of the Lithuanian average farm (15 ha). He thus belonged to the one third of Lithuanian small farmers, whose aggregate land accounted for only 10 percent of Lithuania's total farmland.[42] As a smallholder, Frišenbrūderis suffered from the increasing practice of buyers not paying purchases in full and the inability of peasants to negotiate prices and payments versus the almighty cooperative *Lietūkis*. "Finally, after a month or so, you get 70 per cent, but even from that they still deduct the advances made in the spring, and they leave the 30 per cent still standing," Frišenbrūderis wrote in 1932: "Meanwhile, the taxes don't wait. Then again, Mr. *Lietūkis* demands the redemption of bills for fertilisers, here municipal taxes are rising year after year, here is the salary of the mayor, there are other expenses, and so on."[43]

Like much of East-Central Europe, Lithuania witnessed a proliferation of small banks across the 1920s, many of which were forced to shut down their business during the depression and were either liquidated or absorbed by Lithuania's national bank (*Lietuvos bankas*), or the Land Bank (*Žemės bankas*). In 1929, more than 400 small-credit associations operated in Lithuania, a figure that shrank by one quarter across the 1930s. Of 24 mutual credit associations, 9 closed during the depression.[44] As a measure to sustain their business during the depression, many small banks increased their interest rates, significantly impacting small farmers, who traditionally preferred local banks or private individuals—often neighbors. Forced to engage with nonlocal banks, the depression brought many farmers into contact with the Land Bank for the first time. Frustrated by its bureaucracies, many returned to local

41 Dragomir, "Development Characteristics," 59.

42 Valčiukienė, Atkocevičienė, and Sudonienė, "Changes of Land Users," 9.

43 Jonas Frišenbrūderis, "Mūsų skaitytojų žodis," *Lietuvos ūkininkas* 4 (1932): 4.

44 Irena Čepienė and Vladas Terleckas, "Kooperatinės bankininkystės sektorius Lietuvoje 1918–1940 m.," *Ekonomika* 47 (1999): 30–39.

lenders, accepting significantly higher interest rates.[45] A farmer called Stankaitis complained that "the various small credit societies and private banks have spawned like ticks, making millions of litas of profit from the interest they earn" and thus contributing to a deepening divide between large and small farmers: "Since 1927, the abyss has grown wider and deeper every year." Moreover, smallholders felt that state support benefited export-oriented large farms and estates only.[46] Stankaitis suggested the creation of a hardship fund for small farmers from the 20 million Litai collected in land tax each year. This led to strong opposition among owners of larger farms, who blamed the troubles of smallholders on laziness, profligacy, and alcoholism ("He who works and saves will have").[47] A peasant owning a 25-ha pig-breeding farm argued that such a fund would mean "awarding farmers for not wanting to produce."[48] However, several smallholders wrote in support of such a fund. Leveling the increasing gap between small and large farmers would, in their words, "create equality for all farmers and make everyone feel like children of the same father and more energetic and more committed to the work of rural culture."[49]

However, the depression had its most profound impact on the divide between rural producers and urban workers. This was closely linked to debates around unemployment, which was mostly an urban phenomenon. Although unemployment figures—as in other countries—are unreliable, a surge is discernible in the numbers of those employed in public works, which were introduced during the depression to battle unemployment. In 1932, the number of people employed in industries had dropped for the first time since 1926. In Kaunas alone, 6,500 people became employed in public works in 1932 and 10,500 in 1933. In summer 1932, the Ministry of the Interior demanded the expansion of public works into smaller towns, which

45 S. Strimaitis, "Kai kurie privatiniai bankai tebelupikauju," *Lietuvos ūkininkas* 27 (1932): 4

46 K. Stankaitis, "Ar nes tas pats, kas iš vienos kišenės kiton," *Lietuvos ūkininkas* 6 (1932): 6.

47 Taikos angelas, "Kas dirba ir taupo, tas ir turi," *Lietuvos ūkininkas* 11 (1932): 5.

48 Ūkn. Taučius, "Ar premijuotinas eksportas?" *Lietuvos ūkininkas* 11 (1932): 5.

49 Virbalietis, "Mūsų skaitytojų žodis," *Lietuvos ūkininkas* 13 (1932): 4.

had hitherto never experienced unemployment at all.[50] At the end of 1933, the mayor of Kaunas, Antanas Gravrogkas, told a representative of the International Labour Organization (ILO) that the worst was yet to come, as the postwar reconstruction of Lithuanian towns and cities was coming to an end and public works had to be phased out.[51]

Yet peasants writing to *Lietuvos ūkininkas* had little sympathy for the plight of urban workers who, they claimed, considered farm labor beneath them. When unemployed workers went on strike in Šiauliai, a major center of Lithuania' emerging industries, this was met with disdain. A farmer claimed that unemployment "was invented either by utter sluggards or by those who do not want to work as a 'poor man's man' and flee to the cities." The unemployed did not mind "splitting a wagon of firewood for a Jew, or driving a barrel of kerosene and herrings into a wheel, or stacking iron in a cellar . . . But try to hire them for farm work!" Due to falling agricultural prices, the urban population were benefitting from the crisis and preferred urban unemployment over farm work: "The city has completely corrupted the worker. He knows all the laws that protect his rights to the best of his ability, but he does not want to think about his duties or work."[52] Of course, farm labor was not the outlet for urban unemployment that many farmers claimed it to be. There was indeed a severe lack of farmhands across the 1930s, with rural workers often emigrating to neighboring Latvia, where higher wages were paid.[53] But this was true for some large farms only. Falling prices led many owners of small- and medium-sized farms to rely on their own labor and lay off farmhands, thus contributing to unemployment. A nationalist newspaper quoted a farmer as saying: "Why do I need to hire farm hands if I have to earn their bread and wages?" Instead, farmers resorted to selling off their livestock,

50 Norbertas Černiauskas, *Nedarbas Lietuvoje 1918–1940 metais* (PhD diss., Vilnius University, 2014), 275, https://www.lituanistika.lt/content/70352.

51 "Rapport Nr. 1 sur la Lithuanie au Directeur du B.I.T," December 30, 1933, Internal Labour Organisation Archive, C 39-2-1, unnumbered.

52 Nuliūdęs berželis, "Nedarbas Lietuvoje," *Lietuvos ūkininkas* 41 (1932): 5

53 Leonas Sabaliūnas, *Lithuania in Crisis. Nationalism to Communism, 1939–1940* (Bloomington, IN: Indiana University Press, 1972).

ploughing the fields themselves, or sowing clover instead of crops, which they could harvest and sell on their own.[54]

Unsurprisingly, the urban readership of *Lietuvos ūkininkas* was outraged. A farmhand from near Šiauliai stressed that the blame for rotting crops was with the farmers, who hired farmhands only when "their crops or fodder are in imminent danger."[55] Another said that Lithuanian farmers themselves were to blame: Since the depression, they had started to hire farmhands for a few weeks during the harvest time only—too little to feed a family:

> You will see how our workers are running to the field work in Latvia or Germany. If there is a demand, they are running in masses with their wives and children and are seen as exemplary workers there. And why? Because there they get work for the whole summer season, for 6–7 months. Moreover, the farmers there are much more cultured and accept the worker as a human being, they know that a worker cannot work on an empty stomach, so they provide good food and better wages. And how do you feed us? An old piece of bacon for breakfast and some smelly concoction on top of that bacon. You try so hard to make us eat less.[56]

Angry letters to *Lietuvos ūkininkas* were so plentiful that the editors felt the need to justify publishing letters in the first place: "It has long been known to the editorial staff that the farmers blame the workers, and the workers blame the farmers," they wrote: "But now, after the explanation of the workers, they (the land owners—K. R.) will probably not be angry anymore."[57]

The depression deepened a divide that had existed for centuries. Many rural Lithuanians were traditionally wary of the multiethnic towns, which they associated with immorality, vice, and "Jewishness."[58] In 1933, a farmer complained that corruption spread

54 "Nedarbo simptomai mūsų kaime," *Tautos balsas*, October 27, 1932.

55 Darbininkas, "Argi taip iš tikrųjų yra?" *Lietuvos ūkininkas* 43 (1932): 6.

56 P. Čiuprinskas, "Darbininko balsas," *Lietuvos ūkininkas* 43 (1932): 6.

57 "Redakcijos prierašas," *Lietuvos ūkininkas* 43 (1932): 6.

58 Klaus Richter, *Antisemitismus in Litauen: Christen, Juden und die "Emanzipation" der Bauern (1889–1914)* (Berlin: Metropol, 2014).

from the cities, poisoning the countryside and "wiping out the most resilient pillar of our Republic—the farmer." Fellow farmers were beginning "to live in an unusually gentlemanly manner," spending times in towns with "intellectuals . . . playing cards and gambling." Town bureaucrats refused relief to farmers, but lived as if no crisis existed.[59] Farmers recounted stories of lawyers and doctors charging exorbitant sums for short journeys into the countryside: "All in all, the villagers are now sniffing at the learned people. I remember before the war, trained people were much more honoured. Now you often hear them called usurers . . . So, instead of scolding us, the intelligent professionals should curb their appetites, because they recently came out of the straw-roofed hut themselves and should thus live more austerely."[60]

Not least, peasants became aware of the considerable increase in social spending designed to relieve the urban unemployed and low-wage earners. Social transfers dropped at the beginning of the depression, but then increased considerably from 1931 to 1933.[61] Several farmers argued that the government should introduce an austerity-focused policy and cut back on benefits: "It is not only the holiday allowances that should be scrapped, but it is absolutely necessary to scrap: any personal allowances, children's allowances, three-year allowances, five-year allowances, all kinds of per diems, all kinds of additional salaries, in short, to leave only the basic salaries and to prohibit more than one salaried post." The government should tax "lawyers, doctors, clergy, engineers, etc." No farmer "should be made to pay for the things mentioned here."[62] In November 1931, peasants organized in cooperatives in Pagiriai district petitioned the government to fight syndicates as "illegal operations," as these were "operating solely for the purpose of usury," to drastically cut the salaries of state and local officials, and to punish

59 J. Žvelgaitis, "Krizis ir dar šis tas," *Lietuvos ūkininkas* 43 (1933): 8

60 "Per daug iš kaimiečių reikalauja," *Lietuvos ūkininkas* 21 (1932): 7

61 Zenonas Norkus, Vaidas Morkevičius, and Jurgita Markevičiūtė, "From Warfare to Welfare States? Social and Military Spending in the Baltic States 1918–1940," *Scandinavian Economic Review* 69, no. 1 (2021): 1–21.

62 K. A., "Bendrai kovokime su ekonominiu kriziu," *Lietuvos ūkininkas* 15 (1932): 4; Also: "Valdininkų algų mažinimo reikalu," *Lietuvos ūkininkas* 2 (1933): 4.

by law farmhands who leave work before the end of the contract.[63] When rural discontent boiled over in summer 1935, culminating in the rural strikes in the Suvalkija region, strikers distributed leaflets urging peasants not to deliver any foodstuffs to towns, actively obstructed the delivery of agricultural produce, and poured milk into ditches.[64]

The experience of Lithuanian farmers in the early 1930s was structured by debt. By 1931, the collapse in prices meant that loans taken out to compensate for the 1928 crop failure had become three times as expensive to service.[65] It is important to note that debt differed regionally: Sources indicate that peasants in Northern Lithuania—a region the relative prosperity of which was historically based on flax cultivation—were hit particularly severely due to the collapse in flax and linseed prices. From 1928 to 1932, the value of flax dropped from 46.59 million Litai to just 9.12 million and the value of linseed exports from 14.21 million Litai to 2.46 million.[66] As stories about wasteful, profligate, and uneducated peasants proliferated in Lithuanian towns and cities, debts became a deeply personal issue that transcended economic implications. When the summer harvest of 1932 failed, causing a further widening of the scissors between falling agricultural prices and stable prices of manufactured goods, peasants again turned to *Lietuvos ūkininkas* to explain the circumstances that caused them to become indebted. Not least, peasants expressed their frustration with admonitory calls—both from state officials and private businesses—to rationalize their farms to overcome the depression, claiming it was modernization that had brought them into debt in the first place.[67] "The farmer is forced into debt by the constant calls for them to buy livestock and poultry, to modernise their buildings," one farmer complained:

63 "Jo Ekscelencijai Ponui Ministeriui Pirmininkui," 1931, Lietuvos centrinis valstybės archyvas (=LCVA), f. 923, ap. 1, b. 717, l. 14.

64 "Žemės Ūkio Rūmai kviečia ūkininkus griežtai atsispirti agitatorių peršamai netvarkai," 1935. LCVA, f. 923, ap. 1, b. 857, l. 36.

65 "Jo Ekscelencijai Ponui Ministeriui Pirmininkui," 1931. LCVA, f. 923, ap. 1, b. 717, l. 14.

66 Simutis, *The Economic Reconstruction*, 51; "Dėl skolos už sėklą išdėstymo šiaur. Lietuvos ūkininkams," *Lietuvos ūkininkas* 51 (1932): 4.

67 K. Stankaitis, "Mūsų skaitytojų žodis," *Lietuvos ūkininkas* 4 (1932): 4.

> Many farmers have already begun to take less care of their farms in anticipation of even more difficult years. They sow their winter crops on poorly cultivated soil, they no longer select the best seeds, they sow sprouts, they also use less mineral fertiliser, they no longer take care of their buildings, and so on. They sell off their livestock . . . You all should remember that the edifice of the state was created and defended under a straw roof, in the village, which is now in trouble.[68]

Indebted farmers demanded a moratorium on rural debt and cuts to the salaries of state officials as the only way out of the crisis for both peasants and the state, which suffered from the low income from land taxes.[69] *Lietuvos ūkininkas* provided space for creditors to respond to these debt-moratorium proposals ("What the other side says"). One well-to-do farmer, who had borrowed money from the bank to lend to farmers in financial distress, emphasized that some of his debtors had borrowed out of necessity, whereas others had borrowed "in order to become gentlemen." A debt moratorium would only create "a new queue of borrowers," he warned."[70] Another lender stressed that "most private lenders are not moneylenders. They are mainly people of the same ilk who have saved over the years in the hope of acquiring some assets." They were already losing money because of the debtors' ruin. If a debt relief were to be granted, "it would be imperative to sort out the debtors, as grain from chaff," with some whose farms "must be sold off without mercy."[71]

8.3 Economic Nationalism and the Great Depression as Opportunity

While those most affected by the Great Depression were deeply discontented with the government's responses to their hardship, for

68 L. M., "Kaip išbristi iš bėdos," *Lietuvos ūkininkas* 38 (1932): 6.

69 S. B., "Moratoriumo reikalu," *Lietuvos ūkininkas* 49 (1932): 4; "Ar tuojau bus suteikta tikra pagalba ūkininkams?" *Lietuvos ūkininkas* 51 (1932): 7.

70 Alb. Naš., "Nesąžiningi skolininkai neturi teisės palenginimų reikalauti," *Lietuvos ūkininkas* 1 (1933): 8.

71 Žemaitis, "Skolininkus susirūšiuoti," *Lietuvos ūkininkas* 1 (1933): 8.

others, the dynamics unleashed by the depression represented an opportunity to reshape Lithuania as a nation state centered around ethnic Lithuanians. Lithuania's dictator, Antanas Smetona, articulated little sympathy for the complaints of small farmers. To overcome the depression, Smetona argued, cooperative dairy and pig farming and state enterprises had to be further expanded. In fact, the reduction of small farms and the laying off of farmhands gave Lithuania an upper edge: "Our farmers are better able to look after and rear their animals if they are tending to them themselves than if hired farmhands were to do this."[72]

Accordingly, government economic responses were designed with nationalist objectives in mind. Since independence, Lithuanian governments had pursued a policy of empowering the mostly rural Lithuanian speakers vis-à-vis those minorities that were regarded as economically privileged—especially Polish speakers (3.2 percent of the population in 1923), who dominated large land ownership, and Jews (7.6 percent), who were predominantly engaged in urban professions, including trade.[73] While these policies were initially of limited success, they accelerated during the Great Depression, as increasing state control over the economy provided new possibilities to shift both material resources and economic agency, and to encourage impoverished peasants and farmhands to seek work in towns and compete with the urban minorities. Between 1923 and 1930, the urban population had fallen from 16.1 to 13.5 percent (possibly due to higher birth rates in the countryside)—but it increased to 14.9 percent in 1934 and 19.5 percent in 1939.[74] While the share of ethnic Lithuanians accounted for only 13 percent of all those engaged in trade in 1923, their share climbed to one-third in 1935, mostly through their involvement in the burgeoning cooperative sector.[75] According to *Maistas* director Jonas Lapėnas, the depression was wiping out the "weaker," "parasitic" merchants, thus

72 "Ankieta krizės klausimais," *Tautos ūkis* 5 (1932): 129–135.

73 *Lietuvos gyentojai. Pirmojo 1923 m. rugsėjo 17 d. visuotino gyventojų surašymo duomenys* (Kaunas: Lietuvos Respublikos Centrinis Statistikos Biuras, 1923).

74 Klimantas, "Lithuanian Economy," 5.

75 Jacob Lestchinsky, "The Economic Struggle of the Jews in Independent Lithuania," *Jewish Social Studies* 8, no. 4 (1945): 276, 281.

making it possible to centralize and nationalize trade.[76] Social discontent was often countered with nationalist arguments. Seeking to quell the 1935–36 rural strikes in the Suvalkija region, Lithuania's Chamber of Agriculture, for instance, appealed to peasants by stressing the success of land reform: "Instead of estates that were alien to us, today we have tens of thousands of Lithuanian homesteads." These were "the tremendous, miraculous deeds of a nation that has emerged from the ruins of war and the yoke of foreigners."[77]

The Klaipėda region, annexed by Lithuania in 1923 with a vision of turning it into the country's outlet to the sea, is a striking example of how the dynamics of depression could be harnessed for the ends of economic nationalism. Economically dominated by German speakers, the region's integration turned out to be a challenge. Yet when the Central European banking crisis caused panic withdrawals from Klaipėda's banks, *Lietuvos bankas* specifically targeted struggling businesses with low loans. In addition, the bank provided inexpensive loans to Lithuanians from outside the Klaipėda region ("Lithuania Major") to buy up businesses that had been foreclosed. These loans, in turn, stipulated that the new owners should hire only workers from "Lithuania Major."[78] At the same time, the Lithuanian government created jobs for Lithuanian day laborers through ambitious public works in those areas of the city that were under their direct control—the port and the railways. Accordingly, labor migration increased. Over the course of the depression, 8,000 day laborers migrated from "Greater Lithuania" to the Klaipėda region. By the late 1930s, the cooperative Bisdom & Zoom, which came under the control of *Lietuvos bankas* in 1935, employed only 38 Klaipėda-born workers and 420 workers who had migrated from Lithuania Major. The port of Klaipėda employed 47 workers from Klaipėda and 489 from Lithuania Major. The share of Lithuanian speakers in the total population of the city of Klaipėda increased

76 "Ankieta krizės klausimais," *Tautos ūkis* 5 (1932): 129–135.

77 "Žemės Ūkio Rūmai kviečia ūkininkus griežtai atsispirti agitatorių peršamai netvarkai," 1935, LCVA, f. 923, ap. 1, b. 857, l. 36.

78 "Die wirtschaftliche Lage des Memelgebiets," March 16, 1932, The National Archives, Kew, GFM33, 3483: E683723-E684692; Kriminalpolizei des Memelgebiets, Öffentliche Versammlung der Landwirte. April 22, 1933, LCVA, f. 1636, ap. 1, b. 96, l. 133.

from merely 3 percent in 1920 to between 35 and 38 percent in 1938. In 1937, for the first time, the majority of those born in Klaipėda were registered as "Lithuanians."[79]

Such strategic policies were conceived of earlier, but catalyzed by the Great Depression. On December 15, 1933, at the annual assembly of Smetona's Lithuanian Nationalist Union (*Lietuvių Tautininkų Sąjunga—LTS*), a speaker stressed that, in its efforts to overcome the crisis, the LTS had to ensure "that all jobs and professions are accessible to Lithuanians and that they are properly prepared; to tend towards the organization of work and trades which correspond best to national aspirations, where all the Lithuanian resources are used and where the Lithuanian is not forced to emigrate for abroad."[80] LTS members were acutely aware that the Great Depression provided an unexpected opportunity to shift the economic hierarchies between Lithuanians and national minorities. One member stressed in September 1932 that the Lithuanians were "still in almost complete economic slavery" of "strangers and foreigners," by which he meant primarily Jews. Yet trade and industry were "intimately connected with the interests of the nation and the state," meaning Lithuania would not attain genuine sovereignty unless ethnic Lithuanians seized control of these sectors. Jewish merchants, who served as intermediaries between Lithuanian peasants and the large state-sponsored cooperatives, were "nothing more than legalized robbers" working in the interest of foreign powers, funneling Lithuanian money into foreign banks. The state had to make sure that intellectuals and the unemployed were provided with support to compete with Jews in urban professions. "The money works in good times, the mind works in bad times," he claimed, and promoted a policy that would get more Lithuanians into vocational schools, schools of commerce, and university to be able to enter the commercial sector, "which is much easier to enter at the moment." "The economic depression itself has already begun to purge the foreign, dirty merchants and industrialists from our land through massive

79 Julius Žukas, "Soziale und wirtschaftliche Entwicklungen Klaipedas/Memels von 1900 bis 1945," *Nordost-Archiv* 10 (2001): 95.

80 "Rapport Nr. 1 sur la Lithuanie au Directeur du B.I.T." December 30, 1933, Internal Labour Organisation Archive, C 39-2-1, unnumbered.

bankruptcies. That is why today those positions are becoming free . . . If we have learnt to work in this field in difficult times, we will be all the more capable to do so in normal times."[81] The LTS general secretary, Vincas Rastenis, stressed the liminal nature of the crisis for Lithuania's becoming a nation-state:

> We are not daunted by the fact that we are embarking on this difficult work at a time of severe crisis. On the contrary, this latter circumstance even encourages us. Times of general upheaval sometimes shatter convictions which, until recently, seemed to be indisputable truths, but which now appear to be merely windswept. And these times of crisis have already revised more than one truth of yesterday, which now appears to be a handful of sand.[82]

The Lithuanian Businessmen's Association (*Lietuvių verslininkų sąjunga*—LVS) was founded in 1930 for exactly this purpose—to educate ethnic Lithuanians to become engaged in those economic sectors they were hitherto underrepresented in. In September 1933, at a meeting of the LVS branch in Kaunas, economist Kazys Sruoga painted the crisis as a time of embittered economic struggle between Lithuania's nationalities, as the minorities were closing their ranks and providing work and capital "only to their own countrymen."[83] At another congress, an LVS representative from Alytus gave a passionate speech and stressed that "if we are able to survive and strengthen in this time of crisis, it shows that the Lithuanians are talented and resilient entrepreneurs." However, the same representative warned that minorities in the trade sector were still attracting 80 percent of all customers, mainly because of a lack of Lithuanian warehouses, which he urged the government to set up.[84]

The 1938 program of the LTS is a striking amalgamation of the key tenets of economic nationalism and the popular sentiments

81 "Susirupinkime savo ekonomine būkle," *Tautos balsas*, September 24, 1932.
82 Vincas Rastenis, "Ko mes norime?" *Verslas*, February 25, 1932.
83 "Lietuvių Verslovininkų Sąjungos Kauno skyriaus visuotinio susirinkimo, įvykusio 1933 m. rugsėjo m. 24 d. Šaulių S-gos salėje protokolas," LCVA, f. 605, ap. 1, b. 3, l. 21.
84 "Lietuvių Verslovininkų Kongreso 1933 mt. Spalių 7-8 d. Kaune protokolas," LCVA, f. 605, ap. 1, b. 10, l. 7.

produced by the Great Depression. The government concentrated in its hands all instruments to fix prices, thus abolishing cartels, syndicates, and trusts. "In the case of poor management," the state could intervene by taking over the management from the owners. To ensure the "harmonious solidarity" in agricultural and industrial production, strikes were banned. The LTS promised to further expand livestock and dairy exports through an ambitious program of construction of modern slaughterhouses, cold stores, and dairies.[85] However, unlike neighboring Latvia, Smetona's Lithuania never became fully corporatist, although the Lithuanian Nationalist Union did promote corporatist principles.[86] At the height of the depression, and in line with fascist rhetoric, the LTS had advocated for a "return to an organic society, to an organic state, to an organic economy, and to begin the work of rehabilitation," thus healing divides in Lithuanian society. By implementing corporatist principles, the LTS would ensure more planning and thus more certainty and stability. Through a targeted financial policy, the government would support those sectors it considered "more useful" over those that were "more profitable." Not least, the LTS would "alleviate and reduce" the agricultural crisis, as farmers would benefit from the greater degree of planning in production and consumption.[87] In its 1938 program, the LTS defined its key task "to defend and support the economically weaker segments of the Lithuanian producers and to increase the wealth and productivity of the Lithuanian nation." The LTS allocated specific significance to increasing the engagement of ethnic Lithuanians in the trade sector, preferably through cooperatives. It would use "all means . . . to combat speculation and the undercutting of farmers" by supplanting "unnecessary intermediaries"—an implicit reference to the minorities (especially Jews) engaged in trade. Only by "increasing the ethics of trade and

85 "Sąjungos programa," 1938. LCVA, f. 554, ap. 1, b. 115, l. 1-3, 6, 9, 12–21.

86 Vytautas Petronis, "Opting for the National: The Failure of the Lithuanian Committee for the Universality of Rome, 1934–1939," *Journal of Baltic Studies* (2023), https://doi.org/10.1080/01629778.2023.2275581.

87 Staugirdas, "Liberališkoji ar korporatyvynė valstybė?" *Tautos balsas*, November 26, 1932.

capacity of honest, reputable traders" could prices be decreased and government control over prices relaxed.[88]

8.4 Conclusion

With the fall in global agricultural prices, the Great Depression made a considerable impact on Lithuania. Lithuania's geopolitical situation, including its conflict with Poland and its dependence on trade relations with Germany, prolonged and deepened the slump. Although Lithuania's agricultural economy, which was in the process of diversification and modernization, proved fairly resilient against the crisis, the depression fragmented Lithuanian society. Small farmers saw their very existence under threat as private debts soared and agricultural markets dried up. Pre-existing divides between small and large farmers, between towns and the countryside, and between ethnic Lithuanians and the national minorities deepened. However, while peasants demanded a moratorium on debts and a shifting of privileges from the urban and state sector to the countryside, government policies were designed with nationalist objectives in mind, harnessing the disruptions caused by the depression to "Lithuanianize" those sectors of the economy that were previously dominated by national minorities such as Jews, Germans, or Poles.

88 "Sąjungos programa," 1938. LCVA, f. 554, ap. 1, b. 115, l. 1-3, 6, 9, 12–21.

Chapter 9

ROMANIA

SERVING FEWER BY DESIGN: AUSTERITY WELFARE POLITICS DURING THE GREAT DEPRESSION[1]

Alexandra Ghiț

In the interwar period, Romanian statesmen were at first unwilling and then very much unable to steer the priorities of domestic politics toward social rights. In the 1920s, National Liberal Party governments reluctantly expanded employment-related social entitlements—which Linda Gordon termed the "first track" of welfare—as a way of minimally keeping up with international commitments.[2] In 1929, politicians opposed to the Liberals' capital-friendly approaches won elections based on a promise to create policies that were more supportive of peasants and workers. The progressive platform of the 1929 National Peasant government was undermined by the economic crisis and the Peasantists' own authoritarian turn by 1932. This political shift is how, at the peak of the crisis, increases in social spending became explicitly prohibited as part of internationally agreed austerity packages accompanying foreign loans. Social assistance policies, "the second track of welfare," meant to support those who could not benefit from contributory schemes, also became stingier.

The world crisis arrived in Romania on the coattails of an already present agrarian crisis. Like its other agrarian neighbors, Romania began experiencing a drop in revenues from its raw material exports,

1 This chapter develops on and integrates two sections in chapter 2 of my PhD thesis, Alexandra Ghiț, "Loving Designs: Gendered Welfare Provision, Activism and Expertise in Interwar Bucharest" (PhD diss., Central European University, Vienna, 2020). Part of the work on this chapter was done while the author was a fellow of the Imre Kertész Kolleg Jena in January–June 2022.

2 Linda Gordon, *Women, the State, and Welfare* (Madison, WI: University of Wisconsin Press, 2012).

primarily grain, before the crash of autumn 1929. Like Hungary, Bulgaria, or Yugoslavia, between 1926 and 1928, the country borrowed increasing amounts.[3] Similarly to Hungary, the country's economy and the stability of its banking system became bound to increasingly fickle financial markets.[4] Romania would continue to borrow throughout the crisis. The 1931 failure of the Viennese Credit-Anstalt generated capital flight throughout Europe, including from Romania. Whereas many Western European countries departed from the Gold Standard and allowed their currencies to devalue, Romania—and many other Eastern European countries—did not, possibly to avoid further increases in the costs of external debt servicing.[5] In fact, Romania was one of the last countries to depart from the Gold Standard, in 1932.

The crisis arrived rather quietly, in 1929. It was felt by all in 1931, reached its nadir in 1932, and lingered into 1934. The prices of stocks at the Bucharest stock market were already declining in October 1929. However, neither economists nor politicians seemed to be aware yet that the kind of depression occurring in Germany and the Netherlands would be reaching Romania,[6] even if newspapers noted the steady rise in desperate job seekers, especially in the more heavily industrialized Western part of the country. Yet a little over one year later, in 1931, the value of plant-based agricultural production was less than half of its 1928 value; by 1933, plant-based agricultural production had declined to a little more than a third of the 1928 value. Prices for oil and coal, important sources of revenue for the state, fell even more dramatically, with the noticeable

3 Derek H. Aldcroft and Steven Morewood, *Economic Change in Eastern Europe since 1918* (London: Edward Elgar Publishing, 1995), 56.

4 Richard S. Grossman, "The Shoe That Didn't Drop: Explaining Banking Stability during the Great Depression," *The Journal of Economic History* 54, no. 3 (1994): 678.

5 Aldcroft and Morewood, *Economic Change*, 65.

6 Anca Mândru, "From Far Away to Closer to Home: Early Perceptions of the Great Depression in Romania—The Liminality of Failing Democracy: East Central Europe During the Interwar Slump," Project Webpage, *The Liminality of Failing Democracy: East Central Europe During the Interwar Slump* (blog), February 15, 2022, https://blog.bham.ac.uk/interwarslump/2022/02/15/from-far-away-to-closer-to-home-early-perceptions-of-the-great-depression-in-romania/.

drop beginning already in 1929.[7] Urban living conditions worsened quickly due to a decrease in the nominal value of wages and because of unemployment. In the countryside, conditions became dire.[8] As this chapter will show, government relief did not arrive. Whereas neighboring countries began combating unemployment first through unemployment aid and, from the mid-1930s on, through public works schemes, such central-government-managed schemes never quite arrived in Romania, despite promises.[9] On the whole, the economy picked up once Romania could resume its exports to Germany and could engage in a politics of rearmament, the latter from 1935 on.[10] In cities, the situation began to improve somewhat from the second half of 1934. In the countryside, recovery was much slower, partly because the price of wheat for export remained low; in 1937 it was still slightly lower than in 1929.

In recent scholarship on policy directions in interwar Romania, the focus is on state expansion or state intervention in the economy, rather than the lack of intervention that became highly visible during the crisis. A recent account of the emergence of the welfare state in interwar Romania claims that these interwar welfare policies emerged as part of a cross-ideological process of building up a "missing [middle class] core," itself integral to a broader agenda of nationalizing state-building.[11] Other scholars of the interwar era have stressed in their accounts the Romanian state's drive toward economic development after the mid-1930s, particularly its political orientation toward economic dirigisme. For instance, Grama argues that the 1920–30 period saw a kind of capital-friendly state expansion: "an explosion of labor legislation," albeit one that neutralized social conflict and kept the cost of labor low. Grama stresses

7 Nicolae N. Constantinescu, *Situația clasei muncitoare din România, 1914–1944* (Bucharest: Editura Politică, 1966), 222.

8 Constantinescu, *Situația clasei muncitoare*, 227–48.

9 Aldcroft and Morewood, *Economic Change*, 69. Between 1928 and 1931, the Ministry of Labour asked various local authorities to open roadworks (especially) in several counties most affected by unemployment – this depended on local resources available. Gheorghe Banu, *Şomajul în România* (Bucureşti: s.n., 1931), 23–25.

10 Constantinescu, *Situația clasei muncitoare*, 278–81.

11 Sergiu Delcea, "A Nation of Bureaucrats or a Nation of Workers? Welfare Benefits as Nation-Building Modernization Tools in Interwar Romania," *Journal of European Social Policy* 32, no. 1 (2022): 75–90.

that employers' dissatisfaction with the mildly interventionist labor laws of the late 1920s paved the way for Romania's embrace of economic nationalism after the mid-1930s.[12] Certainly, for most of the 1920s and again after 1932, Romanian governments pursued economic nationalism policies, which included placing limits on certain kinds of imports, introducing exchange controls, and controlling (but not limiting) the influx of foreign workers.[13] But this was not the case during most of the Great Depression years.[14] And, in general, economic nationalism did not translate into redistributive policies—neither in the 1920s nor after the middle of the 1930s, when a modicum of prosperity returned. As Murgescu has shown, Romania's social indicators were consistently the lowest in its region.[15]

A steady topic of inquiry in historical production during the state socialist period in Romania, the Great Depression, its social toll, and its political aftereffects has been left unexplored in recent scholarship. This chapter's analysis of changes in social insurance and social assistance between 1929 and 1933 will show that new labor laws and welfare laws passed during this period were designed around the goal of limited coverage. The tendency toward limiting, rather than expanding, welfare can be detected in politicians' statements of intent, but most often in policy design and the nitty gritty of new laws and regulations.

In his historical study on social spending in Malawi, Luke Messac argued that the notion that resources for welfare are scarce is a political construction, with colonial authorities and, more recently, international organizations fostering the idea that economic development and higher social spending are mutually exclusive in practice.[16] Despite international constraints, Romanian politicians had,

12 Adrian Grama, "The Cost of Juridification: Lineages of Cheap Labor in Twentieth-Century Romania," *Labor* 17, no. 3 (2020): 37.

13 Bogdan Murgescu, *România și Europa: Acumularea decalajelor economice (1500–2010)* (Bucharest: Polirom, 2010), 256.

14 Bogdan Murgescu, *România și Europa: Acumularea decalajelor economice (1500–2010)*, 255.

15 Bogdan Murgescu, *România și Europa: Acumularea decalajelor economice (1500–2010)*, 219.

16 Luke Messac, *No More to Spend: Neglect and the Construction of Scarcity in Malawi's History of Health Care* (New York: Oxford University Press, 2020).

in principle, greater space for political maneuver than that available in colonial and postcolonial settings.

How did actual and constructed scarcity shape the emerging welfare state in Romania? This chapter argues that Romania's welfare politics during the world economic crisis was defined by a politics of austerity. Drawing on critical analyses of the welfare state, I look at how welfare policies from the late 1920s until the middle of the 1930s were primarily shaped not by ideologies of development but by medium- and short-term policymaking oriented toward cost cutting.

In the first section of the chapter, I discuss the budgetary austerity measures adopted by Romania's governments. I show how a social-spending austerity principle linked to "open door" economic policies led to politicians downplaying or outright denying the scale of urban unemployment and stalling the creation of government-level relief and public works schemes for the jobless. This, in turn, opened the door for various municipal-level assistance schemes and, eventually, a desperate struggle for funds for relief. In the second and third parts of the chapter, I widen the frame, probing into some of the broader causes and effects of the government's attitude toward the crisis. Thus, in the second section of the chapter, I show how the government's capacity to be a direct provider of social assistance had been reduced by successive rounds of cuts to the budget of the Direction of Social Assistance, while in the third part of the chapter, I discuss the drop in living standards in the period 1929–33, emphasizing the massive scale of the crisis in the already very poor countryside. In the fourth part of the chapter, I provide a gendered analysis of key welfare and health-care laws adopted during the Great Depression, showing—with particular reference to maternity benefits—that for most citizens these laws had few effects due to austerity-based design principles as well as implementation issues.

9.1 Misconstruing Unemployment

The commitment to economic orthodoxy in Romania sprang from the National Peasant Party's (NPP) out-of-step embrace of "an open door" trade and customs policy in early 1929.[17] After a decade of economic nationalism, as other countries were beginning to protect their economies, the Romanian government encouraged foreign direct investment and strengthened financial ties with banks abroad. During most of the Depression years, Romania was governed by the NPP and its electoral coalition partners. After running on a progressive platform "to end the misery of the population," in both national and local elections of 1928–30, the NPP governed in an austere manner in the years that followed (1928–31; 1932–33).[18] Originally, the NPP was a center-left group created in 1926 through the fusion of the regional centrist Romanian National Party from Transylvania and the more radical agrarianist Peasant Party originating in the Old Kingdom. For the 1928 campaign, the new NPP concluded electoral alliances with conservatives and social democrats, among others, as part of an intense opposition campaign against the Liberals (NLP). In 1930, Prince Carol, in exile since 1925 when he refused to break off a love affair, returned to the country. With the support of key politicians and public personalities, the Prince was crowned King Carol II that year.[19] Notably, the NLP opposed the "restoration."[20] In the first 2 years after his coronation, Carol II's policy preferences aligned with the priorities of the Peasantist governments and of a short-lived "government of technicians" led by veteran politician Constantin Argetoianu and prominent historian Nicolae Iorga. In 1932, the National Peasantists were recalled to government. Notably, the party was now electing prime ministers from among their more conservative leaders.

As outlined in the introduction, starting in 1929, the NPP government contracted sovereign loans from the Banque de France,

17 Dietmar Müller, *Agrarpopulismus in Rumänien. Programmatik und Regierungspraxis der Bauernpartei und der Nationalbäuerlichen Partei Rumäniens in der Zwischenkriegszeit*, vol. 1, Rumänien-Studien (St. Augustine, FL: Gardez! Verlag, 2001), 124–29.

18 Ioan Scurtu, *Istoria Partidului Naţional Ţărănesc*, 2nd ed. (Bucharest: Editura Enciclopedică, 1994); Simion Cutişteanu and Gheorghe I. Ioniţă, *Electoratul din România în anii interbelici: mişcarea muncitorească şi democratică în viaţa electorală din România interbelică* (Cluj-Napoca: Dacia, 1981).

19 Ioan Scurtu, *Istoria românilor în timpul celor patru regi (1866–1947)*, vol. III: *Carol al II-lea* (Bucharest: Editura Enciclopedică, 2004), 7–70.

20 Ioan Scurtu, *Istoria românilor în timpul celor patru regi (1866–1947)*, 1–32.

granted in exchange for a commitment to keeping the state budget balanced.[21] The 1929 "monetary stabilization" loan was accompanied by the Rist technical mission—one of several "Money Doctor" delegations to Eastern Europe at the time—dispatched by the French bank to provide assistance to the Romanian National Bank.[22] The "Charles Rist mission" recommended public sector downsizing as one of the main measures to be taken by the government.[23] In Cornel Ban's recent assessment of this interwar situation: "Romania was, practically, in Greece's situation from 2010, with the French central bank playing the part of the IMF."[24]

The government dutifully applied the harsh and publicly very visible "sacrifice curbs [cuts]" required by the lenders as part of monetary stabilization programs. Three successive rounds of cuts (in January 1931, January 1932, and January 1933) reduced the salaries of all public employees by 50 percent. In addition, public sector pensions decreased by 33 percent in 1932. The cuts affected white-collar workers but also thousands of blue-collar workers employed by the railways and several state-owned enterprises.

In conjunction with cuts, the government engaged in early and sustained denial of unemployment. Articles construed unemployment as a problem of industrialization and therefore, not a possible issue in Romania, an agrarian country imagined to be inhabited overwhelmingly by subsistence farmers. The typical preamble of most articles discussing unemployment in state-supported publications in the early 1930s claimed that the lack of jobs had never

21 Dominique Torre and Elise Tosi, "Charles Rist and the French Missions in Romania 1929–1933. Why the 'Money Doctors' Failed?" in *Economic and Financial Stability in Southeast Europe in a Historical and Comparative Perspective (Conference Proceedings of the 4th Meeting of the South-Eastern European Monetary History Network)* (2009), https://www.nbs.rs/en/drugi-nivo-navigacije/publikacije-i-istrazivanja/seemhn/seemhn_conf/, 91–106.

22 The mission was considered a failure. Romania rescheduled payments in 1933 and officially defaulted on the loan in 1941. Rist complained that the stabilization loan was not used for its intended monetary policy purposes but rather to service existing arrears. Torre and Tosi, "Charles Rist," 7, 11.

23 Torre and Tosi, "Charles Rist," 5.

24 Cornel Ban, *Dependență și dezvoltare. Economia politică a capitalismului românesc* (Bucharest: Tact, 2014), 36.

been a genuine issue in the country and that the phenomenon had emerged recently due to global developments.[25]

In the beginning of a study on unemployment relief published in the government's Labor Bulletin (1932), social researcher Veturia Mănuilă argued:

> Although it was never an acute issue in our country, unemployment became a current issue as the international economic crisis deepened. As our country is overwhelmingly agrarian, 80% of the population was employed in work in the countryside. The rest of the population number is in all 3.600.000 souls, about 828.000 heads of families. Evidently, this number is much too low for all the non-agricultural occupations in the country, such that under normal conditions, it was not even possible to speak in Romania about unemployment. [. . .] However, the economic crisis determined a contraction of activity in the various commercial and industrial enterprises, and this reduction created a state of lack of work, which took both officialdom and public opinion by surprise; a social phenomenon that is highly familiar abroad has produced here such confusion that a significant part of public opinion does not recognize the existence of unemployment in Romania.[26]

This assessment was contradicted by a government publication which argued that unemployment was felt in Romania as early as 1927, when public works tied to postwar reconstruction ended. Written in 1930, at the height of Banque de France influence, by C. Stănescu, the director charged with managing unemployment in the Ministry of Labor, the text recognized that the government could not afford to become involved in public works, but that it had concluded a workers' exchange treaty with France (itself hit by unemployment). Congruent with the general government tendency

25 Veturia Manuilă, "Principii de organizarea ajutorării şomeourilor în sectorul I al Municipiului Bucureşti," *Buletinul Muncii, Cooperației și Asigurărilor Sociale* 12, no. 10–12 (1932): 437.

26 Veturia Manuilă, "Principii de organizarea ajutorării şomeourilor în sectorul I al Municipiului Bucureşti," 437.

of downplaying unemployment, even this more clear-eyed piece ended on the hopeful note: "It must be mentioned that lack of employment in Romania presents itself as something unnatural and passing. Both the density of the population and the development stage of our industry, which has so many still unexploited natural resources, confirm this."[27]

If some considered unemployment "unnatural and passing," other policy stakeholders had been pushing for systematic measures for combating growing unemployment since before the crisis. In 1927, representatives of the social democratic General Confederation of Labor (Confederația Generală a Muncii, CGM) had met with the Minister of Labor to propose measures for combating the rising unemployment level. Trade unionists Mirescu and Flueraș asked for controls on imports for goods that could be made in the country, mechanization credits for small producers and craftsmen, public works, bans on mass layoffs in the public sector, the reduction of working hours, emergency relief for unemployed workers and clerks, and the rapid passing of legislation on unemployment insurance (*alocații de șomaj*). A commission of specialists was created to study the matter the same autumn, but no nationwide measures were taken.[28]

Yet rather than setting up national-level unemployment relief schemes, from 1930 on, the government encouraged municipalities to organize such aid themselves (mostly in-kind food aid and soup kitchens [*cantine populare*]). Occasionally, the Ministry of Labor transferred small sums to various localities that simply could not shoulder the burden of too many unemployed. However, by 1931 the government had made it clear that municipalities were to collect their own funds for relief and, otherwise, push back to the countryside any nonresident job seekers. Cities organized charity balls and various other collections, but by 1931 a medium-sized industrial

27 C. Stănescu, "Piața muncii," in *Zece ani de protecție socială în România,* ed. Ministerul Muncii, Sănătății și Ocrotirilor Sociale (Bucharest: Ministerul Muncii, Sănătății și Ocrotirilor Sociale, 1930), 198.

28 Arhivele Naționale Istorice Centrale (hereafter ANIC), Fond 3086- Amintiri și memorii (Collection 60), File 241/567 "Mirescu Ion, Vol II (1926–1932)," ff. 350, 386, 519.

city such as Cluj-Napoca announced that it could no longer provide assistance for any unemployed.[29]

In September 1931, the national government appeared to finally have a plan for the distribution of aid for the unemployed. Previously, in March 1931, the government had introduced a bill for a 10 million lei credit to the Ministry of Labor, for assistance toward the unemployed. Such assistance would largely be organized in accordance with the vision of State Undersecretary in the Ministry of Labor, Dr. Gheorghe Banu. In a brochure on unemployment published later that year, Banu legitimized the government's stance that far: the "truly" jobless were to be helped especially through in-kind aid (such as food and fire wood) and the existing local and regional committees were to research what kind of public works could potentially be opened in order to hire the unemployed.[30] In effect, the new plan continued the same practices, but switched some coordination tasks from municipalities to the central government.

In the March plenum discussion on the bill, social democratic MPs spoke against it, arguing that the 10 million sought were wholly insufficient and that the plan entailed the continuation of a form of distribution of welfare that treated workers in an undignified way. Rather than "charity," MP Mirescu demanded that unemployment be considered an issue to be dealt with through social insurance. In addition, since the beginning of the crisis, social democrats had also repeatedly demanded a ban on foreign "specialist" workers as well as a ban on the import of goods which could be manufactured in Romania. Minister of Labor Hațieganu and other supporters of the plan replied curtly that the issue of unemployment was being blown out of proportion in Romania and that the government had helped and would continue to help the unemployed.[31] Later, a 1932 plan proposed by social democratic MPs for the tackling of

29 "Cluj—Ajutorarea şomerilor," *Universul*, March 21, 1931.

30 Gheorghe Banu, *Şomajul în România* (Bucureşti: s. n., 1931); For a slightly different reading of Banu's stance, see Dragoş Sdrobiş, "Elitele şi universitatea în România interbelică," *Anuarul Institutului de Istorie "George Barițiu"* 60 (2012): 13.

31 "Desbaterile parlamentare—Camera—Şedința din 24 Martie," *Dreptatea*, March 26, 1931, Arcanum Digitheca Online Database, https://adt.arcanum.com/en/view/Dreptatea_1931_03/?pg=92&layout=s.

unemployment as a social insurance issue, through a tripartite contributory scheme, did not pass.[32]

Reluctance to address unemployment was visible in the Romanian government's international dealings. At the 1932 conference of the International Labour Organization (ILO), Romania stood out as the only country represented that would not vote for a proposed "Resolution concerning action to be taken to remedy the present crisis."[33] Whereas the Romanian government had submitted to the International Labour Organization a list of public works it was going to open in the country, MP Mirescu was surprised when informed about them by ILO representative Staal in a postconference letter.

Reluctance to deal with unemployment was discernible in Romanian employers' reactions to even quite unambitious legal initiatives. A 1932 law introduced to Parliament by the municipality of Timişoara, which proposed that funds for local committees for unemployment relief be collected from workers' contributions and various local taxes, was opposed by employers' representatives across the country. In connection to that law, a memorandum submitted to the Ministry of Labor by various Chambers of Commerce and employers' unions emphasized that it was unfair that "those who do not work should receive, whereas those who do work should not receive."[34]

When not misrepresenting and denying unemployment during the crisis years, Romania's governments engaged in suppressing popular protests against austerity and immiseration. This violent tactic culminated in the 1931 bloody crackdown of a railway workers' strike in Bucharest, an event that outraged not only sympathizers of the left wing but also enthusiasts of the extreme right wing. In the short and medium term, the local fascist organization, the Iron

32 "Mirescu Ion, Vol II (1926–1932)," 567.

33 "Mirescu Ion, Vol II (1926–1932)," 575; see list of resolutions of the 16th International Labour Conference, Geneva 1932. "Resolutions Adopted by the International Labour Conference (1919–2019)," accessed February 25, 2023, https://www.ilo.org/global/about-the-ilo/how-the-ilo-works/organigramme/jur/legal-instruments/WCMS_428590/lang--pt/index.htm.

34 "Mirescu Ion, Vol II (1926–1932)," 581.

Guard, stood to profit from established parties' repressive turn and seeming indifference to social demands.[35]

9.2 Central Government Frameworks for Social Assistance

By 1931, when the government was under increasing pressure to engage with growing unemployment and the immiseration of both urban and rural families, the capacity of the central government to act as a distributor of welfare had been curtailed. In fact, from the early 1920s founding of the Social Assistance Direction, the "second pillar" of welfare provision was only assumed to be a state duty in an indirect sense. Between 1921 and 1929, the official goals of the Ministry of Labor, Health and Social Protection's (hereafter MMSOS) Social Assistance Direction were to "organize, lead and supervise all actions related to mandatory social assistance."[36] The Direction's head, popular writer and social reformer Eugen Botez, explained that the office he led strove to "develop and support private initiative" rather than create new state-owned and state-administered institutions or programs.[37]

The goal of developing and supporting "private initiative" was achieved through the subsidies distributed by the Social Assistance Direction. To a lesser degree, the Direction was a direct welfare provider as well—in the middle of the 1920s, it maintained several "work colonies" meant to reform beggars and vagrants. During the Direction's first decade of functioning, "mandatory assistance" entailed indoor (in institutions like orphanages or homes for the elderly) and outdoor (cash and in-kind aid) assistance to those "in a physical, moral or material state of inferiority" who "could not

35 Marin C. Stănescu, *Stânga politică din România în anii crizei (1929–1933)* (Bucharest: Editura Mica Valahie, 2002), 46; Dylan Riley, *The Civic Foundations of Fascism in Europe*, 2nd ed. (London: Verso Books, 2019), 161.

36 Eugen Botez, "Asistența Socială," in *Zece ani de politică socială în România (1920–1930)*, ed. Ministerul Muncii, Sănătății și Ocrotirilor Sociale (Bucharest: Ministerul Muncii, Sănătății și Ocrotirilor Sociale, 1930), 249.

37 Botez, "Asistența Socială," 250.

support themselves through their own efforts."[38] Within this definition, poor mothers and children, widows, the disabled, and the elderly were categories of special interest. Assistance could also be provided to "the valid indigents," that is, those capable of work who needed support in finding employment.[39]

In 1927, the Social Assistance Direction lost its budgetary autonomy and, as a result, much of its revenues. A year later, the ability of the Social Assistance Direction to fund and monitor private initiative social assistance, while also serving as a direct welfare provider, decreased further. During that year, the National Liberal government was dealing with monetary instability and increasingly strong opposition. In this context, according to Eugen Botez, the government's social assistance body had to deal with additional cuts:

> The critical situation in which the Assistance found itself [in 1928] only became worse as the cost of living became higher and instead of expanding, the Assistance had to limit its activity. It decreases and cuts aids and subsidies for charitable organizations, it halts the construction of institutions and even shuts down part of the existing ones, so that it could sustain the remainder.[40]

These 1928 second round of cuts, occurring soon after the 1927 reduction of revenues, managed to derail a post-World War I vision of social policymaking for various categories of "dependents" as having to occur, at least to a certain extent, at the level of the national government. Notably, this contraction of central state

38 This category included "poor new mothers and infant children," "poor and orphaned children, foundlings, the disabled, the morally-abandoned vagrants and those children whose poor parents are unable to work," the poor disabled and invalids, "the poor wounded, convalescents, and the ill," "widowers and old people who can no longer work, the blind and the deaf-mute, the abnormal and the feeble." Botez, "Asistența Socială," 229.

39 In fact, the Social Assistance Direction within the Ministry of Labor energetically took it upon itself (rather than leaving the task to private charities) to "combat and repress those who refuse work" and engage in begging and vagrancy instead. The law saw vagrants rounded up by police and interned into work colonies; it was only abolished in 1936.

40 Botez, "Asistența Socială," 252.

social assistance provision and policymaking did not occur against the backdrop of a severe economic crisis. Rather, the priorities of the NLP shifted away from social policy expansion likely due to mismanagement, the mounting costs of administrative unification, and the repositioning of foreign policy.

In late 1929, under the new NPP government, the Ministry of Labor's Social Assistance Direction became the Social Assistance Service. Eugen Botez commented bitterly that this was the culmination of a longer trend: "The Social Assistance Direction, which had been conceived in a grand spirit as a great autonomous house with juridical personality, for social aid, with certain revenues, ends up through successive transformations as a simple and rigid Ministry office."[41] None too pleased about the NLP budget cuts in the late 1920s, Botez was even more upset by the NPP's enthusiasm for downsizing.

Downsizing was visible in the 1930 reorganization of health and social assistance services. The so-called "Moldovan Law" was one of the key acts passed by the eugenicist Health Minister of the first NPP government. The voluminous, detailed legal document actually bore the official title of the "Sanitary and Protection Law" (M. Of. 236/July 14, 1930). It was rooted in two principles: decentralization (budgetary and administrative) and the primacy of certified experts' authority (doctors especially, but also statisticians and social assistants) over other categories of persons involved in welfare provision.[42] Maria Bucur suggests that the most striking feature

41 Botez, "Asistența Socială," 252.

42 The 572 articles of the Law detailed employment requirements and attributions for most positions within the Ministry of Labor, Health and Social Protection involving sanitary intervention and social assistance. The act focused on preventative medicine, insisting on the combating of venereal disease. Through the creation of an autonomous Regie of the Sanitary and Protection Fund, the Law intended to safeguard a budget meant to cover health-care costs for the very poor. Parliament of Romania, *Legea Sanitară și de Ocrotire* [Sanitary and Protection Law]. In the version that was enacted, the Law also switched the regime of sex work from regulationist to abolitionist (through the banning of brothels). However, Lucian Dărămuş points out that the measure was tacked onto the Law during debates, likely at the separate insistences of hygienist doctors, clergy, and feminists. Lucian Dărămuş, "Prostituţie feminină şi heterosexualitate în România interbelică," in *Familia în România-Oincursiune diacronică pluridisciplinară*, ed. Anca Dohotariu (Bucharest: Editura Universităţii Bucureşti, 2017), 91–119.

of the Moldovan Law was its "combin[ing] a system of centralized decision-making by a group of elite technocrats—doctors—with a decentralized system of implementing these policies. [. . .] The law empowered local technical officials at the expense of the central administrative bureaucracy, while allowing the technocratic elite at the top of the ministerial hierarchy to retain control over long term policies."[43] The provisions of the law certainly aimed toward this change in legal oversight.

The new legal framework devolved most social assistance tasks from the national level to the municipal level. Consequently, the ministry-level Social Assistance Direction was replaced by the Service of Social Assistance, a strictly technical and supervisory body. The law now stated that the "Social assistance of individuals and families incapable of supporting themselves, and obliged to appeal to public support, falls to the communes, in collaboration with the private societies for social assistance" (Art. 466). At the same time, the state's authority over the voluntary welfare sector (dominated by women welfare workers) was to be expanded. The 1930 "Moldovan" Sanitary and Protection Law placed charitable associations under additional ministerial technical control and more stringent financial supervision.

The twist in the state's planned expansion of the municipal social assistance bureaucracy—as a way of controlling private initiative welfare provision—was represented by the massive budget cuts enacted in 1931. That year, the Ministry of Labor, Health and Social Protection lost one-fifth of its funding. The two largest charitable organizations, as well as new institutions created for the training of certified social assistants, lost all their funding.[44] In an analysis of the slashed categories of expenses, a writer for the eugenicist publication *Revista de Igienă Socială* (*Social Hygiene Review*) blamed the retrenchment on the government's "sacrifice curbs": "In principle, cuts could have been made from anywhere else but from the miserable budget of the Ministry of Health. [. . .] This is a truth lost from

43 Maria Bucur, *Eugenics and Modernization in Interwar Romania* (Pittsburgh, PA: University of Pittsburgh Press, 2002), 198–99.

44 "Bugetul pe 1931 al Ministerului Sănătății și Ocrotirilor Sociale," *Revista de Igienă Socială* 1, 1931, 65–71.

sight—whether with ill will or in good faith is of no importance—by the masters of balanced budgets, who slashed at random, left and right."[45]

These budgetary cuts impoverished private and public social assistance organizations in Bucharest when the inhabitants of the capital were experiencing the peak of the Great Depression. The Encyclopedia of Romania admitted as much 8 years later, stating:

> Social Assistance was included in the budget of the Ministry of Labor, Health and Social Protection, which we all know the hardships it went through [*sic*] and how many savings it had to make. When it came to such savings, the Social Assistance always came first. Because of the financial crisis the private initiative did not have a better situation in any way. Exactly at the time when it was entitled to greater support from the State Social Assistance, the latter was going through its hardest period.[46]

In 1931, the ministry's Service of Social Assistance had neither funding for direct assistance nor subsidies for private charities. Against the background of these 1931 massive cuts to the central budget, the legally emboldened Social Assistance Services of the Municipality further gained authority. However, even if these city and sector bureaus had greater coordination power, they could not implement many of their coordination initiatives, also because of a lack of funds.

For instance, besides unemployment relief, local budgets were meant to cover most or all the costs for indoor assistance institutions considered of "national importance" (large orphanages, schools for the deaf). However, the Direction reported that most cities and towns in Romania could not afford to do so, leaving these "nationally important" institutions' budgets to be provided by the central government.[47] By 1931, administrators quoted in the press

45 "Bugetul pe 1931 al Ministerului Sănătății și Ocrotirilor Sociale," 67.

46 Asociația Științifică pentru Enciclopedia României, *Enciclopedia României*, vol. 1 (Bucharest: Imprimeria Națională, 1938), 524.

47 ANIC, Fond MMSOS – Oficiul pentru Studii Sociale, File 79/1934 "România-Serviciile Sociale 1933 – Asistența Socială," vol. 2, ff. 74–80.

laid the blame for the situation on the central government. Popular NPP mayor Dem. I. Dobrescu complained that the central government effectively confiscated the revenues of most municipalities, leaving most cities in difficult situations when it came to organizing relief or providing longer-term social assistance.[48]

9.3 Without Relief: The Drop in Living Standards during the 1930s

Nationally, 300,000 individuals in urban and industrialized areas were laid off between 1929 and 1933. Articles published after 1945 pointed out that another 300,000 persons were let go from among the agrarian proletariat or were working in the private sector on reduced schedules and/or docked pay.[49] Small-scale social surveys from 1930s Bucharest confirm the tendency toward the de-regularization of employment during and after the crisis.[50]

The progressive deterioration of the situation of the workers in Bucharest since the beginning of the world crisis in 1929 was described by Veturia Mănuilă, head of the Superior School for Social Assistance, who was tasked by the city council with organizing unemployment relief in one of Bucharest's districts, in 1932:

> The economic crisis and lack of jobs have sensibly reduced the living standards of all the laboring classes. Among approximately 60% of our unemployed [assisted in Sector I Yellow] we could verify the gradual reduction of their earnings in the last 5–6 years. In 1925–26–28, a skilled worker had on average a wage of 5000–7000 lei per month. In 1930–31 monthly earnings have decreased to 3500–4000 lei, but most are around the 3000 lei limit. Fixed salaries have been

48 D. Dbr, "Congresul Uniunii Orașelor din România -Primarii orașelor cer ca statul să restituie fondul comunal pe care-l înstrăinează," *Adeverul*, January 27, 1931.

49 Teodor Necșa, "Date privind situația clasei muncitoare în perioada crizei economice 1929–1933," *Studii- Revista de Istorie* 9, no. 1 (1956): 108.

50 Gheorghe Banu et al., "Etudes concernant la situation de la femme ouvriere en Roumanie," *Revista de Igienă Socială* 7, no.7–8 (1937), 351–89.

> reduced by 50% over three years. At the same time, rents have constantly remained at the same level.[51]

In the countryside, already low living standards plummeted. In party programs and during their first round in government (1928–30), the National Peasantists promised to support small and middling peasants, especially by encouraging the creation of rural cooperatives to help modernize the small plot subsistence agriculture which characterized most peasant households.[52] These ambitious plans were an ill fit for the actual circumstances of the Romanian peasantry and the other economic (monetary and fiscal) policies of the government.

In 1928, many peasants were already deep in debt to the state and private lenders. The 1921 agrarian reform had expropriated estates and distributed them as small plots (around 5 ha) to 1.4 million peasants.[53] Formerly landless peasants, now propertied, became taxpayers. They were also paying the state back for two-thirds of the total amount paid in bonds to landlords whose estates had been expropriated in the reform.[54] In 1929, peasants were permitted to sell the land received in the agrarian reform. As holdings of 5 ha and under could not provide the food needed in the average peasant household, owners sold their plots or incurred high-interest debts, generally used to cover basic household consumption, tools, or seeds.

In 1930, following an unfavorable Rist report spotlighting inefficient tax collection, the government "ordered that [peasants' unpaid taxes] be recovered 'at all costs', so the tax collector and the gendarme resorted to all kinds of pressures, including the auction sale

51 Manuilă, "Principii de organizarea ajutorării şomeourilor," 444.

52 Economist Virgil Madgearu, the architect of the NPP rural development platform, believed the Romanian peasantry had not yet been incorporated into world markets and considered the peasant household, based on the free labor of family members, economically self-sustaining and suited to peasants' individualistic mentality. Rural cooperatives were meant as an intermediary phase in Romania's small-scale agriculture's integration into world markets by ensuring that peasant households would not be affected by the process. Keith Hitchins, *Rumania, 1866–1947* (Oxford: Clarendon Press, 1994), 323.

53 Hitchins, *Rumania, 1866–1947*, 323.

54 Hitchins, *Rumania, 1866–1947*, 323.

of household items" during that year.[55] The measure was dramatic considering that peasants' homes were already generally sparsely furnished and more than half of Romanian peasants had no cows or other animals that could be confiscated.[56]

Despite belated government measures and some failed attempts at banning speculative lending, halving the land tax (1932), and attempting a rescheduling ("conversion") of agricultural debt, the crisis re-created a large group of landless, seasonally mobile agricultural workers.[57] Peasants with too little land hired themselves and family members as agricultural laborers on larger holdings. Thus, a 1937 questionnaire on women's work prepared for the ILO could report that the single largest category of paid women workers in Romania comprised the 4,181,000 individuals employed in agricultural work as "family auxiliaries."[58] Such circumstances also pushed some peasant families in poor conditions to migrate to cities, Bucharest foremost among these.[59] Likely, as in other places in Europe at the time, rural poverty also determined the rural-urban migration of great numbers of girls and young women, in search of domestic service or occasional employment in cities.

9.4 A Gendered Analysis of National-Level Social Policies in the 1930s

If social assistance, the "second track" of welfare, contracted, the "first track" of welfare, social insurance, expanded during the early 1930s, at least in a formal sense. This was because in 1933

55 Scurtu, *Istoria românilor în timpul celor patru regi (1866–1947), vol. al III-lea (Carol al II-lea)*, 112.

56 Hitchins, *Rumania, 1866–1947*, 342.

57 Hitchins, *Rumania, 1866–1947*, 340, 353, 354.

58 Calypso Botez, "Răspunsul dat de Calypso C. Botez la chestionarul Biroului Internaţional al Muncii referitor la condiţiile de muncă ale femeilor în România," in *Din Istoria Feminismului Românesc*, ed. Ştefania Mihăilescu, vol. 2 (Iaşi: Polirom, 2006), 298.

59 National Statistical Institute director Sabin Manuilă made a harsh assessment of peasants who "sold everything" in the countryside and moved to Bucharest without means. Sabin Manuilă, "Importanţa Recensământului populaţiei pentru asistenţa socială," *Asistenţa Socială—Buletinul Şcoalei Superioare de Asistenţă Socială "Principesa Ileana"* 2, no. 1 (1931): 111–17.

the government managed the long-planned unification of the existing three regionally distinct, preunification systems of social insurance. However, in substance, the new laws were designed to explicitly exclude large categories of workers that should have been included—based on the ILO recommendations at the time—and to implicitly put others at a disadvantage. It fostered the continuity of a system of minimal social insurance and health-care provision. This section analyzes the Depression-era changes in social policy and its effects on public healthcare, focusing especially on how women (as workers or as the coinsured of insured men) were disadvantaged within the system.

The 1930s saw a process of administrative unification and cost cutting in the area of social policy. Most workers were not insured or insurable. For those insured and their families, in practice, all components of contributory social insurance offered limited protection against social vulnerability during the Great Depression. Women, be they insured as workers themselves, as the partners of insured men, or most often be they uninsured and uninsurable citizens, were affected by the stinginess and malfunction of the modern welfare policies introduced.

Categories of risk covered by mandatory insurance in the 1920s and 1930s included disease, maternity, death, and invalidity due to illness and (solely for public employees) old age.[60] Until 1933, "first track" policies functioned on the basis of laws passed in the different now-Romanian provinces by their respective governments before World War I. For instance, the more industrialized region of Transylvania governed insurance through Hungarian Law XIX from 1907, amended—significantly—in 1919 to mandatorily cover all agricultural workers, a massive expansion of the number of those technically insured. Until 1933, the Old Kingdom (and hence Bucharest) applied the 1912 "'Nenitescu' Law for the organization of crafts, credit and workers' insurance"; it insured disease, maternity, death, and invalidity due to illness and old age. In 1932,

60 Parliament of Romania, "Senatul: Ședința dela 17 martie 1933," *Monitorul Oficial* 34 (April 7, 1933): 1100, 1116; Sergiu Delcea, "The Welfare-State as a Means of Nation-Building in Interwar Romania, 1930–1938" (MA Thesis, Central European University, Vienna, 2014), 30.

Transylvanian agricultural workers' coverage was revoked by the central Bucharest government, leaving thousands uninsured.

Finally, in 1933, a Law for the Unification of Social Insurance was passed. Its supporters in government and parliament argued that although the economic crisis did not allow an expansion of insured categories, administrative simplification was going to translate into broader access and small increases in the levels of benefits for all those covered. The risks insured in the 1933 Law were the same as in the 1912 Nenitescu Law. Neither unemployment nor old-age pensions for nonpublic employees were provided under the new legislation. Whereas legislators admitted that both widows and orphans would have to become fully insured in a more prosperous future, agricultural workers received no mention and became (to be clear, purposefully) "locked out" of the emergent "welfare state."

The 1933 Romanian Law for the Unification of Insurance (MO. 83/April 1933), which created uniformity in insurance among older and newer provinces of the country, included categories of workers that were previously uninsured in the Old Kingdom, such as craftsmen whose crafts occurred in clients' homes, within compulsory insurance for illness, maternity, death, accident, and invalidity.[61] As a result, self-employed persons carrying out a recognized trade in clients' homes became assimilated to entrepreneurs, while the many domestic servants working in Romania were implicitly demoted to a position of low-skill, nonartisan, home-based workers.[62]

Because insurance unification was both an opportunity to meet ILO standards and an occasion for the cost cutting made necessary by the Depression, precarious or "low-skill" workers, in effect most of the workforce in agrarian Romania, were excluded either explicitly or due to the cultivation of implementation faults. Thus, "employees of agricultural enterprises" were exempted from

61 Parliament of Romania, "Legea pentru unificarea asigurărilor sociale," *Monitorul Oficial* 83 (April 8, 1933), 2300

62 MMSOS, *Dare de seama asupra activității Casei Centrale a Asigurărilor Sociale pe anii 1912–1934* (Bucharest: Imprimeria Națională, 1935), 59; Parliament of Romania, "Senatul: Ședința de vineri 17 martie 1933," *Monitorul Oficial* 34 (April 7, 1934): 1148.

insurance, ostensibly due to the protests of medics' associations who feared being overwhelmed by rural patients in city hospitals.[63]

Means-testing applied to some social insurance entitlements, such as the inheritance of a deceased person's invalidity or old-age pension by their legally recognized dependents. The persistence of means-testing procedures like pauperism certificates points to the convenient incorporation of the instruments that defined minimalist poverty policy in Western Europe into the austerity policymaking of the NPP in 1933.[64]

The 1933 Law for the Unification of Social Insurance provided that: "The legitimate wife or husband of a pensioner has the right to 50% of the deceased person's pension, when it is ascertained that she or he is unable to work and when the state of poverty is proven through a pauperism act (orig. 'act de paupertate') issued by the habilitated financial administration." Minor children could benefit from a third of the pension of a deceased person if they could prove pauperism through the same type of document, attesting to their lack of income and property and that they were devoid of means.[65]

Also beginning in 1933, morality-related criteria could be applied to deprive insured persons of benefits. According to an amendment introduced by Parliament to the original project presented by the government:

> The insured person who provoked their injury, purposefully or through serious oversight, by taking part in fights, or commission of a crime, or if the disease is owed to alcoholism,

63 MMSOS, *Dare de seamă asupra activității Casei Centrale a Asigurărilor Sociale pe anii 1912–1934*, 59.

64 James Midgley, "Poor Law Principles and Social Assistance in the Third World: A Study of the Perpetuation of Colonial Welfare," *International Social Work* 27, no. 1 (January 1, 1984): 21, https://doi.org/10.1177/002087288402700105; On the traditions of philanthropy in Valachia (later Kingdom of Romania), see Ligia Livadă-Cadeschi, *De la milă la filantropie. Instituții de asistare a săracilor din Țara Româneasca și Moldova în secolul al XVIII-lea* (Bucharest: Nemira, 2001); "Săracii din Țările Române la începuturile timpurilor moderne," in *Sărăcie și asistență socială în spațiul românesc sec. 18–20* (Bucharest: New Europe College, 2002), 11–60, http://www.nec.ro/data/pdfs/publications/relink/saracie-si-asistenta-sociala/Saracie_si_asistenta_sociala.pdf.

65 Senate of Romania, "Senatul: Ședința dela 17 Martie 1933," 1187.

> will not have the right to financial compensation [during illness]. If it will be proved that the family was being supported through the Labor of the insured person, in the cases specified in the previous two paragraphs, it will be possible to grant to the family up to 50 percent of the legal compensations and only within the limits of the family's needs.[66]

The amendment created a large loophole in workmen's accident insurance, guaranteeing that only those workers and families considered well-behaved in work discipline, personal morality and habits, or political convictions would have their needs recognized by the state in case of an accident.

The state-backed system for interwar health-care provision has been described as "heterogeneous."[67] In Bucharest, hospitals were maintained from the state budget. Specifically, in 1921, the state took over the public interest foundation which had administered the city's major hospitals since the nineteenth century (the Eforia [Foundation] of Civil Hospitals) and redistributed its considerable landholdings in that year's agrarian reform. Due to the Eforia's loss of income, hospitalization in Bucharest state institutions could no longer be free of charge for the neediest persons, as it seems to have been the case since the 1840s.[68] The system of workers' social insurance covered only professionals and skilled workers, who were a minority, even in the capital city. In addition, nationally, there were smaller associations and religious organizations that provided health-care services and maintained hospitals or sanatoria.[69]

Just how limited access to healthcare was made clear by pregnant women's difficulties in benefiting from any kind of medical assistance during this period, even in Bucharest and even when insured. Between 1931 and 1937, nationally, only 15 percent of births occurred in hospitals and 4 percent occurred outside

66 Senate of Romania, "Senatul: Şedinţa dela 17 Martie 1933," 1184.

67 B. Duţescu and N. Marcu, "Medicina în perioada dintre cele două războaie mondiale," in *Istoria medicinii româneşti*, eds. V. L. Bologa et al. (Bucharest: Editura Medicală, 1972), 302.

68 Arhivele Nationale Istorice Centrale, "Inventar. Eforia Spitalelor Civile. Centrala (1890–1948)" (Bucharest: ANIC, 2009), 1.

69 Duţescu and Marcu, "Medicina în perioada dintre cele două războaie mondiale," 307.

hospitals but with medical assistance, whereas more than half of women gave birth at home, at best assisted by midwives. By the late 1930s, Romania's European-high maternal mortality rate was visible in statistical data, referenced nationally and internationally. In 1932, a sanitary inquiry into one of Bucharest's districts noted that most births occurred at home, while in 72 percent of cases prenatal supervision had been nonexistent.[70] By 1936, Dr. L. Mavromati, director of the Center of Maternal Assistance functioning within Bucharest's Central Insurance House, described that the Center employed two doctors and fifteen midwives, working in ten dispensaries throughout the city.[71] Due to the lack of a maternity house run by the Insurance House, Mavromati encouraged home births by the well-prepared midwives working in the ten dispensaries, accompanied by improved prenatal and postnatal supervision.

In slashing the Ministry of Health's funding, the budgetary austerity of the 1930s enhanced the heterogeneity of the health-care system. The expansive 1930 Sanitary and Protection Law (MO236/July 14, 1930) created by the NPP government used the principle of decentralization in part to mask budget cuts.[72] Thus, decentralization of the sanitary system meant that hospital budgets were to be administered by hospital managers.[73] At the same time, decentralization meant a strong encouragement from the government for health institutions to secure their own revenues beyond the state budget.[74] In Bucharest's Eforia hospitals, the application of this principle led to the eventual forging of a partnership with the Superior

70 Ștefania Negrescu, "Date și concluzii din ancheta internațională asupra cauzelor mortalității infantile la copiii născuți vii, între 0-1 an, precum și asupra mortalității în circumscripția medicală X (periferică) din București pe anul 1931," *Revista de Igienă Socială* 2, no. 3 (1932): 279–90.

71 He described that before his reorganization of the Center's functioning, "a midwife assigned to home births would be told 'you are a homebirth midwife in dispensary X'; fullstop. How she will function, how she will orient herself, how she will procure the medication and emergency instruments, no detail, no guidance concerning these issues." L. Mavromati, "Asistența Maternă la Casa de Asigurări București," *Revista de Igienă Socială* 6, no. 3 (March 1936): 175.

72 Parliament of Romania, "Legea Sanitară și de Ocrotire," *Monitorul Oficial* 236 (July 14, 1930), 5338–5398.

73 Bucur, *Eugenics and Modernization*, 198.

74 Duțescu and Marcu, "Medicina în perioada dintre cele două războaie mondiale," 302.

School of Social Assistance (SSAS), a private but state-subsidized higher-education institution training women in social work.

In 1938, before the participants of the National Congress of Social Assistance, sociologist and social worker Xenia Costa-Foru explained the functioning of the "general social services" and the "special social services" functioning alongside various hospitals and clinics in Bucharest. Created in 1930 by the SSAS, mostly as a way of providing practical training for students, "the hospital social service" aimed to assist sick persons with "social matters," collaborate closely with all those involved in the care of a patient, and conduct research on "matters of social dependence" created or aggravated by disease. Costa-Foru reported that between 1930 and 1936, the assistants had created 10,938 patient fiches for only one of the four Bucharest major hospitals where assistants were present.[75]

However, the most important function of the SSAS's Hospital Social Services and the feature that made them first tolerated components and then essential parts of hospitals' administrations were assistants' investigations into the patients' ability to pay for healthcare. Because of the crisis and possibly due to the formalization of health-care provision through the 1933 law, healthcare was now offered free of charge only under increasingly stringent conditions.

The small scale of Romania's health and social insurance programs as well as lapses in implementation are abundantly evident in relation to care for recent mothers. Technically, insured employed women were covered for maternity along the lines of the 1919 ILO Maternity Protection Convention (C003) through the 1928 Law for the Protection of Minors' and Women's Work (MO 85/April 13, 1928).[76] This meant that, in Romania, women working in industrial

75 Over the course of 5 years (1933–38), volunteer assistants for the general social services had rendered the following services to patients: 777 job placements "with families" or establishments, 1,669 transportation of sick persons in the city and the rest of the country, 4,891 "correspondence services," 8,523 "connections to other assistance organs," 1,311 commitments to institutions, "material aid" for 7,497 persons and "incidental assistance services" for 4,564 persons. Xenia Costa-Foru, "Serviciile sociale generale şi serviciile sociale speciale pe lângă diferite spitale şi clinici," *Asistenţa Socială—Buletinul Asociaţiei pentru Progresul Asistenţei Sociale* 7, no. 2 (1938): 129–37.

76 International Labour Organization Convention C 3: Maternity Protection Convention (Convention concerning the Employment of Women before and after Childbirth)

and commercial enterprises were entitled to a maximum 6 weeks of leave before childbirth and a mandatory leave of 6 weeks afterward, for a full total of 12 weeks of leave; during this time they could not be laid off by employers and benefited from "an indemnity for her and her child's maintenance, as well as free medical care under the conditions established through the law on health insurance (Art. 31)."[77] However, eligibility for parts of this indemnity was not automatic. Access to benefits connected to maternity was conditional; employed women had to have contributed to insurance for a minimum of 26 weeks in the year before childbirth.[78]

The number of those insured for maternity was expanded in 1933 with the passing of a new general insurance law, which included all servants and other categories of "homeworkers." The nursing wives of insured men were also covered. However, from 1933 onward, only the wives of those men who had been insured for a longer period could avail themselves of this right. An insured man's wife could be coinsured and benefit from maternity healthcare if her legal husband had contributed for at least 52 weeks in the previous 2 years.[79] This placed the high number of women in common-law marriages, usually the most precarious ones, entirely outside coverage. The same category of insured men could receive, "when the financial situation of the [Insurance] House allows it, an amount of money for the wife and baby."[80] The condition of uninterrupted employment penalized most blue-collar workers, especially in times of economic crisis when stable employment was hard to come by. Furthermore, an aid in money that could be received by a nursing mother was conditioned upon her submitting to a doctor's advice on child-rearing, a measure considered to be in the woman's own best interest.

(1st Conference Session, Geneva, November 28, 1919); Parliament of Romania, "Lege pentru ocrotirea muncii minorilor şi femeilor şi durata muncii," *Monitorul Oficial* 85 (April 13, 1928), 3127–3132.

77 Parliament of Romania, "Lege pentru ocrotirea muncii minorilor şi femeilor şi durata muncii."

78 Parliament of Romania, "Senatul: Şedinţa dela 17 martie 1933," 1126.

79 Parliament of Romania, "Senatul: Şedinţa dela 17 martie 1933," 1187.

80 Parliament of Romania, "Senatul: Şedinţa dela 17 martie 1933," 1127.

Overall, the advantages of the formal existence of maternity insurance in Romania seem to have been minimal. Financial benefits associated with maternity leave received higher allocations in 1933, but the ineffectiveness of all "protective" labor laws in Romania radiated onto working women's entitlements to components of the social insurance system. A 1938 report by social democratic women in Romania stated tersely: "The employers do not respect the law which provides that women shall be paid their wages six weeks before, and six weeks after confinement. It is much simpler to give them the sack."[81] Similarly, a report submitted to the ILO Correspondence Committee on Women's Work by a liberal progressive group of women described the same situation: "In the great enterprises, women receive maternity leave. In the smaller enterprises, they show pregnant women the door, other women are employed in their place."[82]

9.5 Conclusion

In this chapter, I have sought to reconstruct the Romanian central government's policy and political response to the Great Depression's social effects, arguing that in the period 1929–33 the young welfare framework of the state did not see a substantial expansion, despite the adoption of key (and seemingly very comprehensive) welfare laws. Instead, I pointed out that the period was characterized by institutional downsizing, exclusionary policymaking, and a tendency toward denying the social cost of the crisis. The chapter reconstitutes a broad chronology of the evolution of the crisis in cities and rural areas, and the insufficient responses to the situation by the Bucharest-based central authorities. In particular, I have discussed the obstruction of systematic relief for the unemployed as being in part caused by political reluctance and in part by the institutional lack of capacity created by successive rounds of cuts. Also, I have analyzed how new laws on social insurance and healthcare

81 "Letter from Roumania," *International Information—Women's Supplement*, 1937. Courtesy Prof. Susan Zimmermann.

82 Calypso Botez, "Reponse au questionnaire du BIT sur les conditions de travail des femmes," in *Din Istoria Feminismului Românesc*, ed. Ştefania Mihăilescu, vol. 2 (Iaşi: Polirom, 2006), 301.

were designed to cover a limited number of beneficiaries and malfunctioned in practice. In particular, I have shown how maternity benefits and healthcare for expectant or new mothers—an area for which the legal framework had expanded continuously between the early 1920s and 1933—offered little meaningful protection.

PART FOUR

The Depression as Catalyst for Economic and Political Thought

Chapter 10

HUNGARY

SOCIAL AND POLITICAL CONSEQUENCES OF THE GREAT DEPRESSION

Béla Tomka

The scholarly literature tends to present a fairly somber portrayal of the economic conditions in East-Central Europe, including Hungary, during the interwar period. The dominant interpretation suggests that the Great Depression hit East-Central and Southeast Europe particularly hard because of their specific structural economic problems.[1] According to these views, the economic development and the overall progression of the crisis in Hungary during the interwar period differed little from this general narrative. What may have distinguished the Hungarian case were the impacts of the comprehensive border changes implemented after the Treaty of Trianon and the dissolution of the economic unity of the Austro-Hungarian Monarchy. These factors only served to make the country's return to its previous growth trajectory that much more challenging.[2]

1 Iván T. Berend and György Ránki, *Economic Development in East-Central Europe in the 19th and 20th Centuries* (New York: Columbia University Press, 1974); Iván T. Berend, *Válságos évtizedek. A 20. század első fele közép- és kelet-európai történetének interpretációja* (Budapest: Magvető, 1987).

2 For a different interpretation of the economic impact of the Treaty of Trianon, see Béla Tomka, "Az első világháború és a trianoni béke gazdasági hatásai Magyarországon," in *Háborúból békébe: a magyar társadalom 1918 után. Konfliktusok, kihívások, változások a háború és az összeomlás nyomán*, ed. Zsombor Bódy (Budapest: MTA Bölcsészettudományi Kutatóközpont Történettudományi Intézet, 2018), 47–80; Béla Tomka, "The economic consequences of World War I and the Treaty of Trianon for Hungary," *Regional Statistics* 10, no. 1 (2020): 82–100.

Some recent studies give a more nuanced picture of the economic development of the region between the two World Wars.[3] Matthias Morys points out that "the critical assessment of the interwar achievements carries a subtext, namely to justify, very subtly, the heavy state intervention, collectivisation of agriculture and forced industrialisation which materialised after World War II under communist regimes."[4] However, these newer, more optimistic approaches cover the entire interwar period. This is essential to understand the longer-term processes, but it does little to answer the economic and sociopolitical impact of the Great Depression. For the moment, the newer interpretations can hardly be reconciled with the radical sociopolitical changes that took place in the region in the 1930s.

Accordingly, this chapter examines how the Great Depression affected Hungary. We first describe the background to the Great Depression and then discuss its advance and the government measures taken to alleviate it. Particular attention will be paid to the economic restructuring and foreign trade reorientation taking place in the era, both of which were crucial factors in terms of the progression of the economic crisis. We will then present the growth trajectory of the Hungarian economy during the depression era from an international perspective. Finally, we will examine the wider social and political consequences of the Great Depression and summarize our findings.

3 Joan Roses and Nikolaus Wolf, "Aggregate Growth, 1913–1950," in *The Cambridge Economic History of Modern Europe. Vol. 2: 1870 to the Present*, eds. Stephen Broadberry and Kevin O'Rourke (Cambridge: Cambridge University Press, 2010), 181–207; Matthias Morys, "Economic Growth and Structural Change in Central, East and South-East Europe, 1918–1939," in *The Economic History of Central, East and South-East Europe: 1800 to the Present*, ed. Matthias Morys (London and New York: Routledge, 2021), 161–87; Nathan Marcus, Stefan Nikolič, and Tobias Straumann, "Economic Policy, 1918–1939," in *The Economic History of Central, East and South-East Europe: 1800 to the Present*, ed. Matthias Morys (London and New York: Routledge, 2021), 188–215.

4 Morys, "Economic Growth and Structural Change," 162.

10.1 Path to the Great Depression

As a consequence of World War I and its aftermath, the conditions under which the Hungarian economy operated changed significantly.[5] The actual military operations only affected a limited part of Hungary's territory. Moreover, the impacted areas lay beyond the country's post-1920 borders and therefore fall outside the scope of our study. As such, there was no direct physical destruction affecting the present territory of Hungary; however, the war had a profound impact on the depletion of the country's human resources. There were also other ways in which the war effort depleted the country's economy. By 1918, there were severe shortages of fuel, raw materials, and food, causing disruption to transport, industrial production, and public services.[6] It was not only certain consumer goods industries that saw their output fall by 60–70 percent in the final stages of the World War; even those sectors geared specifically toward supplying the military with materiel experienced a decline in their production output. The 1920 output of the processing industry was stagnating at 35–40 percent of the prewar levels.[7]

The war also wrought devastating fiscal consequences, exacerbating the instability of the national currency. During the final years of the war, military spending accounted for a large share—around half—of the total national product. The budget could not cover these expenses from traditional revenue sources. The Hungarian government did not seek to increase taxes; instead, it resorted to borrowing and covered more and more of its expenditure by printing

5 On this period, see Iván T. Berend and György Ránki, *Magyarország gazdasága az első világháború után. 1919–1929* (Budapest: Akadémiai Kiadó, 1966), 7–129; Max-Stephan Schulze, "Austria–Hungary's Economy in World War I," in *The Economics of World War I*, eds. Stephen Broadberry and Mark Harrison (Cambridge: Cambridge University Press, 2005), 78–111; on the wider region, see Derek H. Aldcroft and Steven Morewood, *Economic Change in Eastern Europe since 1918* (Aldershot: Edward Elgar, 1995), 1–127.

6 József Szterényi and Jenő Ladányi, *A magyar ipar a világháborúban* (Budapest: Franklin Társulat, 1934); Iván Berend T. and György Ránki, "Ungarns wirtschaftliche Entwicklung, 1849–1919," in *Die Habsburgermonarchie Bd. I.: Die wirtschaftliche Entwicklung*, ed. Alois Brusatti (Vienna: Österreichische Akademie der Wissenschaften, 1973), 520–27.

7 Dezső Laky, *Csonkamagyarország megszállásának közgazdasági kárai* (Budapest: Eggerberger, 1923), 362.

money. Inflation commenced already with the outbreak of the war, and the process of internal and external depreciation of the korona continued for a decade, sometimes slowing down, but generally accelerating, giving an entirely new framework for the development of the Hungarian economy. At the end of 1918, the war debts of the Hungarian state amounted to 33–34 billion koronas. But the innovative methods used for financing the war were later to come at a heavy price.[8]

Economic disorganization was exacerbated by the postwar revolutions of 1918–19 and the conflicts emerging with several neighboring countries. These—and especially the Romanian invasion of Hungary in 1919—caused considerable losses also in the means of production.[9] The economic difficulties were further aggravated by the loss of about two-thirds of the country's territory and half of its population. The 1920 Treaty of Trianon merely sanctioned these losses and added to them, among other things, a slew of adverse financial and economic measures such as reparations and economic restrictions. The Entente maintained the economic blockade for some time even after the war.

Hungary ceased to be part of the economic integration of the Monarchy, which meant that its traditional supplier and trade relations were severed. Raw material sources and processing plants were cut off from each other by the new, difficult-to-cross borders, which meant that transactions that had previously been considered domestic trade became foreign trade transactions that were more cumbersome and expensive to carry out. Furthermore, the border adjustments of 1920 led to considerable underutilization of capacities in specific industries and sectors, concurrently presenting market challenges for agriculture. Moreover, they also made Hungary's preexisting government bureaucracy disproportionately large for a country and an economy that had in the meantime undergone

8 János Teleszky, *A magyar állam pénzügyei a háború alatt* (Budapest: Magyar Tudományos Akadémia, 1927); Tibor Rácz, *Valutaügyünk története a Magyar Nemzeti Bank alapításáig* (Budapest: Magyar Nemzeti Bank, 1934).

9 István Varga, "Csonka-Magyarország gazdasági fejlődése," in *Emlékkönyv Kenéz Béla negyedszázados professzori munkásságának évfordulójára*, ed. Dezső Laky (Budapest: Statisztikai Hivatal, 1932), 179–214.

a substantial reduction in size.[10] At the same time, a significant number of officials and professionals formerly employed by the Hungarian government left the newly enlarged neighboring countries and migrated to Hungary, adding to the country's human capital. Despite the often apocalyptic predictions of contemporary commentators, the territorial changes had little impact on the country's growth opportunities in the longer term.[11]

In the early 1920s, there were several attempts to suppress inflation. The failure of these attempts can be attributed, first, to the substantial budget deficit, and second, to the fact that many economic agents temporarily benefited from inflationary financing, as it effectively reduced the real value of their debts over time. Inflation ended with the stabilization of 1924–25. By this time, gross domestic product had reached its prewar level, and the increase in tax revenues enabled the restoration of fiscal balance. On the other hand, a substantial loan from the League of Nations also helped financial stabilization, as did tax increases and a significant reduction in the number of government employees.[12] Legislation was adopted on stabilization, and the Hungarian National Bank was also established as an autonomous institution.[13] On January 1, 1927, the country adopted the korona as its new currency.[14]

With stabilization, the immediate consequences of the war were averted. The stabilization of the Hungarian korona, the rebalancing

10 László Buday, *Magyarország küzdelmes évei* (Budapest: self-published, 1923); Elizabeth Boross, *Inflation and Industry in Hungary, 1918–1929* (Berlin: Haude und Spener, 1994), 224; István Varga, "Tőke és infláció," *Közgazdasági Szemle* 50 (1926): 586.

11 Tomka: "Az első világháború és a trianoni béke gazdasági hatásai Magyarországon," 68–70.

12 On the League of Nations loan for Hungary, see Mária Ormos, *Az 1924. évi magyar államkölcsön megszerzése* (Budapest: Akadémiai Kiadó, 1963).

13 On the details of the financial sanation of the country's economy, see *Magyarország pénzügyi újjáépítése. A Nemzetek Szövetsége magyarországi főbiztosának első–huszonharmadik jelentése. 1924. május–1926. március. Budapest, 1924–1926;* Ágnes Pogány, "A Magyar Nemzeti Bank alapításának nemzetközi és belföldi előzményei," in *A Magyar Nemzeti Bank története. I*, ed. Tamás Bácskai (Budapest: KJK, 1993), 501–85; György Péteri, "Montagu Norman és a magyar 'szanálási mű'. Az 1924-es magyar pénzügyi stabilizációról," *Századok* 119, no. 1 (1985): 121–52.

14 Béla Tomka, *A magyarországi pénzintézetek rövid története, 1836–1947* (Budapest: Aula, 2000), 88–105.

of the country's public finances, and the deregulation of exchange controls allowed the country to take advantage of the global economic boom. Hungary's economic reconstruction in the 1920s benefited from relatively favorable opportunities for the sale of the country's agricultural products on the world market as well as from significant capital imports. The new customs regime introduced at the beginning of 1925 protected a wide range of industrial products with very high customs duties, which were considerably higher than those applied under the Monarchy. Tariffs were also raised for many industrial products heavily used for agricultural purposes, effectively making the agricultural sector finance the losses of the country's uncompetitive industrial production. One of the key aims of the new customs policy was to support the country's previously underdeveloped textile industry.[15]

The boom of the second half of the 1920s was a major success in Hungary, as by 1929 per capita gross domestic product was about 18 percent above the level of the last prewar year. This compares favorably with, for example, the performance of Austria, where growth was only 6.8 percent over the same period.[16]

10.2 Evolution of the Crisis and Economic Policy Measures Taken to Alleviate It

The relatively successful growth process of the second half of the 1920s was brought to a close by the Great Depression: the relative price level of agricultural products fell, while export prospects deteriorated in other ways as well; industrial production fell sharply; and international financial relations were severely hampered or even disrupted from 1931. However, Hungary's economic output did not decline to the same extent as in many Western countries.

In Hungary, the Great Depression first manifested itself in the agricultural sector: the industrial boom was still going on in 1928, when there was already talk of a crisis in agriculture. Because of

15 József Buzás and András Nagy, *Magyarország külkereskedelme, 1919–1945* (Budapest: KJK, 1961); Berend and Ránki, *Magyarország gazdasága az első világháború után*, 172–84.

16 Angus Maddison, *The World Economy: Historical Statistics* (Paris: OECD, 2003), 60–101.

the structural characteristics of the Hungarian economy—first and foremost, the high proportion of agricultural employment—the overall economic impact of the agricultural crisis was greater than that of the industrial crisis, which also arose later.

The downturn in agriculture did not actually lead to a fall in production: pursuing a strategy of reducing production in order to maintain price levels was simply not an option for a large number of landowners. The value of agricultural production increased by 1.3 percent between 1929 and 1934 (when calculated at constant prices), that is, it remained essentially stagnant during the crisis.[17] Thus, the impact of the crisis on agriculture can be observed in three main—and interrelated—areas:

1. The price of agricultural products plummeted, reducing farmers' incomes.
2. As a result of the diverging dynamics of industrial and agricultural prices, an "agricultural scissors effect" manifested itself.
3. The country's export markets shrunk.[18]

The decline in agricultural prices began at the end of 1928 and continued for several years afterward. Among the early causes of the agricultural crisis was, first and foremost, the transformation of the global agricultural market, which continued apace in the post-World War I period. Intense competition from overseas producers, particularly those in the United States, Canada, Argentina, and Australia, led to a sharp fall in world wheat prices. This also reduced sales opportunities for Hungarian producers. In 1933, agricultural prices hit their nadir, with wheat prices plummeting to 35.1 percent of the 1928 price level. Similarly, maize, potatoes, fattened hogs, and cow's milk experienced comparable declines, registering at 25.5

17 *Magyarország története. Vol. 8. 1918–1919/1919–1945*, eds. Tibor Hajdu and Loránt Tilkovszky (Budapest: Akadémiai Kiadó, 1976), 601–2; Péter Gunst, *A mezőgazdasági termelés története Magyarországon (1920–1938)* (Budapest: Akadémiai Kiadó, 1970), 62; for a set of slightly different data, see Mathias Matolcsy and Stephen Varga, *The National Income of Hungary 1924/25–1936/37* (London: P. S. King and Son, 1938), 45.

18 Iván T. Berend and György Ránki, *Közép-Kelet-Európa gazdasági fejlődése a 19–20. században* (Budapest: KJK, 1976), 344.

percent, 25.4 percent, 46.8 percent, and 74.4 percent, respectively.[19] Overall, agricultural prices in 1933 amounted to 45.1 percent of the 1928 level.[20]

The situation of farmers was further exacerbated by the adverse development of the ratio between industrial and agricultural prices, which, even though it was a global phenomenon, was particularly marked in the East-Central and Southeast European regions. Hungary experienced a less prominent agricultural scissors effect already in the 1920s,[21] but in 1928 it was only 9.9 percent compared with the 1913 price levels, that is, the price index for industrial products was only that much higher than the price index for agricultural products. By 1933, however, the difference was as high as 45.7 percent.[22]

The fall in domestic demand could not be offset by exports, as the country's external markets were partially closed. Hungary was a major agricultural exporter, but the markets for its agricultural products were rather keen to protect their own producers. Hungary's foreign market opportunities were also hampered by the production structure of the country's agriculture, in which cereals and maize played a prominent role, while world prices for these crops fell more than average during the crisis. Because of the fall in world prices and the deterioration in export prospects, agricultural exports fell by 27 percent in volume and 61 percent in value by 1934 compared with 1929.[23]

Agricultural products accounted for a key portion of Hungary's exports, making up 73.8 percent of the total 1928.[24] Therefore, the fall in their prices on the world market had broad economic effects, particularly in terms of a deterioration in the terms of trade. The

19 Gunst, *A mezőgazdasági termelés története Magyarországon*, 73.

20 Gunst, *A mezőgazdasági termelés története Magyarországon*, 75.

21 A set of different data is cited in Béla Csikós-Nagy, *A XX. század magyar gazdaságpolitikája. Tanulságok az ezredfordulón* (Budapest: Akadémiai Kiadó, 1996).

22 *A magyar mezőgazdaság árhelyzete az utolsó évszázadban (1867–1963).* (Statisztikai Időszaki Közlemények. 73.) (Budapest: KSH, 1965), 34.

23 Iván T. Berend and György Ránki, "Polen, Ungarn, Rumänien, Bulgarien und Albanien, 1914–1980," in *Handbuch der europäischen Wirtschafts- und Sozialgeschichte*, vol. 6, ed. Wolfram Fischer (Stuttgart: Klett-Cotta, 1987), 812.

24 Gunst, *A mezőgazdasági termelés története Magyarországon*, 82; cf. Norbert Csáki and Balázs Szitó, *Magyarország mezőgazdasági kivitele* (Budapest: KJK, 1963), 7.

unfavorable development of the terms of trade was already visible in the first half of the 1920s, but the crisis accelerated this process. Using the level of foreign trade prices in 1925–27 as a benchmark, there was a deterioration in the terms of trade of 8 percent in 1929, 10 percent in 1930, 15 percent in 1931, and 19 percent in 1933. Thus, the deterioration in the terms of trade was already about 30 percent compared to the period before World War I, which was due to the high share of agricultural products and raw materials in the export mix. In Czechoslovakia, for example, which had a more favorable export structure, import prices fell by an average of 52 percent over the period, while export prices fell by only 35 percent.[25]

In this situation, government policy sought to mitigate the impact of the crisis in several ways. These included seed access facilitation programs to promote quality production, efforts aiming to restrict the total cultivated area, and, first and foremost, offering financial support for the marketing of the crops produced, creating public institutions for marketing, offering bank debt restructuring to producers, and export promotion.[26] Financial support to promote sales started in the mid-1930s when the fall in the prices of agricultural products accelerated. The main instrument for this was the so-called "boletta" system, which operated for 4 years. In addition to the agreed price, buyers were also required to pay an additional amount of three to 6 pengős per quintal (100 kg) of wheat in "bolettas" (grain vouchers), which the producers could use toward paying their taxes or, alternatively, redeem for cash.[27] Another form of subsidy was the monopolization of selling the produce through state-owned sales organizations, which paid a guaranteed minimum price for the produce purchased for centralized resale. Entities such as Hangya ("Ant") Cooperative—in which the government owned a 70 percent stake—or the purely state-owned share company Futura

25 Zdenek Drabek, "Foreign Trade Performance and Policy," in *The Economic History of Eastern Europe, 1919–1975, Vol. I: Economic Structure and Performance between the Two Wars*, eds. Michael C. Kaser and Edward A. Radice (Oxford: Clarendon, 1985), 444–46.

26 Miklós Szuhay, *Az állami beavatkozás és a magyar mezőgazdaság az 1930-as években* (Budapest: Akadémiai Kiadó, 1962), 103–38.

27 János Honvári, *XX. századi magyar gazdaságtörténet: Transzformációk, rendszerek* (Budapest: Aula, 2006), 55.

Rt., as well as a number of other organizations, were granted exclusive rights to trade in and export certain agricultural products. By the late 1930s, they accounted for 80–85 percent of all agricultural exports.[28]

Another form of state support was offering debt restructuring facilities to farmers who became insolvent. From 1931 onward, several government decrees stipulated a ban on auctioning off landed estates during debt restructuring procedures. This, of course, severely affected the financial institutions lending to the producers, above all the smaller rural banks and savings banks, as their claims were consequently frozen. As the debt restructuring program progressed, the protection of the indebted landed estates was gradually removed, making the debt recoverable.

The government's engagement in agro-exports notably intensified during the mid-decade period, a development closely linked to the simultaneous expansion of Hungary's trade relations with Germany, a topic we will explore in greater detail later. The bulk of all exports during this period was already made on the basis of intergovernmental trade agreements.

These government interventions certainly helped agriculture to recover from the crisis, but other factors also played a role. On the one hand, in 1934 and 1936, unfavorable weather conditions reduced world grain production, improving market opportunities for Eastern European producers. On the other hand, as other sectors of the economy began to grow, the internal market also started to expand from 1933.

The agricultural crisis as such had its own impact on the industry as well by reducing the purchasing power of a large part of the population. Nevertheless, the industrial crisis was not as severe in Hungary as in Western countries. Overall, industrial output reached its lowest point in 1932, plummeting to 23 percent below the 1929 level, accompanied by a 27 percent reduction in the industrial workforce compared to the same base year. By 1935, industrial

28 Szuhay, *Az állami beavatkozás és a magyar mezőgazdaság az 1930-as években*, 255–62; Iván T. Berend, *An Economic History of Twentieth Century Europe: Economic Regimes from Laissez-Faire to Globalization* (Cambridge: Cambridge University Press, 2006), 66.

production not only recovered to the 1929 level but also exceeded it by 11 percent.[29] Moreover, the crisis affected different sectors differently. The largest declines were seen in the sectors producing capital goods and capital equipment, including iron and steel, machinery and equipment, construction materials, and wood. By 1932, their combined production plummeted to only 52 percent of the 1929 level. The food and certain other consumer goods industries experienced considerably smaller losses during the Great Depression, as demand for their products was less elastic. Food and clothing production contracted by 23 percent. However, there were some industries which, after an initial minimal decline, managed to increase their output even during the years of crisis. They included the textile, leather, and paper industries, whose combined output was 2 percent lower in 1931 and 4 percent lower in 1932 than back in 1929, but by 1933 it was already 10 percent higher as compared to the same base year.[30] The chemical and electricity industries emerged practically unscathed from the crisis. Notably, sectors such as oil refining and pharmaceuticals witnessed increased production, and even a new electric power plant was commissioned amid the economic downturn.

These sectors were also hit by a fall in domestic consumption, but state intervention compensated domestic producers by introducing import tariffs and other restrictions that largely squeezed foreign products out of these market segments. This process had begun long before the crisis: the tariff on manufactured goods in Hungary averaged 18% in 1913, rising to 27 percent in 1925 and then to 42.6 percent in 1931. This process was similar or even more pronounced in other East-Central and Southeast European countries (see Table 10.1).[31] Direct import restrictions played an increasingly important

29 "Az ipari termelés nemzetközi alakulása," *Magyar Statisztikai Szemle* 15, no. 3 (1937): 210; *A M. Kir. Kormány 1929. évi működéséről és az ország közállapotairól szóló jelentés és statisztikai évkönyv* (Budapest: Athenaeum, 1931), 105; *A M. Kir. Kormány 1932. évi működéséről és az ország közállapotairól szóló jelentés és statisztikai évkönyv* (Budapest: Athenaeum, 1933), 120.

30 *Magyarország története Vol. 8*, 604–5.

31 József Buzás, "Magyarország külkereskedelme, 1919–1938," in *Magyarország külkereskedelme, 1919–1945*, eds. József Buzás and András Nagy (Budapest: KJK, 1961), 33–34.

Table 10.1 Customs Tariffs on Processed Industrial Goods in European Countries, 1913–31

	1913	*1925*	*1931*
Hungary	18	27	42.6
Poland		32	52
Czechoslovakia	18	27	36.5
Bulgaria			90
Romania			55
Germany	13	20	18.3
United Kingdom	0	5	
France	20	21	29
Netherlands	4	6	
Belgium	9	15	13
Austria	18	16	27.7
Switzerland	9	14	22
Sweden	20	16	23.5
Denmark	14	10	
Italy	18	22	41.8

Source: Ronald Findlay, Kevin H. O'Rourke. *Power and Plenty: Trade, War, and the World Economy in the Second Millennium*, Princeton: Princeton University Press, 2007, 494 (Europe 1913, 1925); Heinrich Liepmann. *Tariff Levels and the Economic Unity of Europe: An Examination of Tariff Policy, Export Movements and the Economic Integration of Europe, 1913–1931*. London: Allen & Unwin, 1938 (Europe 1931); League of Nations. *Tariff Level Indices. Economic and Financial Section, 1927.II.34. Documentation for the International Economic Conference*. Geneva: League of Nations, 1927.

Notes: The data are simple unweighted averages.

role in curbing imports during the crisis: the government introduced quotas to limit the amount of certain products that could be imported from abroad. Such quotas had also existed before, but during the period under review they were usually set well below pre-crisis levels. The crisis intensified economic nationalism: the logic and consequences of this are illustrated by the customs war that broke out between Czechoslovakia and Hungary after the expiry of their foreign trade agreement at the end of 1930. Czechoslovakia introduced a 90 percent import tariff and other restrictions on Hungarian grain, as a result of which total Hungarian exports to that country plummeted by 85 percent from 1 year to the next. Czechoslovak exports to Hungary dropped by 71 percent as a result of the increased tariffs Hungary imposed on the import of Czech industrial products in response. The trade relationship between the two countries did not recover for the rest of the decade.[32]

As we have seen, the Hungarian economy was already severely affected by the decline in the prices of agricultural products from the late 1920s, which significantly reduced export revenues and thus worsened the country's balance of trade. In addition, it became more difficult to secure new foreign loans, as the protracted period of stock market bullishness that the New York Stock Exchange experienced in 1928–29 not only kept American capital at home but even attracted European funds overseas. The ability to raise capital thus also deteriorated in Hungary, creating significant tensions in the financial market.[33] The export problems and the difficulties in obtaining new loans were particularly threatening because in the second half of the 1920s Hungary received about 2 billion pengős ($400 million) in foreign loans, which accounted for about a third of the gross domestic product and contributed significantly to the success of economic consolidation.[34] Because of the stagnation of capital imports, in 1929 the combined amount of principal and interest repayments exceeded the amount of foreign capital flowing into the country by 16%, creating a completely new situation for the Hungarian economy. In 1930, Hungary's per capita debt service was the highest among the East-Central and Southeast European countries, accounting for 22.1% of its exports, which was also the highest such ratio in the region.[35]

But the real financial turmoil came in the year 1931. In the first half of the year, Hungary, like many other countries, experienced a large-scale wave of foreign debt defaults, accelerated by the collapse of Credit-Anstalt, a giant Viennese bank with a long history behind it, which was announced in mid-May 1931.[36] Due to the mounting

32 Drabek, "Foreign Trade Performance and Policy," 441; Szuhay, *Az állami beavatkozás és a magyar mezőgazdaság az 1930-as években*, 61–62.

33 Tomka, *A magyarországi pénzintézetek rövid története, 1836–1947*, 115.

34 Alexander Eckstein, "National Income and Capital Formation in Hungary, 1900–1950," in *Income and Wealth, Series V*, ed. Simon Kuznets (London: Bowes and Bowes, 1955), 219.

35 Marcus, Nikolič, and Straumann, "Economic Policy, 1918–1939," 193.

36 *A Magyar Gazdaságkutató Intézet gazdasági helyzetjelentései*, no. 12 (Budapest: Magyar Gazdaságkutató Intézet, 1931), 11; on the bank failure of Credit-Anstalt, see Dieter Stiefel, *Finanzdiplomatie und Weltwirtschaftskrise* (Frankfurt/M.: Fritz

uncertainty, there was also a surge in domestic demand for foreign exchange. Ever since the stabilization, this was the first time that the gold reserve ratio dropped under the 40 percent level, but by the end of July, it was only 28 percent. Despite the fact that Hungarian financial institutions were able to meet all requests, there was still a risk of panic withdrawals, as happened in Bucharest, Sofia, and Athens in early July, and in Germany on 13 July. The Hungarian government, therefore, decided to follow the German example and declared the 14th, the 15th, and the 16th as bank holidays. The stock exchange was also closed, and it was not until April 1932 that the sale of some government securities and then some shares began. The temporary restrictions on bank withdrawals were, however, gradually lifted in the following months. This was helped by the fact that—contrary to expectations and the experience of other countries—the public in Hungary did not rush the institutions. This was helped by the fact that, from the onset, depositors were free to dispose of the funds they had deposited with their banks after the bank closure/government ban on bank withdrawals, but the main reason for the relief was that no major financial institution in Hungary became insolvent during this period.[37]

The issuance of the so-called "gold pengő decree" in mid-August also served to provide reassurance to creditors and depositors, who had been left with a bitter taste in their mouths due to their past experiences of currency depreciation with the korona. The decree stipulated that debts incurred before 15 August should automatically be considered to be payable in so-called "gold pengős," while also allowing monetary claims to be denominated in gold pengős after that date. The exchange rate of the gold pengő to the standard pengő was determined by the Hungarian National Bank under instructions from the minister of finance. The 1:1 ratio used initially

Knapp Verlag, 1989); Karl Erich Born, *Die deutsche Bankenkrise 1931. Finanzen und Politik* (München: R. Piper & Co. Verlag, 1967).

37 Ágnes Pogány, "Válságok és válaszások. Pénzügyi politika Magyarországon és Ausztriában, 1931–1936," *Aetas* 15, no. 4 (2000): 32–49; Ágnes Pogány, "Zwillingskrisen oder Multiple Krisen? Finanzielle Krisen in Ungarn und Österreich in den dreißiger Jahren," in *Krisen/Geschichten in mitteleuropäischem Kontext*, eds. Márkus Keller, György Kövér, and Csaba Sasfi (Vienna: Institut für ungarische Geschichtsforschung in Wien, 2015), 227–53.

was never changed. The introduction of the gold pengő undoubtedly had a beneficial psychological effect in the short term.[38] However, as a result, the Hungarian currency became a "managed currency," because it was not the value of the gold reserves backing it but the policy of the central bank that guaranteed its domestic stability.[39]

A number of measures, which, in retrospect, foreshadowed the gradual implementation of exchange controls, proved to be much more permanent than the restrictions on deposit withdrawals, which were fully lifted after just a few weeks. The most important exchange control measure stipulated that no payments could be made in foreign currency, no foreign currency could be physically taken out of the country, and no foreign loans could be procured without the express permission of the Hungarian National Bank. This effectively ended the convertibility of the Hungarian pengő. The monopoly of the central bank was also ensured by the fact that the foreign exchange obtained from export transactions had to be surrendered to the central bank. Reporting any debt accrued, cash held, or securities owned in foreign exchange was also soon made mandatory above a threshold of 5,000 pengős.[40]

Despite the strict exchange controls, the foreign currency holdings of the National Bank of Hungary significantly decreased by the end of 1931. It became apparent that the foreign currency needed to service the debt, some 270 million pengős a year, was not available, while procuring new foreign loans had become virtually impossible.[41] The experts of the Financial Committee of the League of Nations, sent at the request of the Hungarians, therefore offered the creditors a standstill agreement—in the vernacular of the time, "*Stillhalte*." At the end of December, the government implemented a transfer moratorium, which prohibited the transfer of any principal or interest to foreign lenders, except for payments related to the loan from the League of Nations. Instead, all the amounts affected by the transfer moratorium had to be paid into the newly created

38 István Varga, "Az aranypengő," *Közgazdasági Szemle* 55, no. 12 (1931): 759.

39 Ernő Makai, *Pénz és hitel a világválság tükrében* (Budapest: TÉBE, 1934), 242.

40 Zoltán Óvári Papp, *A devizaforgalom szabályozása Magyarországon* (Budapest: A Gazdasági Jog Kiadványa, 1941), 77–82.

41 Rudolf Nötel, "Money, Banking and Industry in Interwar Austria and Hungary," *Journal of European Economic History* 13, no. 2 (1984): 186.

Foreign Creditors Fund, which was managed with the involvement of creditors' representatives. Initially, the moratorium was meant to defer only the repayment of principal amounts, but the Hungarian currency situation deteriorated so rapidly that there was insufficient foreign currency available to pay even the interests. Therefore, in 1932, an agreement was reached with the British and American creditors to postpone the repayment of the principal. Under the terms of this agreement, creditors were permitted to use the pengő equivalent of the interest payments to purchase goods, among other possibilities. Such exports were subsidized by a surcharge, which made it possible to reduce the debt considerably and also encouraged the export of otherwise unsaleable products. This was the first time that currency policy was deliberately used as an instrument of economic and trade policy in Hungary.[42]

Overall, Hungarian banks weathered the crisis with relatively little sacrifice in international comparison. The long-standing banking supervision authority and the measures taken by the government and by the central bank may have contributed to this. However, one of the reasons for the relative strength of the Hungarian credit system was the sound business policy of the leading institutions, which was primarily based on liquidity considerations. As a result, unlike in Austria or Germany, among other countries, the state was not compelled to dig deep into its pockets, nor were any banks nationalized even temporarily. Legislative measures proved sufficient to avoid the severe consequences of the credit crisis.[43]

Although the financial crisis in Hungary did not bring about any spectacular bank failures, the closure of the banks from July 14 to 16, 1931, and the subsequent measures mark a dividing line in the history of Hungarian lending, primarily because there had never been a direct state intervention like this before. The dynamics of state intervention are illustrated by the fact that, just as the crisis period saw the introduction of banking supervision in Germany, the United States, and the United Kingdom, the development of ever stricter state control over financial institutions also continued

42 On the government measures, see *A magyar hitelpolitika az 1920–1944. években* (Budapest: s. n., 1946), 33–36.

43 Tomka, *A magyarországi pénzintézetek rövid története, 1836–1947*, 122–23.

in Hungary, a country with a long history of such supervision. An important step in this direction was the establishment of the National Credit Council in October 1931.[44] The extensive powers of the Council clearly limited the business freedom of financial institutions. It could, for example, set a ceiling on interest rates, order the Centre for Financial Institutions to carry out an audit, or, in the last resort, order the compulsory winding-up of a financial institution. In other words, the central bank took on more and more tasks as a regulatory authority. Without its permission, it was not possible to buy securities from foreign sellers or sell them to foreign buyers, and any gold reserves had to be declared. Its articles of association also changed significantly. In 1933, the government was allowed to borrow 100 million pengős from the Hungarian National Bank to pay off agricultural debts. At the same time, the mandatory gold reserve ratio was reduced to 24 percent. Even more significant amendments to the articles of association followed in 1938, when the rules on the Gold Standard were completely abolished and the central bank was also empowered to carry out open market operations. The provision that the heads of the financial institutions no longer became members of the General Council of the Hungarian National Bank further solidified the bank's role as a public administration agency.[45]

By the late 1930s, the supervisory powers of the Hungarian National Bank and the Centre for Financial Institutions were expanded to such a degree that they no longer left the banks' personnel policy unaffected: bank directors could only be hired with the permission of these two institutions. This decree was related to the persecution of Jews rather than to the official justification, which claimed a risk of the government losing its most qualified administrators to financial institutions. This example shows that the state played a far greater role in financial life during the depression period than would have been strictly necessary to deal with the

44 Aladár Holbesz, *A magyar hitelszervezet története* (Budapest: May János Nyomdai Műintézet, 1939), 314–18.

45 Tomka, *A magyarországi pénzintézetek rövid története, 1836–1947*, 128.

crisis and its aftermath. Hence, the increase in state intervention can by no means be explained by economic factors alone.[46]

The economic role of the state soon went beyond the regulation of financial lending, trade in agricultural commodities, and foreign trade, and the introduction of monopolies in these areas. After the announcement of the major government development plan of 1938, known as the Győr Programme, the state's dominance in the field of finance further increased. This was primarily because the government heavily relied on loans to finance the implementation of its program, a significant portion of which was related to armament.[47] Act II of 1939 empowered the government to regulate the circulation of money as well as the operation of the central bank and of the Centre for Financial Institutions for national defense purposes. It also expanded the government's authority to access foreign loans and thereby incur sovereign debt. Even loans taken from private banks were eventually sourced from the central bank, because they were paid out on treasury bills that were then rediscounted at the central bank.

10.3 Restructuring and the Reorientation of Foreign Trade

The obvious ways out of the crisis were to increase efficiency and solve producers' market access issues. Efficiency improvements could come from efficiency gains within individual sectors on the one hand, and, on the other, from shifts in favor of sectors and activities with higher added value.

In agriculture, little progress was made in improving efficiency during the 1930s. It required significant investment, for which there

46 Ágnes Pogány, "Wirtschaftsnationalismus in Ungarn im 19. und 20. Jahrhundert," in *Für eine nationale Wirtschaft: Ungarn, die Tschechoslowakei und Polen vom Ausgang des 19. Jahrhunderts bis zum Zweiten Weltkrieg*, eds. Ágnes Pogány, Eduard Kubů, and Jan Kofman (Berlin: Berliner Wissenschaftsverlag, 2006), 11–71.

47 Iván T. Berend and György Ránki, *Magyarország gyáripara a második világháború előtt és a háború időszakában, 1933–1944* (Budapest: Akadémiai Kiadó, 1958), 374–75; György Lengyel, "Az irányított gazdaság kialakulásának néhány tényezője Magyarországon," in *Budapest Főváros Levéltára Közleményei* 1 (1978): 290–301; György Lengyel, "Irányított gazdaság és tervgazdaság," *Medvetánc* 1 (1981): 109–19; Csikós-Nagy, *A XX. század magyar gazdaságpolitikája*, 98–105.

was little scope during the years of the crisis. In fact, the drop in revenues prevented the acquisition of the necessary modern machinery and equipment, fertilizers and pesticides, and, in general, the industrial products needed for modernization. The agricultural scissors effect was also a factor in its own right, making the transformation of agriculture more difficult.

As an indication of this, tractors spread rapidly in the 1920s, but between 1929 and 1938, their numbers barely increased: In 1929, there were 6,800 tractors in operation in the country. By 1934–35, their number dropped to 3,600 before returning to precrisis levels by 1938. The proliferation of engine-driven threshers also came to a grinding halt. Because of mass unemployment, the use of live labor—instead of machines—could also serve social purposes, although this did not become government policy in Hungary—unlike in Yugoslavia, where a decree banned the use of tractors for a time. Fertilizer use increased sharply in the 1920s but then fell during the depression years from 26 kg per hectare in 1929 (values expressed in kilograms of actual nutrient content) to 3 kg in 1933, and even in 1938, it only reached a level of 10 kg per hectare. Despite this, there were also positive trends in yields: although the yields of rye and potatoes fell slightly in Hungary, wheat yields increased by an average of 10 percent and maize by 15 percent between 1924–29 and 1933–38.[48]

Nevertheless, a slow structural transformation of agriculture can be observed during the crisis years. From 1930 to 1934, the area devoted to vegetable crops increased by 37 percent, while the average area dedicated to cereal production during the period 1935–38 was three percentage points lower than the average of the years 1920 through 1924. Grape, wine, and fruit production also increased. However, some livestock sectors were hit particularly hard by the crisis. In 1934, the number of cattle decreased by 8 percent, the number of pigs by 3 percent, and the number of sheep by 31 percent compared to 1929 livestock levels.[49] At the same time, there was a positive trend in the rapid development of poultry produc-

48 Péter Gunst, *Magyarország gazdaságtörténete (1914–1989)* (Budapest: Nemzeti Tankönyvkiadó, 1996), 70–71.

49 Gunst, *A mezőgazdasági termelés története Magyarországon*, 310, 358, 378.

tion, which was reflected in the doubling of poultry exports in the decade after the mid-1920s. During the crisis, the value of exports of live animals and products of animal origin expressed as a share of total food exports increased significantly, with a slight increase in the share of processed agricultural products within this.[50]

As far as the shifts across the sectors are concerned, we see more significant changes. Economic restructuring progressed at a relatively fast pace during the crisis, with agriculture losing weight to industrial and service sectors producing a higher added value. While in 1928 agriculture accounted for 38.8 percent of the country's total output, in 1937 it was only 32.2 percent. In contrast, the share of industry increased from 29.9 percent to 31.8 percent and that of services from 31.9 percent to 36 percent.[51] This structural shift was much stronger than what happened in, for example, Czechoslovakia or Bulgaria during this period.[52]

Two of the most important ways for the government to alleviate the demand shortages faced by Hungarian economic actors were to protect the internal market and to expand the external markets. While the former mainly concerned industry, the expansion of the export markets was mainly seen as feasible in agriculture. The measures to protect industry have been described earlier. Between 1929 and 1933, the value of imports fell to less than a third. As a result of the economic policy, which favored import substitution, the share of consumer goods in total imports was 62 percent in 1913, but by 1925 it had fallen to 49 percent and by 1937 to 27 percent.[53] This decline in consumer goods helped the corresponding sectors of domestic industry—especially textiles. As imports were displaced, production in this sector continued to grow dynamically in the 1930s, even though domestic demand fell. This also contributed to a reduction in trade openness. While in 1929 the combined share of exports and imports (trade openness) was 32.7 percent of the country's gross domestic product (GDP), in 1937 it was only 20

50 *Gunst, A mezőgazdasági termelés története Magyarországon,* 89–90.
51 Eckstein, "National Income and Capital Formation in Hungary, 1900–1950," 165.
52 Morys, "Economic Growth and Structural Change in Central, East and South-East Europe, 1918–1939," 179.
53 Drabek, "Foreign Trade Performance and Policy," 461.

percent.[54] At the same time, the import substitution measures had a beneficial effect on the balance of trade and on the balance of payments, and, as a matter of fact, even on the terms of trade. Indeed, the drastic restrictions on imports of consumer goods affected precisely those groups of goods for which world prices fell the least. The surge in consumer goods production, on the other hand, boosted the imports of raw materials and semifinished products—such as, for example, cotton and yarn—whose prices on the world market fell the most during the crisis.[55] The share of the latter in Hungarian imports was only 38 percent in 1913, rising to 60% in 1929 and 73 percent in 1937. Partly as a result of this and partly as a result of price movements on the world market, the terms of trade, which had deteriorated sharply in the early years of the crisis, began to improve from the mid-1930s onward and roughly recovered to precrisis levels.[56]

During the crisis, the country's traditional export markets became even more closed than before and exports fell sharply. In 1929, exports amounted to 1,038 million pengős, in 1933 to only 391 million pengős, and even in 1937 the figure only rose to 588 million pengős.[57] Thus, in addition to curbing imports, Hungary's governments were also keen to promote exports. With the introduction of state control over international payments and with state supervision being extended over foreign trade, the government's options—as well as its responsibilities—only expanded. An official license was required for all export and import transactions. In 1932–33, a surcharge system was introduced for exports, following the German model. The background of the measure was that the government wanted to stimulate exports but did not want to devalue the pengő, as this would have increased the interest payments on foreign debt, which would have also been calculated in pengős. The export premiums introduced corresponded to a de facto devaluation of 20–50% against foreign currencies.

54 Marcus, Nikolič, and Straumann, "Economic Policy, 1918–1939," 202.

55 Drabek, "Foreign Trade Performance and Policy," 463.

56 Berend, *Válságos évtizedek*, 326.

57 *A Magyar Gazdaságkutató Intézet gazdasági helyzetjelentése*, no. 45 (Budapest: Magyar Gazdaságkutató Intézet, 1940), 9.

Some industries were able to adapt to external market needs, and some sectors within those industries achieved particularly good export performance. One of these sectors was the production of canned fruit and vegetables. Exports of canned food sold under the Globus brand increased, with exports of tomato paste in particular growing twentyfold. In other branches of industry, areas with advanced technology and export potential only emerged as isolated pockets of development. It was during the Great Depression that Hungary's bauxite deposits began to be explored, and by 1937 half a million tons of bauxite were being mined annually. Much of this was exported to Germany. Already internationally important in the production of incandescent lamps, Egyesült Izzó Rt. (United Incandescent Ltd.) was a world leader in the development of krypton lights but also ventured into new fields such as the production of radio tubes.[58] Among the new and successful exports of the engineering industry was the electric motor train developed by Ganz. The world market share of Hungarian electrical engineering companies peaked during the crisis: their weight in this cutting-edge technological segment of the economy was 0.7 percent in 1929, 2.2 percent in 1933, and 1.7 percent in 1937.[59] Another important export of Ganz & Co. was Jendrassik's diesel locomotive, of which more than five hundred were exported until the outbreak of the war. In 1939, for example, two-thirds of Argentina's railway locomotives were Hungarian-made.[60] There were also important innovations in the pharmaceutical industry.

Of course, these examples do not mean that most Hungarian industry was of such a high standard nor that these sectors dominated the country's exports. Quite the contrary: the industrial development of the 1930s in Hungary was not so much the result of exports based on technological innovations but rather of import-substitution industrialization, which gained new momentum during the crisis. Exports continued to be dominated by agricultural rather than industrial products.

58 Mária Hidvégi, *Anschluss and den Weltmarkt: Ungarns elektrotechnische Leitunternehmen, 1867–1949* (Göttingen: Vandenhoeck & Ruprecht, 2016), 195–97.

59 Hidvégi, *Anschluss and den Weltmarkt*, 248–49.

60 Hidvégi, *Anschluss and den Weltmarkt*, 254.

As in other countries in the region, the importance of clearing arrangements in foreign trade increased, which, in the space of just a few years, completely eclipsed trade transactions involving foreign exchange. In 1935, two-thirds of Hungary's foreign trade was conducted in this way; by 1938, this ratio increased to 85 percent.[61] The essence of a clearing arrangement was that the two countries involved did not settle the value of their reciprocal deliveries on a continuous basis, but instead transferred only the difference in the annual balance.

The direct economic involvement of the state became particularly pronounced in the context of the country's increasingly close economic relations with Germany. This was due to the fact that from the mid-1930s onward, Hungary found itself within a radically altered international political and economic force field, one in which Germany's influence had significantly intensified. In the early days of the crisis, Germany tried to limit agricultural imports from East-Central and Southeast Europe. After Hitler came to power, Germany appeared to be more open to such imports, in line with its improving economic situation and the arms build-up. The *Neuer Plan*, announced in Germany in 1934, put the German foreign economy on a new footing by introducing centralized import control. This made it possible for Germany to conclude comprehensive bilateral agreements with the countries of Southeastern Europe using clearing arrangements. Germany also used these agreements to achieve its foreign policy goals. In Germany's "Greater Space Economy" (*Großraumwirtschaft*), the *Südostraum* or southeastern region, which included Hungary, occupied an important place. It was in this spirit that the German-Hungarian trade agreement was concluded in early 1934 as the first of Germany's new type of clearing agreements and the one that later became a model for similar agreements negotiated with other countries in Southeastern Europe.[62]

61 Berend and Ránki, "Polen, Ungarn, Rumänien, Bulgarien und Albanien, 1914–1980," 815.

62 György Ránki, "Hitel vagy piac," in *Mozgásterek, kényszerpályák*, ed. György Ránki (Budapest: Magvető, 1983), 341–82; György Ránki, *Gazdaság és külpolitika. A nagyhatalmak harca a délkelet-európai gazdasági hegemóniáért, 1919–1939* (Budapest: Magvető, 1981), 249.

Under the agreement, the German government provided tariff reliefs and other concessions for the sale of Hungarian agricultural products in Germany, using a complex system of reimbursements, and also committed to purchasing significant quantities of grain, live animals, meat, and fat at prices above world market prices. In return, the German side received substantial tariff reductions for its industrial exports to Hungary in the context of the clearing arrangement. German-Hungarian trade expanded rapidly: In 1929 Germany's share of Hungarian exports was 11.7 percent, rising to 24.1 percent in 1937 and 40 percent in 1938. This was complemented by German capital investment, which accounted for half of all foreign capital investment in Hungary before World War II. In the eyes of many contemporary observers, this was seen as Germany's "sacrifice" to help the region.[63] This in itself is an indication that these processes clearly strengthened Germany's economic and political influence in Hungary and the wider Southeastern European region.

10.4 Hungary's Growth in International Comparison

GDP per capita in Hungary grew by 2.5 percent in 1929, then declined by 2.2 percent in 1930 and by a further 4.8 percent in 1931. At the depth of the Great Depression in 1932, the contraction was 11.5 percent compared to 4 years earlier. After that, however, the reconstruction of the economy was relatively rapid. By 1935, GDP per capita had reached the previous peak of 1929 and—after a small decline in 1937—exceeded it by 7.2 percent in 1938 and by 14.6 percent in 1939.[64] If we compare this growth trajectory with the countries of the narrower region, we see that Hungary was one of the most successful countries to emerge from the depression: By the end of the 1930s, Hungary's economic performance—in terms of

63 Derek H. Aldcroft, *Europe's Third World: The European Periphery in the Interwar Years* (Aldershot: Ashgate, 2006), 122.

64 Béla Tomka, *Gazdasági növekedés, fogyasztás és életminőség: Magyarország nemzetközi összehasonlításban az első világháborútól napjainkig* (Budapest: Akadémiai, 2011), 267; Maddison, *The World Economy. Historical Statistics*, 100.

Table 10.2 Trends in Gross Domestic Product Per Capita in Hungary and East-Central European Countries, 1913–38 (in 1990 Geary-Khamis International Dollars)

	1913	*1921*	*1929*	*1938*	*Growth 1929–38 (%)*
Hungary	2,098	1,709	2,476	2,655	7.2
Czechoslovakia	2,096	2,085	3,042	2,882	–5.3
Poland	1,739	n/a	2,117	2,182	3
Bulgaria	1,137	1,000	1,285	1,499	16.6
Yugoslavia	973	959	1,256	1,249	–0.6

Compiled by the author on the basis of the following sources: Angus Maddison. *The World Economy: Historical Statistics*. Paris: OECD, 2003, 100–101 (1913–39 data for Czechoslovakia, Hungary, and Poland); Matthias Morys. "Economic Growth and Structural Change in Central, East and South-East Europe, 1918–1939." In *The Economic History of Central, East and South-East Europe: 1800 to the Present*, edited by Matthias Morys. London and New York: Routledge, 2021, 169 (1913–38 data for Bulgaria and Yugoslavia).

Notes: For Czechoslovakia, the data are given for 1937 (instead of 1938); for Hungary, the data are given for 1920 (instead of 1921).

per capita output—was closer to that of Czechoslovakia, leaving Poland far behind (see Table 10.2).[65]

A longer-term international comparison of Hungary's growth trajectory provides an additional opportunity to characterize the impact of the crisis in a comprehensive way. To this end, it is quite enlightening to examine the evolution of economic convergence and divergence trajectories between Hungary and Western European countries. As for the background, we might note that at the end of the nineteenth century, per capita GDP in Hungary—based on its present territory—was only slightly more than half the average of thirteen Western European countries and lagged behind every single Western European country. In the early twentieth century, Hungary converged slightly with Western Europe, and this process reached its peak in the years before World War I. World War I and its economic consequences led to a more severe decline in Hungary than in most Western European countries, and this was reflected in the development of economic output ratios. But the boom came

65 Morys, "Economic Growth and Structural Change," 169; Maddison, *The World Economy: Historical Statistics*, 100–1.

relatively quickly in Hungary, with per capita GDP reaching 57.1 percent of the Western European average by 1929. The crisis did not cause a disruption, as Hungary actually slightly surpassed this level on the eve of World War II: With a value of 58.3 percent in 1939, it almost returned to its pre-World War I level of relative economic development (see Table 10.2). If we also take into account the evolution of internal divergences in Western Europe and work with the standardized Hungarian data for the purposes of this exercise, the dynamics found will be slightly different from those presented above: Hungary came closest to Western Europe around 1890, but after that, the trend reversed, and by 1913 Hungary was lagging behind Western Europe even more than back in 1890. The standardized Hungarian data between 1920 and 1938 initially show a convergence, but as a result of increasing unification within Western Europe, this turned into a divergence. Thus, between the two World Wars, there was no significant shift in this respect.[66]

When Hungary is compared to Austria, significantly different convergence and divergence trajectories are observed. Such a comparison may be justified by the fact that historically, Hungary and Austria formed an economic unit in varying forms and degrees over quite a long period. On the other hand, during the period between the two World Wars, when these close ties were severed, the two countries shared a similar political and economic heritage and had comparable endowments. Moreover, the two states are akin by virtue of their geographical location and size. After 1870, Hungarian economic output was slightly approaching that of Austria, reaching 60.3 percent of Austrian per capita output by 1890. It then remained at roughly the same relative level until World War I. However, the gap between the two neighboring countries narrowed significantly between the two World Wars, and especially during and after the crisis. As a result, before World War II, Hungary's per capita economic output increased to 74.6 percent of the Austrian level (see Table 10.3). This was the closest Hungary had ever come to Austria in this respect during the entire twentieth century. This result also indicates that Hungary emerged from the Great Depression in a relatively favorable position.

66 Tomka, *Gazdasági növekedés, fogyasztás és életminőség*, 270.

Table 10.3 Trends in Gross Domestic Product Per Capita in Hungary in International Comparison, 1890–2005 (in 1990 Geary-Khamis International Dollars)

	1890	*1900*	*1910*	*1913*	*1920*	*1929*	*1930*	*1938*	*1939*
Hungary	1,473	1,682	2,000	2,098	1,709	2,476	2,404	2,655	2,838
Western Europe (average)	2,535	2,910	3,269	3,474	3,247	4,336	4,301	4,667	4,867
Hungary/Western Europe (average) × 100	58.1	57.8	61.2	60.4	52.6	57.1	55.9	56.9	58.3
Hungary/Austria × 100	60.3	58.4	60.8	60.5	70.9	66.9	67	74.6	69.3

Compiled by the author on the basis of the following sources: Angus Maddison. *Monitoring the World Economy, 1820–1992.* Paris: OECD, 1995, 194–195, 198 (1890–1939 data for Germany, 1890–1900 data for Ireland); Angus Maddison. *The World Economy. Historical Statistics.* Paris: OECD, 2003, 60–69, 100–101 (1890–1913 data for Austria, Belgium, Denmark, Finland, France, Italy, the Netherlands, Norway, Sweden, Switzerland, and the United Kingdom; 1920–39 data for Austria, Belgium, Denmark, Finland, France, Italy, the Netherlands, Norway, Sweden, Switzerland, and the United Kingdom; 1913–39 data for Ireland; 1890–1939 data for Hungary).

Notes: Western Europe: the United Kingdom, France, the Netherlands, Belgium, Ireland, Germany, Austria, Switzerland, Sweden, Denmark, Norway, Finland, and Italy. For Ireland, 1913 and 1921 data were used (instead of 1910 and 1920).

10.5 Social and Political Impact of the Crisis

The most immediate social impact of the crisis was a deterioration in the living conditions of the general population. Comprehensive data on the income situation of the agricultural population, the largest social group, are not available, but the trend is well illustrated by the evolution of the real value of daily wages for agricultural day laborers. Compared with 1929 levels, the real value of daily agricultural wages fell by 37.1 percent in 1934, the year of the lowest point, and was back to its previous level by 1939.[67] At the same time, the social impact of declining real wages was exacerbated by the decline in job opportunities during the crisis. In 1935, the officially recorded proportion of unemployment and underemployment in agriculture was 10.3 percent and 20.1 percent of the total workforce in the sector, but it is important to note that this count was highly incomplete.[68] Often those who found work could only work for shorter periods.

During the crisis, unemployment among industrial workers was particularly high. In 1929, 75,600 people were registered as unemployed in industry, while in 1933 the figure rose to 241,900. This was 36 percent of the precrisis workforce.[69] Average workers' earnings declined by 23 percent between 1929 and 1933.[70] This, however, did not imply a proportionate decline in real terms. On the one hand, the decline in average earnings also reflected certain structural changes in the labor force—namely, the increasing share of unskilled and female workers. These latter categories of labor were overrepresented in the light manufacturing sectors that were less affected by the crisis. On the other hand, the drop in food prices

67 Mátyás Matolcsy, *Az életszínvonal alakulása Magyarországon, 1924–1944* (Budapest: Magyar Ipari Munkatudományi Intézet, 1944), 35.

68 Péter Gunst, *A paraszti társadalom Magyarországon a két világháború között* (Budapest: MTA Történettudományi Intézet, 1987), 62; for alternative calculations, see *Magyarország története, vol. 8*, 603.

69 Miklós Incze, ed., *Az 1929–33. évi világgazdasági válság hatása Magyarországon* (Budapest: Akadémiai Kiadó, 1955), 333.

70 Without mining. *A M. Kir. Kormány 1929. évi működéséről és az ország közállapotairól szóló jelentés és statisztikai évkönyv* (Budapest: Athenaeum, 1931), 105; *A M. Kir. Kormány 1934. évi működéséről és az ország közállapotairól szóló jelentés és statisztikai évkönyv* (Budapest: Athenaeum, 1936), 131.

compensated for part of the decline in wage levels. According to trade union calculations, the cost of living for industrial workers at the depths of the crisis was actually 20–24 percent lower than back in 1929.[71] Taking all of this into account, industrial wages fell by 5.4 percent between 1929 and 1933 in real terms.[72] While this was true for those employed full time, unemployment and part-time employment led to a larger decline in the average income of households.

The crisis also eroded the living standards of the middle classes. The purchasing power of the incomes of artisans and retailers diminished, while civil servants were also affected by rising unemployment. The salaries of some public employees were cut by central measures, but it was only in the highest income brackets that the reduction of salaries significantly exceeded the decrease in the cost of living.[73] At the end of 1931, the ratio of unemployed white-collar workers was about 10–12 percent of the corresponding group.[74]

The crisis led to a revival of mass political movements. The change was not so much in the number of political rallies or the number of participants, but rather in the radicalization of the strikes and demonstrations, including the increased frequency of confrontations with law enforcement. In autumn 1929, 5,000 miners went on strike in Salgótarján and Pécs for 4 weeks. For the first time in 10 years, the illegal communist party was able to mobilize a significant number of workers. In 1930, for the first time since 1921, the Social Democratic Party organized a May Day march in Budapest with 10,000–15,000 participants, which was followed by several similar demonstrations in the following months. The political mobilization that unfolded in the wake of the Great Depression also affected small and landed peasants, which manifested itself mainly in protest rallies and the formation of political groups. Although this was by no means a revolutionary situation, the developments were

71 György Borsányi, *Válságévek krónikája. Az 1929–1933-as gazdasági világválság hatása Magyarországon* (Budapest: Kossuth, 1986), 27.

72 Iván Kádár, Gyula Bedő, and Györgyné Falus, eds., *A munkásosztály helyzete a Horthy-rendszer idején* (Budapest: Szikra, 1956), 223.

73 I. Gábor Kovács, "Az értelmiségi keresetek változása (1920–1975)," in *Értelmiségiek, diplomások, szellemi munkások*, ed. Tibor Huszár (Budapest: Kossuth, 1978), 227–38.

74 Tibor Hajdú, "Az értelmiség számszerű gyarapodásának következményei az első világháború előtt és után," *Valóság* 24, no. 7 (1981): 2–22.

viewed with concern by a significant part of the ruling elite and the middle class, who had already experienced a major social upheaval a decade or more before that had threatened their very existence.[75]

In Hungary, as in many other countries, the crisis brought about a transformation in the relationship between society and the state. There was a growing perception in political thinking and in wider public opinion that economic and social problems could be solved by increasing the involvement—and therefore the powers—of the state. The changes were driven to a large extent by the international environment: the spill-over effect of the authoritarian regimes in the neighboring states and later the Italian and German dictatorships.[76]

The deepening economic crisis and the intensifying political mobilization in its wake, coupled with the broad ideological changes indicated, posed a challenge to Prime Minister István Bethlen and his regime, which had primarily pursued political consolidation in the 1920s. Bethlen established and maintained a parliamentary system with authoritarian elements for a decade after 1921. This system was based to a large extent on restrictions on political participation and political mobilization, the most prominent of which were limited suffrage and the open ballot system used outside the big cities.[77]

During his premiership, Bethlen relied on his dominance over the ruling party, the Unity Party (*Egységes Párt*), often through informal means. During the crisis, Bethlen was able to keep his system of government running for a while, but more and more people within the political elite were inclined to believe that the system established by Bethlen and operated for a decade was not capable of dealing with the consequences of the economic and social crisis. Within the Unity Party, rifts soon developed that Bethlen could no longer bridge.[78]

Following Bethlen's resignation in August 1931, Gyula Károlyi became prime minister. His 1-year rule did not yet bring significant

75 *Magyarország története, vol. 8.*

76 György Ránki, *Állam és társadalom a két világháború közötti Közép-Kelet-Európában* (Budapest: MTA Történettudományi Intézet, 1986), 17.

77 Gábor Gyáni, "Politikai rendszer és választói magatartás," in *Magyarország társadalomtörténete a reformkortól a második világháborúig*, eds. Gábor Gyáni and György Kövér (Budapest: Osiris, 1998), 332–42.

78 Ignác Romsics, *Bethlen István—Politikai életrajz* (Budapest: Helikon, 2019).

changes to the political system. The turning point was the autumn of 1932 when Gyula Gömbös came to power. Gömbös was a prominent figure in the post-1919 counterrevolution. Initially, he was the leader of a far-right military organization, the Hungarian National Defence Association (*Magyar Országos Véderő Egyesület*; MOVE). Between 1923 and 1928, he was the head of the Hungarian National Independence Party (*Magyar Nemzeti Függetlenségi Párt*), an opposition party also known as the Party of Racial Defence (*Fajvédő Párt*). Eventually, he crossed the aisle and joined the governing party. Gömbös's premiership brought a whole range of previously marginal far-right politicians to prominent positions.[79]

He held overtly racist views, and his goal was an Italian-style corporatist reorganization of society with severe restrictions on political rights and freedoms. Initially, he was forced to make considerable compromises, as the governing party—now renamed the National Unity Party (*Nemzeti Egység Pártja*)—remained under the control of Bethlen. In the years that followed, Gömbös fought constantly within his party to implement his plans. In 1935, he succeeded in dissolving parliament and calling early elections, which changed the composition of the parliamentary faction of the National Unity Party: the extreme right was greatly strengthened and came under the control of Gömbös. The dualism of power that had prevented a radical transformation of the political system was abolished: Bethlen left the party and his supporters were now a minority within the parliamentary group.[80]

Gömbös then set about implementing his ideas with great vigor, in particular the creation of a mass party and an accompanying mass movement that would encompass not only political life but also the social, economic, and cultural spheres. In his program, great emphasis was placed on the creation of a "national community" based on a "unified Hungarian world view." He placed emphasis on the protection of private property but promised to eliminate the harmful phenomena of capitalism. Meanwhile, he also aimed to

79 József Vonyó, "Gömbös kormánypártjának ideológiája és programja," *Századok* 145, no. 1 (2011): 3–38; Vonyó József: *Gömbös Gyula és a hatalom. Egy politikussá lett katonatiszt* (Pécs: Kronosz Kiadó, 2018), 186–280.

80 Levente Püski, "Magyarország politikai berendezkedése a két világháború között)," *Korunk* 23, no. 11 (2012): 22–23.

integrate the working class into what he called the "national society." Gömbös presented himself as a charismatic strongman leader, and his supporters wanted to put the principle of dictatorial leadership into practice. Overall, he aimed to achieve rule by decree by curtailing the powers of parliament; essentially, his goal was to create a dictatorship.

The governor, Miklós Horthy, was suspicious of Gömbös's dictatorial aspirations and his many domestic policy initiatives, such as his attempts to curb the system of large estates. By the spring of 1936, Gömbös's efforts had foundered, and his illness and death ended his attempt to transform the constitutional system. Thus, during Gömbös's premiership, there was a significant shift in political relations in favor of the extreme right, but no dictatorial turn took place just yet.

However, the trend toward political realignment continued after his death. The change that proved to have the greatest impact was the one in the structure of the political party system.[81] The political mobilization mentioned above led to the formation of new parties and political organizations but also to major internal movements within the ruling party. By the mid-1930s, the extreme right-wing tendencies had clearly gained strength and were seeking a radical transformation of the political and social system. They aimed at the elimination of political pluralism, thus reducing civil liberties and freedoms, and severely limiting the role of parliament. Much in line with Gömbös's earlier plans, they wanted to create a corporatist regime.[82]

One of the signs was that in the mid-1930s, Hungary saw the emergence of a fascist mass party—the Party of National Will (*Nemzet Akaratának Pártja*)—under the leadership of Ferenc Szálasi. However, several other far-right parties—such as the National Socialist Hungarian Workers' Party (*Nemzetiszocialista Magyar Munkáspárt*) and the Socialist Party for Racial Defence (*Fajvédő Szocialista Párt*)—were also active and growing in influence.[83] At

81 Levente Püski, *A Horthy-rendszer (1919–1945)* (Budapest: Pannonica, 2006), 265.
82 Püski, "Magyarország politikai berendezkedése a két világháború között," 22–23.
83 Rudolf Paksa, "Szélsőjobboldali mozgalmak az 1930-as években," in *A magyar jobboldali hagyomány, 1900–1948*, ed. Ignác Romsics (Budapest: Osiris, 2009), 275–304.

the end of 1937, the Hungarian National Socialist Party (*Magyar Nemzeti Szocialista Párt*) was formed from the merger of several parties, which—as its name readily reveals—adopted the program of the German National Socialist Party (NSDAP) almost in its entirety. The governments of the second half of the 1930s tried to suppress these movements and parties for a time by banning them and imprisoning their leaders: even Szálasi himself was imprisoned.[84] But the shift to the right was continual even in government policy. Among the countless signs of this, the anti-Semitic laws of the late 1930s should be highlighted.[85]

Although in 1937–38 the conservative forces succeeded in strengthening the powers of the governor under the banner of protecting the constitution, the introduction of a comprehensive election system by secret ballot could no longer be avoided—which, in the given political context, actually favored the extreme right. In the elections of May 1939, the moderate conservatives—and even the former supporters of Gömbös—were crowded out from the governing party, which was renamed once again—this time as the Party of Hungarian Life (*Magyar Élet Pártja*). Replacing the moderate conservatives, various groups on the far right took the lead. Meanwhile, the opposition was dominated by the National Socialist parties.[86]

The late 1930s saw further significant structural and institutional changes in the Hungarian political system, such as the extension of Horthy's powers as governor. These were partly aimed at curbing extremist parties, but overall they led to the almost complete elimination of the controlling role of parliament. While in the period of the Great Depression the Hungarian system of state and government could be considered a parliamentary system with authoritarian elements—or, according to alternative assessments, a system of hegemonic party authoritarianism—after 1939 the political system was fully authoritarian.[87]

84 Rudolf Paksa, *Magyar nemzetiszocialisták. Az 1930-as évek új szélsőjobboldali mozgalma, pártjai, politikusai, sajtója* (Budapest: Osiris, 2013), 104–20.

85 Krisztián Ungváry, *A Horthy-rendszer és antiszemitizmusának mérlege. Diszkrimináció és társadalompolitika Magyarországon, 1919–1944* (Pécs: Jelenkor, 2016).

86 Ignác Romsics, *Magyarország története a XX. században* (Budapest: Osiris, 2010).

87 Püski, "Magyarország politikai berendezkedése a két világháború között," 25.

The change in the relationship between state and society and the expansion of the powers and functions of the state were also reflected in the intersection of economics and politics: social policy. After World War I, the Hungarian welfare system was characterized by a strong dualism. Although the first social security laws appeared in Hungary relatively early by international standards, in the late nineteenth and early twentieth centuries, they—like the corresponding measures in most European countries—only provided social rights for workers employed in large industries, while state employees received pensions and other social benefits through special schemes.[88] These groups had access to relatively high levels of social benefits. In contrast, the social rights of the agricultural population, who made up the majority of the population, remained marginal. The development of public health, which had already led to significant results in the villages since the 1920s—especially in terms of substantially reducing mortality—showed a somewhat different picture.

From the mid-1930s, another wave of changes swept through the system. On the one hand, the social rights of industrial workers were further increased from this period onward, and on the other hand, welfare systems slowly began to open up to the agrarian population. In 1937, the 8-hour working day was introduced in industry and the minimum wage was differentiated by occupation. It was also the time when paid leave was introduced in industry. Six days of paid leave per year were granted to industrial workers who had worked in the same job for at least one year without interruption. The number of paid days of absence increased with further years of seniority. In practice, however, this provision affected only a small number of industrial workers—some estimates put the number at around one-tenth of the total, or 60,000—because only that many had worked continuously for the same company for at least a year.[89] A further welfare measure introduced in 1938 was the so-called family wage,

88 Dorottya Szikra and Béla Tomka, "Social Policy in East Central Europe: Major Trends in the 20th Century," in *Post-Communist Welfare Pathways: Theorizing Social Policy Transformations in Central and Eastern Europe*, eds. Alfio Cerami and Peter Vanhuysee (Basingstoke: Palgrave Macmillan, 2009), 17–34.

89 Gábor Gyáni, *A szociálpolitika múltja Magyarországon* (Budapest: MTA Történettudományi Intézet, 1994).

which provided industrial workers with a monthly education allowance of 5 pengős per child, which amounted to roughly 55 percent of the average wage. Some of these welfare measures, however, remained in place for only a short time because in the autumn of 1939—when World War II broke out—both the 8-hour working day and the paid leave provisions were suspended. Nevertheless, they unquestionably pointed the way toward future developments.

Farm servants and some agricultural workers were already guaranteed accident insurance by law, and in 1939, coverage was also extended to all agricultural workers. Old-age and widows' pension insurance for agricultural workers was introduced in 1938 and 1939. An old-age pension, similar in its benefits to the industrial workers' pension scheme, was introduced for agricultural workers over the age of 65. The scheme included a 15-year waiting period, that is, it was to be first implemented for the cohort that still had at least 15 years to contribute to the social insurance scheme. The amount of the pension was also adjusted to that provided for in the insurance scheme for industrial and commercial employees.[90] At the same time, from the end of the 1930s, tendencies toward ethnicization and discrimination against the Jewish population also appeared in social policy.[91]

10.6 Conclusion

The Great Depression interrupted the relatively successful period of growth that Hungary was going through post-World War I. The growth of the 1920s relied heavily on the import of foreign capital and was marked by import-substitution industrialization. The first sector to be hit by the crisis was agriculture, where it manifested itself not in a decline in production but in the falling prices of agricultural products and, hence, in lower incomes for producers. The opening of the agricultural price scissors in the first half of the 1930s, and the sharp contraction of export opportunities, further aggravated the situation of the agricultural producers. In contrast,

90 Béla Tomka, *Szociálpolitika a 20. századi Magyarországon európai perspektívában* (Budapest: Századvég, 2003), 83–84.

91 Ungváry, *A Horthy-rendszer és antiszemitizmusának mérlege.*

the crisis brought about a sharp decline in industrial production: at its lowest point in 1932, industrial output was down by about a quarter as compared to 1929 levels. After the financial crisis that unfolded in 1931, capital imports came to a halt. The tertiary sector, in essence, experienced stagnation during this period.

Governments sought to alleviate the crisis through vigorous state intervention. Assistance to farmers took many forms and included, in particular, direct financial support, price regulation, debt rescheduling, granting a monopoly to newly established, fully or partially state-owned entities as the sole authorized purchaser of specific crops, and the promotion of agricultural exports through financial support. Support for industry was, first and foremost, a matter of economic nationalism: In order to protect the market, customs tariffs, which were not low to begin with, were raised even further, and quotas were introduced to discourage imports of foreign manufactured goods. This gave a new impetus to the import-substitution industrialization that had already been prevalent in the 1920s.

From 1931, particularly drastic measures were taken to combat the financial crisis, which then affected the entire economic policy arsenal of the state for the rest of the decade. To prevent a financial collapse, a transfer moratorium was declared and a fully fledged system of exchange controls was swiftly established. This brought international financial relations and foreign trade under full state control. The change helped to bring about a complete reorientation of Hungary's foreign trade from the mid-1930s onward, as a result of which Germany gained a dominant position in Hungary's foreign economic relations. On the one hand, this reorientation was the result of economic necessity, as Germany was the country most open to Hungarian agricultural products. On the other hand, it was very much in line with Hungarian revisionist foreign policy ambitions, which encouraged cooperation with Germany, another country seeking to change the international status quo.

During the crisis, the Hungarian economy also underwent beneficial adjustment processes, partly as a result of government interventions and partly independently of them. Among these, it is essential to highlight certain structural changes that were significant even by international standards. Specifically, we observe an increase in the share of sectors generating higher added value on the one hand and a shift toward more profitable activities within each sector on the other. Agriculture did show some innovation, but it was outpaced by industry and services, where innovation was much stronger.

Overall, our results on the depth of the economic crisis in Hungary differ in several respects from the views that have dominated the literature thus far. Applying several types and methods of comparisons, we have found that in terms of its economic performance in the period of the Great Depression, Hungary was among the better performers by international standards.

Nevertheless, the crisis had a significant social impact and catalyzed broad political changes. First and foremost, it contributed to political mobilization, which brought with it—in several stages—the strengthening of the far right. The main mediator of this was the transformation of the party system. This impact of the crisis was linked to the characteristics of Hungarian political culture between the two World Wars. The revolutions after World War I discredited liberalism and the political left, and the country's defeat in the war strengthened revisionist aspirations. This was accompanied by the rise of extreme antiliberal or outright fascist and/or national socialist political currents in Central Europe from the mid-1930s onward, which had a profound demonstration effect. As a result, the limited parliamentarism that had developed in Hungary in the early 1920s gradually eroded, and from 1939 onward the political system could be considered an autocracy. In other words, the crisis in Hungary was somewhat milder and the recovery was faster than in most European countries. Nevertheless, while—in line with general trends in Central Europe—the crisis certainly contributed to the decline of democracy, it was far from being the sole, or even most important, factor of that decline.

Chapter 11

BULGARIA

ECONOMIC THOUGHT AND STRUCTURAL CHANGE DURING THE GREAT DEPRESSION

Nikolay Nenovsky and Tsvetelina Marinova

The Great Depression in the Balkans, including Bulgaria, has not been the subject of any special analysis in the Western literature.[1] Nevertheless, the Bulgarian economy and society during these years has been object of a number of in-depth studies by Bulgarian authors from different periods. The ideological and scientific preferences of the authors, characteristic of each period, inevitably left their mark on their interpretations. Yet, each of them has contributed to the overall understanding of the profound changes that occurred in Bulgaria between the two World Wars.[2]

1 Apart from reviews such as League of Nations, *Situation Economique Mondiale, 1932–1933* (Geneva: League of Nations, 1933) and the RIIA, there are several interesting studies by Western and Bulgarian authors published abroad, but almost all of them cover the period before the depression, that is, until the stabilization of the lev, or until the financial crisis of 1931. Leo Pasvolsky, *Economic Nationalism of the Danubian States* (London: George Allen & Unwin, 1928); Henri Prost, *La Bulgarie de 1912 à 1930. Contribution à l'Histoire Economique & Financière de la Guerre et des Conséquences* (Paris: Editions Pierre Roger, 1932); Henri Prost, *La Liquidation Financière de la Guerre en Bulgarie* (Paris: Marcel Gard, 1925); J. Petkof, *Prix, circulation et change en Bulgarie de 1890 a 1924* (Paris: Jouve & Cie Editeurs, 1926); Angelo Focarile, *Bulgaria d'Oggi. Nei Suoi Aspetti Sociali, Economici, Commerciali e Finanziari* (con una carta delle ferrovie bulgare) (Milano: Ulrico Hoepli, 1929); Panayot Ilieff, *La Banque Nationale de Bulgarie et L'Histoire de sa Politique Monétaire* (Lyon: Bosc and Riou, 1930); J. P. Koszul, *Les Efforts de Restauration Financière de la Bulgarie (1922–1931)* (Paris: Félix Alcan, 1932); Vladimir Mollof, *La Crise Mondiale et la Banque Nationale de Bulgarie*, Etude de Documentation Economique (Paris: Domat-Montchrestien, F. Loviton & Cie, 1934); Adam Tooze and Martin Ivanov, "Disciplining the 'Black Sheep of the Balkans': Financial Supervision and Sovereignty in Bulgaria, 1902–38," *The Economic History Review* 64, no. 1 (2011): 30–51.

2 Among the Bulgarian scholars who have studied various aspects of the Great Depression are Andrey Lyapchev, Alexandar Tsankov, Slavcho Zagorov, Georgi

The main objective of this text is to present in a synthesized form the general dynamics of the Great Depression in Bulgaria, the causes and factors that have given specific shape to its manifestation in the country, its phases and forms, and the subsequent structural change and trajectory of the Bulgarian economy and society. Along with reconstructing the historical facts, we are presenting the history of economic thought and the debates that accompanied them. Without falling into determinism, we argue that the overall dynamics of the causes, phases, and consequences of the Great Depression has an internal logic and causal consistency.

11.1 Bulgaria on the Eve of Crisis and Depression

The initial conditions of the Bulgarian economy set the direction for how the Great Depression evolved and determined the consequences, the policy response, and the overall dynamics of the Bulgarian economy. They also determined the political development of the country as well as the spread of certain economic and political views and theories among the Bulgarian elites. Initial conditions can be reduced to two groups—first, the internal characteristics of the economy that determined its external and internal vulnerability, and second, the different types of external and internal shocks and impulses that provoked the crisis.

The domestic economic, social, and political conditions can be considered a continuation of trends that emerged after World War I, as well as before it in the years after the restoration of statehood, that is, since the liberation from Ottoman rule in 1878. First, like most

---

Svrakov, Kiril Popov, Kiril Nedelchev, Konstantin Bobchev, Naum Dolinsky, Oscar Anderson, Iliya Palazov, Georgi Danailov, Nikola Stoyanov, Nikola Sakarov, Ivan Stefanov, Dimitar Kalinov, Todor Vladigerov, Assen Hristoforov, and so on, and subsequently Lyuben Berov, Atanas Leonidov, David Cohen, Roumen Avramov, Diyana Mishkova, Roumen Daskalov, Pencho Penchev, Mitko Dimitrov, Martin Ivanov, Daniel Vachkov, and so on. We have also used some archival documents, especially those of the Bulgarian National Bank, Balgarska narodna banka: *Sbornik ot dokumenti (1915–29). Glavno upravlenie na arhivite*, vol. 3, 2001. We have studied the history, the consequences, and the policy development during the Great Depression in Bulgaria (see Nikolay Nenovsky and Tsvetelina Marinova, "Parvite stapki na kreditora ot posledna instantsiya v Balgaria. Istoriya i debati v godinite na Velikata depresiya," *Ikonomicheska missal* 67, no. 1 (2022): 28–53.

Table 11.1 Structure of Land Ownership in 1908 and 1926 in Bulgaria

Farm Groups (Dekari)	*Number of Farms*		*Land Owned by Farms*			
			In Million Dekari		*In % of Total Area*	
	1908	*1926*	*1908*	*1926*	*1908*	*1926*
Up to 10	120,946	89,040	1.29	0.44	2.8	1.0
11–50	241,438	338,479	9.04	9.68	19.6	22.6
51–100	162,271	210,441	12.41	14.81	26.8	34.5
101—300	107,146	107,951	16.89	15.71	36.5	36.6
Over 300	8,710	4,682	6.57	2.25	14.3	5.3
Total	640,511	750,613	46.25	42.91	100	100

Source: Lyuben Berov, ed., *Ikonomikata na Balgariya do sotsialisticheskata revolutsiya* (Sofia: Nauka i izkustvo, 1989), 436.

European peripheral countries, and especially the Balkan ones, Bulgaria was a poorly diversified agrarian country (over 80 percent of the population was employed in agriculture, where two-thirds of the national income was generated).[3] Bulgaria suffered from rural overcrowding, permanent fragmentation of land and farms, weak technological armament, and generally low productivity (Tables 11.1 and 11.2).[4]

These characteristics not only severely constrained the fiscal base of the government but also largely determined the political and ideological forces and movements in the country. For example,

3 The total agricultural production in 1929 was 25,618 million levs (crop production 16,379 million levs and livestock production 9,239 million levs), and industrial production amounted to 12,714 million levs, or a 66%/33% ratio, see Assen Chakalov, *Natsionalniat dohod i razhod na Balgaria* (Sofia: Knipegraf, 1946) and Lyuben Berov, ed., *Ikonomikata na Balgariya do sotsialisticheskata revolutsiya* (Sofia: Nauka i izkustvo, 1989).

4 On the agrarian development of Bulgaria, see Atanas Yaranov, "Nashata zemedelska politika," *SBID* 30, no. 1 (1931): 5–17; Naum Dolinsky, "Proyavite na krizata v balgarskoto zemedelsko stopanstvo," in *Godishnik na Vissheto targovsko uchilishte* 8 (1936): 1-92; Anastas Totev, "Indeksni chisla za obema na zemedelskoto proizvodstvo," *TSISP pri Sofiyskiya Universitet* 2–3 (1935): 25-48, and from contemporary authors such as Marko Dimitrov, "Balgarskoto selsko stopanstvo po vreme na svetovnata ikonomicheska kriza 1929–1934," *Godishnik na Yuridicheskiya fakultet pri UNSS* 3 (2010): 197–217.

Table 11.2 Indices of Agriculture, Peasant Incomes and Industrial Output at 1908–12 in Bulgaria, Base = 100

Year	*Agricultural Output Volume Index*	*Index of Real Income of Peasants against Industrial and Imported goods*	*Total Industrial Production Index*	*Production Index of the Promoted Industry*	*Manipulated Tobacco Production Index*	*Tobacco Production Index*
1921	82	81	100	100	100	100
1924	98	109	116	104	157	97
1925	106	128	186	210	167	129
1926	101	118	150	165	136	108
1927	100	114	189	228	134	108
1928	112	140	213	270	111	117
1929	108	123	209	262	110	115

Source: Lyuben Berov, ed., *Ikonomikata na Balgariya do sotsialisticheskata revolutsiya* (Sofia: Nauka i izkustvo, 1989), 439, 443.

Table 11.3 Structure of Exports as % of Total Annual Average Exports in Bulgaria

Group of Goods	*1906–10*	*1926–29*
Cereals and flour	64.3	18.7
Tobacco	1.3	39.1
Live animals	5.6	4.4
Livestock works	11.0	13.9
Rose oil	4.1	4.0
Skins	3.5	5.7
Cloth and other textile articles	6.8	3.6
Molasses and other waste	0.3	1.8
Other goods	2.0	4.0
Total	**100**	**100**

Source: Berov, ed., *Ikonomikata*, 439, 443.

Bulgaria was the only country in Europe where the peasants actually ruled from 1919 to 1923. During these four years, the Bulgarian Agricultural National Union, led by Aleksandar Stamboliyski, made a number of radical reforms and reform attempts in favor of the rural population.[5] Despite the efforts, industry did not develop; it remained primarily light, and, that is, linked to local raw materials (food, tobacco, and textiles) (see Table 11.3).

Despite the aforementioned backwardness, the Bulgarian economy stabilized and revived in the period after 1924–25 until 1929. This dynamism followed the global revival. The protectionist and supportive policies of the Bulgarian government were also an important factor.

At the onset of the Great Depression, there was also a shift in the agrarian structure, with grain production giving way to tobacco, which became the main export commodity (see Table 11.3).[6] Among the relative successes during this period should be noted the stabilization of the Bulgarian currency, the lev, with the support of two external loans (1926, refugee loan and 1928, stabilization loan). Price increases were contained.

5 John Bell, *Peasants in Power: Aleksandar Stamboliyski and the Bulgarian Agrarian National Union: 1899–1923* (Princeton, NJ: Princeton University Press, 1977).

6 Georgi Kremenski, "Targoviyata s tiyutiyuni na Balgaraia," *Stopanska missal* 3 (1932): 3–57.

A second important characteristic of the Bulgarian economy, despite the development of the market and monetary economy and the development of the private and cooperative sectors, was that the state was positioned at the center of economic life. All sectors were nationalized, controlled, or subsidized by the state. The private sector and intellectual elites were "attached" to the state and to political parties, and their economic lives depended on them.[7] Trade protectionism and foreign exchange control were applied, as well as interventionist policies (the 1928 law is particularly important here).[8] The central role of the state was a universal phenomenon in Europe in those years, especially in the European periphery. What was specific was that in Bulgaria a form of path dependence could be observed in the dominance of the state, which resulted from the fact that Bulgaria founded its independent statehood only in 1878, after five centuries of existence within the framework of the Ottoman Empire (which was also dominated by the state economy). With the gaining of independence, the public administration concentrated the Bulgarian elite, while the private initiative was born under the tutelage of the state, and this largely determined the statist trajectory for decades to come.

Third, despite some relief of the debt burden in 1925, Bulgaria, as a defeated country in the Balkan Wars and World War I, entered the depression with a high debt burden.[9] This burden included external economic and political debts (reparations) and domestic debts (direct debt to the Bulgarian National Bank, BNB). Public deficits were high and public savings were low. As a result of the wars and peace treaties (the Bucharest Treaty of 1913 and the Treaty of Neuilly of 1919), Bulgaria lost important economic territories, for exam-

7 Roumen Avramov, *Komunalniyat kapitalizam. Iz balgarskoto stopansko minalo* (Sofia: Fondatsia Balgarska nauka i izkustvo, 2007); Roumen Daskalov, *Balgarskoto obstestvo 1978–1939*, vol. 1: *Darjava, politika, ikonomika*; vol. 2: *Naselenie, obstestvo, kultura* (Sofia: Gutenberg, 2005).

8 Konstantin Bobtcheff, "La Politique du Commerce Extérieur de la Bulgarie Après la Guerre," Publications of the Statistical Institute for Economic Research, no. 4 (Sofia: State University of Sofia, 1938) and on the foreign exchange monopoly, see Lyubomir Vladikin, "Kambialniyat monopol v Balgaria," *Stopanska misal* 3, no. 1 (1932): 3–32.

9 Henri Prost, *La Bulgarie de 1912 à 1930. Contribution à l'histoire économique & financière de la guerre et des conséquences* (Paris: Editions Pierre Roger, 1932); Henri Prost, *La liquidation financière de la guerre en Bulgarie* (Paris: Marcel Gard, 1925).

ple, the granary of the country, Dobruja, which was annexed by Romania. The country also suffered financial losses in the transfer of population between the Balkan countries, the refugee problem. All external burdens expressed in gold did not allow devaluation of the national currency.

Fourth, after the wars, the budget and the monetary system were entirely under the direct control of the League of Nations Finance Committee, the Reparations Commission, and the Representatives of the Bondholders. In the period 1926–28, monetary stabilization based on gold was implemented. External debts and loans prevented an official devaluation of the lev. It should be noted that the stabilization of the Bulgarian lev was carried out within the framework of a strict foreign exchange monopoly by the BNB. This allowed the Bulgarian authorities, in a foreign exchange monopoly regime, to legally maintain the level of the fixed exchange rate by introducing a number of technical instruments (premiums, etc.) and to informally deviate from the nominal parity.[10]

Fifth, we need to bear in mind the rapid and uncontrolled expansion of the banking sector and credit, especially after the monetary stabilization. After 1928–29, there was an increased inflow of foreign capital, especially into the banking sector, as parent banks transferred deposits to their branches in Bulgaria. Banking institutions became numerous—in addition to the few state-owned and foreign banks, there were hundreds of cooperative and popular banks as well as dozens of small and local private credit institutions. Capital inflows from parent banks, protectionism, and good harvests led to lower interest rates and a significant increase in investment,

10 For the stabilization of the lev, see Nikolay Nenovsky, *Exchange Rates and Inflation: France and Bulgaria in the Interwar Period and the Contribution of Albert Aftalion, 1874–1956* (Sofia: BNB, 2006), and for the evolution of the monetary and exchange rate system under foreign exchange controls, see Assen Hristoforov, *Kurs po balgarsko bankovo delo* (Sofia: 1946), 186, and Nikolay Nenovsky, Giovanni Pavanelli, and Kalina Dimitrova, "Exchange Rate Control in Italy and Bulgaria in the Interwar Period. History and Perspectives," in *The Experience of Exchange Rate Regimes in South-Eastern Europe in a Historical and Comparative Perspective*, ed. P. Mooslechner (Vienna: Österreichische Nationalbank, 2007), 80–117.

including in construction and real estate. At the same time, there was a lack of systematic banking regulation and supervision.[11]

The internal vulnerability outlined so far, which in itself indicated an unstable situation potentially leading to a crisis, was also provoked by shocks coming from outside. These shocks were linked to the agrarian crisis in Europe and the closure of the market for Bulgarian goods as well as the subsequent crisis in the European money market and the European banks. We must also take into account the geostrategic shifts between the great powers.

The external impulses of the Great Depression are generally well studied by economists. In the case of Bulgaria, they amount to three, namely, (1) a sharp fall in prices of agricultural products at the end of 1929, due to the contraction of external demand; (2) the complete disintegration of the network of world trade; and finally, (3) chronologically, the banking crisis in Austria and Germany (summer of 1931). As far as the geopolitical dimensions are concerned, France and England, the leading powers at the time of the stabilization of the lev, began to give way to a revanchist Germany and Italy. Bulgaria was increasingly attracted by Germany, which supported territorial revenge ambitions. It should not be forgotten that Bulgaria as a defeated country was isolated in the Balkans. It subsequently refused to participate in the economic initiatives to form a Balkan Union, due to the nonrecognition of its borders in the postwar treaties.[12]

In summary, the geopolitical dimension was of utmost importance, and this was noted by the Royal Institute of International Affairs (RIIA) in 1939:

11 Konstantin Kossev, *Bankoviyat sector po vreme na Golyamata depresiya v Balgaria 1924–1938* (Sofia: BNB, 2008). This was not a Bulgarian phenomenon as it was observed in all countries after the monetary stabilization; Charles Kindleberger, *The World in Depression, 1929–1939* (Berkeley, CA: University of California Press, 1973).

12 For a comprehensive geopolitical and economic analysis, see Royal Institute for International Affairs (RIIA), *South-Eastern Europe. A Political and Economic Survey* (London: Oxford University Press, 1939). For the Balkan initiatives, see the review in Nikolay Nenovsky and Pencho Penchev, "Between Enthusiasm and Scepticism: Bulgarian Economists and Europe (1878–1944)," *History of Economic Theory and Policy* 1 (2018): 27–56.

> The student of politics who would try to reduce to their simplest expression the factors which have been chiefly responsible for the shaping of the history of South-Eastern Europe, might well be content with restricting them to three basic factors: geography ("the mother of history"), the striking mixture of peoples, and the perpetual and disturbing intrusion of the Great Powers.[13]

11.2 Crisis and Depression in Bulgaria—Dynamics and Debates

The crisis and the subsequent depression in Bulgaria can be reduced to two phases—agrarian and financial.

The first and most vivid manifestation of the Great Depression was the agrarian crisis. It manifested itself as a brutal decline in the prices of industrial and agricultural products, leading to indebtedness and bankruptcies of rural producers. The decline in prices was extraordinarily severe and was accompanied by the widening of the price scissors, that is, by changes in relative prices. Although it had already appeared after the war, at the peak of the depression the dissolution of the scissors reached threatening proportions. According to Bobchev (1934, 212), "agricultural products depreciated by 59 percent, industrial products by 28 percent, and the purchasing power of agricultural products declined by 43 percent."[14] The dissolution of the price scissors led to strong redistributive processes in which rural households lost income. Compared to 1926, agricultural prices dropped by exactly half (Table 11.4), and with a 1929 base year, the decline was even more significant. The farmers' purchasing power shrank by almost half.

The total liabilities of the farmers to the state banks (BNB, Bulgarian Agricultural Bank, Bulgarian Central Cooperative Bank) were about 5.5 billion levs, to the private banks (several foreign and 134 Bulgarian)—about 5.8 billion levs, and to the credit cooperatives (212 popular banks and 1,386 agricultural credit

13 RIIA, *South-Eastern Europe*.

14 Konstantin Bobchev, "Nesaotvetstvieto mezhdu tsenite na zemedelskite i tsenite na industrialnite proizvedeniya," *SBID* 33, no. 4 (1934): 203–50.

Table 11.4 Wholesale Price Indices Based on 1926 = 100 in Bulgaria

	Agricultural Goods				*Nonagricultural/Industrial Goods*			
	Plant Foods	*Animal Foods*	*Raw Materials*	*Total*	*Local Goods*	*Foreign Goods*	*Total*	*Purchasing Power of Agricultural Commodities*
1927	106	96	107	103	104	97	102	100
1928	128	100	113	114	102	101	102	112
1929	125	108	133	121	101	100	101	120
1930	69	83	131	91	94	94	94	96
1931	49	64	90	65	77	85	80	81
1932	45	55	75	56	67	85	72	78
1933	35	49	71	50	69	84	73	68
1933 Q1	37	51	76	52	66	86	71	74
1933 Q2	35	45	74	43	70	85	74	65
1933 Q3	34	46	68	47	68	83	72	67
1933 Q4	30	55	66	48	70	83	73	66

Note and source: We have chosen the index constructed by Bobchev "Nesaotvetstvieto," because of its methodological soundness and argumentation. Mollof's index has interesting breakdowns. There are other indices of price decline that generally yield similar dynamics. According to testimonies from that time on the commodity exchanges in Varna and Burgas, the price of grain collapsed by 50 percent; see Todor Bliznakov, "Pogled na stopanskoto i finansovoto polojenie na Balgariya prez 1930 g.," *SBID* 30, no. 5 (1931): 285–97.

Table 11.5 Protested Bills of Exchange, Insolvencies (Bankruptcies), and Moratoriums (Bulgaria)

Years	*Protested Bills of Exchange (Number)*	*Protested Bills of Exchange (Million BGN)*	*Insolvencies (Number)*	*Moratoriums (Number)*
1928	200,000	1,432	95	153
1929	250,000	2,213	107	211
1931	350,000	over 3,000	224	619

Source: Hristoforov, *Kurs po balgarsko bankovo delo*, 186. See the data in Mollof, *La Crise*, 137; Assen Kemilev, "Parichnoto obrastenie v Balgaria," *VTU* 1, no. 4 (1936): 287–300 and Konstantin Kossev, *Bankoviyat sector po vreme na Golyamata depresiya v Balgaria 1924–1938* (Sofia: BNB, 2008).

cooperatives)—about 4.1 billion levs, or a total of 15.4 billion levs.[15] As for the debts of the farmers, Tsankov estimates these at 9 billion gold levs, about 75–80 percent of which was owed to public credit institutions, and 92 percent of this amount was short-term debt.[16] Again, according to Tsankov, about 20 percent of this debt was debt for subsistence. The situation of citizens was also dire, with total debts amounting to 142 gold levs per capita. In order to preserve their income level, peasants responded to the fall in prices with an increase in production. However, this led to even greater indebtedness and financial difficulties, which could be illustrated by the dynamics of protested bills of exchange, bankruptcies, and credit moratoriums (Table 11.5).

In this environment, agriculture rapidly became naturalized, abandoning market and monetary mechanisms:

> The crisis means for them [the peasants] a return to greater subsistence, as, in fact, the whole national economy, with a view to the development of domestic production and the curtailment of imports, may be considered to be leading towards greater self-sufficiency during the crisis.[17]

15 Iliya Palazov, "Problemat s oblekchavaneto na dlazhnitsite," *SBID* 31, no. 4 (1932): 205–24.

16 Alexandar Tsankov, "Stopanskata i sotsialna kriza," *SBID* 31, no. 1 (1932): 1–24.

17 Bobchev, "Nesaotvetstvieto," 203–50.

The problems of agriculture (but not only) were very quickly transferred to the banking system. As mentioned, the banking system was particularly vulnerable because of the credit boom that began in 1925 and gained momentum after the monetary stabilization of 1928–29.[18] There was an inflow of capital, not only through the two official external loans but also through the transfer of private capital from foreign parent banks to their Bulgarian subsidiaries. Leading economist Dimitar Yordanov noted the dangers of this credit crunch:

> The world economic crisis of 1929–30 found the Bulgarian banking system in a state of disorganization and fragmentation. At that time there were over 2,000 banking institutions in Bulgaria which functioned in a fragmented and competitive manner. There was extensive and in many cases indiscriminate lending to agriculture, industry, crafts and commerce. Extensive credit enabled the accumulation of large stocks of goods and materials. This accumulation has been carried out with a passion, without taking into account what will be the purchasing power of our national economy in the coming year, which is directly dependent on the agricultural production of Bulgaria. And this production in 1930 was very unsatisfactory. A considerable part of the crops of 1929 froze, with the result that the harvest was insufficient.[19]

The banking crisis in Bulgaria has come in three waves. These were two "internal" waves on the line of the real economy and the regulatory policy of the government, those in 1929–30 and in 1933–34, and an "external" wave—triggered by a banking panic, a reflection of the crises of Credit-Anstalt and Deutsche Bank. The first crisis of 1929–30 was a typical twin crisis, that is, both a banking crisis and a balance of payments crisis (i.e., capital flight and currency crisis).

18 The banking crisis, the BNB's policy as Lender of Last Resort and safety net, and the debates of those years are detailed in Nikolay Nenovsky and Dominique Torre, "Debates, Plans and Interventions to Overcome the 1931 Banking Crisis in Romania and Bulgaria," *Jahrbuch für Wirtschaftsgeschichte* 63, no. 2 (2022): 1–31.

19 Dimitar Yordanov, "Nadzorat varhu chastnite banki v Balgaria i negovoto vliyanie varhu deinostta," *SBID* 42, no. 1–2 (1943): 23–43.

Table 11.6 Deposits, Own Funds and Placements of Banks (million levs) (Bulgaria)

Years	*Own Resources*	*Deposits and Foreign Funds*	*Total*	*Placements (Loans)*	*Number of Banks*
1929	1,157	6,959	8,116	8,442	135
1930	1,247	5,888	7,135	7,412	138
1931	1,376	4,464	5,840	6,510	131
1932	1,343	3,918	5,261	5,361	128
1933	1,256	3,293	4,549	4,406	119

Source: Minko Rusenov, ed. *Istoriya na finansovata i kreditna sistema v Balgaria. Ot Osvobojdenieto do 9. IX. 1944,* vol. 2 (Varna: Knigoizdatelstvo "Georgi Bakalov," 1983), 728.

Banks lost deposits and the central bank lost reserves. In response, the BNB increased the discount rate from 9 percent to 10 percent and kept it high until 1934 (when it reduced it to 7 percent). The high discount rate further intensified deflation and recession (Table 11.6).

The second crisis was liquid and systemic; it came in the summer of 1931. The leading banks were affected, such as the Credit Bank (*Kreditna banka*), whose main shareholder was *Deutsche Bank*. The panic was extraordinarily strong, and only the rapid intervention of the BNB and the contacts of the director of the Credit Bank, Marko Ryaskov, managed to prevent a systemic bank failure:

> However, I calculated that if the run (mass withdrawal) continued the next day, the bank would be put in an untenable position. I therefore went to the management of the central bank to describe the situation and ask for assistance. The Board of the central bank was watching with great anxiety the development of the first event in the life of banking in our country and was ready to listen to my suggestions. I was easily able to convince the management of the Bank that if the Credit Bank saw itself forced to close its counters, the crisis would inevitably affect the other banks and spread throughout the country. [. . .] Both sub-governors went to report to then Finance Minister Alexandar Girginov, who in turn took them to then Prime Minister Alexandar Malinov

> for a decision. To my honour, Prime Minister Malinov had said that he had absolute confidence in me and gave his opinion that I should be helped at any cost, so that our country would be kept from financial ruin.[20]

Finally, the third crisis (1933–34) can be interpreted as a response to the regulatory policies of the government, in particular, and the BNB, in part. Regulatory policy led to the emergence of a moral hazard (in the words of those years—"undermining payment morality"). Following the 1931 elections, a new political formation came to power, the People's Bloc (1931–34) and the governments of Alexandar Malinov and Nikola Mushanov. They raised the slogans of debt forgiveness. Thus, in 1932, two laws were adopted—the "Law on the Relief of Debtors" and the "Law on the Protection of the Landowner-Farmer." Debates began for the creation of a Sinking Fund, which was launched in 1934. At the same time, the banking sector was nationalized through consolidations and state intervention. In 1931, the Bankers' Council was established and regulations on deposit insurance, liquidity, equity, and large exposures were adopted.

Of particular interest is the Sinking Fund, which issued 2, 10, 15, and 20 year 3 percent bonds in exchange for 30 percent of farmers' total debt. These bonds replaced about one-third of the total debt, and the assumption of the debt was according to the degree of indebtedness; the debtors were grouped into three categories. In effect, the state took on the burden of making contributions to the Sinking Fund. Bonds replaced debts in the banking system's assets, and in 1938 they accounted for about one-fourth of their balance sheets. The two state banks, the Bulgarian Agricultural Bank and the Bulgarian Central Cooperative Bank, concentrated about 36 percent of these bonds, 21 percent were held in the popular banks, and only 7 percent in the private banks.[21] These bonds could be discounted at the BNB; thus, the Sinking Fund became a kind of intermediate form of Lender of Last Resort. "Bulgarian agriculture should set itself two big goals," Slavcho Zagorov claimed in 1933:

20 Marko Ryaskov, *Spomeni i dokumenti* (Sofia: BNB, 2006), 65–66.
21 Hristoforov, *Kurs po balgarsko bankovo delo*, 186.

"1. To reduce the debt burden of our farmer without upsetting the credit in the country and 2. to restore the payment morality of our peasantry." According to Zagorov, "material sacrifices will, however, go in vain unless a moral basis is created for strengthening credit in the country by distinguishing between the possibility and the impossibility of scaring off existing agricultural debts in the short term and by providing for a different fate of the good and bad debtors."[22] Another leading economist, Iliya Palazov, stressed:

> In 1920, 1921, 1922, 1923, when the lev depreciated and the debtors repaid with insignificant sums the old golden levs, nobody thought then of the creditors whose capitals melted. For example, the Bulgarian Agricultural Bank was completely invalidated because the farmers sent to it their debts, which they had made in gold levs, in paper levs, devalued 30 times. Just as nobody thought of the creditors then, it is not fair today to ask that the debtors be helped, with the entire burden falling on the creditors alone, and as only the private creditors are being asked. [. . .] Our assumption of the defeat of these two laws on our lending organization was unfortunately borne out very early. Already during the debate on the two bills, small joint-stock banks suffered a heavy defeat. The majority of them stopped payments. And only the dispute whether or not to privilege the popular banks caused them to withdraw about 150 million levs in deposits.[23]

Kiril Nedelchev provided a similar appraisal of the laws on debtors:

> An across-the-board thirty per cent relief of all debts up to two hundred thousand levs, as projected, instead of relieving, will further aggravate the debtors' situation, because it is small, unfair and dangerous. Small, because he who cannot pay a thousand will not be able to pay seven hundred. Dangerous, because it will kill credit to small, already

22 Slavcho Zagorov, "Podpomagane na zatrudnenite dlazhnitsi zemedeltsi i zazdraviyavane na kredita v Balgaria," *SBID* 32, no. 1 (1933): 1–9.

23 Palazov, "Problemat s oblekchavaneto," 205–24.

> poorly creditworthy persons. Unfair, because large debtors who have used other people's money not for consumption but for productive purposes, and whose enterprises are facing disaster, get no relief.[24]

The process of large-scale consolidation of the banking system, which practically led to its nationalization, had similarly damaging "behavioural" consequences. Thus, in 1930, twelve small joint-stock banks were merged into the United Bulgarian Bank, and in 1934, seven joint-stock banks were merged into it to form the Bulgarian Credit Bank, in which almost half of the capital became state-owned (through a loan from the BNB).

Politically, in May 1934, a military coup took place: The National Assembly was dissolved, parties were closed down, and from 1935 an authoritarian regime of the Tsar was imposed. This continued until May 1938, when the National Assembly was restored. Despite being drawn into the German economic zone, Bulgaria managed to maintain political neutrality until March 1, 1941, when, in Vienna, Prime Minister Bogdan Filov signed the accession to the Tripartite Pact.[25] The country thus became an active participant in World War II, joining the side of Germany. As such, Bulgaria occupied Macedonia, Western Thrace, and part of Serbia, after having previously, in 1940, peacefully regained Southern Dobruja.

11.3 In Search of a New Economic and Social Model

The Great Depression caught Bulgarian economists in a state of theoretical diversity in conceptual and practical terms. It can be summarized into five groups: (1) classical liberals, (2) adherents of the historical and evolutionary school, (3) adherents of the subjective Austrian school, (4) scholars with quantitative and monetary views, and (5) Marxists-Leninists. The majority (with the exception of the Marxists) initially considered the Great Depression a cyclical phenomenon, related to the disturbance of the equilibrium of the

24 Kiril Nedelchev, *Zadachi na balgarskoto stopanstvo* (Sofia: Poligrafiya, 1941).

25 The Tripartite Pact was signed in September 1940 by Germany, Italy, and Japan.

market and prices, as a result of changes in supply and demand.[26] They did not see the depth of the crisis. For example, the 1929 BNB Annual Report, in its analysis of the Bulgarian economic situation at the onset of the Great Depression, stated:

> The exchange rate situation, as well as the measures taken by the bank's management, do not give any cause for concern regarding the stability of the lev. Unfortunately, such disturbing rumours find rich soil in our society, constantly worrying about various phantasmagorical fears, such rumours get out and cause great damage to our finances. The bank's management is doing its best to dispel all worries and doubts and to assure the public that, despite the adverse economic developments, the BNB, together with other economic representatives, is capable of maintaining the stability of the lev.[27]

It should be noted that during all the years of attempts at stabilization, on the eve of the crisis as well as during the crisis, mass behavior and, in general, social psychology shaped not only specific economic and political decisions but also decisions on the general development trajectory of the country.[28] The role of the media, especially the press, which creates or reinforces social fears, rumors, and so on, is growing significantly. In this regard, the role of Petar Cholakov-Zarin (former representative of the BNB) can be given as an illustration. In a number of journalistic publications, he reveals

26 A comprehensive analysis of the approaches and evolution of Bulgarian economists during the depression years is made in Bulgarian in Nikolay Nenovsky and Roumen Andreev, *Balgarskite ikonomisti za Goliyamata depresiya* (Sofia: Izd. UNSS, 2013) and Nikolay Nenovsky, "Theoretical Debates in Bulgaria during the Great Depression. Confronting Sombart, Marx and Keynes," *OEconomia* 1 (2012): 67–101.

27 BNB, *Balgarska narodna banka: Sbornik ot dokumenti (1915–1929)* (Sofia: Glavno upravlenie na arhivite, T. 3., 2001), 262.

28 In this connection, it is appropriate to note the growing popularity among Bulgarian economists of the psychological theory of exchange rate formation and monetary stabilization developed by the French economist Albert Aftalion (who, by the way, was born in Bulgaria).

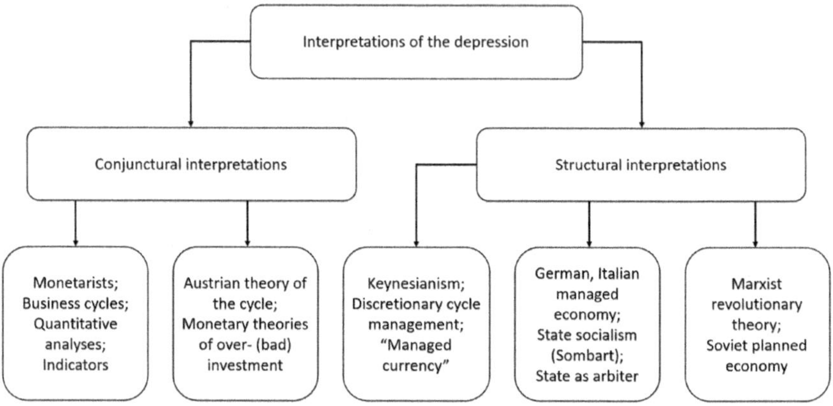

Figure 11.1 Bulgarian Interpretations of the Great Depression

(*Source*: Nenovsky and Andreev, *Balgarskite ikonomisti.*)

abuses, "robberies," and incompetence in the central bank and in general of the political elite.[29]

Very quickly, however, and especially after the aggravation of the agrarian crisis, Bulgarian economists realized that this was a deep structural crisis. They evolved toward structural interpretations, and eventually, the model of governance and state economy was imposed as vision and policy. This was a corporate model characteristic of the German and Italian economy (see Figure 11.1).

The diagram presents the two groups of interpretations of the Great Depression by Bulgarian economists, namely conjunctural (cyclical), which considered the crisis as a momentary phase of the normal business cycle, and structural, where changes in the structure of the economy were assumed. Within the framework of the first group, the approaches of business cycle indicators stood out as well as the Austrian school of over and malinvestment. Within the second group, we can single out (1) the Keynesian elements, which reflected upon the new role of the state and managed currency, (2) the models of the corporate economy, and "third way" model, through the influence of the Italian and German economists, and

29 Petar Cholakov-Zarin, *Vav vihara na grabezhite* (Sofia: Izd. Boris Kozhuharov, 1929).

finally (3) the radical Marxist approaches to the new society and the need for Soviet planning.

The economic, financial, political, and geopolitical factors made it possible for Bulgaria to shift to the model of state capitalism and eventually to become part of the German economic zone. What was the manifestation for Bulgaria of this nationalization and subsequent incorporation into the German economic space? How did it change the nature of the Bulgarian economy, economic policy, and, in general, the social and political model of the country? First of all, nationalization, protectionism, and encouragement were gaining more and more momentum. The state intervened in and controlled more and more economic sectors, processes triggered by the adjustment of the Bulgarian economy to the needs of Germany. As we have shown, the banking system was de facto nationalized, the Credit Bank (*Kreditna banka*) becoming the main transmission institution during this period. Public bail-out mechanisms were set up for peasant debtors, which put a heavy burden on the budget. Second, entry into the German clearing zone led to the introduction of total exchange controls, centralized in the BNB.[30] Foreign trade flows were almost completely transferred to the state and various state-owned organizations, such as the specialized agricultural export company Food Export. Nominally, the exchange rate was maintained after the devaluation of the franc in 1936, but a number of exchange rate coefficients (currency premiums, etc.) were introduced and constantly changed throughout the period.

In particular, Bulgaria concluded a number of agreements and clearings,[31] starting with Austria (October 1931–33), Switzerland

30 Roughly speaking, there were three zones: the devaluers led by England, the Gold Standard maintainers led by France, and the exchange controls and clearing led by Germany (Derek Aldcroft, *From Versailles to Wall Street, 1919–1929* (Berkeley and Los Angeles, CA: University of California Press, 1981 [1977]); Charles Kindleberger, *The World*; Alan Milward, *War, Economy and Society* (Berkeley and Los Angeles, CA: University of California Press, 1979).

31 Technically, in the clearing system, the importer pays in their own currency by depositing the money with the national central bank, and the exporter receives the foreign exchange proceeds in their own currency in an account at its central bank (see detailed analysis in Dimitar Georgiev, *Clearing Payments in International Trade* (Sofia: Bulgarian Academy of Sciences, 1955); Nenovsky, Pavanelli, and Dimitrova, "Exchange Rate Control," 80–117; Heinz Wolfgang Arndt, *The Economic Lessons of*

(April 1932–33), Germany (June 1932), and Italy (April 1934). The partial agreements were followed by Bulgaria's general and extended clearing agreements with Germany and Czechoslovakia (concluded in September 1932); with Austria, Poland, Switzerland, Belgium, France, Yugoslavia, and Hungary, concluded in 1933; with Yugoslavia, Turkey, Italy, and Spain in 1934; and with the Netherlands and Romania in 1935 and Finland in 1936. According to Michaely's (1962) calculations, Bulgaria ranked first out of the sixty countries surveyed in clearing, with bilateralism (bilateral clearing) covering about 87 percent of its trade in 1938 (against an average of 70 percent for all countries).[32] Other economists give similar figures[33] (Table 11.7).

Difficulties in clearing, the need for greater flexibility, and the need for free currencies led to the emergence in Bulgaria of private compensation, a form of barter, which became particularly widespread in 1933–35. In general, this form was particularly common in the Balkan countries, where exchange rates were overvalued, and where active balances with Germany were observed. As a result, these countries sought to diversify and stimulate their trade toward countries with free currencies. In contrast to clearing, where the exchange rate is fixed, private compensations allow it to deviate and fluctuate (in private compensations, imports are allowed only

the Nineteen-Thirties (London: Routledge, 2014 [1944]). This is done at a predetermined exchange rate (there are different possibilities for its determination, notional, official, official with a premium, parity, market, etc.). Usually, the country with the strong currency (overvalued) loses and accumulates a positive clearing balance that cannot be satisfied. The country with the overvalued currency seeks to increase its purchases outside the clearing because inside it loses. One country becomes a creditor of the other (this was the case with Bulgaria in its relations with Germany, as we will see later).

32 Michael Michaely, "Multilateral Balancing in International Trade," *American Economic Review* 52, no. 4 (1962): 685–702.

33 Frederic Benham, *South-Eastern Europe: A Political and Economic Survey* (London: Royal Institute of International Affairs, 1939); Larry Neal, "The Economics and Finance of Bilateral Clearing Agreements: Germany 1934–8," *Economic History Review* 32, no. 3 (1979): 391–404. On the state of the Bulgarian economy under German auspices, see David Cohen, *Voennovremennata ikonomika na Balgaria, 1939–1944* (Sofia: UI "Sv. Kliment Ohridski," 2002); Kurt Hauke, *Balgaria. Strana, narod, istoriya, kultura, stopanstvo* (Sofia: Iztok-Zapad, 2017 [1942]); Mariya Koleva, *Germanskata ikonomicheska politika kam Balgaria mejdu dvete svetovni voini 1919–1939* (Sofia: Izd. "Marin Drinov," 2012).

Table 11.7 Clearing and Nonclearing Trade of Bulgaria

Years/ Shares	*Export (Shares, %)* Clearing in Total export	Germany in Total Export	Germany in Total Clearing	Nonclearing in Total Exports	*Imports (Shares, %)* Clearing in Total Imports	Germany in Total Imports	Germany in Total Clearing	Nonclearing in Total Imports
1934	78.97	48.05	60.84	21.03	78.3	48.87	62.43	21.7
1935	77.25	49.48	68.09	22.75	80.19	59.82	75.11	19.81
1936	69.44	50.53	72.78	30.56	81.7	66.67	81.58	18.3
1937	65.52	47.11	71.91	34.48	79.9	58.22	72.82	20.1
1938	77.24	58.86	76.21	22.76	74.02	51.43	70.22	25.98
1938a	71.68	51.49	71.78	21.4	74.74	54.1	72.38	25.32
1939a	72.81	59.43	81.63	27.19	80.89	61.04	75.46	19.05

Note and source: Export/import data refer to the first five/four months of the year; see Assen Hristoforov, *Razvitie na konyunkturniya tsikal v Balgaria, 1934–1939* (Sofia: Pridvorna pechatnitsa, 1939).

in exchange for exports of certain goods, and part of the currency can then be sold on the open market). This is done through the so-called currency premiums, which in Bulgaria reached 20–40 percent above the official exchange rate. These premiums are a form of informal devaluation and they help exports to countries with convertible "free" currencies, but they make imports more expensive and lead to a number of structural distortions.[34]

After 1934, and especially after the beginning of the war, trade with Germany mobilized the entire Bulgarian economy. The controversy over the "exploitative" clearing trade with Germany is still a subject of analysis today.[35] In reality, Bulgaria's ties with the German economy were the result of geopolitical choices. As sociologist Nikola Aganski commented in 1936: "In international relations, the principle that the exchange of goods between states rests not only on an economic basis but is either the result of a particular policy or is a prerequisite for a political orientation is strongly established."[36] Clearing agreements were a matter of forming geopolitical blocs, within which Bulgaria fitted into the German zone due to territorial and political ambitions, as a result of severe debt problems, as well as the complementarity of the two economies. The political, economic, and cultural processes of rapprochement go hand in hand.[37] In fact, the strong economic dependence and lack of diversification were seen as a danger by a number of Bulgarian economists (including the aforementioned Aganski).

34 For these mechanisms, see Nenovsky, Pavanelli, and Dimitrova, "Exchange Rate Control"; Dimitar Kalinov, "Svetovnata stopanska kriza i avtarkiyata kato glaven nein izraz," *SBID* 34, no. 5 (1935): 275–88.

35 Cohen, *Voennovremennata*.

36 Nikola Aganski, "Germanskiat pazar i dunavskite darjavi," *ASSP* 11, no. 2 (1936): 132–41.

37 Georgi Markov, *Balgaro-germanski otnoshenia, 1931–1939* (Sofia: Nauka i Izkustvo, 1984). There are numerous testimonies about the German leaders' interest in and respect for Bulgaria. For example, the visit of the Reich Minister of Finance Graf Schwerin von Krosigk in November 1941, and the publication of his book: Lutz Graf Schwerin von Krosigk, *Fragen der Gegenwärtigen Wirtschafts und Finanzpolitik. Öffentliche Finanzen und Wirtschaft*, Das Neue Europa. Staatsrechtliche Probleme der Neuen Ordnung (Sofia: Drei Vorträge, 1943). In the book, he explicitly emphasizes the geopolitical and strategic connection and proximity of Germany to Bulgaria (see Markov, *Balgaro-germanski*).

An important moment in Germany's relations with Bulgaria was the intergovernmental clearing agreement signed in 1940. This allowed Germany to transfer resources from Bulgaria. Since German purchase prices were significantly higher than those of other countries[38] and Germany limited its exports in order to concentrate resources domestically,[39] Bulgaria exported significantly more to Germany than it imported from it. The terms of trade were favorable for Bulgaria, which exported agricultural products and imported raw materials for industry.

After 1934, Bulgaria accumulated a significant positive clearing balance with Germany, which was not covered either by imports of machinery and raw materials or by capital inflows (subsequently, after the end of the war, these amounts were lost). In the last years of the war, in order to clear the balances, the German negotiators on the clearing lists offered unnaturally high and "arbitrary" prices for their machinery and artificially low prices for Bulgarian goods, even becoming aggressive at certain times. In his memoirs, the High Commissioner of the Bulgarian military economy, Petar Aladzhov, noted at the end of 1943:

> Recently, the German side has been arbitrarily increasing the prices of its export goods, while the Bulgarian prices have remained almost at the same level as before [. . .]. Germany was no longer able to supply the required quantities of certain machines, but at best only supplied single units [. . .]. The German side was very anxious to receive the entire quantity of tobacco produced in Bulgaria. The Reich's plenipotentiary for tobacco was named Dr. Wenkel. He had an injured leg and walked with a cane. During discussions with our Minister of Trade, Nikola Zahariev, it had come to the point that Dr. Wenkel had reached out to hit our Minister with the cane. Apparently, how much the passions about Bulgarian tobacco had heated up.[40]

38 Hristoforov, *Razvitie na konyunkturniya*.

39 Adam Tooze, *The Making and Breaking of the Nazi Economy* (London: Penguin Books, 2008).

40 Petar Aladzhov, *Varhoven komisar. Edin zhivot v slujba na stopanstvoto* (Sofia: UI "Sv. Kliment Ohridski," 2000).

Table 11.8 Bulgaria's Foreign Trade with Germany (incl. Austria, and from 1941 incl. Bohemia and Moravia (in Million Levs))

Years	*Export*	*Import*	*Balance*
1939	4,311.1	3,613.6	+698.2
1940	4,378.0	5,209.2	–830.3
1941	6,743.7	8,148.3	–1,404.6
1942	976.7	8,503.2	+1,473.5
1943	13,109.7	10,555.3	+2,554.4
1944	10,099.5	4,865.2	+5,234.3
Total	48,620.3	40,894,8	+7,725.5

Source: Cohen, *Voennovremennata,* 183.

In fact, in the foreign trade contracts with Germany, there was no clause for a ceiling on the clearing balance, and for the ways and terms, which put Bulgaria under constant pressure (the BNB issued levs for this amount without any real imports). The clearing balance also included nontrade payments as well as "domestic" exports to Germany (the cost of supplies for German troops in the country). According to Cohen, by 1944 the total amount of the active balance was 25,406.1 million levs, of which only 30.4 percent was on foreign trade, a balance of 7,725.5 million levs (see Table 11.8).

Third, it is appropriate to note the structural change of the Bulgarian economy, aimed entirely at satisfying the military needs of Germany, which was revealed by two leading scholars such as Dimitar Georgiev and David Cohen. They both expressed similar views. Here we take the liberty of quoting the best expert on the military economy of this period, David Cohen, who wrote with some Marxist overtones:

> Bulgaria's economy during World War II developed under the growing influence of Germany. In relation to Bulgaria, this was a policy of developing it as a source of agricultural produce, with mainly light industry, and turning it into a supplier of minerals for the needs of German heavy industry. Through its unequal trade agreements Germany aims to import Bulgarian products cheaply, to export at high

> prices its sometimes obsolete and low-quality manufactured goods, to use the mechanism of Bulgarian-German clearing to credit the German economy, and to transfer the maintenance of German troops in Bulgaria to its finances. The government, which had submitted to the economic aims of Germany, tried to reorganize the national economy on military lines [. . .]. A policy of complete centralization of the management of the economy, of the German and Italian type, was unsuccessfully pursued [. . .]. The structure of sown and planted land was changing, with an increase in the relative share of extensive crops, which was a retrograde development of agriculture.[41]

According to Dimitar Georgiev:

> A typical example of this is provided by the overvalued rate of the German mark in all clearings with the south-eastern countries, which upset their trade with the rest of the world and turned them into an agrarian appendage of the Hitler's war machine. Through brutal interference and political pressure, the Hitler's aggressors imposed different mark-ups on individual countries and thereby achieved the redemption of vast masses of goods in exchange for the formation of clearing balances. [. . .]. Thus clearing payments during the war brought the following benefits to Nazi Germany: the supply from abroad of vast quantities of goods for the civil and military economy, the use of hundreds of thousands of workers from abroad in return for payment of their rationed supplies alone, the maintenance of its troops in occupied and conquered countries, the lending of capital and working capital to its military enterprises abroad without interest and without return, facilities in the financing of the war economy.[42]

41 Cohen, *Voennovremennata*.

42 Dimitar Georgiev, *Kliringovite plastaniya v mejdunarodnata targoviya* (Sofia: Balgarska akademia na naukite, 1955).

The economic and structural changes outlined above inevitably led to the emergence of new social forces and movements, the spread of views, ideas, and theories that argued for and modeled the new social and political order.

After the depression, and especially after 1933–34, with Hitler coming to power, new ideas began to make their way, based on the Italian fascist model. They sought a third way, different from that of market capitalism and Bolshevik socialism. The third system is mostly seen as a manifestation of a corporatist model of class peace in which the state is the supreme arbiter, a model generally authoritarian and built on the principle of leadership. The economic dimension of this model was the guided/directed, planned, and autarkic economy. These ideas quickly found their social and political bearers as well as their theoretical exponents among economists, lawyers, and sociologists.

The new economic system called by some Bulgarian economists "socialist or national social"[43] was a reaction to the exacerbation of social and class pretensions in those years, taking into account that Bulgaria already had experience of radical rule. It was that of the peasants who ruled the country between 1919 and 1923 and were overthrown in a coup. To this experience can be added the active workers' and communist movements and the growing influence of the Comintern and Bolshevism.

We mentioned that from 1934 until the end of the war, Bulgaria was under authoritarian rule, the military (1934–35), and the personal regime of the monarch Boris III (1935–43), the regents, who tried to stop the proliferation of even more radical authoritarian movements like that of Alexandar Tsankov's "National Social Movement," Iliya Minev's "Union of the Bulgarian National Legions," the Union of the Ratniks, and organizations such as the Association of the Reserve Officers in Bulgaria, the Bulgarian Popular Union "Kubrat," the Union of Bulgarian Fascists, the

43 Alexandar Tsankov, *Trite stopanski sistemi. Kapitalizam, komunizam i natsionalsotsializam* (Pleven: "Edelvais," 2020 [1942]).

Union "Bulgarian Homeland Defense," the political circle "Zveno," the Bulgarian youth organization "Brannik," and so on.[44]

In theoretical terms, the ideas of Italian fascism and the corporative model gained traction in the late 1920s already. Here, the most serious theorist was Alexandar Staliiski, who published his fundamental work, *The Fascist Doctrine of the State*, in 1929. Later, the models and experiences of National Socialism of Hitler's Germany gained in influence. Parallel to German practices, the ideas of the directed, guided economy, which were developed in France and the French-speaking countries, began to be increasingly commented upon.[45] The French ideas carried a certain nuance not only in purely economic terms but also in political terms. They served to argue for a general tendency to increase the role of the state without being exclusively tied to German practices.

All kinds of models of a new economy have one philosophical source, that of universalism, which evolved into corporatism (Otto Spahn), of solidarism (Léon Duguit), and of "integralism" (here the main authors were Italian). And precisely because these theories are philosophical and legal, one can assume that Bulgarian lawyers were significantly ahead of economists in their knowledge of the structure of the state, and economists followed them and copied some of their formulations (even due to the fact that both economists and lawyers in general worked at the Faculty of Law of Sofia University as Lyubomir Vladikin, for example).

Later, as a final result of his research, the famous economist and politician Alexandar Tsankov, published the book *The Three Economic Systems. Capitalism, Communism and National Socialism* (2020 [1942]), in which he summarized his views on the three possible ways of organizing society. In this work, Tsankov defined the three economic models with poster simplicity. National socialism, in Tsankov's eyes, transcended the other two; he synthesized them

44 A detailed documentation of this authoritarian movement, as well as its main programmatic documents, is collected in Nikolay Poppetrov, *Sotsialno naliyavo, natsionalizmat—napred. Programni i organizatsionni dokumenti na balgarski avtoritaristki natsionalsotsialisticheski formatsii* (Sofia: Gutenberg, 2009).

45 See the overview of the guided economy in Todor Vladigerov, *Rakovodentoto stopanstvo. Teoriya i praktika* (Sofia: Pechatnitsa "Odeon," 1939).

in a Hegel style into some third higher state that brought together the best of both systems and rejected their harmful elements.

Another important topic is that of autarky in the new economic model. An important point in the discussion is two visits of foreign scholars. The first one was Werner Sombart's visit to Bulgaria. Sombart, one of the main ideologues of autarky and the new economic system, gave two lectures from October 25 to November 2, 1932, in the presence of the leading economists of the time, Prime Minister Nikola Mushanov, as well as many of his former students (Georgi Svrakov, for example).[46]

The second significant event was the visit to Bulgaria of the Romanian protectionist Mihail Manoilescu. Manoilescu's book found wide resonance in Bulgaria, and Konstantin Bobchev (1933) made his own counter-theory.[47] Manoilescu's protectionist theory later evolved into the model of integral corporatism, [48] largely shared by Dimitar Mishaykov.[49] In 1937, Bobchev set out his protectionist theory based on the postulates of marginalism and criticized

46 Sombart was extremely popular among Bulgarian economists, and in general on the Balkans (his second wife was Romanian), and this happened in the first years of the twentieth century, with his books and publications on modern capitalism and before it evolved in the direction of autarky, organic economy, and so on (he did this much later in the 1930s). A particular propagandist of Sombart's ideas was the leading Bulgarian economist in those years, Georgi Danailov (see Nenovsky, "Theoretical Debates," 67–101). After Sombart's noted visit to Bulgaria, his books *The Crisis of Capitalism* (1932), *German Socialism* (1935), and *World Perception, Science and Economics* (1938) were translated and published.

47 Nikolay Nenovsky and Dominique Torre, "Productivity Based Protectionism: A Marxian Reconstruction of Mihail Manoilescu's Theory," *Journal of Economic Issues* 49, no. 3 (2015): 772–86.

48 Mihail Manoilescu, *Le Siècle du Corporatisme: Doctrine du Corporatisme Intégral et Pur* (Paris: Félix Alcan, 1938 [1934]).

49 Mishaykov speaks of an "integralist economic system" alongside an "individualist economic system" and a "socialist economic system," Mishaykov (1933, cited in Nikolay Poppetrov, *Sotsialno naliyavo, natsionalizmat—napred. Programni i organizatsionni dokumenti na balgarski avtoritaristki natsionalsotsialisticheski formatsii* (Sofia: Gutenberg, 2009).

Manoilescu's system, resting on a labour and cost theory.[50] This monograph was highly appreciated by Bulgarian economists.[51]

11.4 Conclusion

The Great Depression had a fundamental impact on the Bulgarian economy and society as well as on the political and scientific life in the country. The agrarian nature of the country and Bulgaria's defeat and "humiliation" in the two previous wars (the Second Balkan War and World War I) and the peace treaties, with heavy economic and political debts, highly dependent on geopolitical processes, determined the trajectory of the Bulgarian economy and society during the years of the depression and after.

The Bulgarian elites responded to the Great Depression with an intensification of the inherent tendency to nationalize economic life—nationalism, protectionism, control of domestic and foreign trade, exchange controls, and planning (the first attempts at multiyear planning, especially of agriculture[52]). Rapidly, for the purposes of revenge or for purely economic reasons (complementarity of the structures of the Bulgarian and German economies), Bulgaria became fully integrated into the German clearing, economic, and political orbit. This not only changed the nature of the economy but also had a comprehensive impact on political and social processes. In the field of economic theory, the theories of managed and planned economies, autarky, and protectionism gained prominence. The political system was also profoundly realigned toward a nonparty and authoritarian model.

50 Bertrand Blancheton and Nikolay Nenovsky, "Protectionism and Protectionist Theories in the Balkans in the Interwar Period," *Cahiers du GREThA* no. 2 (2013), https://cahiersdugretha.u-bordeaux.fr/2013/2013-02.pdf.

51 Slavcho Zagorov, "Novi metodi i novi idei v politicheskata ikonomiya," *SBID* 36 no. 10 (1937): 569–84.

52 See, for example: Ministerstvo na zemedelieto i darzhavnite imoti, *Petgodishen zemedelsko-stopanski plan 1942–1946* (Sofia: Ministerstvo na zemedelieto i darzhavnite imoti, 1941); see also Bogdan Filov, *Slovoto na Bogdan Filov. Rechi na 28-miya minister-predsedatel* (Pleven: Edelvais, 2022 [1942]).

Chapter 12

GREECE

INSTITUTIONAL STRATEGIES AND POLITICAL ACTORS IN A PERIOD OF INCREASING ECONOMIC PROTECTIONISM

Catherine Brégianni

12.1 Global Recession and Domestic Crisis as an Economic and Political Challenge

This chapter builds on research on the regulatory but heterogeneous space of political strategies designed as a response to the Great Depression.[1] It focuses on the application of westernizing economic models in Greece regarding the modernization efforts undertaken by the local political elites from the end of the 1920s to the early 1930s and on the impact of the Great Depression on this process of economic and social modernization. On this nonlinear economic surface, the Greek crisis of the early 1930s had a pivotal role as it diversified the interference of international institutions (i.e., the League of Nations and its advisory body, the Financial Committee) in the country during the 1920s and consequently intensified the

1 Research Project "Transnational Monetary and Economic Alternatives in the Interwar Politics. The 1930s Greek Crisis in the European Context," directed by Catherine Brégianni, funded by the Hellenic Foundation for Research and Foundation and hosted by the Academy of Athens, https://transmonea.academyofathens.gr/index.php/en/. As a follow-up to this research, the interference of the League of Nations in Greece is the object of the author's personal research project in the Modern Greek History Research Centre (Academy of Athens) "Geopolitical Challenges of the Greek Interwar Economy: Greece and the International Financial Centers," http://www.academyofathens.gr/en/node/3318. The question of the League's agency regarding the interwar population transfers in Europe is addressed in her research project in the CRH-EHESS "Systèmes monétaires transnationaux dans l'Europe de l'entre-deux-guerres et le 'pivot' de la Grande Dépression: Modèles de gouvernementalité par la Société des Nations," http://grheco.ehess.fr/category/membreassocies.

intervention of the state in the regulation of the internal market. The domestic crisis had a decisive role in the decline of democracy in the country from the early 1930s onward.

The Greek interwar crisis was a local (i.e., national) facet of the Great Depression, which developed specific domestic characteristics that corresponded to the historical context, the peripheral character of the Greek economy, and its position within the capital market. In general terms, the increasing Greek protectionism of the 1930s follows the general tendency of the continental European states (especially the Eastern European countries) toward centralized politics,[2] after the failure of liberal monetary models and particularly after the abandonment of the Gold-Exchange Standard and the French failure to establish a Gold Franc. In this interpretation of the Greek crisis within a transnational framework, one should also consider the fact that Greece has participated in the Gold-Exchange Standard since 1928.

The liberal views that dominated the 1920s that the state should exert the least possible influence on the economy,[3] as expressed at the international monetary conferences of the early 1920s, and the relevant efforts to homogenize global monetary circuits and establish an autonomous character for the central banks,[4] the rationalization of the markets and the dynamics of entrepreneurial activity were insufficient to avoid recession, as the applied politics focused

2 See also Paul Brasslay, "The 1929 Crisis from the Perspective of a Food-Importing Country—The United Kingdom, 1928–35," in *Agriculture and the Great Depression. The Rural Crisis of the 1930s in Europe and the Americas*, eds. Gérard Béaur and Francesco Chiapparino (London: Routledge, 2023), 59–76; Michalis Sarras, "'Εκθεση για την ερευνητική προσέγγιση και αξιολόγηση ειδικών ποσοτικών πηγών: η κρίση του 1929 στην περιοχή της Νοτιοανατολικής Ευρώπης," TransMonEA Working Papers No. 11, https://transmonea.academyofathens.gr/index.php/en/publications/working-papers-ppt-presentations.

3 See Harold James, *The German Slump. Politics and Economics. 1924–1936* (Oxford: Clarendon Press, 1986), 324–28.

4 Catherine P. Brégianni, *The Great Depression and Greece: Monetary and Economic Perspectives in a Transnational Context* (Athens: TransMonEA Research Project/ Academy of Athens Research Committee—Hellenic Foundation for Research and Innovation, Alfeios, 2023), 43–53. See also on this subject Jamie Martin, *The Meddlers: Sovereignty, Empire, and the Birth of Global Economic Governance* (Cambridge, Mass.: Harvard University Press, 2022).

on monetary stability.[5] This failure was not, of course, a European exception: In the United States, "the Hoover Administration and Congress . . . raised taxes in the early 1930s in a futile effort to balance the budget, but only reinforced the collapse of private demand."[6] In the second half of 1929, the US central administration failed to take effective steps to halt the fall in prices and to stabilize the banking system; the political establishment took no measures to restart investment spending until 1933, when the implementation of the Keynesian New Deal functioned as a precursor of the postwar mixed economy.[7]

The current recession in Europe has prompted historians and economists to analyze, once again, the history of past economic crises. Not least, these inquiries are based on a psychological aspect: Economic recovery can be expected, as was the case regarding previous crises. The current interpretations of the Great Depression contribute to a sense of security but also underline the challenges of financial "reproduction." On the other hand, as Barry Eichengreen remarks, "the analogy with the Great Depression informed the policy response to the crisis more generally."[8] Consequently, we can say that the interpretation of the crisis of the 1930s also had a real aspect related to responses to the current financial recession by the state authorities, in Europe and mostly in the United States. Nevertheless, analyzing earlier crises cannot produce a generalized model concerning the evolution of economic and social phenomena, as each crisis has its own structural character.[9] However, the analysis of previous periods of economic decline can indicate the multiplicity of the directions and the economic alternatives among

5 Cf. Dani Rodrik, *The Globalization Paradox. Why Global Markets, States, and Democracy Can't Coexist* (Oxford: Oxford University Press, 2011), 99.

6 Barry Eichengreen, "The Great Recession and the Great Depression: Reflections and Lessons," Working Paper No. 593, Central Bank of Chile, 2010, http://www.bcentral.cl/esp/estpub/estudios/dtbc, 1.

7 Eichengreen, "The Great Recession and the Great Depression," 1.

8 Barry Eichengreen, "Economic History and Economic Policy," *The Economic History Journal* 72, no. 2 (2012): 290.

9 Youssef Cassis, *Crises and Opportunities: The Shaping of Modern Finance* (Oxford: Oxford University Press, 2011)

which a society can choose so as to ensure its continuing existence and development.[10]

Historical interpretation associates economic mechanisms with social context, combining structure with institutional agency.[11] In other words, it describes the evolution of the crises in a dialectic and multidimensional way when evaluating the change of property rights, labor force, and exchange rates during economic crises. From this methodological perspective, material cultural practices are taken into account to explain the organization of the economy and social relations as well as their points of intersection. This interpretation is in fact not very different from Keynes's perception that the crisis can be further correlated with social and psychological factors,[12] as far as the negative expectations for investment rates are among the recession's characteristics.[13]

From this perspective, a revision of the 2008 economic crisis reveals primarily similarities with the economic depression of the last quarter of the nineteenth century, not only in terms of its prolonged effects but also because of the strong implication of the monetary factor: the nineteenth-century system of balance, the expansion of entrepreneurial activity, the evolution of capital market mechanisms (based, of course, on less sophisticated financial instruments), and the stabilization of international financial centers that were partially created and supported by supranational monetary institutions, especially by the classical Gold Standard.[14] Inherently, the nineteenth-century monetary stability must be seen

10 Serge Latouche, "Contribution à l'histoire du concept de développement," in *Pour une histoire du développement: Etats, sociétés, développement*, eds. Catherine Coquery-Vidrovitch, Daniel Hemery, and Jean Piel (Paris: L'Harmattan, 2007), 44–46.

11 C. Brégianni, "Introduction: Researching the Economy," in *Shaping and Reshaping the Global Monetary Order During the Interwar Period and Beyond. Local Actors in-between the International Institutions*, eds. C. Brégianni and Roser Cussó (Athens: Alfeios, 2023), 15–22.

12 For further analysis see Michelle Baddeley, "Keynes' Psychology and Behavioural Macroeconomics: Theory and Policy," *The Economic and Labour Relations Review* 28, no. 2 (2017): 177–96.

13 George Chouliarakis and Sophia Lazaretou, "Déjà vu? The Greek Crisis Experience, the 2010s versus the 1930s. Lessons from History," Bank of Greece Working Paper, No. 176 (2014), https://ssrn.com/abstract=4184601, 7–8.

14 See Laure Quennouël-Corre and Y. Cassis, eds., *Financial Centres and International Capital Flows in the Nineteenth and Twentieth Centuries* (Oxford: Oxford University

within the ideological framework of economic liberalism.[15] The interwar Gold-Exchange Standard represents a different quality of international reserve, as far as one could comprehend the stabilization of national currencies pegged to the British currency as creating a zone of global monetary hegemony of the sterling,[16] which since 1925 was repegged to gold.[17] During the interwar years, the Gold Standard was mostly a precondition for broader financial transactions, with the result of turning London's market into the center of international reserves.[18] Through the lens of global monetary order, we see that 1930s Greek economists and political actors associated the domestic crisis with the workings of the Gold-Exchange Standard and more broadly with monetary factors.[19] This type of analysis focuses on the features of the crisis in Greece. The decrease of gold-based exchange reserves in the central Bank of Greece led to the abandonment of the Gold-Exchange Standard and to the discontinuation of the free convertibility of banknotes.[20]

The major studies of the Great Depression identify the decrease of exchange reserves in the central banks and the instability of the Gold-Exchange Standard as important factors of the crisis,[21] or they focus on the influence of the banking crisis on the workings of the monetary standard.[22] Western European economists of the interwar period associated the Great Depression with pre-1929 structural

---

Press, 2011); Luca Einaudi, *Money and Politics. European Monetary Unification and the International Gold Standard, 1865–1873* (Oxford: Oxford University Press, 2001).

15 I.a. Marc Flandreau, "The Economics and Politics of Monetary Unions: A Reassessment of the Latin Monetary Union, 1865–1871," *Financial History Review* 7 (2000): 25–27.

16 Gérard Duménil and Dominique Lévy, *The Crisis of Neoliberalism* (Cambridge, Mass.: Harvard University Press, 2011).

17 I.a. Robert Boyce, *The Great Interwar Crisis and the Collapse of Globalization* (Basingstoke: Palgrave Macmillan, 2009), 151–52.

18 Barry Eichengreen, *Golden Fetters. The Gold Standard and the Great Depression, 1919–1939* (New York: Oxford University Press, 1992), 203.

19 Brégianni, *The Great Depression*, 82–89.

20 Cf. Rodrik, *Globalization Paradox*, 40.

21 Ben Bernanke and Harold James, "The Gold Standard, Deflation, and Financial Crisis in the Great Depression: An International Comparison," in *Financial Markets and Financial Crisis*, ed. G. Hubbard (Chicago, IL: The University of Chicago Press, 1991), 35–64.

22 Michael D. Bordo, Christopher Erger, and Charles Evans, "Money, Sticky Wages and the Great Depression," *The American Economic Review* 90, no. 5 (2000): 1447–63.

factors and causes as well as with the consequences of World War I.[23] The Greek economic circles of the period also stressed that World War I created conditions of spontaneous protectionism for the European economies, which in the postwar period caused and aggravated the crisis.[24] In addition, scholars have highlighted the contribution of military expenditure to the crisis because of the early 1920s hyperinflation as well as the uncontrolled character of monetary stabilization.[25] Finally, we need to look at industrial production, which grew up to early 1929 and declined globally afterward.[26] Broadly, we can conclude that the Great Depression had roots in the years after World War I, but also structural characteristics associated with the instability of capital markets and the disequilibrium between production and consumption in the late 1920s.[27] Greece faced similar challenges to most countries in Eastern Europe, from the Baltics to the European borderlands of the former Ottoman Empire,[28] where the existing structures of the rural economy multiplied—in economic and social terms—the effects of the global economic recession.[29]

Examining the depression in Greece from a geo-historical perspective involves looking at collective economic processes and institutional aspects as well as investigating ideological underpinnings

23 Guy M. Henry, *La crise de 1929* (Paris: A. Colin, 2000), 27–28.

24 This was the point of view of the liberal politician Emmanuel Tsouderos (1882–1956), Governor of the Bank of Greece between 1931 and 1939, and later Prime Minister (1941–1944). Brégianni, *The Great Depression and Greece*, 88–89.

25 Pierre-Cyrille Hautcoeur, "Crise de 1929 et politique internationale," *Politique Etrangère* 3–4 (2000), http://www.parisschoolofeconomics.com/hautcoeur-pierre-cyrille/crise29politiqueinternat.html and idem, *La crise de 1929* (Paris: La Découverte, 2009).

26 Richhild Moessner and William A. Allen, "Banking Crises and the International Monetary System in the Great Depression and Now," BIS Working Papers, Monetary and Economic Department, No. 333 (December 2010), https://ideas.repec.org/p/bis/biswps/333.html, 2.

27 Cf. Joseph Schumpeter, *Capitalisme, socialisme et démocratie*, French translation by Gaël Fain, 2nd ed. (Paris: Petite bibliothèque Payot, 1946), 2nd part: "Le capitalisme peut-il survivre?".

28 See also Nathan Marcus, Stefan Nikolić, and Tobias Strauman, "Economic Policy, 1918–1939," in *The Economic History of Central, East and South-East Europe. 1800 to the Present*, ed. Matthias Morys (London: Routledge, 2021), 188–215.

29 Chryssos Evelpidis, "Η γεωργική κρίσις ιδίως εν Ελλάδι," *Αρχείον Οικονομικών και Κοινωνικών επιστημών* 11, no. 2 (1931): 145–204.

of applied economic policies. The approach of this chapter zooms in on the political and scientific discourse regarding development and on the representations of financial and monetary mechanisms—the metonymy of economic activity. From this perspective, the chapter incorporates fragments of public debates that took place after the Greek default of 1932. Nevertheless, this chapter focuses on the formulation of a descriptive overview of sectors of the national economy based on empirical historical analysis, so as to reconstitute the multiple facets of the interwar period—via the Greek paradigm—and the interaction among the various economic components of reality.[30] Reconstructing the evolution of economic and political views on the interwar crisis intersects with the analysis of applied politics.

12.2 A Failed Modernization? Greek Monetary Stabilization, Rationalization of the State, and Rural Change in the Late 1920s

During the regime of the First Greek Republic (1924–35), the 1928–32 administration of Eleftherios Venizelos was characterized by political efforts to modernize the national economy and reform the Greek banking system. The monetary stabilization, the reorganization of the banking sector, and the agrarian reform accomplished at the end of the 1920s were indicators of the economic role of the state.[31] The latter was thus progressively enlarged and, by the 1930s and under the influence of the Great Depression, took the form of strong interventionism. At the same time, these modernizing processes reflect the interference of the League of Nations in the rationalization of a peripheral economy such as Greece.

Interwar Greece was primarily a rural country with over 67 percent of its population living in rural and semirural areas, according

30 Cf. John-Mayard Keynes, *The General Theory of Employment, Interest and Money* (London: Macmillan, 1936).

31 Marc Mazower, "Η Ελλάδα και η οικονομική κρίση του 1931," in *Ελευθέριος Βενιζέλος. Κοινωνία-Οικονομία -Πολιτική στην εποχή του*, eds. Thanos Veremis and G. Goulimi (Athens: Gnosi, 1989), 237–66, in Greek.

to the rural census of 1929,[32] while 61.1 percent of the labor force worked in the agricultural sector.[33] Farming and small agricultural holdings had been the object of state protectionism under the liberal administration of the 1920s already, with the aim to forge a social alliance between the bourgeois and rural classes in order to preserve the "social regime." For this objective, the massive settlement of the refugees in rural areas and the agrarian reform were a precondition for agrarian change.[34]

The Venizelos government tried to increase the capital flow directed to the rural sector through the foundation of the State Agricultural Bank of Greece (henceforth ABG) in 1929. In the late 1920s, cultivated land and yields were expanded; at the same time, Greek agriculture underwent a qualitative transformation, moving away from cereal monoculture to products destined for the market, like tobacco.[35] On the other hand, until the beginning of the 1930s and the Great Depression, traditional commercialized commodities, like currants, underwent an important decrease in production.[36]

The modernization of the rural sector also reflects the Greek efforts to contract a new international loan, following a first loan contracted under the aegis of the League of Nations in 1924. The country's international loans during the 1920s were part of the League's agenda to address the challenges of demographical changes in Europe.[37] Cases in point were the extensive displacement of populations in the Balkans, and substantial population transfers (whether voluntary or forced), such as the forced population

32 Babis Alivizatos, "Η γεωργική Ελλάς και η εξέλιξίς της," *Δελτίον ΑΤΕ* [Bulletin of the Agricultural Bank of Greece] 4 (1939), no. 3: 304.

33 Alivizatos, "Η γεωργική Ελλάς," 306.

34 C. Brégianni, *Les banques, l'agriculture et l'Etat. Stratégies de crédit et politique agraire en Grèce de 1861 à 1940* (Lille: Presses Universitaires de Septentrion, 2002), 180–225.

35 Cf. Juan Carmona Zaballa, "Underfunded Modernization: Tobacco Producers and Agricultural Policy in Interwar Greece," *Journal of Modern Greek Studies* 39 (2021): 191–214.

36 Brégianni, *Les banques, l'agriculture et l'Etat*, 160–61.

37 For the archival documentation of the connection between financial support to states and refugee settlement in Europe and the Balkans established by the League's agents, see the 1930 commemorative report of the Financial Committee: IATE, Emmanuel Tsouderos Archives, A3S1Y1F26T0005, 6.

exchange between Turkey and Greece after the Greek defeat on the Asia Minor front in August 1922.[38] In 1923, the Lausanne Treaty between the Allies and the Ottoman Empire included the exchange and resettlement of populations: namely, the Orthodox subjects of the former Ottoman Empire and the Muslim population of Greece. Only the Orthodox minority of Istanbul and the Muslim population of Thrace were exempted. The criterion for this massive transfer of people was religious, in tandem with the League's promotion of an ideal of ethnic homogeneity for nation-states.[39] The total number of refugees settled in Greece was estimated in the Greek general census of 1928 at 1,222,000 individuals, while other sources estimated the number of refugees, before and after the forced exchange of populations and the Lausanne Treaty, at about 1,500,000 million.[40]

An important percentage of the refugees were settled in Hellenic Macedonia, a process that provoked a deep demographical change leading to the "hellenization" of the area. According to synchronically collected data, the Greek population of the region, representing 42 percent of the inhabitants in 1912, had reached 88 percent by 1928. At the same time, the Muslim inhabitants of Hellenic Macedonia, who represented 39 percent of the total population in 1912, had become statistically almost irrelevant by 1926 (0.1 percent of the total population).[41]

Regarding the rural refugee settlement, despite the uncertainty of the data, the refugees settled in rural areas represented about 45 percent of the settled population after the Lausanne Treaty. According to the data quoted by Emmanuel Tsouderos, out of the 147,215 refugee families settled in the countryside in 1928, 76 percent were wheat producers, 14 percent produced tobacco, and 3 percent cultivated

38 See for the abovementioned topic, Brégianni, *The Great Depression*, 48–53. For the international loans of the period, see also Michalis Psalidopoulos, *Τα δάνεια της Ελλάδας. 200 χρόνια ανάπτυξης και κρίσεων* (Athens: Papadopoulos, 2019).

39 See Sarah Shields, "Forced Migration as Nation-Building: The League of Nations, Minority Protection, and the Greek-Turkish Population Exchange," *Journal of the History of International Law* 18, no. 1 (2016): 120–45.

40 A. A. Pallis, "Les effets de la guerre sur la population de la Grèce," in *Les effets économiques et sociaux de la Guerre en Grèce*, ed. A. Andréadès (Paris; New Haven, CT: Presses Universitaires de France/Yale University Press, 1928), 136–50. This source also reflects the estimations of the League.

41 Pallis, "Les effets de la guerre," 136–50.

vineyards.[42] According to 1933 data of the ABG, a total number of 167,089 refugee families were settled in rural areas.[43]

Regarding the preponderance of wheat and tobacco cultivators among the refugees settled in rural areas, one must consider the necessity to cultivate products not only for the market, as with tobacco, but also for self-consumption, as with wheat, this variable being a consequence of the rural estates' minimum size.[44] As such, the rural settlement of refugees, the agrarian reform, and the stabilization of small-scale agriculture did not automatically lead to the breaking of the closed cycle of local economies.

As mentioned, the League supported the rural settlement of the refugees by facilitating Greek international borrowing and by creating the international autonomous Refugee Settlement Commission, which had two Greek representatives. Thus, in 1927, the Greek state applied to the League for a new international loan,[45] to fund especially the rural settlement of the refugees and public works programs, such as the drainage drying works in Macedonia and the construction of technical infrastructure (e.g., electrification and the water supply in Athens).

The League made the rationalization of the Greek banking system contingent on its support for the contraction of a new loan. In this framework, the Greek state stabilized the national currency, that is, the drachma; a policy of financial stabilization was attempted, and the Greek banking system was modernized with the foundation of a central and autonomous bank, the Bank of Greece, as its essential axis. According to the global principles established in 1922 by the Genoa International Monetary Conference, the Bank of Greece was

42 Emmanuel Tsouderos, *L'indemnisation des réfugiés grecs* (Paris: Librairie du Recueil Sirey, 1928), 25–26.

43 Babis Alivizatos, "Η ρύθμισις των αγροτικών χρεών," *Bulletin of the ABG* 3, no. 2 (1938): 123, 129.

44 See C. Brégianni, "Crise agraire et mutations agricoles. La dépression internationale de l'entre-deux-guerres et l'économie rurale grecque (1928–1935)," *Histoire & Sociétés Rurales* 51, no. 1 (2019): 125–57.

45 Archives of Contemporary Social History, Private Archives of A. Mylonas, D. 1, Participation to international Conferences, 1930–1936, "Protocol signed in Geneva, 15 September 1927 on the approval of the loan issuing from Greece for the stabilisation of the Greek currency, liquidation of budget deficits and reestablishment of the refugees" [in Greek and French].

Table 12.1 Proportion of Gold and Net Foreign Gold Exchange to Sight Liabilities at Bank of Greece

Gold	876,306,261	**Notes**	4,863,352,808
Net foreign gold exchange	3,087,697,849	**Other sight liabilities in Drachmas**	2,522,756,836
Reserve	3,964,004,110		7,386,109,644
According to Article 62 of Statutes	Total (a)		Total (b)
Proportion of gold (total a to total b)		53.67%	

Source: Bank of Greece Archives, Emmanuel Tsouderos Archives, A3S1Y1F17T3_0005.

granted the exclusive privilege to issue banknotes, and the drachma was tied to the Gold Standard (Tables 12.1–12.3). This obliged the central bank to maintain convertibility of its banknotes into gold-based exchange. By pegging the drachma to the pound sterling (1 sterling = 375 drachmas), the Greek state was integrated into an enlarged monetary zone, a policy consistent with the stabilization of national currencies at the time (like the stabilization of the French franc in 1928 or the efforts to stabilize the Italian lira by Mussolini's regime). Monetary stabilization could thus improve the solvency of the drachma and ameliorate its position in the international capital market.[46] On the other hand, the transfer of Western European frameworks of monetary rationalization to Greece led to the creation of new financial institutions like the Bank of Greece and the ABG.[47] The modernization of Greek banking reflects the regulatory role of the specialized, economic and financial committees of the League of Nations,[48] a role that created parallel interferences in the

46 For the abovementioned topic, see C. Brégianni, "Οι διεθνείς θεσμοί του Μεσοπολέμου, η Μεγάλη Ύφεση και η Τράπεζα της Ελλάδος," in *Η κρίση και η Τράπεζα της Ελλάδος*, eds. Sotiris Rizas and Andreas Kakridis (Athens: Bank of Greece, 2021), 135–65; Brégianni, *The Great Depression and Greece*, 54–65. See these studies for further archival documentation and related literature.

47 Ioanna Pepelassis Minoglou, "Transplanting Institutions: The Case of the Greek Central Bank," *Greek Economic Review* 19, no. 1 (1997): 33–64.

48 Patricia Clavin, "'Money Talks': Competition and Cooperation with the League of Nations, 1929–1940," in *Money Doctors. The Experience of International Financial Advising, 1850–2000*, ed. Marc Flandreau (New York: Routledge, 2003), 219–48.

Table 12.2 Bank of Greece—Statement at the Beginning of Business on May 14 (Morning), 1928—Assets in Drachmas

Assets	
1. Gold coin and bullion	876,306,261
2. Foreign gold exchange (Article 62 of Statutes)	3,191,081,165
3. Other foreign exchange	9,827,590
4. Inland bills and notes: commercial bills and notes	49,999,309
5. State debt	3,759,525,381
6. Other assets	42,938,226
Total	**7,929,677,932**

finances of other Balkan countries, like Bulgaria, during the same period.

This policy of currency stabilization ended in April 1932 as the impact of the Great Depression on the Greek economy was amplified. The government abandoned the Gold Standard, and the national currency entered the regime of floating parity.[49] Britain's departure from the Gold Standard in September 1931 dealt a strong blow to Greece's public finances, as London was the main source of foreign borrowing that permitted the continued implementation of public works programs as well as a major export market for Greece. Despite the determination of the Venizelos administration to pursue a liberal policy of monetary stabilization (as other states, like Italy and Turkey, did) by attaching the drachma to the US dollar and legislating a number of measures for the protection of the national currency, the important reduction of the foreign exchange reserves at the Bank of Greece and the continuous devaluation of the drachma against the dollar on the black market made this target illusional.[50] The central bank's reserves decreased significantly and fell to

49 For the relevant bibliography and archival documentation of the 1931–1932 Greek monetary policy summarized here, see Brégianni, *The Great Depression and Greece*, 75–111.

50 Georgios Mitrofanis, "Τιμές και ιστορικοί αριθμοδείκτες τιμών," in *Οικονομική Ιστορία του Ελληνικού* Κράτους, eds. Th. Kalafatis and E. Prontzas, vol. 3 (Athens: Cultural Foundation of the Piraeus Bank, 2011), 479.

Table 12.3 Bank of Greece—Statement at the Beginning of Business on May 14 (Morning), 1928—Liabilities in Drachmas

Liabilities		*Totals*
7. Capital paid up		400,000,000
8. Reserve Funds:		
9. Bank notes in circulation		4,863,352,808
10. Other sight liabilities in drachmas		
Current and deposit accounts:		
(a) Government accounts	666,738,254	
(b) Banker's accounts	964,587,723	2,522,756,836
(c) other accounts	891,430,859	
11. Foreign exchange liabilities:		
(a) *Foreign gold exchange (Article 62 of Statutes)*	103,383,316	113,210,906
(b) *Other foreign exchange*	9,827,590	
12. Other liabilities		30,357,383
Total		**7,929,677,932**

one-third from the stabilization period (1928) up to February 1932. This decrease was of major importance as the diminution of the commercial balance and, in general, the fall of capital input under the crisis's negative effects made obligatory to cover the national budget deficit using the Bank of Greece's exchange reserves.[51]

A social parameter of the recession of the Greek economy was the increase in unemployment. Despite the uncertainty of the statistical data, it is possible to reach some conclusions.[52] According to the 1928 general census, the active population was 2,415,078 out of

51 Archives of Eleftherios Venizelos, Benaki Museum/Athens, 062. Société des Nations. Comité Financier. Rapport au Conseil sur les travaux de la quarante-cinquième session du Comité (Paris, 3–24 mars 1932), 13.

52 For the calculation of the active population in the following years, upon a linear interpolation, see L. Tsoulfidis, "The Interwar Depression and the Greek Economy—Lessons Learned and Not Learned," in *Shaping and Reshaping the Global Monetary Order During the Interwar Period and Beyond. Local Actors in-between the International Institutions*, eds. C. Brégianni and Roser Cussó (Athens: Alfeios, 2023),204.

a total population of 6,204,684.[53] Around 60 percent of the active population were employed in agriculture and animal husbandry. However, female labor in agriculture was not always officially registered. The available information on unemployment requires contextualization. In 1928, 75,000 were registered as unemployed. This increased to 218,000 in 1931 and to 237,000 in 1932.[54] It must be underlined, however, that officially registered unemployment included contractual employment only while excluding those who were self-employed in all sectors.[55] Considering the high level of the active population in the primary sector, which is not included in the calculation of the official unemployment, we can estimate that in the maelstrom of the crisis the percentage of unemployment in Greece was around 17–20 percent (i.e., the same unemployment rates as registered during the peak of the current recession in Greece).

By January 1932, the Bank of Greece, via its economic and financial consultants, Kyriakos Varvaresos and Horace Finlayson, consulted the League's Financial Committee to ensure continued collaboration. With the agreement of the Greek government, the Bank of Greece invited a delegation of the League of Nations' Financial Committee to Greece to examine the Greek budget and the central bank's financial conditions.[56] At the same time, the Greek government demanded from the League the suspension of the sinking funds of the public debt, internal and external, for a period of 5 years.[57] Greece also demanded the mediation of a new

53 General Statistical Service, *Annuaire Statistique de la Grèce 1931* (Athens: National Printing Office, 1932), 23.

54 Alivizatos, "Η γεωργική Ελλάς": 306. Anotaton Ikonomikon Symvoulion [henceforth AOS = Supreme Economic Council]," in *Οι δείκται της οικονομικής δραστηριότητας της Ελλάδος κατά τα έτη 1928–1934*, ed. Supreme Economic Council (Athens: National Printing House, 1935), 103.

55 According to the Greek Confederation of Workers, I thank Dr. Zizi Salimba for bringing that information to my attention.

56 Archives of Eleftherios Venizelos, Benaki Museum/Athens, 062. SdN. Comité Financier. Rapport au Conseil sur les travaux de la quarante-quatrième session du Comité (Genève, 11–22 janvier 1932), 9. See also "Le renforcement des finances des puissances danubiennes," *L'avenir*, August 16, 1932, Historical Archives of the Bank of France, 1069199121/ 14, Crise Economique mondiale, 1931–1939.

57 Archives of Eleftherios Venizelos, Benaki Museum/Athens, D. 062. Neville Chamberlain to Eleftherios Venizelos, January 28, 1932.

international loan of 50 million US dollars[58] to complete its public work programs and more specifically the drainage projects in Greek Macedonia.[59]

In March 1932, the Financial Committee gave its approval for the suspension of the sinking funds of the public debt as well as its support for the contraction of a new international loan. This was under the condition that the Greek railways would be privatized, the Bank of Greece's independent character reinforced, public works suspended, public expenditure restricted, and imports controlled to avoid capital outflow for any purpose other than servicing of public debt.[60] The new loan could sustain the irrigation of agricultural land, as this was deemed to result in the servicing of national debt through a growth of national production. It is obvious that the Financial Committee suggested a program of shrinking the national economy to ensure Greece's financial and monetary recovery. As a final precondition for its financial support, the League insisted on a closer cooperation with the Bank of Greece's financial consultant and on the nomination of a League consultant in the Greek Ministry of Finances, who would steer the government in the domains of financial policy and national budget.[61] At this point began a failed cycle of negotiations of the Greek government with its creditors and the League about a new loan. The terms of the League were rejected by the Venizelos government (and in particular by the Finance Minister G. Maris[62]) and so, in April of the same year, the League refused to grant a new loan.[63] More specifically, Venizelos had declared that the 1-year moratorium on the sinking fund was insufficient, insofar as Greece would almost certainly have to demand a new suspension of the debt's servicing in the near

58 Chamberlain to Venizelos, January 28, 1932.

59 SdN. Comité Financier. Rapport au Conseil sur les travaux de la quarante-cinquième session du Comité Rapport au Conseil sur les travaux de la quarante-cinquième session du Comité (Paris, 3–24 mars 1932), 13.

60 Rapport au Conseil sur les travaux de la quarante-cinquième session, 14–15.

61 Rapport au Conseil sur les travaux de la quarante-cinquième session, 16.

62 See in particular documents from the Emmanuel Tsouderos's Private Archives, Historical Archives of the Bank of Greece.

63 See also Mark Mazower, *Greece and the Inter-War Economic Crisis* (Oxford: Clarendon Press, 1991).

future. Venizelos informed the League that from the May 1, 1932, Greece would be unable to pay its obligations.[64]

On May 5, 1932, the Greek state declared a moratorium on the country's public debt, while in July the forced conversion to drachmas of private loans (contracted in Greece) in foreign currencies was imposed by law.[65] In fact, the Greek case confirms the argument that the League's ability to influence European monetary cooperation in the negative conjuncture of the Great Depression was severely limited.[66]

The debt moratorium yielded some immediate results. The public debt service, constituting 31.1 percent of the total state expenditure just before the default, decreased to 18.9 percent in the following year, with a further downward trajectory in the years to come (Table 12.4).[67]

After the default and up to World War II, the Greek state went through different phases of negotiations with its creditors, concerning the quota of the debt service.[68] Nevertheless, priority was given to the service of the nineteenth-century loans consolidated in gold exchange at the end of the century and put under the control of the International Financial Committee in 1898, when Greece re-entered the capital market after the earlier state's default in 1893.[69]

64 "Le renforcement des finances des puissances danubiennes," *L'avenir*, August 8, 1932.

65 For a further elaboration of the arsenal concerning the protection of the national currency, see C. Brégianni, "The Gold-Exchange Standard, the Great Depression and Greece. Lessons (?) from the Interwar Greek Default." University Bayreuth, Germany, Symposium on "The Euro: (Greek) Tragedy or Europe's Destiny? Economic, Historical and Legal Perspectives on the Common Currency," January 11–12, 2012, http://www.euro.uni-bayreuth.de.

66 S. A. Schuker, "Money Doctors between the Wars: The Competition between Central Banks, Private Financial Advisers, and Multilateral Agencies, 1919–1939," in *Money Doctors. The Experience of International Financial Advising, 1850–2000*, ed. Marc Flandreau (New York: Routledge, 2003), 49–77.

67 Aggelos Aggelopoulos, "Τα δημόσια οικονομικά της Ελλάδος κατά την δεκαετίαν 1924–34," *Ergasia* 5 (1934): 601–3.

68 TransMonEA Database, https://dbstramon.academyofathens.gr.

69 See A. Antoniou and C. Brégianni, "Public Debt as a Key Variable of Public Finances and the Escalation of the Crisis," TransMonEA Project, Academy of Athens/HFRI, https://transmonea.academyofathens.gr/index.php/en/research-data/quantitative-data/public-finances.

Table 12.4 Greek State Expenditure during the Years 1924–34 (Total Percentages)

Financial Year	*Public Dept*	*National Defense*	*Education*	*National Economy*	*Administration*	*Other Expenditure*	*Total*
1924–25	23.8	33.6	5.5	3.9	19.6	13.6	100
1925–26	23.9	28.4	5.7	6.4	22.8	12.8	100
1926–27	36.2	24.5	4.7	5.5	18.7	10.4	100
1927–28	30.9	24.5	5.5	6.3	21.3	11.5	100
1928–29	43	17.5	6.1	5.8	18.2	9.4	100
1929–30	34.1	17.3	7.1	13.5	18.9	9.1	100
1930–31	34.3	17	7.2	9.9	21.4	10.2	100
1931–32	31.1	14.1	5.8	19.9	19.8	9.3	100
1932–33	18.9	17.4	7.5	18.6	27	10.6	100
1933–34	15.4	19.5	7.6	18.5	27.7	11.3	100

Source: Aggelos Aggelopoulos, "Τα δημόσια οικονομικά της Ελλάδος κατά την δεκαετίαν 1924–34," *Ergasia* 5 (1934): 601–3.

12.3 Protectionism and Centralized Economic Strategies after the Interwar Greek Default

Regarding the responses of the Greek state to the effects of the 1932 default, we clearly see an ever-increasing influence of the state over the national economy. After the moratorium and the abandonment of monetary stabilization, the state strengthened its entrepreneurial role and turned toward restructuring the productive sectors with the aim of controlling the national flow of capital to reconstruct the domestic market. For instance, during the year of the default, a series of laws authorized the extension of the public works programs and more specifically the construction of roads and land irrigation works in Greek Macedonia mainly. In an undated manuscript note, Venizelos mentioned the maintenance of public works as a central pillar of his government politics, in spite of the increase in the national debt.[70] Generally speaking, the state's economic interventions of the 1930s tended to create state monopolies in the monetary sector, in the stratification of the internal market, and in the organization of foreign trade. The conceptualization of this type of economic centralization as nationalist capitalism is not recent in economic history; moreover, the term "state capitalism" was in use simultaneously to its application to describe the central regulation of economic activity.[71] In that sense, Greek protectionist policy followed protectionism applied in continental Europe after the onset of the Great Depression, especially within the rural countries of Eastern Europe and the Balkans. Promoting protectionism (even unsuccessfully) in international economic fora was a policy observed since the 1920s.[72] During the 1930s, three basic tenets of economic policies came together: liberalism of the markets, state protectionism, and the regulatory attempts of international organizations.[73] Greece thus, following global developments in interaction with domestic modes of production, turned from liberalism

70 Archives of Eleftherios Venizelos, Benaki Museum/Athens, 290.

71 C. Steuermann, *La crise mondiale, ou Vers un capitalisme d'Etat* (Paris: Gallimard, 1931), 212.

72 Brégianni, "Οι διεθνείς θεσμοί του Μεσοπολέμου," 135–65.

73 Eric Hobsbawm, *L'age des extrêmes. Le court vingtième siècle, 1914–1991* (Bruxelles: Editions Complexe, 2003), 146.

to protectionism, reducing but not eliminating the interference of international institutions in its public finances. An indication of the latter are the negotiations—within the framework of the League—with its creditors (mainly with the British side) from 1933 to the end of the decade concerning the percentages of the national debt servicing. As the geopolitical interest of the United Kingdom was to maintain Greece as an ally, these were, in general terms, favorable to the Greek side.[74]

An indicator of the reinforcement of the state's role in the regularization of the Greek economy is the Greek Government's founding of the National Supreme Economic Council in February 1932. Its role as a national institution was the analysis of national economic activity, the consultation of the Greek government on economic policy issues, and "the observation of the cyclic activity of the international economic activity, in the framework of the economy's monetary and financial interdependence."[75] Given that the analysis of the cycles of the international economy was a declared target of the League's Financial Commission, it is obvious that this local actor—the Supreme Economic Council—followed a "global" methodology, in so far as its publications on the Greek economy during the 1930s more or less applied the statistical protocols and models experimented by the League's specialized committees of statistical experts.[76]

As the Supreme Economic Council pointed out regarding the handling of the crisis from the monetary perspective, Greece's economic policy bordered on the most extreme form of protectionism. Over and above the monopolistic management of foreign exchange, the state prohibited the exportation of foreign currencies for the

74 Brégianni, *The Great Depression and Greece.*

75 Archives of Eleftherios Venizelos, Benaki Museum/Athens, 290. Explanatory Report of the Prime Minister E. Venizelos on the Bill about the foundation of the Supreme Economic Council, February 15, 1932. In the Council, the most eminent Greek economists and jurists of the period, including X. Zolotas, K. Varvaresos, Al. Svolos, and G. Pesmanzoglou, participated.

76 Roser Cussó, "International Quantification and Liberalism: The Early Statistical Activities of the League of Nations' Economic and Financial Organization," in *Shaping and Reshaping the Global Monetary Order During the Interwar Period and Beyond. Local Actors in-between the International Institutions*, eds. C. Brégianni and Roser Cussó (Athens: Alfeios, 2023), 133–57.

payment of commercial debts contracted abroad and imposed restrictions on withdrawals from accounts held in Greece. In parallel, the duties levied on imported goods were increased and tariffs were imposed. As it was pointed out not only by the Greek economic literature of the period but also by the related organs of the League, the deficit of the commercial balance had significantly contributed to the manifestation of the Greek crisis: indeed, this had reached 45 percent for the year 1929 and 40 percent for 1930.[77] In real terms, this represented a deficit from 6 million up to 10 million pounds sterling for the years before 1932, a situation that could only worsen under the influence of the crisis. To deal with this situation, Greece concluded bilateral agreements for foreign trade, a fact that, according also to the Supreme Economic Council, constituted a generalized practice in Europe and was necessary as a measure for dealing with the crisis.[78] Moreover, except for the protectionist legislative framework, it also stressed the creation or intensification of various public organizations—such as the ABG (1929), the Central Committee for the Concentration of Wheat, and the Autonomous Organisation of Greek Tobacco—with an intermediary function between the state and the sectors of production, many of which specifically concerned support to agriculture.[79]

At a political level, the abandonment of monetary stabilization led to changes in governments. Finally, in 1933, the Liberals were succeeded by the Popular Party. This political transition did not alter protectionist policy. During the years 1933–35, the greater part of commercial transactions was carried out on the basis of bilateral agreements, especially after the systematization of clearing mechanisms in 1935. The reinforcement of the clearing system, legislated in July 1935 by the Panagis Tsaldaris government, represented a

77 Archives of Eleftherios Venizelos, Benaki Museum/Athens, 062. SdN. Comité Financier. Rapport au Conseil sur les travaux de la quarante-cinquième session du Comité (Paris, 3–24 mars 1932). Appendices relatifs à la Grèce, 8, 10.

78 The Supreme Economic Council gave a favorable opinion, during its session of July 25, 1932, to Venizelos's question if it was possible to organize Greek trade based on bilateral commercial agreements. AOS, *Το εξωτερικόν εμπόριον της Ελλάδος και αι συμβάσεις ανταλλαγής εμπορευμάτων* (Athens: National Printing House, 1933).

79 C. Brégianni, "Réformes agraires et changement rural en Grèce, du XIXe siècle à l'entre-deux-guerres," *Neohellenica Historica* 4 (2016): 245–82.

new, more centralized, understanding of the state's economic role.[80] For the experts in charge of the application of economic policy, such an organization of international commerce was indispensable as long as the other Balkan states based the greater part of their exports on bilateral agreements. It is thus evident that interventionist politics created new conditions for the position of Greece and the Balkans in the international capital market. Nevertheless, the trade balance in 1935 was still in deficit by 3.5 billion drachmas.[81] As the liberal Alexandros Diomidis,[82] first Governor of the Bank of Greece, stressed, Greek exports were at 50 percent of imports,[83] while the greater part of exported products were not basic necessities. The result of this commercial policy was a closer relation with Germany during the years 1932–35, as the total of the assets of bilateral agreements (surpassing 1 billion drachmas) was derived from exchange trade with Germany. Mainly, the commercial transactions between Greece and Germany involved the export of tobacco and the import of arms. According to French diplomats three-quarters of the Greek commands for arms had gone to German industry since 1935.[84] The policy of clearing agreements, introduced in 1932–33 and intensified after 1935, followed the global models applied to the export-import trade of commodities. Even if the implementation of the clearing system led to the decrease in imports in terms of value and volume and to the progressive growth of exports, across the entire 1930s the external trade balance remained negative. On the other hand, the policy of drachma's devaluation supported exports, as long as their main part concerned rural commodities.

80 AOS, *Η ελληνική οικονομία κατά το έτος 1935* (Athens: National Printing House, 1936), 67. Michalis Psalidopoulos, "Μορφές οικονομικής σκέψης στην Ελλάδα 1936–1940," in *Ελλάδα 1936–1940. Δικτατορία. Κατοχή. Αντίσταση*, eds. Hagen Fleischer and Nicos Svoronos (Athens: MIATE, 1989), 98–144.

81 "Η ελληνική οικονομία κατά το έτος 1935," *Ergasia* 7 (1936): 227 (unsigned article in Greek, based on the Supreme Economic Council's data).

82 On Diomidis, see Nikos Pantelakis, *Αλέξανδρος Διομήδης (1874–1950). Ένας αυθεντικός εκπρόσωπος της αστικής τάξης* (Athens: Metamesonyxties Ekdoseis, 2018), passim.

83 Alexandros Diomidis, "Αι ασθενείς πλευραί της ελληνικής οικονομίας," *Ergasia* 6 (1935): 1298.

84 Archives Historiques de l'Armée de la Terre [Vincennes, Paris], Rapports des Attachés militaires, Grèce/Politique Intérieure, 1930–1939, classified report, December 1938.

12.4 A Recovery?

Focusing on the general trends of the period, it should be noted that at the fiscal level, protectionism was followed by a decrease in direct taxation, at the same time when import duties were imposed on agricultural and industrial products. On the other hand, the rise of the producing and market price of currants—a product intended exclusively for export—led in the beginning of the 1930s to an increase in the product's taxation. In the middle of the 1930s, social agitation in rural areas of Peloponnese, where currants were mainly cultivated, was connected to the crisis in production and the fiscal policy implemented.[85]

Efforts for the stabilization of the national currency seemed to bear fruit as in 1934 the British sterling reached 543 drachmas, an amelioration for the Greek currency compared to an average annual rate of 595 drachmas in 1933. In 1935, the average annual value of the British pound stood lower, at 529 drachmas.[86] In the same year, the Greek economy registered an even more significant growth, as almost all relevant indices improved in comparison to 1934.[87] Public revenue increased by 14.7 percent compared to 1933, but public expenditure expanded in parallel, a fact proving the state's active entrepreneurial role. According to the Governor of the National Bank of Greece, Ioannis Drosopoulos, public expenditure for the financial year 1935–36 increased by 41 percent compared to 1933–34. Because of the protectionist policy, the monetary mass

85 See for the crisis of the currant in correlation to the 1932 state default, Alexis Fragiadis, *1932. Η χρεωκοπία και το τέλος του Βενιζελισμού* (Athens: I Kathimerini, 2019). On social agitation resulting from the currants crisis, see Manolis Arkolakis, *Οπτικές αναπαραστάσεις του Μεσοπολέμου. Παραγωγή, καθημερινότητα και κρίση* (Athens: Ekdoseis ton Synadelfon, 2023), 35–47; Ilias Bitsanis, "Το σταφιδικό ζήτημα στη Μεσσηνία κατά τον Μεσοπόλεμο," TransMonEA Working Paper Series No. 10 (Athens: Academy of Athens & HFRI, 2022). On rural protests in Greece during this period, see Serafeim Seferiades, "Small Rural Ownership, Subsistence Agriculture, and Peasant Protest in Interwar Greece: The Agrarian Question Recast," *Journal of Modern Greek Studies* 17, no. 2 (1999): 277–323.

86 Mitrofanis, "Τιμές και ιστορικοί αριθμοδείκτες τιμών," 479.

87 AOS, *Η ελληνική οικονομία κατά το έτος 1935.*

was increased. At the same time, the Bank of Greece managed to preserve its monetary reserves in gold.[88]

The state's attempt to sustain the internal market was associated with the general growth of private credits, especially those allocated by the National Bank. Nevertheless, the contracted loans were below the demand. Another parameter that must be considered regarding the handling of the crisis was the important decrease in migrant remittance's inputs.[89] As a consequence of the maintenance of the Bank of Greece's gold reserves after the 1932 default as well as a result of transnational developments in the monetary policies of the United States, France, and United Kingdom, the drachma was reattached to sterling in 1936 with a floating parity rate ranging from 542 to 552 drachmas. The "official" devaluation of the drachma for about 40 percent compared to the rate of the 1928 stabilization (1 sterling = 328 drachmas) promised considerable advantages regarding the export of agricultural products, but at the same time considerably intensified domestic inflation pressures from 1936 onward.[90]

The general protectionist conditions were thus favorable to the development of the industrial sector (Table 12.5), while the objective was to respond to domestic demands for industrial products. In 1935, Greek industry was able to cover 74 percent of domestic consumption, as opposed to 1928 when only 58 percent of the internal demand was covered by Greek industrial products. Even if the industrial output was on a rising trajectory across the 1930s, this was of lesser relevance to what was largely an agricultural country. Nonetheless, the industrial development was another factor that diversified the position of Greece in the international market. The

88 M. Psalidopoulos, *Ιστορία της τραπεζας της ελλαδος 1928–2008. Από τράπεζα του κράτους εγγυήτρια της χρηματοπιστωτικής σταθερότητας* (Athens: Bank of Greece, 2014), 120; C. Brégianni, "Stories and Myths: Greek Gold transfers during World War II and beyond," in *Three Conferences on International Monetary History*, edited by Georges Depeyrot, C. Brégianni, and M. Kovalchuk (Wetteren: Moneta, 2013), 261–70.

89 Archives of Eleftherios Venizelos, Benaki Museum/Athens, 063, SdN. Comité Financier. Rapport au Conseil sur les travaux de la quarante-cinquième session du Comité, 13.

90 C. Brégianni, "Νομισματικός χρυσός και προσπάθειες νομισματικής σταθεροποίησης στην Ελλάδα. Από τον Μεσοπόλεμο και την Κατοχή έως την Απελευθέρωση 1928–1946," *Neohellenica Historica* 6 (2021): 87–89.

Table 12.5 Indicators of Industrial Production from 1928 (Base = 100) to 1939 in Greece

1928	*100*
1929	101.79
1930	105.28
1931	108.88
1932	102.67
1933	111.79
1934	127.18
1935	143.17
1936	141.72
1937	153.87
1938	164.24
1939	179

Source: Supreme Economic Council. *Greek economy during the year 1937*. Athens, National Printing House, 1938, 31 & Supreme Economic Council. Greek economy during the year 1939. Athens, National Printing House, 1940, 41.

industrialization of peripheral countries provoked a protectionist response from the core as Germany, England, or Czechoslovakia tried to reinforce their own industrial sectors, using measures such as monetary instruments and the cost of labor, in order to increase competitiveness.[91] Under the conditions of the Depression and the resulting introversion of national economies, the merchant navy, which failed to increase ship ownership to a sufficient degree, stagnated.

The primary sector of production merits closer attention. In 1931, the League documented the progressively negative impact of the Great Depression on the European rural sector, mainly with reference to a slump in prices of agricultural products.[92] In the early 1930s in Greece, agricultural production declined in terms of volume and value. This not only aggravated everyday life in the rural areas but had also a negative impact on the balance of external

91 See Alexandros Diomidis, *Μετά την κρίσιν. Οικονομικαί και δημοσιονομικαί μελέται 1932–1934* (Athens: Kaufman, 1934).

92 Société des Nations-Comité économique, *La crise agricole*, vol. 2 (Genève: SdN, 1931), 4, 9; Archives of Eleftherios Venizelos, D. 062. SdN. Comité Economique. Rapport au Conseil sur les travaux de la trente-septième session du Comité (Genève, 14–19 janvier 1932), 4–7.

trade, at the same time when domestic demand for rural products was plummeting. According to ABG estimates, cultivation costs were rising, while the monoculture could not sustain the rural population. Resuming the state's regulatory interventions in the rural sector, one could remark the creation of specialized national institutions for the protection of a number of agricultural products and the proliferation of agricultural credit. The total sum of agricultural credits during the years 1929–35 increased by 50 percent in comparison to the period before the foundation of the ABG. Half of rural credits were based on the collateral of agricultural products, which demonstrates the centralized character of agricultural development. In addition, short-term rural credits under personal guarantee—reaching about 900 million drachmas in 1929 and more than 1 billion in 1935—supported the costs of production and consequently failed to play a productive role. A main instrument for the distribution of short-term rural credits was credit cooperatives, a mechanism that intensified the dependence of the rural cooperative movement on the Agricultural Bank and the state.[93] Rural credits increased even further during the Metaxas dictatorship. In 1936, short-term credits reached 1.5 billion drachmas, while in 1939 they rose to about 2.2 billion. On the other hand, the credits under rural collateral increased from 1.2 billion drachmas in 1936 to 1.6 in 1939, a growth that can be attributed to the protection of specific products. Therefore, during the years 1937–39 we witness an effort to balance the sums connected to wheat as rural collateral with those connected to tobacco, while this type of rural credit had hitherto been almost exclusively directed to the latter commodity. This constitutes an indicator of the rural policy implemented under the impact of the Great Depression, challenging the monoculture of commodities intended for export. Nevertheless, in the evaluation of the rural credit's proliferation during the 1930s, one should also take into consideration the important devaluations of the drachma after 1932 and, in a second phase, in 1936.

93 For the abovementioned topic and further details on the evolution of the rural credit in the modern Greek state, see Brégianni, *Les banques, l'agriculture et l'Etat*, passim. Concerning the ABG, the quantitative analysis of its credits during the 1930s is based on the elaborated data of the Bank's annual reports for the years 1930–39. See Brégianni, *Les banques, l'agriculture et l'Etat*, 207–9, 281–90.

As a parallel effect of the rural credit's proliferation, the ABG expanded its network to cover the entire national territory.[94] The economic and territorial expansion of the ABG advanced from 1935 onward, in line with the targets of the central rural policy.[95] This chronological point coincides with the recovery of the Greek economy from the symptoms of immediate recession. On the other hand, the growth of agricultural production was initiated by means of the extension of cultivated lands and the improvement of yields. In addition to "healing" purposes, like improving economic conditions and placating social agitation in rural areas, this protectionist policy is associated with the general effort to stimulate the growth of domestic production in order to reduce the deficit of the trade balance and secure the national sovereignty vis-à-vis the unstable international market. The agricultural policy of the period tried to direct capital flow to the rural sector and reorganize agricultural production henceforth oriented toward domestic consumption, retaining at the same time the quota of commercialized products so as to support the equilibrium of the trade balance.[96] The development of the domestic market was a precondition for economic policy, as after the 1932 default Greece had limited access to international capital. According to data from the Supreme Economic Council (Figure 12.1), the protectionist policy resulted in the growth of agricultural production.

From this perspective, we can discern two qualitative developments that elucidate the functioning of the domestic market. In 1935, the statistical data demonstrates, on the one hand, the decrease of official unemployment, which reached the level of 1930.[97] Since

94 For the creation of the Bank's national network, cf. the ABG's relative administrative circulars, Historical Archives of the ABG [PIOP Historical Archives], annual volumes of general circulars, 1930–1939; C. Brégianni, "Forced Population Exchange, Spatial Conceptions and the Agency of International Institutions: League of Nations' Refugee Settlement Commission and Banking Networks in Northern Greece During the Interwar Era," in *Shaping and Reshaping the Global Monetary Order During the Interwar Period and Beyond. Local Actors in-between the International Institutions*, eds. C. Brégianni and Roser Cussó (Athens: Alfeios, 2023), 25–70.

95 C. Brégianni, Les banques, l'agriculture et l'Etat. Stratégies de crédit et politique agraire en Grèce de 1861 à 1940 (Lille: Presses Universitaires de Septentrion, 2002), 417-431.

96 Brégianni, "Crise agraire et mutations agricoles," 128–50.

97 AOS, *Η Ελληνική οικονομία κατά το έτος 1935*, 103.

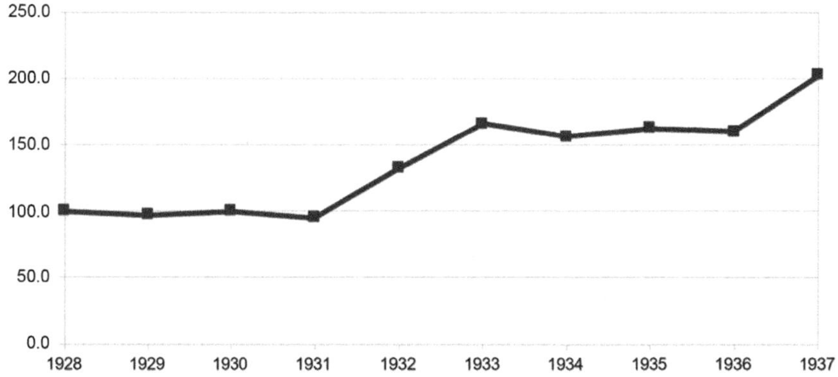

Figure 12.1 Change in Agricultural Production, Greece 1928–37 (Index by Quantities)

1933 unemployment fell, reaching 150,000 people in 1935.[98] On the other hand, we see a slight recovery of bank deposits.[99] The general index of economic activity for 1934 indicates the beginning of an economic recovery.[100]

In addition to the economic recovery indicated by the official data, macroeconomic research has demonstrated different levels of growth represented by GDP (gross domestic product) and GDP per capita.[101] This asymmetrical growth also reflects historical developments, as far as social agitation and riots seemed to intensify in Greece during the years 1932–36, until the imposition of the Metaxas dictatorship. In this order of ideas, the interwar large-scale protectionism of the Greek state in the economic field can be characterized as ever-increasing interventionism, leading to centralized policies that prevented the market's openness without ameliorating the conditions of everyday life.

98 AOS, *Η Ελληνική οικονομία κατά το έτος 1935*, 103.; Alivizatos, "Η γεωργική Ελλάς," 306.

99 AOS, *Η Ελληνική οικονομία κατά το έτος 1935*, 83.

100 AOS, *Οι δείκται της οικονομικής* δραστηριότητας, 5.

101 Giorgos Kostelenos, Dimitris Vasileiou, Emmanouil Kounaris, Sokratis Petmezas, and Michail Sfakianakis, *Ακαθάριστο Εγχώριο Προϊόν 1830–1939* (Athens: IATE Archives - KEPE, 2007).

12.5 Political and "Theoretical" Features of Protectionism

The foundations of the centralized economic policy followed by the People's Party had already been laid by the liberal government, as the governmental change of March 1933 did not signal a rupture in the main principles of economic politics. The continuity in the implementation of economic policies is reflected also in the fact that important political actors among the Liberals retained their positions in the central core of the administration.

The archival research and the analysis of political discourse allow the formulation of a general hypothesis concerning the adoption of an enhanced form of protectionism by the Liberals. As already mentioned, political circumstances led Venizelos in 1932 to reject a moratorium with Greece's creditors and to declare state default. The policy of successive pre-1933 coalition governments was also to focus on the development of domestic production. Despite the decision-making, collective processes were not ruled out, as in the beginning of the 1930s, the liberal model already seemed on the decline in Western Europe. Greek protectionism escalated from regulatory measures of the early 1930s to an economy where the state intervened on a larger scale once the crisis took on a more violent form. Moreover, a distinction between protectionism and economic autarky must be pointed out: the principle of national economic unity, which required the utilization of all national productive forces for its development, can be comprehended as the common base of these systems.[102] Nevertheless, economic protectionism is less expansive than autarky and it is applied in some economic sectors only, while autarky incorporates the entire economic activity.

As the contradiction between liberalism and protectionism is apparent, and as the conservative turn of the interwar Greek Republic cannot be dissociated from the application of this specific policy, liberal perceptions emerged in an effort to rationalize the turning point to economic nationalism [*sic*]: "Economic liberalism

102 Chryssos Evelpidis, "Σύγχρονοι τάσεις κοινωνικής πολιτική," *Agrotiki Ikonomia* 4 (1938): 193.

is the most convenient atmosphere for the Greek genius," declared Alexandros Diomidis. But, he admitted, the current international order was characterized by a global decrease in private initiative and its substitution by the collective forms of economic organization.[103] It is clear from the type of the political elite's public discourse that the antagonism between states on the international market forced nations to develop domestic markets but also to clarify the nature and benefits of capitalism.[104]

It is not adverse to the purposes of this study to stress the high-level public debate concerning the conditions of development after the 1932 default, a debate framed by the analysis of the above-cited tendencies of interwar capitalism but also promoting alternatives of economic organization. We should note that during the 1930s, Greek translations of Western European studies in economic and social sciences were published almost simultaneously to the originals. Furthermore, the conditions of the crisis had already stimulated a blossoming of Greek academic economic thought and the development of statistical methods in the country.[105]

In general terms and simplifying the present analysis, we can conclude that political and social actors put forward various interpretations of the crisis. Even if these had led to the "introversion" of the Greek economy, they were not dissimilar to other European models. Nevertheless, the concentration of the economy that was chosen as a solution led to political centralization, as the creation of a new social reality in Europe collided with the establishment of authoritarian regimes.[106]

103 Diomidis, "Αι ασθενείς πλευραί," 1298.
104 Cf. Steuermann, *La crise mondiale*, 210.
105 Kostas Kostis, *Οι τράπεζες και η κρίση. 1929–1932* (Athens: Eboriki Trapeza, 1986), 20.
106 Peter Wagner, "The Democratic Crisis of Capitalism: Reflections on Political and Economic Modernity in Europe," LSE "Europe in Question" Discussion Paper Series, LEQS Paper No. 44 (2011). https://eprints.lse.ac.uk/53209/1/LEQSPaper44.pdf

12.6 Conclusion

In the Greek case, the First Hellenic Republic was overpowered by the social pressures created by the Great Depression, resulting in the formation of the Metaxas government following a vote of confidence in the Hellenic Parliament. In August 1936, brandishing the danger of a communist takeover of the regime, Ioannis Metaxas imposed a dictatorship, followed by the restoration of the monarchy. Greek authoritarianism had not only a political substratum but also an economic content, as was generally the case for interwar authoritarianism.[107] Even if one can highlight continuities with earlier economic policies, during the dictatorship the planning of economic activity through state mechanisms was a central pillar of public policy. The tendency toward national autarky describes a general outline of economic nationalism, mainly characterized by the intensification of the state's economic role, in order to fulfill the objective of achieving trade-balance equilibrium.[108] These parameters must be comprehended in the framework of an international economic environment of isolated markets, challenged by important difficulties in capital flows and trade transactions.

Clearly, Greek interwar authoritarianism can be included in the analysis of Mediterranean dictatorships of the period, even if enormous differences exist among them.[109] While a principle of Metaxa's "New State" (*Neon Kratos*), the creation of a corporatist state,[110] was

107 *An Institutional History of Italian Economics in the Interwar Period*, vol. 1, *Adapting to the Fascist Regime*, eds. Massimo M. Augello, Marco E. L. Guidi, and Fabrizio Bientinesi (Cham: Palgrave Macmillan, 2020); David Baker, "The Political Economy of Fascism: Myth *or* Reality, or Myth *and* Reality?" *New Political Economy* 11, no. 2 (2006): 227–50.

108 AOS, *Η Ελληνική οικονομία κατά το έτος 1935*; Trapeza tis Ellados [Bank of Greece], *Έκθεσις του Διοικητού της Τραπέζης εξ ονόματος του Γενικού Συμβουλίου επί του Ισο λογισμού του έτους 1939* (Athens: Bank of Greece, 1940).

109 For the economic perception of the Metaxas regime, see C. Brégianni, "Η πολιτική των ψευδαισθήσεων. Κατασκευές και μύθοι της μεταξικής δικτατορίας," *Ta Istorika* 16, no. 30 (1999): 171–90.

110 For the simultaneous perception of corporatism in Greece, see Andreas Notaras, "Το συντεχνιακόν κράτος εις την θεωρίαν και την εφαρμογήν," *Ergasia* 7 (1936): 1285; Sotirios Agapitidis, ""Το πρόβλημα της κυριαρχίας και των τάσεων του συντεχνιακού κράτους," *Ergasia* 5 (1934): 1434–35. Cf. for the corporatist ideology in Greece, Brégianni, "Η πολιτική των ψευθαισθήσεων," 187–91; Spyridon G. Ploumidis, "Ο κορπορατισμός στην Ελλάδα του Μεσοπολέμου," in *Η δύσκολη*

never achieved, it did evoke the fascist model. For the Italian Fascist state, the corporation with a lateral, linear organization was the basic economic form, mirroring the structure of the totalitarian state and being "incorporated" into the dogma of economic nationalism.[111] Corporatism was a conservative institutional collectivity, and it can be considered a major rival of individual freedoms, not only from an economic but also from a philosophical point of view.[112] This type of dystopic collectivity was applied to the planning of a market equilibrium imposed by the state, resulting in the creation of state monopolies and preventing the open functioning of the market in the Mediterranean region. Still, while in the Greek case dictatorial politicians proclaimed the intention to organize the market on a corporatist basis, in practice this was articulated mostly through an effort to reorganize the agricultural cooperative movement as a centralized and regime-controlled structure.[113]

In order to connect the analysis of the Greek case with the interpretation of the concept of crisis, it is to be noted that in Greece the economic recession soon turned into a severe political crisis. Monetary instability forced Greece to abandon the Gold Standard at a time when economic liberalism was on the decline across Europe, while international institutions were incapable of supporting monetary and financial cooperation between nations. The reinforcement of internal productive structures and the progressive centralization of the national economy led to political centralization, while the dominant ideology promoted protectionism. It was not long before this translated into approval of the intervention economist role of the state—even by moderate liberals.

δημοκρατία. Η Ελλάδα του Μεσοπολέμου 1924–1935, eds. Vasilis Panagiotopoulos, Giannis Voulgaris, and Sotiris Rizas (Athens: To Vima, 2024), 95–109.

111 For the documentation of the abovementioned analysis, see the numerous reports of the British attachés in Rome's Embassy. Public Records Office, Foreign Office, 434: Confidential Print. Southern Europe, vol. 1–6, 1934–1939 [copies in microfilm, Modern Greek History Research Center, Academy of Athens].

112 Ludwig von Mises, *Socialism: An Economic and Sociological Analysis*, trans. J Kahane (Auburn, AL: The Ludwig von Mises Institute, 2009).

113 C. Brégianni, "La utopia rural de un régimen autoritario. La política cooperativista durante la dictatura de Metaxas (Grecia, 1936–1940)," *Historia Agraria* 42 (2007): 327–51.

Conclusion

Chapter 13

THE WATERSHED MOMENT OF EASTERN EUROPE'S INTERWAR

Klaus Richter, Jasmin Nithammer, and Anca Mândru

The fall in agricultural prices, the collapse of global trade, and the Central European banking crisis had a catastrophic impact on Eastern Europe. However, although the Great Depression caused profound economic damage, it is impossible to insulate its chronology from the broader interwar crisis that stretched from the end of World War I to the beginning of World War II. World War I had shattered Europe's very economic foundations. In Eastern Europe, this was aggravated by the dramatic territorial reconfiguration brought about by imperial collapse and the postwar peace treaties. Bulgaria lost its granary, Dobruja, to Romania. Austria and Hungary were cut off from the former Habsburg Empire's industrial heartlands. Poland's territory consisted of vastly different developed regions. Outside of the region, this trend toward smaller territories and smaller economic units was interpreted as depreciation, particularism, and irrationality and, increasingly, as a problem that affected the economic recovery of Europe more broadly.

Eastern Europe's agricultural depression began before the Wall Street Crash. In 1927 already, the League noted a dramatic widening of the scissors between prices for manufactured products and agricultural prices, leading to a pauperization of rural producers. Moreover, additional factors, such as the Soviet Union's entry into the European timber market, make it difficult to discern the exact causes for economic dislocations. However, the authors of this volume have shown that, across most of Eastern Europe, the depression was initially regarded as a limited event. This changed by 1932, as no signs of recovery came into sight: The Great Depression was now considered an existential threat to states and societies, a disaster that the "small" states of Eastern Europe had become fully embroiled in, with little agency to influence its outcome. As international cooperation ground to a halt, the depression seemed to confirm what Eastern Europeans had suspected all along: that their fate was decided by the Great Powers, who undertook no meaningful efforts to address the root causes of the downturn. As the world economy recovered from 1934, Eastern Europe recovered, too, but for much of the region, this came at the cost of an increasing economic dependence on Germany, which would translate into a gradual—and then rapid—loss of sovereignty.

Focusing on the subjectivities of the depression and perspectives from within Eastern Europe provides us with a much clearer view of how the crisis changed the way Eastern Europeans viewed the world and their future prospects. Responses to the crisis were shaped by predictions of its duration, expectations toward a future recovery, and broader political and social contextualizations of the crisis. Zachary Doleshal has shown that the business strategies of Czechoslovak shoe manufacturer Baťa and their US counterpart Endicott-Johnson in the face of the crisis differed dramatically, with the former embracing globalization and the latter protectionism. As Boris Nenovsky and Tsvetelina Marinova have demonstrated, Bulgarian economists and bankers were less concerned by their country's financial situation than they were by the fatalistic rumors that spread through Bulgarian society—Bulgaria's depression was certainly an economic depression, but it was also a psychological crisis of Bulgarian society.

The Great Depression thoroughly transformed Eastern European states and societies. Existing scholarship has stressed that the depression furthered "the idea of increased state responsibility and control over the social safety net."[1] This book has further demonstrated that the welfare state was both expanded and contested during the depression. As Béla Tomka has shown, Hungary's recovery from the depression was accompanied by the expansion of social rights of workers and the extension of the welfare system to the countryside. The 8-hour working day was introduced, as well as a considerable education allowance. Yet the depression also led to

1 Tomasz Inglot, *Welfare States in East Central Europe, 1919–2004* (Cambridge: Cambridge University Press, 2009), 59.

substantial cuts in welfare, especially in those countries that were the hardest hit. In Austria, plans to abolish all social insurance benefits were considered, yet the 1935 social insurance law limited itself to reducing pensions and the eligibility for unemployment benefits and sick pay. In Romania, as Alexandra Ghiț has revealed, austerity measures, introduced as a condition for a stabilization loan of the League of Nations, led to a significant reduction in pensions and welfare provisions. This erosion of social systems translated into heightened support for the extreme right.

The transformation of the relationship between states, majority nationalities, and national minorities has traditionally been framed as a result of increasing xenophobia (especially anti-Semitism) in the context of the failure of democracy and the rise of authoritarianism and totalitarianism.[2] However, as the authors of this volume have shown, the Great Depression had a much more immediate impact on the multiethnic fabric of Eastern Europe. Some national minorities, like Belarusians and Ukrainians in Poland, who mostly worked in agriculture, were disproportionately hard hit by the depression. Moreover, in large parts of Eastern Europe, national minorities were concentrated in specific sectors, especially trade and sometimes industrial production, which made them a target for policies that aimed at furthering the national character of the states of Eastern Europe. Katja Wezel has shown how the centralization of the economy in the hands of the government and the "Latvianisation" of the economy were "two sides of the same coin": As the Latvian government brought Baltic German- or Jewish-owned key industrial enterprises under its control, it put ethnic Latvians in charge of running them. Although this policy catalyzed after the 1934 authoritarian coup of Kārlis Ulmanis, it was put in place as a key component of post-1918 state-building already. In Lithuania, as Klaus Richter argues in his chapter, the government pursued a similar policy

2 Stephan M. Horak, *Eastern European National Minorites, 1919–1980: A Handbook* (Littleton, CO: Libraries Unlimited, 1985); Jeffrey S. Kopstein and Jason Wittenberg, "Beyond Dictatorship and Democracy: Rethinking National Minority Inclusion and Regime Type in Interwar Eastern Europe," *Comparative Political Studies* 43, no. 8–9 (2010): 1089–118; Sabrina P. Ramet, "The Failure of Democracy-building, the Fate of Minorities: An Introduction," in *Interwar East Central Europe, 1918–1941*, ed. Sabrina P. Ramet (London: Routledge, 2020), 1–34.

throughout the depression, often in opposition to the very different demands of those groups that were conceived of as the beneficiaries of "Lithuanianization."

Jerzy Łazor has shown that such policies probably went furthest in Poland, where Jewish merchants came under increased pressure by Christian competitors once the depression had hit. Companies owned by national minorities were under constant threat of state takeover. After the death of Piłsudski in 1935, economic anti-Semitism became an accepted political agenda, as the state officially condoned anti-Jewish boycotts. In Hungary, the experience of the depression directly fed into state control of financial institutions through the hiring of bank directors, which was in practice used to exclude Jews. The Law on National Defense in Czechoslovakia was specifically used to target enterprises owned by German speakers. Not least, such measures were legitimized with reference to the alleged role of national minorities as "foreign agents." In Estonia, the Baltic German bank director Klaus Scheel was often portrayed as either a stooge of the German government or as a Jew who felt no loyalty toward the Estonian state. However, these "nostrification" policies also provoked circumvention efforts. For the Czechoslovak shoe manufacturer Bat'a, a "nationally indifferent" company town, where German and English could be heard alongside Czech and Slovak, was existential for its success as a company that conceived of itself as global and that acted as such. In Latvia, the mighty Riga Exchange Committee managed to avoid nationalization by appointing a president who was equally respected among Latvians and Baltic Germans.

The Great Depression fundamentally transformed the relationship of Eastern Europe with the international order. The states of Eastern Europe considered a system based on international cooperation fundamental to the protection of their own sovereignty, which reflected in their enthusiasm regarding the work of the League of Nations and the possibilities of economic cooperation and foreign investment. In rare cases, this enthusiasm survived into the 1930s, as Bat'a expanded its global activities due to the limitations imposed by the small Czechoslovak domestic market (its US counterpart Endicott-Johnson proved too consumed by its own, much larger domestic market, to consider becoming global). However, in most of Eastern Europe, this enthusiasm had dampened in the 1920s already. The League's work was increasingly regarded as colonial in nature and the rosy promises of foreign investments never materialized. International investors regarded Poland as too insecure and volatile a market, which resulted in foreign takeovers of Polish companies rather than greenfield investments. In the run-up to the depression already, the Polish public viewed foreign ownership as a threat to national interests. "The profits are someone else's, the losses are ours," Polish novelist Paweł Hulka-Laskowski wrote.[3]

If these tensions were boiling under the surface in the 1920s, they erupted during the Great Depression. The League, in its failure to understand the implications of national sovereignty in the region, increasingly demanded one-sided concessions from the states of Eastern Europe and blamed their leaders for obstructing Europe's recovery. Demands from within the region to allow preferential treatment for agricultural exports were rejected, only to be implemented one-sidedly by the Great Powers themselves later, as in the case of British Imperial Preference. The League's mediation of stabilization loans came to a halt: While Austria and Romania received new loans on the precondition of accepting budget supervision through a League advisor, Estonia's national bank refused League supervision, stressing that the League's advice had caused Estonia's gold losses. In the most extreme case, Greece rejected a stabilization loan and defaulted on its debts. As Catherine Brégianni has shown, the League's efforts to aid the recovery of European monetary cooperation can only be classed as a failure. The loss of authority of the League directly contributed to the erosion of the most favored nation principle. As preferential treatment and bilateral trade became the norm, much of Eastern Europe moved into Nazi Germany's economic orbit. By the end of the 1930s, Hungary, the first country to conclude a clearing agreement with Berlin in 1934, carried out 40 percent of its entire foreign trade with Germany. As the examples of both Hungary and Bulgaria show, the structural adjustments made to facilitate this clearing trade dramatically enhanced mechanisms and institutions of state intervention.

3 See note 47 in Jerzy Łazor's chapter.

The book has shown that looking at the history of Eastern Europe through the lens of the depression fundamentally enhances our understanding of the dynamics that destroyed democracies and of the broad acceptance of authoritarian rule beyond the traditional explanation of an Eastern European lack of democratic experience.[4] While some countries had turned authoritarian already before the slump (e.g., Poland and Lithuania in 1926), the Great Depression was the decisive event that signaled the end of democracy across the region, with the single exception of Czechoslovakia. It directly led to the 1934 military coup in Bulgaria and the establishment of the Metaxas regime in Greece in 1936. However, as the authors have shown, the end of democracy was not a sudden rupture, but a dynamic process that interacted closely with the depression's downward spiral. In his chapter, Nathan Marcus argues that Austria's depression was so profound and sustained that it damaged the remaining vestiges of parliamentary democracy beyond repair. Perceptions of Nazi Germany's apparent successes in battling the depression enhanced acceptance for Anschluss. In Hungary, Gyula Gömbös's rise to power in 1932 did not lead the Hungarian political class to immediately embrace authoritarianism—but it paved the way for the 1935 dissolution of parliament. In Romania, the failed "open-door" policy enacted by the National Peasant Party undermined the legitimacy of the party and of parliamentary democracy more broadly. In the Baltic States, both Kārlis Ulmanis and Konstantin Päts, who came to power in 1934, legitimized their coups by referring to the democratic governments' inability to overcome the economic crisis—although in both Latvia and Estonia, the economy was by that point already in the process of recovery. Taking ownership of these recoveries decisively contributed to the consolidation of both regimes. As David Feest has shown, the economic crisis in Estonia was connected to a crisis of "our rule," as large parts of the population—not least the Estonian urban middle class, which had emerged only in the 1920s—felt that the post-1918

4 Heidi Hein-Kircher and Steffen Kailitz, "'Double Transformations': Nation Formation and Democratization in Interwar East Central Europe," *Nationalities Papers* 46, no. 5 (2018): 745–58; John Coakley, "Political Succession and Regime Change in New States in Inter-War Europe: Ireland, Finland, Czechoslovakia and the Baltic Republics," *European Journal of Political Research* 14, no. 1–2 (1986): 187–206.

project of building an Estonian state for the Estonian nation was about to fail. This provided the turn to authoritarianism and economic nationalism with a sense of urgency.

The case studies in this volume also contribute to a new understanding of the nature of economic nationalism during the Great Depression and beyond. Whereas traditional historiography has focused on 1930s' economic nationalism as a foreign-trade dogma, the case of Eastern Europe points toward a form of economic nationalism embedded in broader agendas of nationalism.[5] As such, the contributions respond to George T. Crane's 1998 call to "bring the nation back" into the study of economic nationalism, that is, to put the relationship of the state with those conceived of as "the nation" at the center.[6] As the chapter on Poland has shown, the country's policy of taking over "foreign" companies was by no means part of a consistent, coordinated policy, but rather a response to the dislocations of the depression: In a move of "forced statism," the government took over companies because no private buyers were available. As Vojislav Marinković's impassioned speech at the League of Nations showed, the states of Eastern Europe, fearing for a loss of their sovereignty in a hostile international environment, felt they had little choice but to protect their markets. Although a consensus emerged both among economists and the broader public that the state was the only actor that could overcome the economic crisis, many business owners, as the case of Latvia has shown, were deeply dissatisfied with the obstacles of soaring tariffs. However, we can conclude from all chapters that the main battlefield of economic nationalism was not in the arena of international trade, but at home. Governments claimed their policies aimed at protecting and empowering the embattled nations, which, in a multiethnic region such as Eastern Europe, meant delineating a core nationality as bearers of the state and clearly separating them from other groups

5 Harold James, *The End of Globalization: Lessons from the Great Depression* (Boston, Mass.: Harvard University Press, 2009); Douglas A. Irwin, *Trade Policy Disaster: Lessons from the 1930s* (Boston, Mass.: MIT Press); Patricia Clavin, *The Failure of Economic Diplomacy: Britain, Germany, France and the United States, 1931–36* (London: Macmillan Press, 1996).

6 George T. Crane, "Economic Nationalism: Bringing the Nation Back In," *Millennium: Journal of International Studies* 27, no. 1 (1998): 5–75.

that were increasingly viewed, at best, as overprivileged minorities that had to cede economic agency to the core nationalities or, at worst, as foreign agents. This understanding did not neatly map onto how those parts of society felt that were cast as the core nationality—often, the depression had deeply fragmented these socially heterogeneous groups, and their views on how the state should alleviate their plights had more to do with debt relief and social welfare than with alleged "national" concerns.

For Eastern Europe, the Great Depression was the watershed moment of the interwar period. Its consequences have been overshadowed by the larger catastrophe of World War II. Yet its impact has continued far beyond the rupture of 1945. Postwar Communist economic policies in Eastern Europe were deeply influenced by the experiences of the Great Depression.[7] Cold-War communist regimes referred to the depression itself—and the world's inability to fight it—as the most critical historical event showcasing the failure of capitalism and the bourgeoisie. Yet with the end of the Cold War, the slump was gradually relegated from central event in the interwar history of Eastern Europe to the margins of the region's historiography. We hope this book has helped shift it back toward the center.

7 Janusz Kaliński, *Polityka Gospodarcza Polski w latach 1948–1956* (Warsaw: Książka i Wiedza, 1987); Anna Jarosz-Nojszewska, "80 lat Gospodarki Narodowej (1931–2011)," *Gospodarka Narodowa* 1–2, no. 233–34 (2011): 1–18.

Contributors

Catherine Brégianni is Research Director at the Modern Greek History Research Center of the Academy of Athens and an associated member at the CRH-EHESS (*Groupe d'Histoire Économique*). She is currently engaged in research on the evolution of market mechanisms operating within the international monetary system, using a transnational perspective. Part of her research focuses on the postcolonial administrative structures, with a specific focus on the Ionian State under the protection of the British Empire (1814–64).

Zachary Doleshal is a clinical assistant professor at Sam Houston State University. His research looks at intersections of economics, politics, and innovation within the time frame of the "long" nineteenth and "short" twentieth centuries. His first book, *In the Kingdom of Shoes* (University of Toronto Press, 2021), looked at how the shoe company Bat'a globalized and challenged ideas about the nation-state, democracy, and Americanization. He is currently working on a project on parliamentarianism in Austria-Hungary from 1911 to 1918.

David Feest works at the Nordost-Institut, Lüneburg, as a research fellow. His research focuses on the history of the Baltic States, with a special emphasis on Estonia, and the history of Russia. He is a board member of the Baltic History Commission and of the Association of Historians of Eastern European History.

Alexandra Ghiț is a researcher in the History of Feminist Political Thought and Women's Rights Discourses in East Central Europe 1929–2001 (HERESSEE) project at the University of Vienna. From 2020 to 2023, she was a postdoctoral researcher in the ZARAH project, focusing on women's labor activism, at Central European University. She holds a PhD in Comparative Gender Studies from Central European University.

Jerzy Łazor, PhD, is an assistant professor at the Warsaw School of Economics, Poland, where he specializes in twentieth-century economic and business history of Central and Eastern Europe. He is the author of *The Political Economy of Interwar Foreign Investment: Economic Nationalism and French Capital in Poland, 1918–1939* (Routledge, 2024).

Anca Mândru is a honorary research fellow at the University of Birmingham. She received her PhD in Eastern European History from the University of Illinois at Urbana-Champaign. She specializes in the social and cultural history of Eastern Europe and comparative socialisms and nationalisms. She is currently preparing a monograph entitled *Socialism of Sentiment: The Culture of the Left in Romania (1880–1939).*

Nathan Marcus holds a BA in history and economics from the Hebrew University of Jerusalem and earned a PhD in Modern European History from New York University. He was a Max Weber postdoctoral fellow at the European University Institute in Florence, a Golda Meir postdoctoral fellow at the Hebrew University, and a lecturer in Modern European History at the Higher School of Economics in St. Petersburg. Nathan Marcus joined the Department of General History at Ben Gurion University of the Negev in 2018, where he also directs its Center for Austrian and German Studies.

Tsvetelina Marinova is an associate professor of economics at the New Bulgarian University, Bulgaria, and an associate researcher at the LEFMI, University of Picardie Jules Verne, France. Her research is in the fields of the history of economic thought, economic history, social and solidarity economy, and European economic and monetary integration. She is the author of *Economie sociale et solidaire dans les pays des Balkans. Bulgarie, Roumanie, Serbie: Quels enseignements?* (L'Harmattan, 2021).

Nikolay Nenovsky is a professor of economics at the Jules Verne University, France, and an affiliated professor at the University of National and World Economy, Sofia, and at the SU HSE, Moscow. His research is in the fields of the theory and history of money, economic thought, and international economics, mainly the Balkan region. In 2022, together with Eric Magnin, he published the book *Diversity of Capitalism in Central and Eastern Europe: Dependent Economies and Monetary Regimes* (Palgrave Macmillan).

Jasmin Nithammer is a Gerda Henkel research fellow in the project "The Liminality of Failing Democracy: East Central Europe and the Interwar Slump" at the University of Birmingham, in which she investigates the socioeconomic impact of the Great Depression on interwar Poland. Her main research interest lies in the international, social, and economic history of interwar and postwar Poland. She is the author of *Grenzen des Sozialismus zu Land und zu Wasser. Die tschechoslowakische Landgrenze und polnische Seegrenze im Vergleich* (Herder-Institut, 2019).

Klaus Richter is a professor of Eastern European History at the University of Birmingham. His research focuses on nationalism and the social and economic history of Poland and the Baltics. Among his publications are books on anti-Semitism in Lithuania during the late Russian Empire (*Antisemitismus in Litauen: Christen, Juden und die 'Emanzipation' der Bauern, 1889–1914*, Metropol, 2013) and *Fragmentation in East Central Europe: Poland and the Baltics, 1915–1929* (Oxford University Press, 2020). He received his PhD from the Technical University in Berlin in 2012.

Béla Tomka is a professor at the Department of Contemporary History, University of Szeged. His major research area is the social and economic history of Hungary and Europe in the twentieth century, with a special emphasis on international comparisons. He is the author of fifteen books and editor of several other volumes, including *A Social History of Twentieth-Century Europe* (Routledge, 2013) and *Globalization in State Socialist East Central Europe: Looking Beyond Dominant Narratives* (Palgrave Macmillan, 2024).

Katja Wezel is a research fellow at the Institute for Economic and Social History in the University of Göttingen. She received her PhD in 2011 from the University of Heidelberg for a study on Memory Politics in Latvia. She is currently preparing a monograph on *Riga as a Global Port City: From Imperial Russia's Most Successful Port to Latvia's First Capital of Trade (1855–1939).*

Index

For Product Safety Concerns and Information please contact our EU representative GPSR@taylorandfrancis.com Taylor & Francis Verlag GmbH, Kaufingerstraße 24, 80331 München, Germany

Batch number: 10725853

Printed by Printforce, the Netherlands